Equal Play

Equal Play

Title IX *and* Social Change

EDITED BY

Nancy Hogshead-Makar

and

Andrew Zimbalist

TEMPLE UNIVERSITY PRESS
Philadelphia

Temple University Press
1601 North Broad Street
Philadelphia PA 19122
www.temple.edu/tempress

Copyright © 2007 by Temple University
All rights reserved
Published 2007
Printed in the United States of America

☉ The paper used in this publication meets the requirements of the American National
Standard for Information Sciences—Permanence of Paper for Printed Library Materials,
ANSI Z39.48-1992

Library of Congress Cataloging-in-Publication Data

Equal play: Title IX and social change / edited by Nancy Hogshead-Makar and Andrew Zimbalist.
        p.   cm.
    Includes index.
    ISBN-13: 978-1-59213-379-6   ISBN-10: 1-59213-379-7 (cloth: alk. paper)
    ISBN-13: 978-1-59213-380-2   ISBN-10: 1-59213-380-0 (pbk.: alk. paper)
    1. Sex discrimination in sports—Law and legislation—United States.   2. Sex discrimination
in sports—Law and legislation—United States—Cases.   3. Sports for women—Law and legislation—United States.   4. Women athletes—Legal status, laws, etc.—United States.   5. Sex
discrimination against women—Law and legislation—United States.   6. College sports for
women—United States—History.   7. United States. Education Amendments of 1972. Title
IX.   I. Hogshead-Makar, Nancy, 1962–.   II. Zimbalist, Andrew S., 1954–.

KF4166.E68 2007
796.082—dc22   2007020201

031708P

To our families,

Scott, Aaron, Helen Clare, Millicent, Mutti and Big D, Andy, Alex, Scotty, Max, Sally, Rich, Quinton, Azalea, Stan, Buzz, Connie, Honey & Bess, Shelley, Jeff, Mike, Ella & Alex,

To our fathers,

for giving us lessons from the Great Depression about hard work, and

To our mothers,

for teaching us about living in great optimism and possibilities

Contents

PART III

The Initial Backlash: The 1980s

INTRODUCTION • 99

PART IV

Accelerated Pace: The 1990s

INTRODUCTION • 129

PART V

The Second Backlash: 2001–2008

INTRODUCTION • 179

Acknowledgments

I have too many people to thank for their inspiration, encouragement and mentoring. I'll start with the people whose life's work on behalf of girls and women made my full scholarship at Duke University and my three Olympic Gold Medals possible: Donna Lopiano, PhD; Christine Grant, PhD; Marsha Greenberger; Billie Jean King; Senator Birch Bayh; Representative Patsy Mink; Representative Edith Greene; Jean King; Carole Oglesby, PhD; Bernice Sandler; Judy Sweet; Alpha Alexander; and countless others who each believed in sports as a powerful life-altering experience for all.

For my personal journey, I'd like to thank Dr. Jean O'Barr, founding director of the Women's Studies Department at Duke University and my professor. When I needed a course to complete my schedule as an undergraduate at Duke University, I somehow landed in her class, "Women in Third World Countries." Her class ignited an intellectual journey that made me rethink the ideas about women that surrounded my youth and early adulthood, and which expanded into race and ethnicity, class, sexualities, age, and ability. For a sophomore grinding out each day to achieve two modest goals— getting good grades and becoming the world's best athlete—it was a whole new world. She made an indelible mark on the course of my life. (Now, hopefully, she'll forgive me for losing a book she acquired in Africa.)

I grew up admiring Donna de Varona for her swimming accomplishments and broadcasting skills. As a 1964 double Olympic Gold Medalist in swimming, she went on to work for ABC, the network that was broadcasting the 1984 Los Angeles Olympics. She took time out of her schedule to talk to the entire United States Olympic Swimming Team about Title IX, the college scholarships we were already taking for granted, and how the Supreme Court decision in *Grove City* just might eradicate the law's protections for women in education.

She urged us to "use" our impending fame for something good, for something we believed in, and hoped that "something" might be to help save Title IX with a legislative override. In addition to teaching me about Title IX well enough to dialogue with reporters, she and Ken Bastian convinced me to intern at the Women's Sports Foundation (WSF) between my last two years in college. Interning was a weird dual existence. I spoke at corporate events for handsome fees and participated in parades on the weekends, while Monday through Friday I answered the WSF's hotline about Title IX compliance or how to get funding for a recreation league, in between mopping the floor and filing. Eva Auchincloss, Holly Turner, and Alpha Alexander made it a meaningful summer.

While I deeply appreciate her friendship, Donna de Varona's greatest gift was to push me into ever-expanding leadership roles at the WSF. In my twenty-three years with the WSF, I have had the privilege of working with remarkable people—academic leaders in law, sociology, and history; leaders in organizations like the Olympics, the NCAA, professional sports, and municipal recreation leagues; civil rights leaders; physicians; athletic directors; coaches; leaders in journalism and the media; marketing giants; and recruiters in the sports business. The WSF introduced me to good friends Marj Snyder, Deborah Slaner Larkin, Cathy Griffin, Benita Fitzgerald Mosley, Tuti Scott, Richard Lapchick, Lyn St. James, Betty Jaynes, Marian Burton Nelson, Christine Brennan, Yolanda Jackson, Julie Foudy, Wendy Hilliard, Terri Lakowski—all givers in life. Donna Lopiano, CEO of the WSF, has been particularly influential. She has lived the history of the law and is out to empower anyone who shares her commitment to expanding sports and fitness opportunities for everyone. She is not only is a treasure trove of information on Title IX history, but she is inspirational for her ability to get the best out of people around her. I'm lucky to be one of them.

I would also like to thank the many practitioners and academics who have directly or indirectly contributed to this book: Marsha Greenberger, copresident of the National Women's Law Center (NWLC); Neena Chaudhry and Jocelyn Samuels, both senior attorneys working at the NWLC; Arthur Bryant, executive director of the Public Justice Foundation; and Debbie Brake, a professor of law at University of Pittsburgh, each giving me a vision for the type of lawyer I aspired to be. Verna Williams, professor of Law at the University of Cincinnati, and Kristen Galles, a superior plaintiff's lawyer for women athletes and coaches, worked tirelessly for years without pay for good case law on Title IX. Kristen and I are cochairs of the Section on Individual Rights and Responsibilities at the American Bar Association. I also thank Diane Heckman, who has vetted a dozen articles and briefs for me over the years and whose scholarship continues to be a real contribution to the field, and Leslie Annexstein, former chair of the National Coalition for Women and Girls in Education. Linda Carpender, Vivian Acosta, Ellen Staurowsky, Don Sabo, Leslie Haywood, Ellen Vargyas, Athena

Yiamouyiannis, Mary Joe Kane, April Osajima, Charlotte West, John Cheslock, Anita DeFrantz, Welch Suggs, Joe Kelly, and many others have pushed the field. I thank each of them.

My parents, who see the magic in my children, allowed me to work on *Equal Play* worry free. Piyanut Kotaweera, our au pair from Thailand, worked overtime without the first complaint. My faculty assistants, Holly Bolinger and sometimes fill-in Clare Raulerson, found ways to gracefully juggle dozens of other faculty demands while helping me with *Equal Play*. Don Lively gave me an enduring vision of being a professor, and my beloved students read all these materials and much more, vetting out the most impactful ones with their reactions.

I'd like to thank my coauthor, Andy Zimbalist, who had the idea for the project with Temple University Press over two years ago. After agreeing to it, I promptly became pregnant with twin girls, and we had to shelve our ideas for a year. Thank you, Andy, for your collaboration and patience as I juggled 160 students, three small kids, and a husband working in Tallahassee while writing this book.

Finally, and most personally, I'd like to heap appreciation onto my dear husband, Scott Makar. In painstakingly proofreading chapters of *Equal Play* as they developed, he assured that the words matched the vision of the book. But, more than that, Scott finds opportunities to celebrate the best in me (and ignores the rest). He gives me safety to work on hotly contested issues, even when he disagrees. My hope is that his core values, including a steady focus on the big picture, exceptional professional competence, and comfort around strong men and women alike, will be passed on to our son and two daughters. Thank you, Scott, for giving me a solid base to fly from.

—*Nancy Hogshead-Makar*

I may have needed patience to collaborate with Nancy on this project, but my patience was richly rewarded. Nancy's experience, passion, and intellect made this book a labor of love for me. My interest in Title IX has many roots. The first is my sister, Michelle Zimbalist Rosaldo, who was a pioneering writer in women's studies in the 1960s and 1970s, and one of the founders of Signs. Shelly was my guiding light until her untimely death in 1981. The second is my employment at Smith College, a women's college that is firmly dedicated to the promotion of equal opportunities for women. The third is the work I began in sports economics in 1990 and my eventual study of intercollegiate athletics. Throughout I have had many colleagues and collaborators from whom I have gleaned much knowledge and insight. Finally, I would like to thank Donna Lopiano for suggesting that I team up with Nancy for this effort.

—*Andrew Zimbalist*

Introduction

Nancy Hogshead-Makar and Andrew Zimbalist

Title IX of the Educational Amendments of 1972 reflects the nation's collective aspirational belief that girls and boys, women and men, deserve equality in educational experiences and opportunities. Given that American society is governed by principles of equality, tolerance, freedom, and the rule of law, it seems curious by contemporary standards that equality for males and females in federally supported education was ever considered to be a radical idea. Title IX's declaration that "no person in the United States shall, on the basis of sex, be excluded from participation in, be denied the benefits of, or be subjected to discrimination under any education program or activity receiving federal financial assistance" resonates positively with most Americans, many of whom view the law's underlying premise of equality as an unspoken truism. As Birch Bayh, the former United States Senator and one of the drafters of the Title IX legislation, stated: "What we were really looking for was . . . equal opportunity for young women and for girls in the educational system of the United States of America. Equality of opportunity. Equality. That shouldn't really be a controversial subject in a nation [that] now for 200 years has prided itself in equal justice."[1]

Despite the law's promise, athletic departments remain one area of resistance to equity for men and women in higher education. The irony of the battle for gender equality in athletics is apparent in a fundamental way. Athletics on the field is exalted for its embodiment of concepts like fair play, teamwork, sportsmanship, and abiding by the rules. Yet these same concepts could not

---

[1] Senator Birch Bayh, Address at the Secretary's Commission on Opportunity in Athletics 24, August 27, 2002; transcript available at the Department of Education's website http://www.ed.gov/about/bdscomm/list/athletics/transcript-082702.pdf; cited by Ellen J. Staurowsky, *Marquette Sports Law Review* (Fall 2003), 95.

be said to have been widely embraced when women have sought parity of athletic opportunities in their schools. As their efforts at equality were thwarted, women began relying on various strategies via the legislature, executive, and judicial branches of government to assert the right to equality on the playing fields of America.

These efforts paid off in many ways. The effect of Title IX on female participation in interscholastic and intercollegiate athletics over the last thirty-five years has been remarkable. In 1971, only 294,015 girls participated in high-school sports, and 31,852 participated on intercollegiate teams. Today, approximately 3.06 million girls participate in high-school sports, and 166,800 on intercollegiate teams.

Although progress has been extraordinary, it is clear that equality is still an elusive and distant goal. Women continue to lag behind men by every measurable criterion, including participation opportunities, scholarships, budgets, facilities, and recruiting. More disturbingly, the trend toward equality, which accelerated during the 1990s, has essentially come to a standstill since 2000. Much work remains to be done, and some of that work is intellectual.

One mission of this book is to explore the governmental processes that form and continue to shape all public policy, including Title IX. By developing a discussion on the history of women in sports, by analyzing Title IX and the meaning of "equal opportunity" for girls and women to participate in sports, the authors hope to demonstrate how government actions can shape and support the goal of gender equity. The importance of the interconnectedness of the three branches of government and of strategic initiatives in each branch to form public policy is thereby revealed.

Many public policy issues arise under the rubric of Title IX and athletics. Among them are equal scholarship dollars,[2] sexual harassment by coaches or peers in the athletic department,[3] the amount and quality of media coverage,[4]

---

[2]In 2002, the National Women's Law Center (NWLC) filed grievances against thirty colleges and universities to remedy scholarship inequities. NWLC found the annual gap to amount to nearly $6.5 million in lost athletic scholarships to young women at these schools, many of whom depend on scholarships to attend college (http://www.nwlc.org/details.cfm?id=1143&section=newsroom; accessed June 15, 2007).

[3]Nancy Hogshead-Makar and Shelden E. Steinbach, "Intercollegiate Athletics' Unique Environments for Sexual Harassment Claims: Balancing the Realities of Athletics with Preventing Potential Claims," 13 *Marquette Sports Law Review* 173 (2003). Deborah Brake, "The Struggle for Sex Equality in Sport and the Theory Behind Title IX," 34 *U. Mich. J. L.* 13 (2000); see also *Sexual Harassment Guidance: Harassment of Students by School Employees, Other Students, or Third Parties* (1997; available at http://www.ed.gov/about/offices/list/ocr/docs/sexhar01.html (accessed July 9, 2007).

[4]See, e.g., Margaret Carlisle Duncan and Michael Messner, "Gender in Televised Sports: News and Highlights Shows, 1989–2004," *The Amateur Athletic Foundation of Los Angeles* (2005).

girls playing on boys' teams and vice versa,[5] pay equity in coaching,[6] retaliation for championing the rights of female athletes,[7] pregnancy discrimination in athletics,[8] and equal treatment as participants (such as access to equal coaching, training, facilities, equipment, locker rooms, and travel and recruiting budgets),[9] to name just a few. Because having a place on the team is a central issue for most women in athletics, this text focuses on the efforts to increase participation opportunities and on the meaning of "equal opportunity." Without a team, there can be no unequal treatment of that team, no problems with sexual harassment issues, and so on. Furthermore, it is the effort to increase opportunities for women that has encountered the most resistance and is therefore a focus of the material included in this text.

The general principles of governmental policy formation, whether learned in high-school civics or law school, apply to Title IX just as they do to other topics such as workplace safety, protecting the environment, integrating the mentally or physically challenged into society, providing affordable housing, and access to health care or quality education. Major policy initiatives are rarely accomplished with the passage of a single piece of legislation, via a single favorable court decision, or by support from one administration. Instead, achieving a desired result is a continuous process, shaped by ongoing public debate about the policy; about the role of government in forming and implementing policy; and about the outcomes that flow from a policy, including the need to reassess legislation supporting the policy. The interplay among the three branches of

[5]See, e.g., "Co-Ed Participation—Girls Playing on Boys' Teams and Male Versus Female Competition: The Foundation Position" (2002; available at http://www.womenssportsfoundation .org/cgi-bin/iowa/issues/rights/article.html?record=569).

[6]See, e.g., The U.S. Equal Employment Opportunity Commission, *Enforcement Guidance on Sex Discrimination in the Compensation of Sports Coaches in Educational Institutions* (2002; available at http://www.eeoc.gov/policy/docs/coaches.html). (The guidance clarifies how the Equal Pay Act of 1963 and Title VII of the Civil Rights Act of 1964 apply to sex-based differences in the compensation of sports coaches.) Diane Heckman, "The Glass Sneaker: Thirty Years of Victories and Defeats Involving Title IX and Sex Discrimination in Athletics," 13 *Fordham Intell. Prop. Media & Ent. L. J.* 551 (2003).

[7]Diane Heckman, "*Jackson v. Birmingham Board of Education:* Supreme Court to Review Whether There Is a Title IX Cause of Action by an Athletic Department Employee for Retaliation," 194 *Ed. Law Rep.* 1 (2005).

[8]See *Issues Related to Pregnancy & Athletic Participation: The Foundation Position* (2006; available at http://www.womenssportsfoundation.org/cgi-bin/iowa/issues/disc/article.html?record=1145); Deborah Brake, "Legal Challenges to the Educational Barriers Facing Pregnant and Parenting Adolescents," 1994 *Clearinghouse Rev.* 141; OCR, "Dear Colleague Letter Regarding Pregnancy, Athletics, and Scholarships," issued June 25, 2007. Available at http://www.ed.gov/about/offices/ list/ocr/letters/colleague-20070625.html (accessed July 9, 2007).

[9]See, e.g., *Daniels v. Sch. Bd. of Brevard County*, 985 F. Supp. 1458, 1460–1463 (M.D. Fla. 1997); Diane Heckman, "The Explosion of Title IX Legal Activity in Intercollegiate Athletics During 1992–93: Defining the 'Equal Opportunity' Standard," *Det. C. L. Rev.* (1994).

government—the legislative, executive, and branches—oftentimes results in outcomes that are unpredictable. Each branch has its own process by which change is sought or implemented, and each can conflict or concur with the other.

Many times the process starts in the legislative branch with efforts to pass a law. At the federal level, the Senate and the House of Representatives may jointly consider, adopt, or repeal laws that a majority of their members deem appropriate. To do this, Congress typically holds many open hearings to debate the merits or deficiencies in the proposed legislation. The executive branch, via the President of the United States, may approve or disapprove of the proposed legislation passed by the House and Senate either by signing it into law or vetoing it (directly or indirectly, the latter by a "pocket veto"). If signed into law (or if a veto is overridden by Congress), the executive branch then carries out laws through its administrative agencies and other departments under the President's purview. The judicial branch consists of the country's court system, which resolves disputes in individual court cases. Courts resolve factual disputes and explain or interpret laws passed by Congress. In some cases, the courts may find that the executive or legislative branch has failed to comply with the Constitution or that an executive branch agency has failed to conform its actions to congressional intent.

Title IX, as applied to athletics, provides many examples of these governmental dynamics, which have shaped athletic departments and women's participation rates and experience. For example, during the early 1970s and the 1990s, the three branches of government worked in concert to produce a surge in participation opportunities for women. During the 1980s and again after the turn of the century, however, an antagonistic executive branch thwarted new gains for women in sports, resulting in stagnation or a possible backslide of opportunities. Amidst these governmental dynamics are other influences on gender equity and public policy, such as the antitrust laws, the debate over the increased commercialization of collegiate sports, and the controversy over the proper role of the federal government in schools.

As *Equal Play* will show, thus far, the road for women to attain equality in athletics has been far from smooth and effortless. It has been an extremely difficult battle, from the conception of Title IX decades ago, to the current debates on the Department of Education's policy statements. Sport was and often still is seen by some as a masculine activity, thereby posing extraordinary challenges for those who seek a place of equality for girls and women in athletics. Gender-equity advocates have had to shift tactics since Title IX's enactment in 1972, continuously formulating new strategies for achieving the same goals.

As the materials in this text show, Title IX's history consists of episodic legislative, judicial, and administrative gains and set backs. Gender-equity initiatives have required multifaceted approaches and coordination among many organizations, each competing for the same outcome. These initiatives have included gaining access to powerful government representatives; seeking representation on committees responsible for legislation or implementing regulations; and exposing inequities in athletics to government committees, courts, administrative decision-makers, and the public.[10] Title IX's successes also have depended on public-information campaigns that highlight the value of women's sports participation. An informed public debate has helped Title IX by gaining media coverage for women's sports and highlighting academic research on both the health and career benefits of sports participation and the barriers that continue to limit girls' and women's sports participation. This same research has been instrumental in bolstering legislative, administrative, and litigation strategies.[11]

In particular, tireless efforts have been required to demonstrate that sports participation is not a "zero-sum" game; that is, increases in women's sports participation do not have to come at the expense of opportunities for men. Academic research and advocacy positions that directly confront the myth of male-athletic losses have been essential to the overall Title IX strategy.

Unlike a sporting contest, the clock does not run out on public-policy advocacy with one side being able to declare victory. No winner's name is ever chiseled in stone, and no champion returns home victorious to adoring fans. Instead, the materials presented in this book show that the process by which Title IX came into being and continues to exist is a hardscrabble one. The history of Title IX's quest for equality of opportunity for women is marked by many milestones, including: (a) marathon efforts to pass the legislation itself, (b) the writing and adoption of administrative regulations applying to athletic departments, (c) defending the laws and regulations repeatedly in sometimes hostile court battles, (d) legislatively overturning a United States Supreme Court case after four years of hard work, and (e) challenging new administrative regulations that threaten to weaken the law.

These cycles of public-policy formation underlying Title IX both outline and inform the challenges that lie ahead. In the final analysis, the struggle for gender equity in athletics is best understood as an ongoing process whose successes

---

[10]Lopiano, Donna A., Advocating for Gender Equality in Sport: The Experience of the Women's Sports Foundation in the United States (2002), http://www.womenssportsfoundation.org/cgi-bin/iowa/issues/history/article.html?record=908 (accessed June 15, 2007).

[11]Ibid. *See also* Donald Sabo, K. E. Miller, Michael J. Melnick, Leslie Heywood, Women's Sports Foundation Report: Her Life Depends On It: Sport, Physical Activity and the Health and Well-Being of American Girls (2004). (A comprehensive survey of scientific research on girl's health and physical activity.) Available at: http://www.womenssportsfoundation.org/binary-data/WSF_ARTICLE/pdf_file/990.pdf (accessed July 9, 2007).

and stumbling blocks have empowered society generally, and women specifically, in turning back and transforming stereotypes and biases. The successes of Title IX to date, although far from complete, suggest that other social movements can benefit from Title IX's history. It is a story—much like sport itself—that is a testament to our country's enduring and resilient ethic of competition on the field and its passion for fairness and justice.

Women's Sports before Title IX

• INTRODUCTION •

The Industrial Revolution brought a more formal segregation between men and women, as work and home were increasingly separated into what has now become known as the "doctrine of separate spheres." Publicly, men were cast as the competitors in the amoral, economic, legal, and political realms, whereas women were positioned either as decorative acquisitions or as spiritual guardians of men's immortal souls. Women's moral superiority was in direct proportion to their physical inferiority to men. Whereas women at the lowest rung of the socioeconomic ladder have always engaged in heavy physical labor, middle- and upper-class women's roles focused on their central duties in childbearing and homemaking. Physicians and educators noted that women's health was suffering as a result of this limiting definition of femininity, but the call was not for sports and competition; rather, it was for walking and calisthenics to improve women's physical and mental health for the purposes of childbearing and home-making. As the piece by Susan Cahn makes clear, the medical profession warned against exercise that was too strenuous lest it harm women's reproductive functions, while the moralists warned that sports participation would lead to a masculinization of women, either turning them against their prescribed roles or into homosexuals. Homophobia, or the fear of homosexuality, was used (and, indeed, is still used) to keep young women from playing sports.

Yet it is a mistake to assume that girls and women did not participate in sports before Title IX. The article by Welch Suggs provides a brief history of the forces that shaped women's sports experience, and how the female sports leaders hoped to avoid the pitfalls that seemed to plague men's athletic experiences. These visionaries were committed to building a better, more cooperative sporting experience for women than was thought possible for men. The early values of women's sporting competition, however, morphed over the years, especially after women's intercollegiate athletics came to be organized not by the Association for Intercollegiate Athletics for Women (AIAW), but by the historically all-male National Collegiate Athletic Association (NCAA) in the early 1980s. As women came to be involved in organized sports, society did not have an easy time knowing what to make of the new role of women as athletes.

In addition to the experiences of the average female athlete, the article on Babe Didrikson Zaharias makes clear that extraordinary women's accomplishments were widely recognized and respected. The fact that Wilma Rudolph, Billie Jean King, Donna de Varona, and Althea Gibson were household names bears witness to both their athletic feats and the recognition they were accorded for their accomplishments. These women were both elite athletes and the appointed advocates for women's athletics. Despite these isolated success stories, women who were serious about athletics were seen as a bit freakish, not something that parents commonly hoped for their daughters in the same way that they might for their sons. So whereas history books may include shining examples of women excelling in sports, women's accomplishments generally were marginalized, and it took an exceptional person—not just an athlete with outstanding physical skills—to be able to surmount this society-wide position. The *Sports Illustrated* article by Bil Gilbert and Nancy Williamson provides a glimpse of what the sports experience was like for a more typical female athlete.

Coming on Strong: Gender and Sexuality in Twentieth-Century Sports*

Susan Cahn

In the fall of 1911, *Lippincott's Monthly* described the modern athletic woman: "She loves to walk, to row, to ride, to motor, to jump and run . . . as Man walks, jumps, rows, rides, motors, and runs." To many early-twentieth-century observers, the female athlete represented the bold and energetic modern woman, breaking free from Victorian constraints, and tossing aside old-fashioned ideas about separate spheres for men and women. Popular magazines celebrated this transformation, issuing favorable notice that the "hardy sun-tanned girl" who spent the summer in outdoor games was fast replacing her predecessors, the prototypical "Lydia Languish" and the "soggy matron" of old.

With the dawning of the new century, interest in sport had burgeoned. More and more Americans were participating as spectators or competitors in football, baseball, track and field, and a variety of other events. At the same time women were streaming into education, the paid labor force, and political reform movements in unprecedented numbers. Women's social and political activism sparked a reconsideration of their nature and place in society, voiced through vigorous debates on a wide range of issues, from the vote to skirt lengths. Popular interest in sport and concern over women's changing status converged in the growing attention paid to the "athletic girl," a striking symbol of modern womanhood.

The female athlete's entrance into a male-defined sphere made her not only a popular figure but an ambiguous, potentially disruptive character as well. Sport had developed as a male preserve, a domain in which men expressed and cultivated masculinity through athletic competition. Yet, along with other "New

*New York: Free Press (1994), 7–9, 164–165, 181–184, excerpt.

Women" who demanded access to such traditional male realms as business and politics, women athletes of the early twentieth century claimed the right to share in sport. They stood on the borderline between new feminine ideals and customary notions of manly sport, symbolizing both the possibilities and the dangers of the New Woman's daring disregard for traditional gender arrangements.

The female athlete's ambiguity created a dilemma for her advocates. Given women's evident enjoyment of such "masculine" pursuits, could the "athletic girl" (and thus, the modern woman) reap the benefits of sport (and modernity) without becoming less womanly? The *Lippincott's Monthly* article was titled "The Masculinization of Girls." And while it concluded positively that "with muscles tense and blood aflame, she plays the manly role," women's assumption of "the manly role" generated deep hostility and anxiety among those who feared that women's athletic activity would damage female reproductive capacity, promote sexual licentiousness, and blur "natural" gender differences.

The perceived "mannishness" of the female athlete complicated her reception, making the "athletic girl" a cause for concern as well as celebration. Controversy did not dampen women's enthusiasm, but it did lead some advocates of women's sport to take a cautious approach, one designed specifically to avert charges of masculinization. Women physical educators took an especially prudent stance, articulating a unique philosophy of women's athletics that differed substantially from popular ideas of "manly sport."

The tension between sport and femininity led, paradoxically, to educators' insistence on women's equal right to sport and on inherent differences between female and male athletes. Balancing claims of equality and difference, physical educators articulated a woman-centered philosophy of sport that proposed "moderation" as the watchword of women's physical activity. Moderation provided the critical point of difference between women's and men's sport, a preventive against the masculine effects of sport. It was this philosophy, with its calculated effort to resolve the issue of "mannishness," which guided the early years of twentieth-century women's athletics.

By midcentury the persistent attempts of women athletes and their advocates to project an image of attractive femininity had failed to sunder the perceived connection between female athleticism and a rough, ill-bred "mannishness." In fact, the task had become doubly difficult in the conservative post–World War II era. During these years women athletes encountered a growing suspicion that they were not only gender anomalies but might be sexual aberrants as well.

Given the long association between athleticism and male virility, it was not surprising that there should be speculation about lesbianism among athletes.

For decades critics of women's sport had linked "mannishness" to sexual deviance, claiming that masculinized female athletes would inevitably acquire masculine sexual characteristics and interests as well. The fear of female sexuality unleashed from feminine modesty and male control runs like a constant thread through the history of women's sport. However, the nature of such fears and the understanding of "mannish" female sexuality had changed significantly between early and midcentury.

Between 1900 and 1930, the sexual debate in sport centered on the problem of unbridled heterosexual desire, the prospect that "masculine" sport might loosen women's inhibitions toward men. But by the 1930s, female athletic mannishness began to connote failed (rather than excessive) heterosexuality. Citing expert opinion that intense competition would disfigure the athletic woman and make her unappealing to men, author Fred Wittner asserted in 1934 that as an "inevitable consequence" of athletic training, "girls trained in physical education today may find it more difficult to attract the most worthy fathers for their children."

The impression of heterosexual "failure" contained a further possibility as well: The Amazonian athlete might be not only unattractive but unattracted to men—she might prefer women. What began as a vague suggestion of lesbianism emerged as a full-blown stereotype of the "mannish lesbian athlete" in the years after World War II. As a stigmatized figure the mannish lesbian functioned as a powerful but unarticulated "bogeywoman" of sport, silently foiling the ongoing efforts of sport advocates to rehabilitate the reputation of women athletes and resolve the cultural contradiction between athletic prowess and femininity.

By the 1950s, all female athletes and physical educators operated under a cloud of sexual suspicion. The destructive stereotype of the mannish lesbian athlete pressured women in sport to demonstrate their femininity and heterosexuality, viewed as one and the same. Many women adopted an apologetic stance about their athletic skill. Even as they competed to win, they made sure to display outward signs of femininity in dress and demeanor. They took special care in dealing with the media to reveal "feminine" hobbies like cooking and sewing, mention current boyfriends, and discuss future marriage plans.

Leaders of women's sport took the same approach at the institutional level. Physical educators redoubled their efforts to discredit the portrayal of P.E. majors and teachers as social misfits and prudes. In a paper on postwar objectives, Mildred Schaeffer explained that P.E. classes should help women "develop an interest in school dances and mixers and a *desire to voluntarily attend them.*" To this end administrators continued to emphasize lifelong sport and daily-life skills (including occasional lessons on how to lift luggage and dodge oncoming automobiles). The idea of "co-recreation" spread from intramural activities to the regular curriculum, where physical educators began designing coeducational classes to foster "broader, keener, more sympathetic understanding of the opposite sex." Lest there be any confusion about the message, in 1956 the University of Texas brought in Dr. Henry Bowman, author of *Marriage for Moderns*, to lecture first-year women's P.E. classes on how "to be gotten."

In conjunction with curricular reform, physical educators launched internal crackdowns on students and faculty who might feed the public image of mannishness. Departments warned against "casual styles" that might "lead us back into some dangerous channels." They implemented dress codes forbidding slacks and men's shirts or socks, adding as well a ban on "boyish haircuts" and unshaven legs. The Ohio P.E. Association left no doubt about the impression it sought to project. Its 1946 brochure for prospective majors flatly stated, "The mannish concept of a physical educator is no longer acceptable." The pamphlet's cover showed a man in a suit and a woman in high heels and a skirt walking hand in hand *away* from a background of athletic fields.

Popular sports promoters adopted similar tactics. Roxy Andersen responded to the implied connection between mannishness and lesbianism by designing AAU[1] promotional campaigns around the assertion of heterosexuality. In her 1945 article "Fashions in Feminine Sport," Andersen created a historical scenario of growing heterosexual appeal and pursuit. She contrasted "prehistoric femmes who developed their speed running AWAY from the men" with "the glamorous girls of this age," who dated six nights a week. The modern athlete's "luscious . . . decorative . . . long-stem" beauty and frequent dating discredited the "erroneous opinion that men disapprove of women in sport."

Marshaling sexual data as if they were athletic statistics, a 1954 AAU poll sought to sway a skeptical public with numerical proof of heterosexuality—the fact that 91 percent of former female athletes surveyed had married. Publicity for the Midwestern AAGBL[2] supplemented the usual statistics on total hits, runs, and stolen bases with figures on the total number of married players in the league. In the same vein, the professional women's golf tour announced that one-third of its members were married and the rest were on the lookout for attractive marital prospects.

The fear of lesbianism was greatest where a sport had a particularly masculine image and where promoters needed to attract a paying audience. Professional

---

[1]AAU is an acronym for the Amateur Athletic Union, an organization sponsoring many athletic leagues and events. Until Congress passed the newly named Ted Stevens Olympic and Amateur Sports Act in 1978 (section 220510 U.S.C.A.), the AAU was the recognized governing body for many Olympic sports.

[2]AAGBL is an acronym for the All-American Girls Baseball League, founded in the 1940s.

and semipro basketball and softball fit the bill on both counts. Sponsors tried to resolve the problem through beauty contests and other promotional ploys to "prove" the attractive femininity of athletes. While in earlier times such events celebrated the "sexiness" of the emancipated modern woman, in later decades they seemed to serve a more defensive function. Editors of the *Amateur Athlete* made sure that at least one photograph of the national basketball tournament's beauty "queen and her court" accompanied the photo of each year's championship team, as—behind the scenes—teams passed dress and conduct codes designed to allay fears that ball teams attracted "freaks" and "Amazons."

In their efforts to counter pernicious lesbian stereotypes, sports promoters and the media transformed the "unseemly" heterosexual element present in earlier working-class athletics into the basic standard of legitimacy for all women's sport. For decades the overt eroticism of popular sport had sparked internal controversy and external criticism. But by midcentury, promoters of a wide variety of women's sports highlighted the female athlete's sexual allure. The most acceptable athletes were the women whose beauty and sex appeal "compensated" for their athletic ability. Those athletes deemed unattractive by virtue of their size, musculature, facial features, or "unfeminine" bearing met with public censure and suspicion of their sexuality.

Although women's sport advocates did their best to "prove" heterosexuality and to suppress "mannishness," in the end this strategy did little to diminish the lesbian stigma of women's sport. Hostile observers perpetuated lesbian athletic stereotypes through their unrelenting ridicule of skilled athletes as "grotesque," "ugly," "masculine," or "unnatural." Leaders of women's sport unwittingly contributed to the homophobic climate when they began to orient their programs toward a new feminine heterosexual ideal. As organizational policies and media campaigns worked to suppress lesbianism and marginalize athletes who didn't conform to dominant standards of femininity, sport officials incorporated society's fear and loathing of lesbians into the practice and imagery of sport.

The stigmatized "mannish" lesbian athlete did not disappear but rather assumed the stature of a negative symbol of female social and sexual independence. As a powerful representation of deviance her significance reached far beyond the world of sport. She announced to all women that competitiveness, strength, independence, aggression, and same-sex physical intimacy were privileged features of manhood or, conversely, the mark of unacceptable womanhood. She represented the border that must not be crossed, reminding all women to toe the line of heterosexual femininity or risk falling into a despised and liminal category of mannish (not-women) women.

Heroines as Well as Heroes*

Welch Suggs

The public mind-set about women in sports had begun to change in the mid-1960s in part as a result of the Cold War. The public watched women compete on television, mostly in individual sports like tennis and gymnastics. Any competition in which Americans could beat Soviets was met with general approval. Although colleges had cut back on most sports offerings for women in the years following World War II, by the middle to late 1960s more colleges were experimenting with intercollegiate athletics for women.

The first college championship for female athletes was the 1941 golf tournament at Ohio State sanctioned by the National Section on Women's Athletics of the American Association for Health, Physical Education, and Recreation, or AAHPER. The tournament became a yearly event in 1946, and a decade later the various organizations governing women's sports formed the Tripartite Golf Committee. By 1958, that group had expanded to form the Joint Committee on Extra-Mural Sports, which was designed to unite and streamline the efforts of the dizzying array of organizations that had some jurisdiction over sports for women at the time: the AAHPER women's section, which soon became the Division of Girls' and Women's Sports; the National Association of Directors of Physical Education; and the Athletic and Recreation Federation of College Women.

The task of the joint committee was to satisfy the fast-growing interest among college women in competitive sports in the late 1950s and early 1960s.

*A Place on the Team: The Triumph and Tragedy of Title IX (Princeton: Princeton University Press, 2005), chapter 3, excerpt.

14

As women broke down barriers in all facets of society, their interest in sports also grew after watching Wilma Rudolph, Margaret Court, Billie Jean King, and other athletes.

At the same time, the women in charge of the physical-education associations were worried about losing control over women's athletics. Dissatisfied with what they were getting in college settings, some women were playing tennis and competing in semipro sports at private clubs, on corporate teams, and in opportunities provided by the Amateur Athletic Union (AAU) programs.[1] Some women were also competing on men's teams when they could.

"I was playing almost-semipro softball in the 1960s with the Raybestos Brakettes, playing against outside amateur teams," says Donna A. Lopiano, who became women's athletics director at the University of Texas at Austin and later director of the Women's Sports Foundation. "I played in four national championships, and we drew crowds in the thousands in small towns in Connecticut."[2]

Administrators with the Division of Girls' and Women's Sports (DGWS) realized that women were going to find opportunities to compete in elite, Olympic-style sports and decided that it would be better for those women to compete within the American educational system, under the supervision of qualified women, rather than to allow the AAU or National Collegiate Athletic Association (NCAA) to take command. In 1963, Sara Staff Jernigan of the DGWS addressed the NCAA's annual convention, asking the association to stop allowing women to compete on men's teams. She said she and other educators feared that women would be in danger of getting roughed up in games against men, and that women's sports would not develop if the best athletes were skimmed off by men's programs. Women leaders were also deeply suspicious of the regular scandals in men's sports—stories of players being allowed to skate through classes, boosters handing out bribes to recruit talented players, and point-shaving to help gamblers.

"The women in the sixties were historians, students of what had happened in intercollegiate athletics, and one thing they all recognized was that men's sport had gotten to where it was because physical educators, male physical educators, had taken a hands-off approach, saying, 'I don't want to have anything to do with that,'" Lopiano says. Women educators "were faced with repeating history. They took responsibility. They knew highly competitive sport for women was going to come in an educational construct, and that they needed to control it and keep it educational."

[1] Patricia Ann Rosenbrock, "Persistence and Accommodation in a Decade of Struggle and Change: The Case of Women Administrators in Division I-A Intercollegiate Athletics Programs" (PhD thesis, University of Iowa, 1987), 33 and 164.

[2] All quotations from Jernstedt, Lopiano, and Neinas in this article are taken from interviews conducted in 2003 and 2004, unless otherwise noted.

At the time, the NCAA did not object. In 1964, the association satisfied Jernigan by passing a rule to limit championship participation to men. It also created a "special liaison committee on women's athletics" the same year.[3]

At the same time, DGWS officials began to explore the idea of creating an organization to sponsor women's championships, which would involve creating a new structure to govern women's sports across the country. Again, the NCAA approved. In a 1966 memorandum, Charles S. Neinas, the top assistant to NCAA director Walter F. Byers, wrote that the "NCAA limits its jurisdiction and authority to male student-athletes . . . consequently, a national organization assuming responsibility for women's athletics would not be in conflict with this Association."[4]

In 1967, AAHPER announced the formation of the Commission on Intercollegiate Athletics for Women (CIAW) "to give college women more opportunities for high level competition in athletics." A news release announced that a national college championship in gymnastics would be held in March or April 1969, with a track meet scheduled for April or May. The schedule called for swimming, badminton, and volleyball championships in 1970, and the golf tournament was subsumed under the new slate.[5]

Katherine Ley of the AAHPER was to be in charge of the new organization, which would replace all of the competing committees and associations. Her platform for the new organization was as follows: "Children growing up need heroines as well as heroes. We suspect that the naming of national champions each year in the different sports will make sports activity seem more desirable and will motivate less talented girls all over the country to learn sports skills and to enjoy sports on their own."[6]

Within three years, AAHPER officials decided they needed a separate and more formal structure for the championships slate, and they spun off the CIAW into the Association for Intercollegiate Athletics for Women (AIAW) in January 1972.

Developing their own association free from the influence of men, the women of the AIAW had a great feeling of ownership and protectiveness over their organization. They were able to reinvent the "girl for every sport, and a sport for every girl" philosophy from the history of their organizations, and the teams and championships they sponsored were structured to promote broad partici-

[3] Jack Falla, NCAA: The Voice of College Sports: A Diamond Anniversary History, 1906–1981 (Overland Park, KS: NCAA, 1981), 161.

[4] Affidavit of Donna A. Lopiano, president of the AIAW, in Assoc. for Intercollegiate Athletics for Women v. Nat'l. Collegiate Athletic Assoc., 588 F. Supp. 487 (D. D.C. 1983), affirmed, 735 F.2d 577 (D.C. Cir. 1984).

[5] AAHPER, "News Release," December 7, 1967.

[6] Ibid.

pation more than competition. They banned athletic scholarships and placed significant restrictions on recruiting.

These sentiments were reflected in the AIAW Policy Statement, adopted in May 1974:

> We believe sport is an important aspect of our culture and a fertile field for learning. The sense of enjoyment, self-confidence, and physical well-being derived from demanding one's best performance in a sport situation is a meaningful experience for the athlete. These inner satisfactions are the fundamental motivation for participation in sports. Therefore, programs in an educational setting should have these benefits as primary goals.
>
> In keeping with this belief, the following program elements are vitally important:

1. The enrichment of the life of the participant is the focus and reason for the existence of any athletic program. All decisions should be made with this fact in mind.
2. The participants in athletic programs, including players, coaches, and support personnel, should have access to and representation in the policy-making group on campus and in sport governing organizations.
3. Adequate funding is necessary to provide a comprehensive program. Sufficient funds should be provided for:

   - A broad spectrum of sports experiences;
   - A variety of levels of competitive experiences;
   - Travel using licensed carriers;
   - Appropriate housing and food;
   - Rated officials;
   - Well-trained coaches;
   - Equipment, supplies, and facilities which aid performance and appeal to the aesthetic aspects of sport;
   - Competent staff for administering and publicizing the program;
   - Qualified medical and training personnel;
   - And regular opportunities for social interaction with opponents.

4. Careful consideration is needed for scheduling practices and games. The athletic schedule should ensure sufficient time to gain personal satisfaction from skill achievement, but should not deny the student the time to participate in other activities. Factors to be considered include:

- Equitable compensation at all levels;
- Adequate pre-season conditioning;
- Appropriate spacing and length of practice sessions;
- Sufficient number of events in each sport; and
- Comparable length of seasons between sports.

5. Separate but comparable teams should be provided for women and men. In addition to separate teams, intercollegiate coeducational teams comprised of an equal number of women and men competing on opposing teams is desirable in those sports in which such teams are appropriate. Athletic ability is one of the talents which can be considered in the awarding of financial aid to students. However, students should be free to choose the institution on the basis of curriculum and program. Staff time and effort should be devoted to the comprehensive program rather than to recruiting efforts.[7]

This is more a manifesto than a set of playing rules. The women in charge of the AIAW were fighting for equal funding and equal recognition on their own campuses, accustomed as they were to having to pile into players' and coaches' cars to get to a road game. While they wanted their fair share of funding, they really wanted to maintain the independence to conduct their own sports programs with their own values.

Among those values was a certain egalitarianism. In the first AIAW championship in volleyball in 1972, participation ranged from huge urban campuses like UCLA to tiny rural ones like Sul Ross State in Alpine, Texas. In fact, Sul Ross beat UCLA in the championship match. The NCAA had separated into college and university divisions fifteen years earlier, and was on the verge of creating even more divisions.

Early rules were carefully drawn to be restrictive. The AIAW forbade flying recruits onto campuses for visits. Christine H. B. Grant, one of the AIAW's presidents, described the organization's approach to recruiting as "a system that attempted to achieve three goals: (a) to avoid the harassment of high school athletes; (b) to create a system that was financially reasonable to all member institutions; and (c) to prevent the burnout of coaches who spend excessive time in the recruitment of athletes."[8]

The AIAW was accepted widely and quickly. A total of 275 colleges and universities signed on as charter members, including junior colleges, women's

[7]AIAW, "Policy Statement" (AIAW Archives: University of Maryland at College Park, May 1974).
[8]Christine H. B. Grant, "The Gender Gap in Sport: From Olympic to Intercollegiate Level," *Arena Review* (July 1984), 43.

colleges, liberal arts colleges, regional universities, and state flagship institutions. However, women were still in a world of postgame meals of fast-food hamburgers and self-transportation while their male counterparts ate steak and took chartered planes and buses.

The issue of whether female athletes should be competing on male teams remained controversial. The *Athletic Director,* a newsletter published by the National Council of Secondary School Athletics Officials, said in 1974 that "while positive experiences for the exceptional girl competitor may occur through participation in boys' or men's competitive groups, these instances are rare and should be judged acceptable only as an interim procedure for use until girls' programs can be initiated."[9]

This was a crucial issue. The NCAA reconsidered its decision to ban women from its championships in 1972, fearing that it could be sued for violating women's rights under the Fourteenth Amendment to the U.S. Constitution, even before Title IX had been introduced in Congress. Some male athletics directors believed they could accommodate women in sports simply by opening tryouts to everyone, male and female: Women could go out for a team and get cut because they were too small, too slow, or lacked other skills, but the school would have protected its legal obligations.

But that end run around the law never became popular. Women's officials pressed the point that women needed sex-segregated sports programs. Thus, women created perhaps the only context in civil rights law where "separate but equal" was tolerated and even endorsed.

S ome male officials were extremely supportive. The National Association of Intercollegiate Athletics' (NAIA) leadership sent the AIAW a letter saying, "The NAIA Executive Committee is fully aware of the problems which face our member institutions in financing separate programs of intercollegiate competition. . . . We are free to admit we have no magical or painless solution. However, NAIA is most sympathetic to the AIAW program and is committed to giving every assistance to make it possible for opportunities for women to develop."[10]

Even as women won these initial battles for separate teams, however, they found themselves embroiled in a bigger war: the struggle to decide who would ultimately govern women's sports. In the mid-1960s, the NCAA decided that it needed to begin sponsoring women's programs. Its espoused reasons were legal—as the women's movement was so ably demonstrating, institutions

---

[9] National Council of Secondary School Athletics Officials, *Athletic Director* (February 1971), 1.
[10] *AIAW Newsletter* 2, no. 1, 3.

available to men ought also to be available to women. AIAW leaders believe to this day that the NCAA was angling to cement its control over all of collegiate sports.

The first steps were cautious. In 1966 the NCAA's Neinas wrote again to CIAW officials asking if they planned to conduct championships. "Please do not misinterpret this letter," he wrote. "The NCAA has enough problems of its own without irritating DGWS or the gals. It should be recognized, however, that some of the athletic directors in the NCAA believe that national competition for women will stimulate activity at the grass-roots level."[11]

In 1967, the NCAA Council, a group of athletic administrators and college presidents that served as the organization's board of directors, appointed a study committee to consider "the feasibility of establishing appropriate machinery for the control and supervision of women's athletics."[12] In explaining the council's actions, Arthur W. Nebel of the University of Missouri wrote:

> All of us are aware of women's role [in society]. They now are becoming more interested in intercollegiate athletics. NCAA championships are limited to male athletes. Also, the Association's rules and regulations governing recruiting, financial aid, and eligibility apply only to the male student.
>
> It was recently brought to the Council's attention that an increasing number of NCAA institutions are sponsoring intercollegiate athletic activities for women. Some of these institutions have sought the advice of the Association as to the proper administrative procedures for an intercollegiate program for female students.
>
> As a result, the Council has appointed a committee to study the feasibility of establishing appropriate machinery to provide for supervision and administration of women's intercollegiate athletics. . . . This should not be misconstrued as an effort on the part of the NCAA to establish women's championships or extend present Association regulations to women's intercollegiate athletics. It is possible that this may be the eventual result.[13]

That fall, the NCAA became more direct. Walter F. Byers, the association's cantankerous executive director, fired what many women considered a shot across the bow in October 1967. In a letter to women's leaders, he wrote, "The question of whether the NCAA is the organization to take this job [of governing

---

[11]Lopiano, 35–36. Neinas could not confirm the exact wording of the memorandum but recognized the language and the intent.

[12]Ibid., 36.

[13]Falla, 161–162.

women's sports] is a question yet to be determined. Likewise, I presume that the question of whether the AAHPER (through DGWS) is the appropriate organization to supervise and control women's sports has not been determined."[14]

Byers continued to press the question as the decade turned. In 1971, he wrote to Elizabeth Hoyt of the AIAW to say that he had asked the NCAA's lawyer, George H. Gangwere, to evaluate whether the men's association could be held liable for not permitting women to participate in its championships. This letter predated Title IX by a year and a half, and it was written four months before Edith Green held hearings in the House of Representatives about inequities in education. "It appears that the NCAA is in a difficult legal position on the basis of its present posture and I suspect that it is quite likely that we will proceed to remove such barriers and, in fact, provide competitive opportunities for women as well as men," he wrote.[15]

A month later, Byers reported to his members on Gangwere's opinion:

> Because there are numerous opportunities for female athletes to participate (e.g., the Olympic Games), they would have justification to complain that the NCAA does discriminate by preventing females from competing in events against other female athletes. (If the United States constitutional amendment for women's rights is adopted, there probably no longer would be any legally tenable grounds for disqualifying an athletically talented female from competing in an NCAA event against males.)
>
> For the present, action, if any, will more than likely come on the grounds of the equal protection clause of the Fourteenth Amendment . . . It could be argued that any illegal discrimination is that of member institutions, not the NCAA.[16]

Neinas told AIAW officials that he hoped their organization would be the appropriate venue for collegiate female athletes, but that the NCAA had to make plans if AIAW leaders felt "that you cannot make the adjustments necessary to accomplish that end."[17] The implication was that the AIAW's emphasis on participation would not provide female athletes opportunities "comparable" to those of male NCAA athletes.

The NCAA by this time was well established as the largest athletic organization in the country, sponsoring championships for hundreds of schools of all sizes and missions. The NAIA was very viable, especially in basketball, but

[14]Lopiano, 39.
[15]Ibid., 42–43.
[16]Ibid., 43.
[17]Ibid., 49.

NCAA officials controlled the airwaves for football and basketball broadcasts, and their championship events were becoming fixtures on the American sporting scene.

Contempt might be too strong a word, but the men of the NCAA were not very impressed with the AIAW's attitude toward sports. To NCAA officials, the AIAW's model was one of playing sports and having postgame teas, while the men were the "real" athletes. They were dubious that a professional association of educators could manage a sports program, and they certainly did not think the women's organizations were up to the task of administering women's athletics.

Neinas recalls approaching DGWS officials in the 1960s in one of the conversations about improving the United States' medal count in the Olympics. The U.S. Olympic Committee "was willing to put some development money into women's sports, and I said, 'Can you [the DGWS] help us channel it?' Their response was, they weren't interested in competition. That was the group that believed in Play Days, and they didn't want to have too high a level of competition."

Byers's 1971 memo brought a furious response from Rachel Bryant of the AIAW:

> No action the NCAA could take would be a bigger mistake [than to try to co-opt female athletes or the AIAW]. A group of professional women educators have designed an organization and a program in accordance with their accepted philosophy and standards to meet the needs and interests of college women students. To have it now threatened by an organization designed for men and controlled by men would cause such a furor that the NCAA would have a real battle on its hands. The possibility of one girl instituting a court suit to participate on a male varsity team would be a very pale issue in comparison.[18]

The passage of Title IX in 1972 and the kickoff of the AIAW's championships pushed the issue of the NCAA and women's sports to the forefront. The women's movement, according to Byers, made Title IX a national battle instead of a local one: "It's tough for a woman to do battle with the football coach on a Division I-A campus, but a collection of determined women at the national level—with political support and media attention—could take on the NCAA and look very good indeed," he theorized.[19]

While mounting its own challenges to the law through sympathetic congressmen, the NCAA pushed ahead on the question of whether to start champion-

---

[18]Ibid., 45.

[19]Walter F. Byers and Charles Hammer, *Unsportsmanlike Conduct: Exploiting College Athletics* (Ann Arbor, MI: University of Michigan Press, 1993), 242.

ships for women. In 1975 the association sent another of Byers's assistants, Thomas A. Jernstedt, to address the AIAW's convention in Houston. Jernstedt remembers a very chilly reception. "I flew to Houston and made a very brief presentation to say that the NCAA sent me here to share with this organization that the NCAA had been involved in discussions to establish women's championships, perhaps in the next academic year, that hadn't been totally resolved."

According to the AIAW's minutes, Jernstedt says that:

The Association has attempted to cooperate with women's amateur sports organizations for more than eleven years.

This is not a new area of concern for the Association; it is simply that the emphasis and problems involved here have increased markedly over the past two years.

In response to the membership's request for direction in this matter, the Council directed the NCAA staff to prepare a report and recommendations regarding NCAA's role in women's intercollegiate athletics. That report was received by the Council. It recommends that the Association move now to provide the same meaningful services in high quality national championship competition, backed by the same administrative support, for women student-athletes and teams of its member institutions as it does for men student-athletes. It recommends that the only satisfactory approach, considering the demands of court decisions, to the necessary institutional control of all of its intercollegiate athletic programs is to place men's and women's programs under the same administration, the same legislative body, and the same legislative rules. It further recommends that the NCAA begin immediately to offer national intercollegiate competition for women in selected sports. The [NCAA] Council approved the concept of that report and referred the recommendations to the Special Committee on Women's Intercollegiate Athletics for implementation at the earliest possible time.[20]

Before he had finished speaking, Jernstedt says, delegates were streaming off the convention floor, heading outside to call their campuses to see if their presidents would support an effort to quell the NCAA's plan.

Carol Gordon, chairwoman of the AIAW's executive board, fired off a telegram to the NCAA's convention, which was taking place at the same time in Washington:

AIAW views with grave concern the announced intention of NCAA to commence a pilot program of intercollegiate athletics for women. For the

[20]Minutes of the AIAW Delegates Assembly, January 5–8, 1975, Houston, Texas.

sake of future harmony in administration of intercollegiate sports programs for all students and to restore an atmosphere of cooperation in
which a mutually beneficial exchange of views and exploration of future
alternatives might continue, the Executive Board of AIAW urges the Executive Council to reconsider immediately its decision to initiate any pilot
program in women's intercollegiate championships. AIAW has no choice
but to view failure to reconsider as an effort by NCAA to undermine the
existing women's intercollegiate championship program.[21]

"So it was not met with any noticeable enthusiasm," says Jernstedt of his
efforts. "I think there were individuals like Linda Estes [the women's athletic
director at the University of New Mexico], and I'm sure others in the crowd,
who understood it and thought, 'This was very interesting,' and that it may be
better for women student-athletes, and they were silent. This was a very genuine
desire and effort by the NCAA to see if we could provide better and more extensive competitive opportunities. Exposure, I think was one of the primary components. . . . The NCAA, because of the broad scope of programs on the men's
side, was in a stronger position to move women's athletics to a higher level."

The time was not quite right, however. The mass exodus from the convention that Jernstedt's address caused came back to swamp the NCAA. Enough of
the AIAW women had prevailed with their presidents and male athletics directors to force the NCAA convention to table the matter.

The campus debates over the governance of women's sports mirrored the
national one. As college presidents realized they would have to provide "equitable" programs for female athletes, many of them decided they ought to make
women's programs look like men's programs. They moved women's sports out
of physical-education departments, often making the women's athletics director
an associate athletics director (in addition to her teaching responsibilities) and
placing her under the supervision of the men's athletics director.

Said one women's sports administrator: "I think what started us actually
doing anything about moving into 'athletics' as such was a group of students
in the early 1970s who said, 'We are world class and national class athletes. And
when we are swimming in the summer, we are just as good as the guys, and we
get [the same competitive opportunities and benefits].' And it was those students who stirred up such a ruckus in the early 1970s. Then came the emphasis
of Title IX when it started to come along in 1972. The combination of the two
got the attention of the administration in this school."[22]

State legislatures and universities often kicked in money from general funds
to help start women's programs, and the number of women participating in

[21] Ibid.
[22] Rosenbrock, 51–52.

varsity programs spiked immediately after the law's passage. The NCAA puts the number of female athletes on varsity teams at 15,182 in 1966–1967. In 1971–1972, even before the passage of Title IX, that figure had doubled, to 29,977. By 1976–1977, the number of women playing sports had doubled again to 62,886. (The number of male athletes also increased, from 151,918 in 1966–1967 to 168,136 in 1976–1977.)[23]

But the increases were not always comfortable. Many women had to learn that varsity sports were not "church league," according to Judy Rose, who began her coaching and administrative career in 1975. Another female administrator described the transition in the administration of women's sports:

> The first cuts were made in team selection, but you still didn't have extensive schedules and you didn't practice all the time. In 1972 things changed a little bit more and we renamed our women's sports organization the Women's Intercollegiate Sports Association. And several sports were dropped as concentration was put into about five sports, because we had only $5,000 at that point. At that was the beginning of the change to an intensified coaching situation which was mild by comparison with today.
>
> And then in 1973 the chancellor appointed a task force to take a look at women's athletics and decide what to do with it. The upshot of the task force was that women's athletics should become part of the Athletics Department and not be part of physical education any longer, because they determined that it wasn't appropriate, from a financial standpoint nor a philosophical standpoint. And so in June 1974, two weeks after the task force made their report, I was hired as the Assistant Athletics Director, and we moved into the Athletics Department. At that point our women's budget jumped from $10,000 to $83,000. The men's budget at that time was about $2.5 million.[24]

The first major conflict between the AIAW's idealism and the pragmatism of implementing Title IX came a year after the law passed. Female tennis players at Marymount College and Broward Community College sued the AIAW in 1973 over the ban on scholarships. No matter what good reason the AIAW might have for banning scholarships, the plaintiffs argued, if colleges were going to provide men with a certain benefit, they needed to provide women with an equitable benefit.

[23] 1982–2000 Participation Statistics Report (by NCAA), http://www.ncaa.org/library/research/participation_rates/1982-2000/153-164.pdf (accessed July 14, 2004).

[24] Rosenbrock, 53.

Many college administrators believed that they needed to provide scholarships for members of both sexes. Even before the Florida lawsuits were filed, some colleges experimented with scholarship programs, leading to even more chaos among women's programs. A memorandum indicates the precariousness of the situation:

> Pennsylvania State University did not use the DGWS sanctioning approval for the National Intercollegiate Women's Fencing Association Championship held on April 6–8, 1972. Della Durant, Coordinator of Women's Varsity Sports, Penn. St. U., reported that the directors of the event felt that they could not rightfully use the sanctioning since three to four schools would not sign a statement asking for specific information regarding the status of scholarships at their institutions.[25]

The AIAW settled the cases and changed its rules to permit scholarship to avoid losing members, but tried to convince administrators to stick to educational criteria for awarding scholarships rather than athletic ones:

> The DGWS reaffirms its concerns that the provision of scholarships or other financial assistance specifically designated for athletes may create a potential for abuses which could prove detrimental to the development of quality programs of athletics. Specifically, the DGWS deplores the evils of pressure recruiting and performer exploitation which frequently accompany the administration of financial aid for athletes.
>
> The DGWS is concerned that many collegiate athletic programs as currently administered do not make available to female students benefits equivalent in nature or extent to those made available to male students. While a curtailment of programs of financial aid to female students involved in athletics does eliminate the potential for abuses inherent in any such programs, this remedy is overly broad because it operates inequitably to deny to female students benefits available to their male counterparts. Specifically, those benefits might include the recognition of athletic excellence and the opportunity for economic assistance to secure an education.
>
> Therefore, DGWS belies that the appropriate solution in our contemporary society is one directed to avoiding abuses while providing to female students, on an equitable basis, benefits comparable to those available to male students similarly situated.[26]

[25]Addendum to AIAW Executive Board Minutes for Meeting June 1–4, 1972, AIAW archives, University of Maryland at College Park.

[26]DGWS, "Statement of Philosophy" (AIAW archives, University of Maryland at College Park, April 1, 1973).

Many female administrators viewed the awarding of scholarships as a critical change for women's college sports. They had built their paradigm around the idea of providing the best experiences to women who were already enrolled. They did not allow coaches to recruit off-campus, nor to send prospective students anything more than a simple brochure describing their programs. Colleges were not supposed to compete for prized women athletes as they did for males, and coaches were restrained from recruiting so they could devote their time to teaching.

Scholarships shifted the emphasis from women already enrolled to those who could be recruited. Armed with scholarships, coaches needed to go out and find the best possible recipients. They had to choose athletes on the basis of athletic ability, not as a way of providing students with a healthy extracurricular activity.

This may seem like an obscure point to someone familiar with the NCAA's scholarship system, but it meant that women's programs in the 1970s "would take a 180-degree turn," in the words of one administrator. "I'd been here all these years trying to develop a program for the young women who came to this university to get an education, and [also] liked to compete in sport. As they came we tried to allow our program to grow as rapidly as they could take that growth. Now suddenly, with this act, we were going out to find the student-athlete who we thought the university should have. And then we were going to have to provide the program for those student-athletes. And as soon as we began to do that the emphasis for women's sport changed."[27]

Lopiano says that the AIAW held firm to its philosophy, keeping coaches from going off-campus and instead permitting them to hold on-campus "auditions," just like college drama or music programs would. "It was a very healthy experience in that parents came to college with the kid [prior to enrolling], and after it was all over, both parents and kids knew whether they belonged," she says. "The organization didn't look to the NCAA model and say, 'We're going to do this,' but said, 'We don't believe in off-campus recruiting; we believe the kid should recruit the school, and play with the program to see if there's a fit.'"

Grudgingly, the AIAW set caps of eight scholarships a year each for basketball, field hockey, gymnastics, lacrosse, softball, swimming, track and field, and volleyball; and four per year for archery, badminton, bowling, crew, golf, fencing, riflery, skiing, squash, and tennis. Scholarships required athletes to pass minimum academic standards and were limited to tuition, room, board, and fees, excluding books. In men's sports, the NCAA at that time had no limits on the number of scholarships.

NCAA studies show that women's sports grew rapidly in the 1970s. By 1977 women were getting 14 percent of athletics departments budgets nationally, but

[27]Rosenbrock, 53.

55 percent of their budgets were coming from nonathletic sources, such as campus general funds, donors, and state appropriations.[28] Given the meager size of those budgets, colleges were clearly not choosing to cut men's programs to finance women's.

Some colleges even got into a bidding war over coaches. In 1976, the University of Kentucky tried to lure Pat Summitt away from Tennessee by offering her $9,000 a year to coach the Wildcats. The sum was only $100 more than Summitt was making at Tennessee, though, and so she stayed in Knoxville. (Male coaches at the time were making $60,000 to $70,000 in base salaries.)[29]

"Being at Texas, you win a national championship and they love you," Lopiano says. Her budget went up exponentially in those years, often doubling. She and her basketball coach, Jody Conradt, made women's sports a cause célèbre in Austin, taking lessons from the men's department in marketing their programs to the public. "There's nothing wrong in marketing," Lopiano says. "We had great graduation rates, articulate kids, and great coaches. . . . It can be done."

Texas finances its women's program with mandatory student fees, proceeds from campus soft-drink machines and from leasing their facilities back to the university, and "making every effort to find money from nonacademic sources," Lopiano says. Not until the late 1980s, when money began pouring into college football from new television and bowl-game contracts, did the women's department at Texas get funds from the men's athletics department.

At the national level, Byers had not given up. He pressed the NCAA's annual convention every year to inaugurate championships for women, but throughout the 1970s the delegates from the association's colleges turned him down. But a few voices joined his. In 1975, John A. Fuzak of Michigan State University told delegates that the NCAA Council "recognized that the moral obligation to provide meaningful services for the female student-athlete of its member institutions is greater today than ever before, and that to temporize further is to deny the NCAA's own statements of purpose and fundamental policy."[30]

The council further concluded that:

> It is not feasible or desirable for the NCAA to confine future services and programs only to male student-athletes;
>
> It is not possible under the provisions of the law to restrict application of NCAA rules only to male student-athletes competing on intercollegiate varsity teams; and

[28] John R. Thelin, *Games Colleges Play: Scandal and Reform in Intercollegiate Athletics* (Baltimore, MD: Johns Hopkins University Press, 1993), 395.

[29] Ibid., 396.

[30] Falla, 164.

It is not permissible or plausible for the NCAA to enter into agreements with other organizations that, for example, would accord the NCAA exclusive authority over male intercollegiate athletics and accord a like monopoly position to an organization for control of women's athletics.

Existing rules of law and policy contemplate that qualified females will participate on teams which formerly were exclusively male. The NCAA cannot legally or practically limit its services and programs so as to exclude such qualified females.

While the argument may be made that it is legally possible to provide . . . programs through separate but equal facilities and staff, economy probably will dictate that there be a minimum of duplication of personnel and facilities. Furthermore, administrative necessity and the need for equitable eligibility requirements will require coordination and similarity not only at the institutional level, but also on a national level. Integrated or coordinated programs at the national level cannot be achieved if separate male and female national organizations are left to accomplish it through . . . bilateral agreements.[31]

This was a declaration of war, or at least was taken as such by the AIAW. The NCAA had asserted not only its desire to start a national-championship program as an alternative to the AIAW, but also its belief that only one organization ought to govern all of collegiate sport. And that organization was not the AIAW.

In his autobiography, Byers says that some individual women in college sports were less hostile than the AIAW's leaders. He recounts a 1980 meeting with Mary Alyce Hill of San Diego State University and Linda Estes of New Mexico. "They wanted women in key positions in the NCAA, and they wanted the NCAA to be the national governing body for women's athletics," he writes. "Both of them were key players in the burgeoning world of women's athletics, and their decision in favor of the NCAA gave my dwindling confidence a shot of adrenaline."[32]

In 1980, Byers got his wish. Divisions II and III voted to hold women's championships in basketball, field hockey, swimming, tennis, and volleyball beginning with the 1981–1982 academic year. The following year in Miami at the association's annual convention, the entire NCAA membership voted to expand its committees and allocate positions to women, and to create a three-year transition period to allow colleges to adapt from AIAW to NCAA rules. The

[31] Ibid., 164–165.
[32] Byers and Hammer, 244.

vote was 383 for and 168 against. The convention then voted to establish Division I championships in basketball, cross-country, field hockey, gymnastics, softball, swimming, tennis, and outdoor track and field. That measure passed 128–127, and for all practical purposes, the AIAW was rendered irrelevant.[33] Byers was not very sympathetic to those who regretted the undermining of the AIAW. "The men and the NCAA itself didn't discriminate against women," he writes. "Women's athletics leaders discriminated against themselves through the years by refusing to accept competitive athletics as a proper pursuit for teenage women."[34]

The AIAW sued the NCAA to prevent it from starting women's championships, arguing that the association was exercising an illegal monopoly power over college sports. The court disagreed and the lawsuit was dismissed.

Byers and most other NCAA historians largely neglected a crucial fact about his drive to start women's championships: It was Plan B. The NCAA spent much of the 1970s trying to kill off Title IX in Congress and the courts. Once those efforts failed, the next best option was to acquire women's sports.

[33]Falla, 168–174.
[34]Byers and Hammer, 244.

Didrikson Was a Woman Ahead of Her Time*

Larry Schwartz

The first to prove a girl could be a stud athlete, Babe Didrikson began as a muscular phenom who mastered many sports and ended as a brilliant golfer. An exuberant tomboy whose life was athletics, she was accomplished in just about every sport—basketball, track, golf, baseball, tennis, swimming, diving, boxing, volleyball, handball, bowling, billiards, skating, and cycling. When asked if there was anything she didn't play, she said, "Yeah, dolls."

As a teenager she knew her life's ambition. "My goal was to be the greatest athlete who ever lived," she said.

While others dispute her story, Didrikson said that she was nicknamed Babe early in her teens by boys awed at her long-distance homers. As she grew older, there seemed to be more Ty Cobb than Ruth in her, a dark rage that made losing intolerable. Like for Cobb, animosity seemed to be the fuel that stoked Babe's competitive fire.

The Associated Press voted her the Greatest Female Athlete of the first half of the 20th century. The wire service also voted her Female Athlete of the Year six times—once for her track dominance and five times for her golfing prowess.

Babe performed at a time when female athletes were considered freakish at best, downright unacceptable at worst. For most of her life she was the antithesis of femininity; not until her later years did she dress and act less manly. "She was not a feminist, not a militant, not a strategist launching campaigns against sexual liberation," wrote William Johnson and Nancy Williamson in *Whatta-Gal!: The Babe Didrikson Story*. "She was an athlete and her body was her most valuable possession."

*Special to ESPN.com (accessed June 29, 2007).

31

Some writers condemned her for not being feminine. "It would be much better if she and her ilk stayed at home, got themselves prettied up, and waited for the phone to ring," Joe Williams wrote in the *New York World-Telegram.*

Others were enthralled by the 5-foot-5 Babe, who was muscular but never heavy. "She is beyond all belief until you see her perform," famed sportswriter Grantland Rice wrote. "Then you finally understand that you are looking at the most flawless section of muscle harmony, of complete mental and physical coordination, the world of sport has ever seen."

While she excelled in competition, she often alienated teammates and competitors. She frequently acted like a self-centered prima donna, a boastful person who constantly sought attention. Although she became somewhat less arrogant over the years, she still remained flamboyant and cocky—and often overbearing.

Babe didn't seem to have much interest in men until she was swept off her feet when she was paired with George Zaharis at the 1938 Los Angeles Open. Zaharis was a gregarious man, a 235-pound wrestler who as a stock villain was making a fortune as the Weeping Greek from Cripple Creek. They married 11 months later, and Babe would change her name to Babe Didrikson Zaharias.

He would become her manager and advisor, but in the later years of their marriage, problems arose as Zaharias lost influence with his wife. Babe spent more time with good friend Betty Dodd, a young golfer who was a natural athlete and had no interest in looking feminine. She often stayed at the Zaharis' home in Tampa.

As an amateur golfer, Babe won an amazing 13 consecutive tournaments during 1946. The next year, she was the first American to win the British Amateur. Among her 55 tournament victories were three U.S. Women's Opens. With Zaharias, Patty Berg, and Fred Corcoran, she founded the Ladies Professional Golf Association in 1949.

At birth in Port Arthur, Texas, she was Mildred Ella Didriksen (she would later change the spelling of her name). Though Babe wrote in her autobiography that she was born on June 26, 1914, it seems as if the correct year is 1911, which is what it says on her tombstone and on a baptismal certificate. Her parents, emigrants from Norway, moved the family 17 miles inland to Beaumont in 1914 after a hurricane destroyed their Port Arthur surroundings. (It also killed 275 people.)

While playing basketball for Beaumont High School in 1930, Babe was offered $75 a month to work for Employers Casualty Company of Dallas to play for its team. Actually, she was paid to be a secretary because she would have lost her amateur status had she been paid to play. Because she had not yet graduated high school, her parents hesitated before allowing her to go.

She was outstanding from the start, earning AAU All-American honors from 1930–1932. Early in her stay in Dallas, she also took to the track. Soon after taking up the sport in 1930, she won four events in an AAU competition.

Babe single-handedly won the 1932 AAU championships, which served as Olympic qualifying, on July 16 in Evanston, Ill. The sole representative of Employers Casualty, she scored 30 points, eight more than the runner-up team, which had 22 athletes. In a span of three hours, she competed in eight of 10 events, winning five outright and tying for first in the high jump. She set world records in the javelin, 80-meter hurdles, high jump, and baseball throw.

While she qualified for five Olympic events in Los Angeles, women were allowed to compete in only three. She won the first women's Olympic javelin (143 feet, 4 inches) and set a world record in winning the first Olympic 80-meter hurdles (11.7 seconds). In the high jump, she and Jean Smiley both broke the world record at 5-foot-5+, but Smiley received the gold and Babe the silver when Babe was disqualified on a dubious ruling after her final jump. The official ruled Babe's head cleared the bar before the rest of her body, a rule that no longer exists. Also, while Babe had jumped in the same manner throughout the competition, nothing was said to her about her style being illegal.

During the next few years, she performed on the vaudeville circuit, traveled with a basketball team called Babe Didrikson's All-Americans, and toured with the bearded House of David baseball team.

Looking for another challenge, in 1933 she turned to golf, which she had played in high school. Soon after winning the Texas Women's Amateur in 1935, the U.S. Golf Association ruled that "for the best interest of the game," Babe was not an amateur because she had competed professionally in other sports. While Babe continued to golf—as well as play as many as 17 sets of tennis in one day and starring on the bowling lanes—it was not until 1943 that she was reinstated as an amateur.

When asked how she could regularly drive the ball some 250 yards though she didn't weigh more than 145 pounds, she said, "You've got to loosen your girdle and let it rip."

She ripped it far and straight enough, and putted well enough, that not only did she dominate women's golf, but for three straight years (1945–1947) AP named her the Female Athlete of the Year. She turned pro in the summer of 1947 after winning 17 of 18 tournaments.

In 1948, Babe won her first U.S. Women's Open, the World Championship, and the All-American Open. She continued her impressive performance on the LPGA Tour for the next several years.

Shortly after winning the inaugural Babe Zaharias Open in Beaumont in April 1953, Babe learned she had cancer. Surgeons removed the tumor, but discovered the cancer had spread into her lymph nodes, which were inoperable.

Fourteen weeks later, she played in a tournament. By the next year she had completed an incredible golf comeback, winning her third U.S. Women's Open—by an incredible 12 strokes—on the way to five titles and her sixth AP Female Athlete of the Year award.

Pain in her lower spine, caused by cancer, became unbearable in 1955. On September 27, 1956, Babe died of the disease in Galveston, Texas. She was 45.

Sport Is Unfair to Women (Part 1)*

Bil Gilbert and Nancy Williamson

America invests a billion dollars a year in athletic programs with the conviction that games are good for people, developing sound minds and bodies. But the female half of the population has never gotten a run for its money. Now many parents are becoming exercised, schools are growing increasingly concerned, and big changes are in the offing.

There may be worse (more socially serious) forms of prejudice in the United States, but there is no sharper example of discrimination today than that which operates against girls and women who take part in competitive sports, wish to take part, or might wish to if society did not scorn such endeavors. No matter what her age, education, race, talent, residence, or riches, the female's right to play is severely restricted. The funds, facilities, coaching, rewards, and honors allotted women are grossly inferior to those granted men. In many places absolutely no support is given to women's athletics, and females are barred by law, regulation, tradition, or the hostility of males from sharing athletic resources and pleasures. A female who persists in her athletic interests, despite the handicaps and discouragements, is not likely to be congratulated on her sporting desire or grit. She is more apt to be subjected to social and psychological pressures, the effect of which is to cast doubt on her morals, sanity, and womanhood.

As things stand, any female—the eleven-year-old who is prohibited from being a Little League shortstop by Act of Congress; the coed basketball player who cannot practice in her university's multimillion-dollar gymnasium; the professional sportswoman who can earn only one-quarter what her male counterpart receives for trying to do the same work—has ample reasons for believing that the American system of athletics is sexist and hypocritical. There is a publicly announced, publicly supported notion that sports are good for people, that they develop better citizens, build vigorous minds and bodies, and promote a better society. Yet when it comes to the practice of what is preached,

*Sports Illustrated, May 28, 1973, 88–98.

35

females—half this country's population—find that this credo does not apply to them. Sports may be good for people, but they are considered a lot gooder for male people than for female people.

Opportunities for women are so limited that it is a cop-out to designate females as second-class citizens of the American sports world. "Most of us feel that being second-class citizens would be a great advance," says Doris Brown. A faculty member at Seattle Pacific College, Brown has devoted fifteen years to becoming the best U.S. female distance runner. She has been on two Olympic teams, won six national and five world cross-country championships, and set a variety of national and international records in distances from a mile up. Despite her talent and success she has had to pay for nearly all her training and, until recently, all her travel expenses. She was forced to resign from a job at a junior high school because the principal did not believe in women teachers devoting a lot of time to outside athletic participation. She has received far less recognition than male runners who cannot match her record of accomplishment. "Second-class citizenship sounds good," says Brown, "when you are accustomed to being regarded as fifth-class." This is not the whine of a disgruntled individual but an accurate description of the state of things in sports. To document the situation, consider the following:

Money Talks

- In 1969 a Syracuse, New York, school board budgeted $90,000 for extracurricular sports for boys; $200 was set aside for girls. In 1970 the board cut back on the athletic budget, trimming the boy's program to $87,000. Funds for the girls' interscholastic program were simply eliminated.

- New Brunswick (N.J.) Senior High School offered ten sports for boys and three for girls in 1972, with the split in funds being $25,575 to $2,250 in favor of the boys. The boys' track team was allowed $3,700 last spring, while the girls' squad received $1,000. This might be considered a better-than-average division of money except that seventy New Brunswick students competed on the girls' team and only twenty on the boys'.

- The Fairfield area school district in rural south-central Pennsylvania is small: Eight hundred students are enrolled from kindergarten through twelfth grade. Nevertheless, in 1972–1973 the school district budgeted $19,880 for interscholastic athletics. Of this $460 was actually spent on girls' sports, $300 of it on a "play day" in the area and $160 on a volleyball team, which had a one-month season. Boys in the school district are introduced to competitive sport as early as the fifth grade with the organization of soccer and basketball teams that are coached by members of the high-school athletic staff.

- In New York a woman officiating a girls' high school basketball game is paid $10.50, a man receives $21 for a boys' game. Throughout the country and with few exceptions, women who coach girls' sports in secondary schools receive between one-third and one-half the salary of men who coach comparable sports for boys. The woman coach often is expected to supervise candy sales, cooking contests, and raffles to raise money to purchase the girls' uniforms and pay travel expenses.

There are many communities where tax-supported school systems offer absolutely no athletic programs for girls. In fact, until recently no money was spent for girls' interscholastic sports in two entire states—Utah and Nevada.

- In colleges the disparity between men's and women's athletics is even greater than it is in the secondary schools. At the University of Washington, 41.4 percent of the 26,464 undergraduate students enrolled are women. However, when it comes to athletics women get only nine-tenths of 1 percent of the $2 million the university spends annually on sports. The women's intercollegiate budget is $18,000 a year, while the men have $1.3 million to spend over and above the income-producing sports of football and basketball. Despite the enormous discrepancy, the situation at Washington has markedly improved. In 1957 there were no women's intercollegiate athletics at the university. Dr. Joseph Kearney, director of sports at Washington, says, "We want to develop the women's programs that are now in an evolutionary stage." Evolutionary is a clinically accurate term. If the current rate of progress were maintained, women would reach financial parity with men in the year 2320.
- Things are better at Vassar, but hardly as good as one might expect, considering the college's pioneer role in women's education and rights. In 1968 Vassar admitted male students for the first time. There are now 1,400 girls and 700 boys enrolled. Vassar men compete in five sports and have an annual budget of $4,750. The women have three sports and $2,060 to spend.
- Since its organization in 1910 the National Collegiate Athletic Association has governed men's collegiate athletics. The NCAA now has an annual operating budget of $1.5 million and forty-two full-time employees. The female counterpart of the NCAA is the Association for Intercollegiate Athletics for Women. It was established only in 1971. Prior to that, there seemed little need for an organization because there were so few intercollegiate women's programs. The AIAW operates on $24,000 a year and employs one executive (who works part-time) and one assistant.

- In five major collegiate athletic conferences—Southeastern, Big Ten, Big Eight, Southwest, and PAC 8—there are 5,000 students on football scholarships alone. These legitimate scholarships (to say nothing of any under-the-table goodies) are worth some $10 million a year to their recipients. Women are almost totally excluded from the scholarship system which, whatever its deficiencies, is the one used to develop most of our first-class athletes. As many as 50,000 men a year earn a college education by playing games. Figures are hard to come by, but it is likely that less than fifty American women hold athletic scholarships and enjoy the benefits—financial, educational, sporting—that these grants provide.

Whatever the small total of women scholarship holders is, it was reduced by one in January 1973 when Cathy Carr, a swimmer who had won two gold medals at the Munich Olympics, had to resign the four-year grant she had been awarded by the University of New Mexico. The reason: She and the astonished university discovered that a woman holding an athletic scholarship was barred from competing in women's intercollegiate events by, of all things, the AIAW.

Recently, Mary Rekstad, the AIAW's lone executive, explained the *Alice in Wonderland* regulation. "When the AIAW was formed many men told us that scholarships were a bad influence on collegiate sports, that we should avoid making the mistakes they had made and stay out of the mess." On the surface the concern of the admittedly corrupt men for the purity of their female counterparts seems more hilarious than touching—something like a confirmed alcoholic guzzling all the booze at a party to protect the other guests from the evils of drink.

"It might seem that the men were motivated by self-interest," said Rekstad. "But we did not think so. We wanted to protect girls from the excesses of recruiting and exploitation." Last month the AIAW reassessed the situation and decided to drop the regulation. Now women on athletic scholarships can take part in events it sanctions.

- When it comes to pay-for-play situations, unequal scales are established for men and women. As a small but instructive example, one of the leading events of the Northern California tennis circuit is held each May in Mountain View. This tournament is open to men and women and each entrant, regardless of sex, must pay an $8 fee. About an equal number of men and women compete. However, when it comes to prize money, sex raises its miserly head. At Mountain View the men's singles winner receives $1,000, the runner-up $500, the semifinal losers $150 each, quarter-final losers $75 each, and the round of sixteen losers $25 each. On the other hand, the women's singles winner receives $150, and the runner-up $50. The women receive no other money prizes. There also is a doubles competition for men, but not for women. In all, although they have put up the same entry fee, $3,000 is paid to men while the women play for $200. In monetary terms, the Mountain View tournament considers women fifteenth-class citizens.

- In 1971 Billie Jean King became the first woman athlete to win $100,000 in a year. During the same year Rod Laver was the leading winner on the men's tennis circuit, collecting $290,000. To reach her total King won three times as many tournaments as Laver. Last year King captured the U.S. Open at Forest Hills and collected $10,000. Ilie Nastase was the men's winner and earned $25,000. At Wimbledon Stan Smith collected $12,150 for the men's title while King picked up only $4,830 for the women's. At Forest Hills and Wimbledon the women often draw as many spectators, and sometimes more than the men.

- In 1972 on the Ladies Professional Golf tour Kathy Whitworth was the leading money-winner, collecting $65,063 in twenty-nine tournaments. In the same year Jack Nicklaus was the biggest moneymaker among the men pros, winning $320,542 in nineteen tournaments. The discrepancy between men and women professionals is even more notable among lesser competitors. The fifteenth leading money-winner on the women's tour in 1972 was JoAnne Canter, who made $18,901. The fifteenth-place finisher among the men, Jim Jamieson, collected $109,532. Admittedly, the women's tour arouses less interest than the men's, and sponsors feel they receive a better return for their money backing men's events.

- In the Roller Derby it is the women, more than the men, who attract fans and generate publicity. The female star of the Derby is Joan Weston, a superior athlete. She makes between $25,000 and $30,000 a year. There are six men on the Derby tour who play the same game in front of the same crowds as Weston, all of whom earn larger salaries. Charlie O'Connell, the leading male performer, is paid twice as much as Weston. When they join the Derby tour, men and women are paid about $85 a week plus travel expenses. But men's salaries increase more rapidly than women's, and once established a man will receive between $200 and $250 a week, while a woman of equal talent makes only $150.

Big Brother

- Dr. Katherine Ley, a full professor and chairman of the women's physical education department of the State University College of New York at Cortland, is one of the country's leading physical educators. She long has sought better opportunities for women in sports. At Dr. Ley's university (men's budget $84,000 a year; women's $18,000) the situation could hardly be described as one of sweetness, light, and equality. For example, the Cortland women's basketball team cannot practice regularly in the main gymnasium, but it is permitted to play varsity games there. Recently one such game ran overtime whereupon, according to Dr. Ley, the men's basketball coach stormed into the gym and told the girls to get off the court because the boys had to practice. The women's coach asked if he couldn't use the field house, explaining that her team was in the middle of a game and had reserved the space. He said he was in a hurry because he had to leave shortly to scout another leans. He told the women it was silly to finish; the score was lopsided and it was not even a game. The women docilely left the game unfinished and withdrew.

- The Mission Conference, an eight-team league of California junior colleges, agreed not long ago that women could compete in varsity sports with and against men. Last February in a game against San Diego City College, Ray Blake, the basketball coach of San Bernardino Valley College, took advantage of the new ruling. Leading 114 to 85 with three minutes and twelve seconds to play, Blake sent in a substitute, Sue Palmer. The San Diego coach, Bill Standly, responded by calling time and asking his men, "Do you want to be humiliated any further by playing against a girl?" The team, to a man, said no, and San Diego walked off the court.

- At a parochial high school in Maryland, a girls' basketball team was playing a varsity rival. The game was officiated by the male who serves as athletic director of the host school. As the contest drew toward a close, the A.D., bored and feeling that he could spend his time better elsewhere, turned to the timekeeper and, in something less than a whisper, suggested that the clock not be stopped for time-outs, that it be kept running until the game ended. One of the players overheard the conversation and said, "That's unfair." "That, young lady, is a technical foul on you," said the athletic director, ending the argument.

The Feminine Mystique

- Ron Wied is the football coach at coed Pius XI in Milwaukee, the largest Catholic high school in the state. Wied says, "There is cause for concern among our male coaching staff over the pressure for girls' sports. Facilities are a problem. We've got a boys' gym and a girls' gym. Before, we could use the girls' gym for wrestling and B-team basketball a lot more than we can now. I think girls have a right to participate but to a lesser degree than boys. If they go too far with the competitive stuff they lose their femininity. I guess if I had my choice, I'd like to keep boys' teams going up in importance and let the girls stay about where they are now."

- Jack Short is the director of physical education for the State of Georgia school system. Speaking of the physical education program there, Short commented, "I don't think the idea is to get girls interested in interscholastic competition. I don't think the phys ed program on any level should he directed toward making an athlete of a girl."
- At the Munich Olympic Games, Olga Connolly, a female discus thrower, was selected to carry the U.S. flag at the opening ceremonies. Upon learning that Connolly would be the American color-bearer, Russell Knipp, a weight lifter, said, "The flag-bearer ought to be a man, a strong man, a warrior. A woman's place is in the home."
- At Trenton (N.J.) State College the usual man-woman inequality exists, with $70,000 budgeted for men and only $15,687 for women. Joyce Countiss, the women's basketball coach, is paid considerably less than her male counterpart, but as far as she is concerned, the day-to-day discriminations are as humiliating as the monetary inequality. "We aren't supposed to sweat," says Countiss fiercely. "The men's uniforms are laundered by the school, but if we want ours clean we wash them ourselves. We have no athletic trainer; the men have one who even travels with the teams. The school has a training room with whirlpool baths, heat treatments, etc., but women get to use the facilities only in emergencies. The weight room is located in the men's locker room, so naturally we have no access to it. The list goes on and on, but most places are much worse off than we are."
- Susan Hollander is a student at Hamden (Conn.) High School. She had sufficient talent to be a member of her school's varsity cross-country and indoor track teams. There was no girls' team, and she was prohibited by a state regulation from participating on the boys' team. Backed by her parents, she brought suit against the Connecticut Interscholastic Athletic Conference. The case was heard on March 29, 1971, in the Superior Court of New Haven and Judge John Clark FitzGerald ruled against Hollander. In giving his decision Judge FitzGerald stated, "The present generation of our younger male population has not become so decadent that boys will experience a thrill in defeating girls in running contests, whether the girls be members of their own team or of an adversary team. It could well be that many boys would feel compelled to forgo entering track events if they were required to compete with girls on their own teams or on adversary teams. With boys vying with girls . . . the challenge to win, and the glory of achievement, at least for many boys, would lose incentive and become nullified. Athletic competition builds character in our boys. We do not need that kind of character in our girls."
- John Roberts, the executive secretary of the Wisconsin Interscholastic Athletic Association, says many coaches of boys' teams in his state are worried

about the increased interest in girls' sports. "The facilities thing will get worse," says one of Roberts colleagues. "Girls haven't figured out yet how to use the urinals."

The Double Standard

- Last summer a steward at Ellis Park in Kentucky sought to suspend jockey Mary Bacon for cursing in the paddock after a losing ride. Said Bacon, "They expect a girl to get off a horse and say, 'Nice horsey, nice horsey,' like in *National Velvet*. Well, I get mad like everyone else; if I lost a race and didn't cuss, then the Stewards might have something to cuss about."
- When asked why only women were permitted to coach girls' teams, Ada Mae Warrington, director of physical education for women in the Prince George's County (Md.) school system, said, "We have had several instances of a girl assaulting a man. We are trying to protect our coaches."
- In 1971, after a lengthy argument with the New York State Education Department, Katy Schilly was permitted to run on the Paul V. Moore High School cross-country team. After the decision was made, an elaborate security system was set up to protect her. Among other things, a woman had to be present whenever the runner was in her locker room. "Maybe they're afraid I'll slip on a bar of soap in the shower," said Schilly.

Prudery is a major factor contributing to the present low estate of women's sports. This hangup cannot be blamed on our Victorian or puritan ancestors. Early in this century there was widespread participation by girls in competitive athletics. Baseball, bike racing, and track and field were popular pastimes for girls. Basketball was played extensively, and often girls' games were scheduled as doubleheaders with boys' contests. Then in 1923, a national committee of women headed by Mrs. Herbert Hoover was formed to investigate the practice of holding such doubleheaders. The committee was shocked to find girls wearing athletic costumes performing before crowds that included men. Mrs. Hoover and her friends believed the girls were being used as a come-on and that the practice was disgraceful and should be stopped. State after state followed the advice and either abolished all girls' sports or made them so genteel as to be almost unrecognizable as athletic contests.

"When I went to college in the thirties, we were taught that competition was dirty," recalls Betty Desch, head of the women's physical education department of the State University of New York at Stony Brook. Those states that had retained any girls' athletic programs declared that teams should be coached only by women, or else who knows what might transpire. The requirement, still in effect in many states, has stifled the development of competent female athletic programs. While there is no evidence that women cannot be as good coaches as men, it is a fact that there are very few good women coaches. There are obvious reasons for this. Few girls in high school or college have had the same competitive opportunities as men, so they are seldom inspired to take up coaching as a career. Also, few colleges allow girls to take courses in coaching techniques and theory. Where they can attend such classes, there has been little point in doing so, because once a girl graduates she finds few coaching jobs available, and those that are available pay poorly or not at all. When a school needs a coach for a girls' team, the usual practice is to draft a woman from the physical education department for the job. Through no fault of her own, she rarely has much expertise or enthusiasm for coaching competitive athletics. In consequence, girls in her charge do not learn fundamental techniques or skills and seldom become excited about athletics. Thus the vicious circle is continued.

The Same Old Story

The following letter appeared not long ago in the *Washington Post*:

> Your editorial, 'Growing Up by the Book' (Dec. 1), revealed the harmful effects of stereotyped sex roles in children's books and toys. But it seems that the *Washington Post* is extending this same discrimination to its sports pages.
>
> Our specific complaint is that girls' high school basketball scores are completely ignored in your paper while boys' high school basketball is given 500-word articles. There are numerous active, aggressive teams from all-girls' schools as well as public schools. Girls' basketball is not a farce: It is an exciting spectator sport with a four-month season that is of interest to thousands of Washington-area students, including boys.
>
> We suggest that you 'practice what you preach' and print reports on a sport where girls are anything but passive.

The amount of coverage given to women's athletics is meager and the quality is atrocious. Most of the stories that do appear are generally in the man-bites-dog journalistic tradition, the gist of them being that here is an unusual and mildly humorous happening—a girl playing games. Rather than describing how well or badly the athlete performed or even how the contest turned out, writers tend to concentrate on the color of the hair and eyes, and the shape of the legs or the busts of the women. The best-looking girls (by male standards) are singled out for attention, no matter how little their sporting talent may be. Women athletes are bothered by this, because the insinuation is "at least some of them look normal." It is comparable to a third-string defensive back being featured on a college football program cover because of the length of his eyelashes or the symmetry of his profile.

- A fine (in the sense of being typical) example of women's sports journalism appeared in the August 23, 1971, issue of *Sports Illustrated*: "A cool, braided California blonde named Laura Baugh made quite a splash . . . her perfectly tanned, well-timed legs swinging jauntily. The hair on her tapered arms was bleached absolutely white against a milk-chocolate tan. Her platinum hair was pulled smartly back in a Viking-maiden braid. . . ." The account had to do with a women's golf tournament. The difference in reporting men's and women's sporting events is obvious.
- Between August 1972 and September 1973 NBC will televise 366 hours of "live" sport. Only one hour of this (the finals at Wimbledon) will be devoted to women. Til Ferdenzi, manager of sports publicity for NBC, says, "Egad, I never thought about it before. I guess it's not fair." Bill Brendie, his counterpart at CBS, says, "We don't know if women draw an audience—they might not be saleable." During the coming year CBS will televise some 260 hours of sports and 10 hours of women's sports. ABC does not know how its time is divided between men and women athletes, but ABC's Iry Brodsky says defensively, "Women don't play sports."

The paucity and peculiarity of sporting news about females have two effects, both discriminatory. First, girls at all levels of play are deprived of the genuine and harmless satisfaction of seeing their athletic accomplishments publicized. Because the feats of outstanding women athletes are briefly and bizarrely reported, there are few sporting heroines. Boys are bombarded with daily stories about how much fun male athletes are having, how important, dashing, and rich they are. The suggestion is made that getting out and playing games— and playing them well—is an exciting and constructive thing to do. Girls have few such models and seldom receive such subliminal messages advertising athletics.

In an informal survey taken for the purposes of this report, nearly all of some 100 high school girls scattered across the country could name ten male athletes in college or professional sports whom they admired—or at least whose names they knew. But not a single girl to whom the question was put could name ten prominent women athletes. The sportswoman most often identified by the high school girls was not an American but Olga Korbut, the seventeen-year-old Russian gymnast (*SI* cover, Mar. 19) who appeared prominently on television during the 1972 Olympics.

As bad as it is, conventional discrimination has perhaps had less influence on women's position in the sporting world than has another phenomenon that ranges even further. It might be called psychological warfare; its purpose is to convince girls who show an inclination for athletics that their interest is impractical and unnatural. The campaign to frighten girls into accepting notions about their athletic role begins early.

Carol is twelve, an eighth-grade student at a parochial grammar school in Maryland. She is one of the best athletes, regardless of sex, in the school. Last year she was ranked by the AAU among the fifteen best high jumpers of her age in the country. She comes by her athletic interests and talents naturally. Her father was a professional basketball player and now is a college coach. In her family, playing games is a way of life. But Carol is discovering that elsewhere sports are not regarded as suitable for girls. And it makes her angry. "At recess," Carol says, "the boys get the softball and kickball fields. The girls have a parking lot and part of a field with holes in it. Sometimes we don't even get that field because Sister keeps us in to wash off tables. She says that is girls' work."

C.M. Russell High School in Great Falls, Montana, has 2,040 students and an excellent girls' athletic program ($15,000 a year for girls; $35,000 for boys). Yet even there, the members of a six-girl panel discussing sports were aware of forces putting them in their athletic place.

"There's one thing that really doesn't have anything to do with school," said one girl. "If you've got a brother and he's playing football or basketball your folks are going to drive him back and forth to practice and change dinner hours for him. But if you're a girl, your mother says, 'Be home at 5 to set the table.'"

Early on, girls learn to expect and put up with parental edicts and insinuations that the games they play are unimportant. When she is fifteen or sixteen the campaign against a girl's athletic interest takes an uglier turn, being directed against her appearance and sexuality. The six C.M. Russell girls were attractive teenagers. Most of them dated boys who were athletes. "The guys on the teams tease us about being jocks," said a tiny lithe gymnast, "but they are just having fun. They know we work hard and I think they are proud of what we do."

"The mean ones," said a basketball player, "are those who aren't in sports themselves. They don't want to see a girl play because it makes them look bad. They want her to sit in the stands with them. So they try to put us down. They'll come up in the hall and give you an elbow and say, 'Hey, stud.'"

"Some girls are bad, too," a hurdler noted, "They'll say, 'Aren't you afraid you'll get ugly muscles in your legs?'"

"Girls in sports are more careful about how they look," said the gymnast, "We wear skirts more than other girls because we are worried about being feminine."

Some authorities consider the word "feminine" a derogatory term. "When we say 'feminine,'" says Dr. David Auxter of Slippery Rock State College, "we mean submissive, a nonparticipant, an underachiever, a person who lacks a strong sense of self-identity, who has weak life goals and ambitions."

Grosse Pointe (Mich.) North High School has a far different and lesser girls' sports program than that of C.M. Russell in Montana. There are two official girls' interscholastic sports, gymnastics and track. These are financed by a $2,200, hopefully annual, grant from a local boosters club. In contrast, boys receive about $20,000 in school funds. But in at least one respect girl athletes are treated better at Grosse Pointe than in many other places. Girls are awarded school letters that they may wear on a sweater. In many other localities, players are rewarded with inconspicuous pins, printed certificates, or nothing. In practice, winning and being able to wear a letter sweater is an empty honor for Grosse Pointe girls. "Not very many girls wear their letter," says Pam Candler, a senior who is the Michigan girls' trampoline champion and was runner-up last spring in the state tennis championships. "Mostly only freshmen or sophomores—because they don't know what the score is."

What is the score?

"Well, a lot of people think it is freakish for a girl to wear a letter sweater. Like she's a jock. I'm kind of proud of the girls who have enough courage to wear them, but I don't. It would make me feel funny, I guess I've been brainwashed."

"I don't like to think that there are male chauvinists, but I guess there are," says Jan Charvat, another gymnast. "It is degrading that we have to act in a certain way just because we're in sports. A girl ought to be free to be what she is, without people cutting her up."

So far as the "social" acceptability of girls' sports at Grosse Pointe, Candler says, "If a girl is great looking, then maybe the guy she is going with likes to see her in sports. If she isn't good looking and popular, sports are not going to help her. In fact they will do the opposite."

Bruce Feighner, the principal of Grosse Pointe North, is not proud of the weakness of his girls' athletic program. However, like so many of his colleagues, he cites the lack of funds as a major reason for the inequality: "Here and in many other communities in Michigan, taxpayer revolts are brewing. It is hard to establish new programs. This admittedly is unjust, but the fault is not entirely or perhaps even principally with the school. The role of girls in sport is determined by society, and until now that role has been an inferior one. There's another practical side to the matter. Grosse Pointe is a very affluent community. If a girl is interested in athletics, the conventional way of developing her skill is to marry a man who has enough money to belong to a country club, a tennis or yacht club."

Feighner's comment may seem cynical but it is perceptive. Except occasionally in track (where the leading female performers are developed in private AAU clubs) the only women's sports in which the U.S. record is respectable, occasionally outstanding, are tennis, golf, skating, skiing, and swimming, essentially country-club sports and ones that are considered "ladylike." For the girl who lacks country-club opportunities and inclinations, yet somehow has kept her interest in athletics through high school, the question of what to do next is perplexing. For men, the next stage in the American athletic progression is college, where sporting skills are polished and reputations made. However, college sports presently have little attraction or value for good female athletes.

The woman athlete at the university is made to feel unwelcome and an oddity. Beth Miller is a tall, graceful twenty-one-year-old, by any standards a figure pleasing to the eye. She is also one of the best female athletes in the country, having been the National Junior Women's pentathlon and shotput champion, a standout performer on her Lock Haven (Pa.) State College basketball team, a swimmer, softball player, and spelunker. On one weekend last winter, Miller led her basketball team to victory and then hurried to Baltimore where she won the shotput and placed third in the high jump at an all-AAU indoor meet. Word of her accomplishments was received by a Lock Haven radio sportscaster. The commentator spent maybe twenty seconds describing what Miller had done and ended with the comment, "What an animal she must be."

If a talented woman withstands these pressures and decides to become a serious athlete, she often has to cope not just with insinuations but with slanderous gossip. Jo Ann Prentice is a sharp-tongued, sharp-minded woman who has earned her living for seventeen years on the LPGA tour. Asked about the "social" life on the tour, Prentice replied to the euphemistic question in her soft Alabama drawl. "This is kind of how it is. If you get into town at the beginning of the week and you meet some guy whose company you enjoy and have dinner with him once or twice, the gossips start asking what kind of tramps are these babes on the tour. If you stay at the motel where everybody else on the tour has checked in, then the question is what are those girls doing back in those rooms alone."

The vicious paradox that Prentice outlines—women athletes are either heterosexual wantons or homosexual perverts or, simultaneously, both—is the culmination of all the jokes and warnings that began when an eleven-year-old wanted to play sandlot football with her brothers and was teased, in good fun, about being a tomboy.

As a result, a great many girls simply avoid sports completely. Others try to compromise, accommodating their athletic desires to the attitudes of society. They continue to play games, but play them nervously and timidly, attempting to avoid appearances and enthusiasms that might be construed as unladylike.

The few women who survive the pressure may be scarred in various ways, but there are compensations. Jack Griffin, though he has worked for twenty-five years in relative obscurity, is regarded by many who know of him as one of the most distinguished athletic coaches in the nation. He has coached boys and girls, from grade-schoolers to post-collegians, in swimming, track, basketball, and football. Working only with the youth of the small Maryland city, Frederick, he has helped to develop an inordinate number of national and international class athletes. He has been an Olympic coach and is currently a member of the Olympic Women's Track and Field Committee. "I enjoy coaching both sexes," says Griffin, "but strictly from a coaching standpoint, I have noted one important difference between them. Desire is an intangible quality which you like to see in any athlete. Coaches of men's teams often single out an individual athlete and say his most valuable characteristic is his desire. You seldom hear girls' coaches make this sort of comment. The reason, I think, is that any girl or woman who is very much involved in athletics tends to have an extraordinary amount of desire, not only to excel in her sport but to excel as a person. It is so common with the girls that we tend to overlook it, accepting it as normal. I suppose in a sense it is normal for them. The way things are in this country, any girl who perseveres in sport has to be not only an exceptional athlete but an exceptional human being."

PART II

Staking a Claim: The First Decade

• INTRODUCTION •

The accumulation of human capital in the form of education is the primary method by which Americans attempt to improve their income potential and social class in society. For this reason, overt discrimination in educational opportunities limits the upward mobility and financial independence of persons seeking to advance themselves in our country. Yet, for most of American history, women were formally excluded or limited in their participation in higher education opportunities and thereby foreclosed from the types of human capital formation that propelled men's careers in the business world.

Earlier civil rights laws failed to protect women from discrimination in education. Whereas sex-based employment discrimination was prohibited by Title VII of the Civil Rights Act of 1964,[1] Title VII did not help women in education because educational institutions were specifically excluded from the terms of Title VII. Similarly, Title VI of the Civil Rights Act of 1964 prohibited discrimination in education by recipients of federal funds based on race, but women were not a covered class by the terms of this act either.

In 1971 and 1972, Congress held extensive hearings on women in higher education and heard ample evidence of intentional discrimination that presented formidable barriers for admission to institutions of higher education. Testimony revealed that women were required to meet higher admission standards than men. One example was the University of North Carolina where admission of women to the freshman class was "restricted to those who are

---

[1]Title VII also prohibited employment discrimination based on race, religion, and national origin.

49

especially well qualified." No similar heightened restriction applied to male applicants. The 1964 Report of the Virginia Commission for the Study of Educational Facilities found that 21,000 women were denied admission to the Virginia's higher education system, whereas not one male student was rejected.[2] Testimony demonstrated that the possibility of gaining admission into graduate programs was worse. Senator Birch Bayh, referring to the hearings, noted that "over 1,200 pages of testimony document the massive, persistent patterns of discrimination in the academic world."[3] Title IX, it was hoped, would remove these formal barriers to entry into the academic marketplace and open the doors to educational opportunity for women.

Title IX passed on June 23, 1972.[4] Other than women's suffrage, possibly no other piece of legislation has had a greater effect on women's lives. This simple piece of federal legislation has had a powerful impact on American society through its expansion of equal educational opportunities for women. While other civil rights laws allowed women to access the ballot box and to enjoy other civil liberties, it was Title IX that helped to crack the barriers at the foundation of women's inability to have equal opportunity to pursue economic and social advancement through education.

Shortly after its passage, the issue of Title IX's application to college sports emerged. The then-all-male National Collegiate Athletic Association (NCAA), through formal lobbying efforts, attempted to remove the application of Title IX to intercollegiate athletics. In May 1974, Senator John Tower (R-Tex.) introduced legislation (included herein) attempting just that. Senator Bayh's testimony against this amendment and a related speech are reprinted in this section. After the amendment failed, Senator Tower tried a more limited exemption, one that would exclude from Title IX's purview so-called "revenue-producing" sports, including sports that produced donations for the school. Although the Tower Amendment was approved in the Senate, it was eventually defeated.

Another amendment, sponsored by Senator Jacob Javits (R-NY), however, was approved by Congress in 1974 and remains in effect. The Javits amendment (reprinted here) required the Department of Health, Education, and Welfare (HEW) to prepare and publish regulations covering intercollegiate athletics,[5] and those implementing regulations "shall include with respect to intercolle-

---

[2]H.R. Rep. 92-554 (1972).

[3]118 Cong. Rec. 5804 (1972).

[4]20 U.S.C. Sections 1681–1688. The law was renamed as the "Patsy T. Mink Equal Opportunity in Education" on October 29, 2002, upon the death of Congresswoman Patsy T. Mink, one of the authors of the law. The law is still referred to as "Title IX," as it is throughout this book.

[5]S. Conf. Rep. No. 1026, 93d Cong., 2d Sess. 4271 (1974), now *Education Amendments of 1974*, Pub. L. 93-380, Title VIII, Section 844, 88 Stat. 484, 612 (1974).

giate athletics . . . reasonable provisions considering the nature of particular sports."[6] This amendment allows different amounts of monies to be spent on different sports, depending on the distinct needs of the sport. It recognizes that some sports, such as football and equestrian, are inherently more expensive than other sports, requiring costlier equipment or larger budgets for big spectator events. Other sports are relatively inexpensive to operate, such as cross country. At Ohio State University, for example, in 1998–1999 the athletic department spent $5.2 million on the men's football team, whereas it spent only $530,000 on the men's baseball team, $430,000 on the women's softball team and $270,000 on the women's tennis team. Such a pattern might not be considered a violation of Title IX, so long as both genders were receiving the same quality and quantity of equipment. In other words, if both genders are getting either the best equipment, or if both genders are getting average equipment, or if both genders are getting barely functional equipment, it is not a violation of Title IX despite rather large discrepancies in spending, because both genders are considered to be receiving the same educational experience. But a school cannot provide one gender with superior, state-of-the-art equipment and the other gender with lesser quality equipment and still be in compliance under the Javits Amendment.

The NCAA's lobbying efforts were therefore partly successful. After the Javits Amendment, females could not demand half of the athletic department resources or equal per-capita spending on each athlete. Under either of these two tests it would have been far easier to analyze and evaluate compliance than under the tests adopted after the passage of the Javits Amendment. For example, it is much easier to determine whether men and women are being provided equal resources for their sports departments than it is to determine whether both sexes were given equal educational opportunities, "given the nature of the sports." In this way, the NCAA's member schools successfully maintained the large budgets of two men's sports, football and men's basketball, arguing that the "nature" of these sports requires the unequal investment of resources.

Later in 1974, HEW released draft regulations for application to Title IX. These implementing regulations were subject to an extensive administrative comment period during which HEW received approximately 10,000 comments. The process of drafting regulations made it clear that Title IX would have an important role to play in athletic departments, as Casper Weinberger, then-Secretary of the Department of Health, Education and Welfare (the predecessor to the Department of Education), testified:

[6]S. Conf. Rec. No. 1026, 93d Cong., 2d Sess. 421 (1974).

[with] regard to athletics, I have to say, Mr. Chairman and members of the committee, I had not realized until the comment period closed that the most important issue in the United States today is intercollegiate athletics, because we have an enormous volume of comments about them.[7]

Many of these comments were eventually incorporated into the final regulations that HEW issued in the summer of 1975.[8] At that time, Congressional rules required Congress to reject the draft regulations in whole or in part within forty-five days.[9]

The NCAA again tried to marshal its resources against Title IX and its implementing regulations both formally, with proposed bills to weaken Title IX's application to athletics, and informally, through currying favor with influential members of government. In March 1975, John Fuzak, president of the NCAA, wrote to President Ford, who was, not incidentally, the recipient of the NCAA Theodore R. Roosevelt Award that year, saying "the HEW concepts of Title IX as expressed could seriously damage if not destroy the major men's intercollegiate athletic programs."[10] In turn, President Ford communicated a similar concern to Harrison A. Williams, chair of the Senate Committee on Labor and Public Welfare.[11]

Ultimately, none of the proposed bills that would exempt football or "revenue producing" sports were adopted, and the regulations, excerpted here, went into effect in July of 1975. They required all educational institutions to be in compliance within three years—by 1978.

Having failed to convince Congress of a wholesale exemption for athletics from Title IX's purview, the NCAA turned to the courts to get the relief they wanted. In 1976, the NCAA sued HEW challenging the validity of the 1975 regulations as they applied to athletics, seeking to invalidate the newly promulgated regulations. The stakes for Title IX were high, and many parties weighed in, including the AIAW, and several national educational organizations. In its

[7]*Sex Discrimination Regulations,* Hearings before the Subcommittee on Postsecondary Education of the Committee on Education and Labor, 94th Cong., 1st Sess. 438 (1975), 439.

[8]40 Fed. Reg. 24, 128 (1975) (currently at 34 C.F.R. Section 106 (2005)).

[9]Section 431(d)(1) of the General Education Provision Act, Pub. L. 93-380, 88 Stat. 567, as amended 20 U.S.C. Section 1232(d)(1). This provision afforded "Congress an opportunity to examine a regulation and, if it found the regulation 'inconsistent with the Act from which it derives its Authority . . . ,' to disapprove it in a concurrent resolution. If no such disapproval resolution was adopted within forty-five days, the regulation would become effective." *North Haven v. Bell,* 456 U.S. 512 (1982). Currently, the regulatory process does not require Congress to consider whether the proposed regulations reflect congressional intent.

[10]Ellen J. Staurowsky, "Title IX and College Sport: The Long Painful Path to Compliance and Reform," *Marquette Sports Law Review* (Fall 2003), 101–102.

[11]Ibid.

January 1978 decision in the NCAA litigation, the federal district court commented that the case "might be noted the most over-briefed presentation in the court's recent experience."[12]

Among other things, the NCAA argued that: (a) Title IX could not apply to athletic departments when the athletic department was not a recipient of federal funding; (b) NCAA rules conflicted with AIAW rules; and (c) the regulations were too vague to put schools on notice of their responsibilities under the law. As the excerpted decision of the federal appeals court for the District of Columbia makes clear, the case was dismissed when it was found that the NCAA did not have standing to bring the lawsuit. "Standing" is a legal term meaning that the party has the right to bring the lawsuit. The judicial power of the United States is created and defined in Article III of the Constitution, which extends only to hear a "case or controversy" that is ready for judicial determination. Courts do not resolve hypothetical or academic disagreements, or offer advice on the law in the abstract. The standing requirement assures that the right party is bringing the lawsuit so the courts may provide an appropriate judicial remedy.[13] These limitations are part of the Constitution's separation of powers requirement, in theory helping divide law from politics, keeping judges in their place and out of policy-making branches of other branches of government.

In *NCAA v. Califano*, part of the court's analysis, reprinted in this section, concluded that the NCAA, as a membership organization, could not demonstrate any harm that complying with nondiscrimination mandate would force it to suffer, or that any men's intercollegiate athletic programs were "aggrieved, adversely affected, injured, or suffering any legally cognizable 'wrong' as a result of [Title IX's regulations]."[14]

The NCAA's complaint that portions of the regulations were vague, however, may have had some merit. By July 1978, HEW had received "nearly 100 complaints alleging discrimination in athletics against more than 50 institutions of higher education."[15] For both universities and athletes, the central question was whether a school had provided "enough" sports opportunities for female student-athletes to fulfill the 1975 regulations requirement of "equal opportunities." It became clear to investigators that both universities and athletes needed further guidance on how to comply with this aspect of the Title IX regulations. Most other departments were easily integrated—schools were only required to make gender-blind admissions to the math or music department. But when was

---

[12]*NCAA v. Califano*, 444 F. Supp. 425, 428 (D. Kan. 1978), 428.

[13]In addition, the doctrine assures that the parties before them are sufficiently adverse. Parties who were not adverse could collude to force courts to make case law that favored one side, which would be binding on future litigants.

[14]Ibid., 434.

[15]44 Fed. Reg. 71413 (1979).

an athletic department that required separate teams for men and women providing "equal opportunity"? Was a school required to establish a women's
department that was a mirror image of the men's athletic department, including
a women's football team? Was an athletic department required to be 50 percent
female? What about schools that had just 30 percent women in their enrollment? Schools wanted to be sure they were complying with federal law, and
athletes wanted to know when they could legally demand more from their
institution's athletic departments.

In response to this uncertainty, HEW issued a policy interpretation (the
"Policy Interpretation") in 1979 that further clarified the meaning of Title IX's
"equal opportunity" mandate.[16] A key part of the 1979 interpretation, included
here, established a three-pronged test to determine whether or not a school was
providing equal opportunities for athletic participation to both sexes. The validity of the three-pronged test has been heavily litigated over the past twenty
years. It has been upheld by every one of the eight federal appeals courts that
has considered its legality.[17] Later sections will discuss some of the challenges
to the test. The 1979 interpretation also established gender equity guidelines
beyond opportunities for participation, including financial assistance, facilities
and equipment, scheduling, travel and per diem allowances, coaching, support
services, dining and housing, publicity, and recruitment, among others.

The last entry in this section's materials, the case of *Cannon v. University of
Chicago*, which held that Title IX contained an implied right for women to sue
their schools for gender discrimination they suffered in education. The ruling
in *Cannon* allowed athletes themselves to force their schools to comply with
Title IX's mandate of equal opportunity. Without *Cannon*, aggrieved athletes
would have to rely on the Office of Civil Rights to seek and obtain the relief on

---

[16]See U.S. Department of Health, Education, and Welfare, Office for Civil Rights, Office of
the Secretary, HEW, *Title IX of the Education Amendments of 1972: A Policy Interpretation: Title IX
and Intercollegiate Athletics* (1979), at http://www.ed.gov/offices/OCR/docs/t9interp.html [here-
inafter OCR].

[17]See *Chalenor v. Univ. of N.D.*, 291 F.3d 1042 (8th Cir. 2002); *Pederson v. La. St. Univ.*, 213
F.3d 858, 879 (5th Cir. 2000); *Neal v. Bd. of Trs. of Calif. St. Univs.*, 198 F.3d 763, 770 (9th Cir.
1999); *Horner v. Ky. High Sch. Athletic Assoc.*, 43 F.3d 265, 274–275 (6th Cir. 1994), *appeal after
remand*, 206 F.3d 685 (6th Cir. 2000), *cert. denied*, 531 U.S. 824 (2000).; *Kelley v. Bd. of Trs., Univ.
of Ill.*, 35 F.3d 265, 270 (7th Cir. 1994), *cert. denied*, 513 U.S. 1128 (1995); *Cohen v. Brown Univ.*,
991 F. 2d 888 (1st Cir. 1993) (hereinafter *Cohen II*) (upholding the grant of a preliminary injunction to the female student-athletes); *Cohen v. Brown Univ.*, 101 F.3d 155, 170 (1st Cir. 1996), *cert.
denied*, 520 U.S. 1186 (1997) (this case was before the First Circuit twice, first on Brown University's appeal of a preliminary injunction granted by the district court [*Cohen I*], and the second
time after a trial on the merits [*Cohen II*]); *Roberts v. Colo. St. Bd. of Agric.*, 998 F.2d 824, 828 (10th
Cir. 1993), *cert. denied*, 510 U.S. 1004 (1993); *Williams v. Sch. Dist. of Bethlehem*, 998 F.2d 168,
171 (3d Cir. 1993), *cert. denied*, 510 U.S. 1043 (1994); *see also* Diane Heckman, "The Glass
Sneaker: Thirty Years of Victories and Defeats Involving Title IX and Sex Discrimination in Athletics," 13 *Fordham Intell. Prop. Media & Ent. L. J.* 551 (2003), 568–587.

their behalf under Title IX, a remedy that we shall see has been rarely used and is far from satisfactory.

In sum, the 1970s were a heady time for women in athletics. With the passage of Title IX they saw a spike upwards in opportunities offered. Despite the male-dominated NCAA's powerful lobbying arm, Congress did not bow to all the attempts to weaken both Title IX and the regulations implementing it. The courts likewise rejected the attempts of the NCAA[18] and others to weaken Title IX, which gave women a powerful tool to fight discrimination via court claims. As will be seen, any victory party was to be short-lived, because a new presidential administration would work hard to limit the reach of Title IX into athletic departments. In addition, whereas the NCAA was unsuccessful in its lawsuit against HEW, the NCAA did successfully take over the organizing body for women's athletics, the AIAW, so that men would largely be overseeing and administrating women's sports.

---

[18]The United States District Court in *NCAA v. Califano* stated that "however worthy the aims and programs of the NCAA may be within its proper sphere, some might view the purposes of the NCAA as inimical to legitimate overall interests and objectives of particular educational institutions. Whether the NCAA may be deemed an appropriate representative of its members in this proceeding must therefore be examined in light of the fact that its representational capacity may be fairly said to extend to only the interests of its members in promoting intercollegiate athletic programs and activities for male student athletes." 444 F. Supp. 425 (D. Kan. 1978), 433–434.

Speech of Senator Birch Bayh to the New York Women's Political Caucus

New York, November 23, 1975*

The history of all movements for social progress in the United States is not a narrative of uninterrupted success. Before the struggle against slavery achieved its goal in the passage of the Thirteenth Amendment there was the Dred Scott decision and the Fugitive Slave Act.

Before the rights of labor were established, there were the massacres at Homestead and Ludlow.

Before the quest for civil rights culminated in the passage of the Civil Rights Act of 1964, 1965, and 1968, there was Birmingham and Neshoba County.

So it is with the struggle for the Equal Rights Amendment. We accept success with grace . . . but we also must learn to take advantage of our setbacks.

The realities that exist for the American women are on our side. What is the status of most women in our nation—almost half of all American women over the age of sixteen are counted in the ranks of the American labor force. More than eight million workers are single women. Almost seven million women workers are widowed, divorced, or separated, and their reason for working is simple and compelling economic necessity.

More than nine million children under the age of eighteen are in families with a woman head of household. Many of those are young children who need quality child care.

Of the married women in the labor force, almost six million have husbands making less than $7,000 a year.

*Text provided by Kate Cruikshank, PhD, Political Papers Specialist, Indiana University, Bloomington, Indiana.

Almost half of all unemployed persons are women, and of those one-quarter of a million are heads of their families.

The earnings gap between men and woman has not narrowed, it has widened. In 1955, women earned salaries that were about 63 percent of the salaries of similarly employed men. This figure has now dropped to 57 percent.

The performance of the present administration in civil-rights enforcement is dismal. Within the Department of Health, Education, and Welfare [HEW], there is the Office of Civil Rights. This should not be a trivial bureaucratic office.

It is responsible for enforcing most of the nation's antidiscrimination laws—Titles VI and VII of the 1964 Civil Rights Act, and Title IX of the Education Amendments of 1972. This office is deluged with cases, yet the Secretary of HEW made no requests for additional money for additional enforcement and investigative personnel.

Secretary Matthews cannot argue that money is the problem, since his department returned 10 percent of the appropriation for the Office of Civil Rights to the Treasury in fiscal year 1975.

Regional offices, such as the one in Dallas, are openly refusing to handle individual complaints filed by women or by Spanish-speaking citizens.

As bad as HEW has been in processing complaints and pursuing enforcement, the Equal Employment Opportunity Commission [EEOC] has been worse. This agency was created by the 1964 Civil Rights Act to help resolve the thousands of complaints brought by minority people and women who are the victims of discrimination in the work place. The backlog of cases at EEOC is an unbelievable 100,000 cases. This agency is so demoralized and so full of internal conflict that it is almost dysfunctional.

Justice delayed is justice denied, and the backlogs in these fact-finding and enforcement agencies stand as a monument to the denial of the civil rights of hundreds of thousands of minority and female workers.

The response by HEW officials to this shocking situation was a regulation issued last June 4, that HEW will no longer take action on individual complaints, but will rely instead on periodic compliance reviews.

Rather than seeking the money and staff to process complaints, HEW asked to be relieved of the responsibility of virtually all civil rights enforcement responsibilities on behalf of individuals.

I was infuriated by this regulation and, in July, I chaired a full day of hearings before the Labor-HEW Subcommittee of the Senate Appropriations Committee to get to the bottom of this scandalous situation. The HEW witnesses told us they were understaffed, yet they failed to fill fifty positions authorized by the Congress and never got around to asking for staff positions for the enforcement of Title IX until its fiscal 1976 budget request. As a result of these hearings, I authored a resolution, cosponsored by fifty-two of my colleagues, expressing disapproval of the new HEW regulations.

The struggle for the equality of women in America is not a hobby or a fad which can be used for political aggrandizement; it is not a political ruse; it is not a spasm of sympathy which lasts only a moment; it is not a fever of enthusiasm; it is not the product of fanaticism; it is not a spirit of factionalism.

It lies in the heart as a vital principle. It is an essential part of democracy, and aside from it there can be no humanity. Its scope is not confined to the women of the United States, but embraces all people, everywhere. Opposition cannot weary it, force cannot suppress it, and temporary defeat cannot still its message.

Amendment to Title IX of the Education Amendments of 1972

94th CONGRESS
1st Session

(Proposed Tower Amendment)

S. 2106

IN THE SENATE OF THE UNITED STATES
JULY 15 (legislative day, JULY 10), 1975

Mr. TOWER (for himself, Mr. BARTLETT, Mr. HRUSKA, and Mr. LAXALT) introduced the following bill; which was read twice and referred to the Committee on Labor and Public Welfare.

A BILL

To amend Title IX of the Education Amendments of 1972.

Be it enacted by the Senate and House of Representatives of the United States of America in Congress assembled, that section 901(a) of the Education Amendments of 1972 (Public Law 92-318) is amended by—

(1) striking out the word "and" at the end of paragraph (4) of such section; and

(2) striking out the period at the end of paragraph (5) and inserting in lieu thereof a semicolon and the word "and"; and

(3) adding at the end thereof the following new paragraph:

"(6) this section shall not apply to an intercollegiate athletic activity insofar as such activity provides to the institution gross receipts or donations required by such institution to support that activity."

Statement of Hon. Birch Bayh,
a U.S. Senator from the State of Indiana,
on the Tower Amendment*

Mr. Chairman, I thank you and Senator Pell and other members of the committee and staff for the opportunity to testify here today on legislation which seeks to fundamentally alter the original goals of Title IX, goals which included equal opportunity for women in athletics and physical education.

The issue of equal opportunity for women in athletics is not a new one. Congress's decision to uphold the coverage of athletics by Title IX has been buttressed by a number of court decisions which mandated equal opportunity for women in high school and college athletics based upon the due process guarantees of the Fourteenth Amendment. See *Brenden v. Independent School Dist.*, 342 F. Supp 1224 (D. Minn. 1972); *Reed v. Nebraska School Activities Assoc.*, 341 F. Supp. 1212 (W.D. Pa. 1973); and *Morris v. Michigan St. Bd. of Ed.*, 472 F. Supp. 207 (6th Cir. 1973).

The question before this subcommittee today is whether the Congress should retreat from the full commitment it has given to provide equal opportunity for women in athletics by exempting revenue-producing sports from Title IX.

Mr. Chairman, it is interesting to me that in the midst of the highly vocal debate now going on over whether or not Title IX should apply to either revenue-producing sports in particular or intercollegiate athletics in general, no one is making the argument that there is not discrimination against women. No football coach or athletic director is denying that this is something fundamentally wrong with a college or university that relegates its female athletes to second-rate facilities, second-rate equipment, or second-rate schedules, solely because they are women. No one seriously disputes the fact that athletic budgets for

*120 Cong. Rec. 39992 (1974).

women are a fraction of those provided for the men. Instead, the argument has focused on the ability of certain intercollegiate sports to withstand the financial burdens imposed by the equal-opportunity requirements of Title IX. To this end, those who feel such sports as football could not survive such financial strictures are seeking to exempt these sports from the mandates of Title IX through the Tower Bill, sec. 2106.

As the Senate author of Title IX, Mr. Chairman, I am opposed to the Tower Bill, not because I am oblivious to the economic concerns of those members of the NCAA opposing Title IX, but because I think their concern is based upon a misunderstanding of both what is required under the Title IX regulations and the true implications of the Tower proposal.

What does Title IX require of colleges and universities in order to meet their equal opportunity guidelines in intercollegiate athletics?

Do the guidelines require equal aggregate expenditures for either male and female teams or individual male and female players? The answer is no.

Do the guidelines require equal separate facilities for any intercollegiate sports? Again, the answer is no.

Do the guidelines require that equal athletic scholarships be given to male and female athletes? The answer is no.

Do the guidelines require that certain sports must be offered for women? Again, the answer is no.

What the guidelines do require is that when a college or university chooses to offer a particular sport to male athletes, it must provide equality of opportunity for women athletes. Under the guidelines, this equality of opportunity is provided in two ways. First, with regard to contact sports, the college or university may provide separate teams for males or females or may have a single team, composed of players from both sexes. If the college or university chooses to have separate teams, the institution is prohibited from discriminating on the basis of sex in providing the necessary supplies or equipment. Nowhere in the guidelines is there a requirement for equal aggregate expenditures.

I think one example of how Title IX would change things is that in one institution I know of for sport x, say basketball, to be specific, if the men are trying out for the team, and the university feels that buying the shorts and the shirts and attendant equipment is a university expense, but the women, to try out for the women's team, must bear that expense themselves. Now, I think that is probably the best example that I can give you.

In a statement by the NCAA circulated among members of the Congress prior to the congressional approval of the Title IX guidelines, the NCAA maintained:

Throughout the entire, long debate over Title IX and the HEW regulations, the NCAA members have consistently sought—not to have revenue-producing sports exempted from Title IX . . . but merely to make clear that revenues produced by a particular sport would be used to maintain the program in that sport. Excess of revenues over expenses in the sport would, under the NCAA proposal, be available for use throughout the intercollegiate program

It seems clear to me that the NCAA was seeking an exemption, which differs substantially from the Tower proposal in two significant ways. First, the Tower proposal addresses gross receipts and donations, not net profit; and second, the Tower proposal seeks a blanket exemption for any intercollegiate activity which provides gross receipts or donations to any institution for its support.

Under the Tower proposal, any institution's athletic programs could fall under the exemption of Title IX merely by charging a nominal fee at all intercollegiate activities which produce gross receipts or donations required by the institution for the support of that sport.

The original NCAA proposal states that the concern of the NCAA was not with a total exemption for revenue-producing sports, but with an exemption for moneys produced by that sport and necessary to cover the expenses of the sport.

In other words, the net profit of the sport, not its gross receipts or initial donations.

The Tower Amendment does not provide a partial exemption to Title IX for revenue-producing sports, it provides a blanket exemption. The only criteria necessary to achieve the exemption is the production of revenues or donations. The specific wording of the Tower bill is not directed to the moneys necessary to cover expenses of a particular sport; rather it is directed at creating a total exemption for the sport itself from Title IX.

Therefore, despite the initial statement of the NCAA that the NCAA membership was not seeking such a blanket exemption from Title IX, this is exactly what is created by the Tower Amendment, Mr. Chairman.

In conclusion, Mr. Chairman, let me say that from the college coed to the ten-year-old longing to play little league baseball, American women have been consistently denied adequate athletic opportunities, funding, coaching, scheduling, scholarships, and access to facilities are only a few of the areas where inequities are glaring.

Title IX attempts to address these inequities, not through rigid requirements of equal expenditures for males and females, but through an assessment of a variety of factors including student interest and participation, past history of athletic opportunities for members of both sexes, and current fiscal constraints that will vary from institution to institution.

For years women's intercollegiate athletics have had to struggle by with very little institutional assistance. For the first time, under Title IX, women athletes will be afforded a true opportunity to use their skills and aptitudes. I hope that

members of this subcommittee will help make sure that after years of depriva-
tion, support will be there for women's athletic programs throughout this
nation.

I am concerned, Mr. Chairman, that this subcommittee not begin the ero-
sion of our commitment to the women of this nation through Title IX. In this
particular instance we are talking about our commitment to the women athletes
throughout this nation's colleges and universities, but once the Pandora's box
of successful exemptions to Title IX is opened, we will see a host of other deserving exemptions being offered.

Therefore, Mr. Chairman, I urge you and other members of the subcommittee to reject the bill of our distinguished colleague from Texas and leave the
congressional commitment to women through Title IX unscarred.

I might say, Mr. Chairman, I have had the opportunity, I suppose, as much
as anybody in this body to study what we are trying to accomplish through Title
IX. It is unbelievable to me that sports programs so steeped in tradition as most
of our big-ten schools are suddenly going to disintegrate or even be seriously
damaged or even slightly damaged by permitting the women to attend these
same fine institutions and have an equal opportunity to participate in athletic
programs and programs of physical education.

Javits Amendment*

Passed May 20, 1974

PROVISION RELATING TO SEX DISCRIMINATION

SEC. 844 OF THE EDUCATION AMENDMENTS OF 1974. THE SECRETARY SHALL PREPARE AND PUBLISH, NOT LATER THAN 30 DAYS AFTER THE DATE OF ENACTMENT OF THIS ACT, //20 USC 1681 NOTE.// PROPOSED REGULATIONS IMPLEMENTING THE PROVISIONS OF TITLE IX OF THE EDUCATION AMENDMENTS OF 1972 //86 STAT. 373, 20 USC 1681.// RELATING TO THE PROHIBITION OF SEX DISCRIMINATION IN FEDERALLY ASSISTED EDUCATION PROGRAMS WHICH SHALL INCLUDE WITH RESPECT TO INTERCOLLEGIATE ATHLETIC ACTIVITIES REASONABLE PROVISIONS CONSIDERING THE NATURE OF PARTICULAR SPORTS.

*The Javits Amendment became part of the Education Amendments of 1974, section 844.

1975 Title IX Regulations*

Section 106.41   Athletics.

(a) *General.* No person shall, on the basis of sex, be excluded from participation in, be denied the benefits of, be treated differently from another person, or otherwise be discriminated against in any interscholastic, intercollegiate, club, or intramural athletics offered by a recipient, and no recipient shall provide any such athletics separately on such basis.

(b) *Separate teams.* Notwithstanding the requirements of paragraph (a) of this section, a recipient may operate or sponsor separate teams for members of each sex where selection for such teams is based upon competitive skill or the activity involved is a contact sport. However, where a recipient operates or sponsors a team in a particular sport for members of one sex but operates or sponsors no such team for members of the other sex, and athletic opportunities for members of that sex have previously been limited, members of the excluded sex must be allowed to try out for the team offered unless the sport involved is a contact sport. For the purposes of this part, contact sports include boxing, wrestling, rugby, ice hockey, football, basketball, and other sports the purpose or major activity of which involves bodily contact.

(c) *Equal opportunity.* A recipient which operates or sponsors interscholastic, intercollegiate, club, or intramural athletics shall provide equal athletic opportunity for members of both sexes. In determining whether equal opportunities are available, the Director will consider, among other factors:

*34 C.F.R. Section 106.41 (2003).

(1) Whether the selection of sports and levels of competition effectively accommodate the interests and abilities of members of both sexes;

(2) The provision of equipment and supplies;

(3) Scheduling of games and practice time;

(4) Travel and per diem allowance;

(5) Opportunity to receive coaching and academic tutoring;

(6) Assignment and compensation of coaches and tutors;

(7) Provision of locker rooms, practice and competitive facilities;

(8) Provision of medical and training facilities and services;

(9) Provision of housing and dining facilities and services;

(10) Publicity. Unequal aggregate expenditures for members of each sex or unequal expenditures for male and female teams if a recipient operates or sponsors separate teams will not constitute noncompliance with this section, but the Assistant Secretary may consider the failure to provide necessary funds for teams for one sex in assessing equality of opportunity for members of each sex.

(d) *Adjustment period.* A recipient which operates or sponsors interscholastic, intercollegiate, club, or intramural athletics at the elementary school level shall comply fully with this section as expeditiously as possible but in no event later than one year from the effective date of this regulation. A recipient which operates or sponsors interscholastic, intercollegiate, club, or intramural athletics at the secondary or postsecondary school level shall comply fully with this section as expeditiously as possible but in no event later than three years from the effective date of this regulation.

A Policy Interpretation:
Title IX and Intercollegiate Athletics*

Tuesday, December 11, 1979
Department of Health, Education, and Welfare
Office for Civil Rights

I. Legal Background

A. The Statute

Section 901(a) of Title IX of the Education Amendments of 1972 provides:

- No person in the United States shall, on the basis of sex, be excluded from participation in, be denied the benefits of, or be subjected to discrimination under any education program or activity receiving federal financial assistance.

Section 844 of the Education Amendments of 1974 further provides:

- The Secretary of [HEW] shall prepare and publish proposed regulations implementing the provisions of Title IX of the Education Amendments of 1972 relating to the prohibition of sex discrimination in federally assisted education programs, which shall include with respect to intercollegiate athletic activities reasonable provisions considering the nature of particular sports.

Congress passed Section 844 after the Conference Committee deleted a Senate floor amendment that would have exempted revenue-producing athletics from the jurisdiction of Title IX.

*44 Fed. Reg. 71,413, 71,423 (1979); http://www.ed.gov/about/offices/list/ocr/docs/t9interp. html (accessed June 29, 2007).

B. The Regulation

The regulation implementing Title IX is set forth, in pertinent part, in the Policy Interpretation below. It was signed by President Ford on May 27, 1975, and submitted to the Congress for review pursuant to Section 431(d)(1) of the General Education Provisions Act (GEPA).

During this review, the House Subcommittee on Postsecondary Education held hearings on a resolution disapproving the regulation. The Congress did not disapprove the regulation within the 45 days allowed under GEPA, and it therefore became effective on July 21, 1975.

Subsequent hearings were held in the Senate Subcommittee on Education on a bill to exclude revenues produced by sports to the extent they are used to pay the costs of those sports. The Committee, however, took no action on this bill.

The regulation established a three-year transition period to give institutions time to comply with its equal athletic opportunity requirements. That transition period expired on July 21, 1978.

II. Purpose of Policy Interpretation

By the end of July 1978, the Department had received nearly 100 complaints alleging discrimination in athletics against more than 50 institutions of higher education. In attempting to investigate these complaints, and to answer questions from the university community, the Department determined that it should provide further guidance on what constitutes compliance with the law. Accordingly, this Policy Interpretation explains the regulation so as to provide a framework within which the complaints can be resolved, and to provide institutions of higher education with additional guidance on the requirements for compliance with Title IX in intercollegiate athletic programs.

III. Scope of Application

This Policy Interpretation is designed specifically for intercollegiate athletics. However, its general principles will often apply to club, intramural, and interscholastic athletic programs, which are also covered by regulation. Accordingly, the Policy Interpretation may be used for guidance by the administrators of such programs when appropriate.

This policy interpretation applies to any public or private institution, person or other entity that operates an educational program or activity which receives or benefits from financial assistance authorized or extended under a law administered by the Department.

IV. Summary of Final Policy Interpretation

The final Policy Interpretation clarifies the meaning of "equal opportunity" in intercollegiate athletics. It explains the factors and standards set out in the law and regulation which the Department will consider in determining whether an institution's intercollegiate athletics program complies with the law and regulations. It also provides guidance to assist institutions in determining whether any disparities which may exist between men's and women's programs are justifiable and nondiscriminatory. The Policy Interpretation is divided into three sections:

- Compliance in Financial Assistance (Scholarships) Based on Athletic Ability: Pursuant to the regulation, the governing principle in this area is that all such assistance should be available on a substantially proportional basis to the number of male and female participants in the institution's athletic program.
- Compliance in Other Program Areas (equipment and supplies; games and practice times; travel and per diem; coaching and academic tutoring; assignment and compensation of coaches and tutors; locker rooms, and practice and competitive facilities; medical and training facilities; housing and dining facilities; publicity; recruitment; and support services): Pursuant to the regulation, the governing principle is that male and female athletes should receive equivalent treatment, benefits, and opportunities.
- Compliance in Meeting the Interests and Abilities of Male and Female Students: Pursuant to the regulation, the governing principle in this area is that the athletic interests and abilities of male and female students must be equally effectively accommodated.

V. Major Changes to Proposed Policy Interpretation

The final Policy Interpretation has been revised from the one published in proposed form on December 11, 1978. The proposed Policy Interpretation was based on a two-part approach. Part I addressed equal opportunity for participants in athletic programs. It required the elimination of discrimination in financial support and other benefits and opportunities in an institution's existing athletic program. Institutions could establish a presumption of compliance if they could demonstrate that:

- "Average per capita" expenditures for male and female athletes were substantially equal in the area of "readily financially measurable" benefits and opportunities or, if not, that any disparities were the result of nondiscriminatory factors, and

- Benefits and opportunities for male and female athletes, in areas which are not financially measurable,. "were comparable."

Part II of the proposed Policy Interpretation addressed an institution's obligation to accommodate effectively the athletic interests and abilities of women as well as men on a continuing basis. It required an institution either:

- To follow a policy of development of its women's athletic program to provide the participation and competition opportunities needed to accommodate the growing interests and abilities of women, or
- To demonstrate that it was effectively (and equally) accommodating the athletic interests and abilities of students, particularly as the interests and abilities of women students developed.

While the basic considerations of equal opportunity remain, the final Policy Interpretation sets forth the factors that will be examined to determine an institution's actual, as opposed to presumed, compliance with Title IX in the area of intercollegiate athletics.

The final Policy Interpretation does not contain a separate section on institutions' future responsibilities. However, institutions remain obligated by the Title IX regulation to accommodate effectively the interests and abilities of male and female students with regard to the selection of sports and levels of competition available. In most cases, this will entail development of athletic programs that substantially expand opportunities for women to participate and compete at all levels.

The major reasons for the change in approach are as follows:

(1) Institutions and representatives of athletic program participants expressed a need for more definitive guidance on what constituted compliance than the discussion of a presumption of compliance provided. Consequently the final Policy Interpretation explains the meaning of "equal athletic opportunity" in such a way as to facilitate an assessment of compliance.

(2) Many comments reflected a serious misunderstanding of the presumption of compliance. Most institutions based objections to the proposed Policy Interpretation in part on the assumption that failure to provide compelling justifications for disparities in per-capita expenditures would have automatically resulted in a finding of noncompliance. In fact, such a failure would only have deprived an institution of the benefit of the presumption that it was in compliance with the law. The Department would still have had the burden of demonstrating that the institution was actually engaged in unlawful discrimination. Since the purpose of issuing a policy interpretation

was to clarify the regulation, the Department has determined that the approach of stating actual compliance factors would be more useful to all concerned.

(3) The Department has concluded that purely financial measures such as the per-capita test do not in themselves offer conclusive documentation of discrimination, except where the benefit or opportunity under review, like a scholarship, is itself financial in nature. Consequently, in the final Policy Interpretation, the Department has detailed the factors to be considered in assessing actual compliance. While per capita breakdowns and other devices to examine expenditure patterns will be used as tools of analysis in the Department's investigative process, it is achievement of "equal opportunity" for which recipients are responsible and to which the final Policy Interpretation is addressed.

VI. Historic Patterns of Intercollegiate Athletics Program Development and Operations

In its proposed Policy Interpretation of December 11, 1978, the Department published a summary of historic patterns affecting the relative status of men's and women's athletic programs. The Department has modified that summary to reflect additional information obtained during the comment and consultation process. The summary is set forth at Appendix A to this document.

VII. The Policy Interpretation

This Policy Interpretation clarifies the obligations which recipients of Federal aid have under Title IX to provide equal opportunities in athletic programs. In particular, this Policy Interpretation provides a means to assess an institution's compliance with the equal opportunity requirements of the regulation, which are set forth at 45 CFR 88.37(c) and 88.4a(c).

A. Athletic Financial Assistance (Scholarships)

1. The Regulation—Section 86.37(c) of the regulation provides:

[Institutions] must provide reasonable opportunities for such award (of financial assistance) for member of each sex in proportion to the number of students of each sex participating in intercollegiate athletics.

2. The Policy—The Department will examine compliance with this provision of the regulation primarily by means of a financial comparison to determine

whether proportionately equal amounts of financial assistance (scholarship aid) are available to men's and women's athletic programs. The Department will measure compliance with this standard by dividing the amounts of aid available for the members of each sex by the numbers of male or female participants in the athletic program and comparing the results. Institutions may be found in compliance if this comparison results in substantially equal amounts or if a resulting disparity can be explained by adjustments to take into account legitimate, nondiscriminatory factors. Two such factors are:

a. At public institutions, the higher costs of tuition for students from out of state may in some years be unevenly distributed between men's and women's programs. These differences will be considered nondiscriminatory if they are not the result of policies or practices which disproportionately limit the availability of out-of-state scholarships to either men or women.

b. An institution may make reasonable professional decisions concerning the awards most appropriate for program development. For example, team development initially may require spreading scholarships over as much as a full generation (four years) of student athletes. This may result in the award of fewer scholarships in the first few years than would be necessary to create proportionality between male and female athletes.

3. Application of the Policy—

a. This section does not require a proportionate number of scholarships for men and women or individual scholarships of equal dollar value. It does mean that the total amount of scholarship aid made available to men and women must be substantially proportionate to their participation rates.

b. When financial assistance is provided in forms other than grants, the distribution of nongrant assistance will also be compared to determine whether equivalent benefits are proportionately available to male and female athletes. A disproportionate amount of work-related aid or loans in the assistance made available to the members of one sex, for example, could constitute a violation of Title IX.

4. Definition—For purposes of examining compliance with this Section, the participants will be defined as those athletes:

a. Who are receiving the institutionally sponsored support normally provided to athletes competing at the institution involved, e.g., coaching, equipment, medical and training room services, on a regular basis during a sport's season; and

b. Who are participating in organized practice sessions and other team meetings and activities on a regular basis during a sport's season; and

c. Who are listed on the eligibility or squad lists maintained for each sport; or

d. Who, because of injury, cannot meet a, b, or c above but continue to receive financial aid on the basis of athletic ability.

B. Equivalence in Other Athletic Benefits and Opportunities

1. The Regulation—The Regulation requires that recipients that operate or sponsor interscholastic, intercollegiate, club, or intramural athletics "Provide equal athletic opportunities for members of both sexes." In determining whether an institution is providing equal opportunity in intercollegiate athletics the regulation requires the Department to consider, among others, the following factors:

 (1) [No content for item (1)]
 (2) Provision and maintenance of equipment and supplies;
 (3) Scheduling of games and practice times;
 (4) Travel and per diem expenses;
 (5) Opportunity to receive coaching and academic tutoring;
 (6) Assignment and compensation of coaches and tutors;
 (7) Provision of locker rooms, practice and competitive facilities;
 (8) Provision of medical and training services and facilities;
 (9) Provision of housing and dining services and facilities; and
(10) Publicity.

Section 86.41(c) also permits the Director of the Office for Civil Rights to consider other factors in the determination of equal opportunity.

Accordingly, this Section also addresses recruitment of student athletes and provision of support services.

This list is not exhaustive. Under the regulation, it may be expanded as necessary at the discretion of the Director of the Office for Civil Rights.

2. The Policy—The Department will assess compliance with both the recruitment and the general athletic program requirements of the regulation by comparing the availability, quality, and kinds of benefits, opportunities, and treatment afforded members of both sexes. Institutions will be in compliance if the compared program components are equivalent, that is, equal or equal in effect. Under this standard, identical benefit, opportunities, or treatments are not required, provided the overall effects of any differences is negligible.

If comparisons of program components reveal that treatment, benefits, or opportunities are not equivalent in kind, quality, or availability, a finding of compliance may still be justified if the differences are the result of nondiscriminatory factors. Some of the factors that may justify these differences are as follows:

a. Some aspects of athletic programs may not be equivalent for men and women because of unique aspects of particular sports or athletic activities. This type of distinction was called for by the "Javits' Amendment" to Title IX, which instructed HEW to make "reasonable (regulatory) provisions considering the nature of particular sports" in intercollegiate athletics.

Generally, these differences will be the result of factors that are inherent to the basic operation of specific sports. Such factors may include rules of play, nature/replacement of equipment, rates of injury resulting from participation, nature of facilities required for competition, and the maintenance/upkeep requirements of those facilities. For the most part, differences involving such factors will occur in programs offering football, and consequently these differences will favor men. If sport-specific needs are met equivalently in both men's and women's programs, however, differences in particular program components will be found to be justifiable.

b. Some aspects of athletic programs may not be equivalent for men and women because of legitimately sex-neutral factors related to special circumstances of a temporary nature. For example, large disparities in recruitment activity for any particular year may be the result of annual fluctuations in team needs for first-year athletes. Such differences are justifiable to the extent that they do not reduce overall equality of opportunity.

c. The activities directly associated with the operation of a competitive event in a single-sex sport may, under some circumstances, create unique demands or imbalances in particular program components. Provided any special demands associated with the activities of sports involving participants of the other sex are met to an equivalent degree, the resulting differences may be found nondiscriminatory. At many schools, for example, certain sports, notably football and men's basketball, traditionally draw large crowds. Since the costs of managing an athletic event increase with crowd size, the overall support made available for event management to men's and women's programs may differ in degree and kind. These differences would not violate Title IX if the recipient does not limit the potential for women's athletic events to rise in spectator appeal and if the levels of event management support available to both programs are based on sex-neutral criteria (e.g., facilities used, projected attendance, and staffing needs).

d. Some aspects of athletic programs may not be equivalent for men and women because institutions are undertaking voluntary affirmative actions to overcome effects of historical conditions that have limited participation in athletics by the members of one sex. This is authorized at 86.3(b) of the regulation.

3. Application of the Policy—General Athletic Program Components—

a. Equipment and Supplies (86.41(c)(2)). Equipment and supplies include but are not limited to uniforms, other apparel, sport-specific equipment and supplies, general equipment and supplies, instructional devices, and conditioning and weight training equipment.

Compliance will be assessed by examining, among other factors, the equivalence for men and women of: [the quantity, amount, suitability, maintenance and replacement, and availability of equipment and supplies].

b. Scheduling of Games and Practice Times (86.41(c)(3)). Compliance will be assessed by examining, among other factors, the equivalence for men and women of:

(1) The number of competitive events per sport;
(2) The number and length of practice opportunities;
(3) The time of day competitive events are scheduled;
(4) The time of day practice opportunities are scheduled; and
(5) The opportunities to engage in available preseason and postseason competition.

c. Travel and Per Diem Allowances (86.41(c)(4)). Compliance will be assessed by examining, among other factors, the equivalence for men and women of:

(1) Modes of transportation;
(2) Housing furnished during travel;
(3) Length of stay before and after competitive events;
(4) Per diem allowances; and
(5) Dining arrangements.

d. Opportunity to Receive Coaching and Academic Tutoring (86.41(c)(5)).

(1) Coaching—Compliance will be assessed by examining, among other factors: [the availability of full-time, part-time, and graduate assistant coaches].
(2) Academic Tutoring—Compliance will be assessed by examining, among other factors, the equivalence for men and women of: [the availability and procedures for obtaining tutoring].

e. Assignment and Compensation of Coaches and Tutors (86.41(c)(6)). In general, a violation of Section 86.41(c)(6) will be found only where compensation or assignment policies or practices deny male and female athletes coaching of equivalent quality, nature, or availability.

Nondiscriminatory factors can affect the compensation of coaches. In determining whether differences are caused by permissible factors, the range and nature of duties, the experience of individual coaches, the number of participants for particular sports, the number of assistant coaches supervised, and the level of competition will be considered.

Where these or similar factors represent valid differences in skill, effort, responsibility, or working conditions they may, in specific circumstances, justify differences in compensation. Similarly, there may be unique situations in which a particular person may possess such an outstanding record of achievement as to justify an abnormally high salary.

(1) Assignment of Coaches. Compliance will be assessed by examining, among other factors, the equivalence for men's and women's coaches of:

(a) Training, experience, and other professional qualifications; and
(b) Professional standing.

(2) Assignment of Tutors. Compliance will be assessed by examining, among other factors, the equivalence for men's and women's tutors of: [tutor qualifications].

(3) Compensation of Coaches. Compliance will be assessed by examining, among other factors, the equivalence for men's and women's coaches of:

(a) Rate of compensation (per sport, per season);
(b) Duration of contracts;
(c) Conditions relating to contract renewal;
(d) Experience;
(e) Nature of coaching duties performed;
(f) Working conditions; and
(g) Other terms and conditions of employment.

(4) Compensation of Tutors. Compliance will be assessed by examining, among other factors, the equivalence for men's and women's tutors of: [the hourly rate, pupil load and qualifications].

f. Provision of Locker Rooms, Practice and Competitive Facilities (86.41(c)(7)). Compliance will be assessed by examining, among other factors, the equivalence for men and women of:

(1) Quality and availability of the facilities provided for practice and competitive events;

(2) Exclusivity of use of facilities provided for practice and competitive events;

(3) Availability of locker rooms;

(4) Quality of locker rooms;

(5) Maintenance of practice and competitive facilities; and

(6) Preparation of facilities for practice and competitive events.

g. Provision of Medical and Training Facilities and Services (86.41(c)(8)). Compliance will be assessed by examining, among other factors, the equivalence for men and women of:

(1) Availability of medical personnel and assistance;

(2) Health, accident, and injury insurance coverage;

(3) Availability and quality of weight and training facilities;

(4) Availability and quality of conditioning facilities; and

(5) Availability and qualifications of athletic trainers.

h. Provision of Housing and Dining Facilities and Services (86.41(c)(9)). Compliance will be assessed by examining, among other factors, the equivalence for men and women of:

(1) Housing provided; and

(2) Special services as part of housing arrangements (e.g., laundry facilities, parking space, maid service).

i. Publicity (86.41(c)(10)). Compliance will be assessed by examining, among other factors, the equivalence for men and women of:

(1) Availability and quality of sports information personnel;

(2) Access to other publicity resources for men's and women's programs; and

(3) Quantity and quality of publications and other promotional devices featuring men's and women's programs.

4. Application of the Policy—Other Factors (86.41(c)).

a. Recruitment of Student Athletes. The athletic recruitment practices of institutions often affect the overall provision of opportunity to male and female athletes. Accordingly, where equal athletic opportunities are not present for male and female students, compliance will be assessed by examining the recruitment practices of the athletic programs for both sexes to determine whether the provision of equal opportunity will require modification of those practices.

Such examinations will review the following factors:

(1) Whether coaches or other professional athletic personnel in the programs serving male and female athletes are provided with substantially equal opportunities to recruit;

(2) Whether the financial and other resources made available for recruitment in male and female athletic programs are equivalently adequate to meet the needs of each program; and

(3) Whether the differences in benefits, opportunities, and treatment afforded prospective student athletes of each sex have a disproportionately limiting effect upon the recruitment of students of either sex.

b. Provision of Support Services. The administrative and clerical support provided to an athletic program can affect the overall provision of opportunity to male and female athletes, particularly to the extent that the provided services enable coaches to perform better their coaching functions.

In the provision of support services, compliance will be assessed by examining, among other factors, the equivalence of:

(1) The amount of administrative assistance provided to men's and women's programs; and

(2) The amount of secretarial and clerical assistance provided to men's and women's programs.

5. Overall Determination of Compliance. The Department will base its compliance determination under 86.41(c) of the regulation upon an examination of the following:

a. Whether the policies of an institution are discriminatory in language or effect; or

b. Whether disparities of a substantial and unjustified nature exist in the benefits, treatment, services, or opportunities afforded male and female athletes in the institution's program as a whole; or

c. Whether disparities in benefits, treatment, services, or opportunities in individual segments of the program are substantial enough in and of themselves to deny equality of athletic opportunity.

C. Effective Accommodation of Student Interests and Abilities

1. The Regulation. The regulation requires institutions to accommodate effectively the interests and abilities of students to the extent necessary to provide

equal opportunity in the selection of sports and levels of competition available to members of both sexes.

Specifically, the regulation, at 86.41(c)(1), requires the Director to consider, when determining whether equal opportunities are available, whether the selection of sports and levels of competition effectively accommodate the interests and abilities of members of both sexes.

Section 86.41(c) also permits the Director of the Office for Civil Rights to consider other factors in the determination of equal opportunity. Accordingly, this section also addresses competitive opportunities in terms of the competitive team schedules available to athletes of both sexes.

2. The Policy. The Department will assess compliance with the interests and abilities section of the regulation by examining the following factors:

a. The determination of athletic interests and abilities of students;

b. The selection of sports offered; and

c. The levels of competition available, including the opportunity for team competition.

3. Application of the Policy—Determination of Athletic Interests and Abilities.

Institutions may determine the athletic interests and abilities of students by nondiscriminatory methods of their choosing provided:

a. The processes take into account the nationally increasing levels of women's interests and abilities;

b. The methods of determining interest and ability do not disadvantage the members of an underrepresented sex;

c. The methods of determining ability take into account team performance records; and

d. The methods are responsive to the expressed interests of students capable of intercollegiate competition who are members of an underrepresented sex.

4. Application of the Policy—Selection of Sports.

In the selection of sports, the regulation does not require institutions to integrate their teams nor to provide exactly the same choice of sports to men and women. However, where an institution sponsors a team in a particular sport for members of one sex, it may be required either to permit the excluded sex to try out for the team or to sponsor a separate team for the previously excluded sex.

a. Contact Sports. Effective accommodation means that if an institution sponsors a team for members of one sex in a contact sport, it must do so for members of the other sex under the following circumstances:

(1) The opportunities for members of the excluded sex have historically been limited; and

(2) There is sufficient interest and ability among the members of the excluded sex to sustain a viable team and a reasonable expectation of intercollegiate competition for that team.

b. Noncontact Sports. Effective accommodation means that if an institution sponsors a team for members of one sex in a noncontact sport, it must do so for members of the other sex under the following circumstances:

(1) The opportunities for members of the excluded sex have historically been limited;

(2) There is sufficient interest and ability among the members of the excluded sex to sustain a viable team and a reasonable expectation of intercollegiate competition for that team; and

(3) Members of the excluded sex do not possess sufficient skill to be selected for a single integrated team, or to compete actively on such a team if selected.

5. Application of the Policy—Levels of Competition.

In effectively accommodating the interests and abilities of male and female athletes, institutions must provide both the opportunity for individuals of each sex to participate in intercollegiate competition, and for athletes of each sex to have competitive team schedules which equally reflect their abilities.

a. Compliance will be assessed in any one of the following ways:

(1) Whether intercollegiate level participation opportunities for male and female students are provided in numbers substantially proportionate to their respective enrollments; or

(2) Where the members of one sex have been and are underrepresented among intercollegiate athletes, whether the institution can show a history and continuing practice of program expansion which is demonstrably responsive to the developing interest and abilities of the members of that sex; or

(3) Where the members of one sex are underrepresented among intercollegiate athletes, and the institution cannot show a continuing practice of program expansion such as that cited above, whether it can be demonstrated that the interests and abilities of the members of that sex have been fully and effectively accommodated by the present program.

b. Compliance with this provision of the regulation will also be assessed by examining the following:

(1) Whether the competitive schedules for men's and women's teams, on a programwide basis, afford proportionally similar numbers of male and female athletes equivalently advanced competitive opportunities; or

(2) Whether the institution can demonstrate a history and continuing practice of upgrading the competitive opportunities available to the historically disadvantaged sex as warranted by developing abilities among the athletes of that sex.

c. Institutions are not required to upgrade teams to intercollegiate status or otherwise develop intercollegiate sports absent a reasonable expectation that intercollegiate competition in that sport will be available within the institution's normal competitive regions. Institutions may be required by the Title IX regulation to actively encourage the development of such competition, however, when overall athletic opportunities within that region have been historically limited for the members of one sex.

6. Overall Determination of Compliance.

The Department will base its compliance determination under 86.41(c) of the regulation upon a determination of the following:

a. Whether the policies of an institution are discriminatory in language or effect; or

b. Whether disparities of a substantial and unjustified nature in the benefits, treatment, services, or opportunities afforded male and female athletes exist in the institution's program as a whole; or

c. Whether disparities in individual segments of the program with respect to benefits, treatment, services, or opportunities are substantial enough in and of themselves to deny equality of athletic opportunity.

VIII. The Enforcement Process

The process of Title IX enforcement is set forth in 88.71 of the Title IX regulation, which incorporates by reference the enforcement procedures applicable to Title VI of the Civil Rights Act of 1964. The enforcement process prescribed by the regulation is supplemented by an order of the Federal District Court, District of Columbia, which establishes time frames for each of the enforcement steps.

According to the regulation, there are two ways in which enforcement is initiated:

- Compliance Reviews. Periodically the Department must select a number of recipients (in this case, colleges and universities which operate intercollegiate athletic programs) and conduct investigations to determine whether recipients are complying with Title IX. (45 CFR 80.7(a))
- Complaints. The Department must investigate all valid (written and timely) complaints alleging discrimination on the basis of sex in a recipient's programs. (45 CFR 80.7(b))

The Department must inform the recipient (and the complainant, if applicable) of the results of its investigation. If the investigation indicates that a recipient is in compliance, the Department states this, and the case is closed. If the investigation indicates noncompliance, the Department outlines the violations found.

The Department has 90 days to conduct an investigation and inform the recipient of its findings, and an additional 90 days to resolve violations by obtaining a voluntary compliance agreement from the recipient. This is done through negotiations between the Department and the recipient, the goal of which is agreement on steps the recipient will take to achieve compliance. Sometimes the violation is relatively minor and can be corrected immediately. At other times, however, the negotiations result in a plan that will correct the violations within a specified period of time. To be acceptable, a plan must describe the manner in which institutional resources will be used to correct the violation. It also must state acceptable time tables for reaching interim goals and full compliance. When agreement is reached, the Department notifies the institution that its plan is acceptable. The Department then is obligated to review periodically the implementation of the plan.

An institution that is in violation of Title IX may already be implementing a corrective plan. In this case, prior to informing the recipient about the results of its investigation, the Department will determine whether the plan is adequate. If the plan is not adequate to correct the violations (or to correct them within a reasonable period of time), the recipient will be found in noncompliance and voluntary negotiations will begin. However, if the institutional plan is acceptable, the Department will inform the institution that although the institution has violations, it is found to be in compliance because it is implementing a corrective plan. The Department, in this instance also, would monitor the progress of the institutional plan. If the institution subsequently does not completely implement its plan, it will be found in noncompliance.

When a recipient is found in noncompliance and voluntary compliance attempts are unsuccessful, the formal process leading to termination of Federal assistance will be begun. [sic] These procedures, which include the opportunity for a hearing before an administrative law judge, are set forth at 45 CFR 80.8-80.11 and 45 CFR Part 81.

Appendix B: Comments and Responses

The Office for Civil Rights (OCR) received over 700 comments and recommendations in response to the December 11, 1978, publication of the proposed Policy Interpretation. After the formal comment period, representatives of the Department met for additional discussions with many individuals and groups, including college and university officials, athletic associations, athletic directors, women's rights organizations, and other interested parties. HEW representatives also visited eight universities in order to assess the potential of the proposed Policy Interpretation and of suggested alternative approaches for effective enforcement of Title IX.

The Department carefully considered all information before preparing the final policy. Some changes in the structure and substance of the Policy Interpretation have been made as a result of concerns that were identified in the comment and consultation process.

Persons who responded to the request for public comment were asked to comment generally and also to respond specifically to eight questions that focused on different aspects of the proposed Policy Interpretation.

United States District Court, D. Kansas

NATIONAL COLLEGIATE ATHLETIC ASSOCIATION, Plaintiff,

v.

Joseph CALIFANO, Secretary of the United States Department of Health, Education and Welfare, Defendant, et al.*

Decided January 9, 1978

O'CONNOR, District Judge.

The National Collegiate Athletic Association . . . has instituted the above-cited action for declaratory and injunctive relief seeking to invalidate regulations promulgated by the Department of Health, Education, and Welfare under the aegis of Title IX of the Education Amendments of 1972. After having studied the parties' written presentation of the issues—possibly, it might be noted, the most overbriefed presentation in the court's recent experience—the court is now prepared to render its judgment on those motions.

The background of this controversy may be summarized as follows: [The court described the legislative history of the statute and the implementing regulations.] Such regulations became effective on July 21, 1975. Thereafter, on February 17, 1976, the NCAA instituted the instant action seeking, on behalf of itself and its member institutions, declaratory and injunctive relief that the regulations so promulgated are invalid. More specifically, the NCAA's challenge is based upon the following arguments: (1) the HEW regulations purport to extend administrative jurisdiction over programs and institutions beyond the scope of the governing statutes in that they reach collegiate athletic programs that do not directly receive federal financial assistance; (2) the HEW regulations exceed the lawful scope of Title IX in that they purport to govern collegiate athletic programs offered by educational institutions which do not directly receive federal financial assistance but which offer nonathletic educational programs that receive or "benefit from" federal financial assistance; (3) the provi-

*NCAA v. Califano, 444 F. Supp. 425 (D. Kan. 1978).

sions of the regulations that purport to require that there be no difference in the treatment of male and female student-athletes, and thus purport to invalidate NCAA rules, are arbitrary and capricious; (4) the regulatory requirement that athletic scholarships and grants-in-aid must, if provided, "provide reasonable opportunities for members of each sex" creates an arbitrary and capricious sex-based quota system and violates the Title IX legislation as well as the Fifth Amendment of the United States Constitution; (5) HEW violated the literal language of the Title IX legislation and thus exceeded its authority in promulgating the challenged regulations without concurrently making express findings that said regulations were consistent with the objectives of each statute under which federal financial assistance may be awarded; and (6) the regulatory standards under which HEW professes to evaluate "equality of opportunity" are impermissibly vague and indefinite and thus allow HEW "unfettered and unimpeded discretion" in determining the existence of a violation, contrary to the due process requirements of the Fifth Amendment.

Count I

Count I of the plaintiff's complaint alleges that the challenged regulations are not applicable to the intercollegiate athletic programs of its members because no such programs are direct recipients of federal financial assistance. It further alleges that HEW's efforts to regulate said athletic programs on the theory that they "benefit from" the provision of federal financial assistance to nonathletic educational programs is unlawful. Promulgation of the purportedly invalid regulations is alleged to have the following effects at the plaintiff's member institutions: (1) institutions are presently making "substantial changes in the organization, operation, and budgeting of their individual intercollegiate athletic program"; (2) institutions are required to presently engage in "time-consuming and expensive programs of self-evaluation and affirmative action"; (3) institutions must immediately apply "substantial amounts of time and money to satisfaction of (the regulatory) directives, to the detriment of other legitimate educational purposes"; and (4) said institutions are deprived of the "freedom to determine the educational programs most suited to that institution, free from interference or regulation by the Federal Government." These alleged "injuries" to its member institutions form the basis on which the NCAA asserts representational standing to litigate Count I of the amended complaint. They are, in the court's view, an insufficient foundation.

Item (1) above, the only one of the four alleged injuries that could plausibly be said to relate to an issue within the purported representational capacity of the NCAA, does not assert any cognizable injury to the plaintiff's members. The Supreme Court held in *Warth v. Seldin* that representational standing depends upon an allegation that the association's members, or any one of them, "are suffering immediate or threatened injury as a result of the challenged action of the sort that would make out a justiciable case had the members themselves brought suit." Here, the complaint merely asserts that "changes" in the organization and operation of individual intercollegiate athletic programs are now occurring. Significantly, the amended complaint omits any suggestion that the member institutions or, more specifically, their men's intercollegiate athletic programs are aggrieved, adversely affected, injured, or suffering any legally cognizable "wrong" as a result of the unspecified changes. Furthermore, the complaint alleges no facts which would permit any inference that the "changes" have had any such effect. In these circumstances, there appears to be no "case or controversy" between the defendant and the NCAA member institutions and, absent any suggestion of actual injury flowing from the defendant's conduct, the NCAA must be deemed to have failed "clearly to allege facts demonstrating that (it) is the proper party to invoke . . . the exercise of the court's remedial powers."

Items (2), (3), and (4), citing injuries to the institutional members' rights to be free from the self-evaluation and affirmative action programs mandated by [the 1975 Regulations] and the regulatory restrictions of the exercise of their rights of internal budget control and academic freedom, likewise allege no sufficient basis for representational standing by the NCAA. First, the complaint gives no indication that these requirements pose a threat of injury to any of the limited interests that the NCAA is qualified to represent. The NCAA's effort to base standing on these claims must therefore be viewed as an effort merely to vindicate the value preferences of proponents of men's intercollegiate athletic programs through the judicial process. Second, even if the interests for which the NCAA is a qualified spokesman could be deemed "injured" by the fact that institutions of postsecondary education are engaging in self-evaluation and affirmative action programs and are making internal budget realignments, it is highly unlikely that this situation would be redressed by a favorable decision in this case. The plaintiff does not directly challenge the validity of the regulation requiring affirmative action and self evaluation. Therefore, since the interests of men's intercollegiate athletics would not stand to benefit from "redress" of this "injury," the exercise of federal judicial power on this claim at the behest of the NCAA would be gratuitous and thus inconsistent with Article III of the Constitution. Furthermore, even assuming that the interests properly represented by the NCAA have been injured by budget cuts in the funding of intercollegiate athletic programs—an injury not, in fact, alleged in the complaint—there is no indication that such injury directly results from application of the challenged regulations. The NCAA in this regard relies on "little more than the remote possibility, unsubstantiated by allegations of fact, (that) situation (of its members' interests) might have been better had the (defendant) acted otherwise, and might improve were the court to afford relief."

In summary, the court must conclude that Count I alleges no injuries, in fact, that are both causally related to the conduct of the defendant and are inflicted upon interests for which the NCAA is an appropriate representative. In these circumstances, any basis for representational standing by the NCAA is lacking.

Count II

Count I basically alleges that HEW's Title IX regulations cannot be directly applied to or enforced against intercollegiate athletic programs because they do not receive federal financial assistance and they cannot be forced to comply on the ground that they merely "benefit from" the provision of federal financial assistance to other educational programs and activities.

The Supreme Court has recognized that "(w)hen a governmental prohibition or restriction imposed on one party causes specific harm to a third party, harm that a constitutional provision or statute was intended to prevent, the indirectness of the injury does not necessarily deprive the person harmed of standing to vindicate his rights." Nevertheless, in the specific context of Count II, this theory does not confer upon NCAA intercollegiate athletic programs standing to challenge the application of Title IX regulatory standards by institutions of higher education of which they are a component part. In the first place, as the court noted in its discussion of Count I, the amended complaint alleges no specific injuries to intercollegiate athletic programs that are presently occurring or that will occur if the challenged application of the regulations is upheld. Second, even if the requisite injury could be found in the allegation that colleges and universities are presently making "substantial changes in the organization, operation, and budgeting of their individual intercollegiate athletic programs," said injury could not be deemed to be one that any relevant statute or constitutional provision was intended to prevent. It would constitute no "legal wrong . . . within the meaning of a relevant statute," and would thus be insufficient for purposes of standing. Finally, despite the complaint's allegation that many intercollegiate athletic programs are operated on budgets "separate from that of the institution as a whole" and in some instances are operated with a separate corporate framework, Count II is premised upon the fact that, Title IX questions aside, colleges and universities exercise legitimate control over the budgets and administrative and educational policies of intercollegiate athletic programs on their respective campuses. The court is therefore not confronted with a case in which "one party" causes palpable harm to some "third party," but with a case in which one educational program within a university seeks judicial leverage against other educational programs—indeed, against the university as a whole—in order to enhance its intra-institutional political power to garner what it deems to be a "fair share" of the financial resources of the larger educational community and to preserve its departmental autonomy.

Counts III and IV

Counts III and IV, respectively, challenge the defendant's regulatory directives that (1) "no person shall, on the basis of sex . . . be treated differently from another person" in any intercollegiate athletic program offered by a recipient of federal financial assistance; and that (2) such recipients must, if they provide athletic scholarships, "provide reasonable opportunities for such awards to members of each sex participating in interscholastic or intercollegiate athletics." The NCAA does not allege that its members are aggrieved by promulgation of these regulations because they cause any discernible, tangible injury to the men's intercollegiate athletic programs for which the NCAA properly speaks. Rather, the NCAA claims that its members' compliance with said regulations will cause them to violate NCAA rules, "thereby jeopardizing their associational ties with the NCAA and the financial and educational benefits they derive from the reform." In the alternative, NCAA members will allegedly be required to collectively undertake "a costly and arbitrarily imposed revision of NCAA rules." These arguments, for reasons previously discussed, must fall of their own overreaching weight.

In the first place, the NCAA has failed to cite a single example of an instance in which a member's compliance with the challenged Title IX regulations would necessarily violate an NCAA rule. In the second place the NCAA has failed to cite a single example of an NCAA rule that would require "costly" revision if the challenged regulations should be implemented by its members. Finally, the suggestion that NCAA rules and AIAW rules require differential treatment of men and women athletes is totally without support in the record. The court must therefore conclude that the complaint alleges no distinct, palpable, immediate, or threatened injury to the associational ties between the NCAA and its members. Because no member of the NCAA would have standing in its own behalf to litigate Counts III and IV in the absence of such an injury, it follows that the NCAA cannot be accorded representational standing on these claims.

Count V

Count V alleges that, contrary to the requirements of [Title IX] in the course of the rule-making proceedings culminating in issuance of the challenged Title IX regulations, HEW made no express findings that the regulations were consistent with achievement of "the objectives of the statute authorizing the financial assistance in connection with which the action is taken." Significantly, the NCAA does not argue that HEW's failure to make such findings has caused "injury in fact" to it, its members, or anyone else. Further, [Title IX] imposes no requirement that HEW make such "findings" in any event. Finally, the NCAA does not allege that an inconsistency between any federal funding statute and the defendant's regulations in fact exists. Count V therefore fails to allege the existence of a justiciable case or controversy between the NCAA, as the representative of its member institutions, and the Department of Health, Education, and Welfare.

Count VI

Count VI of the amended complaint alleges that [the 1975 Regulations are] so vague and indefinite that the members of the NCAA are provided no meaningful standards by which their compliance with the law can be ascertained. [The court then recites the 1975 Regulations.]

[The 1975 Regulations] further provide, "Unequal aggregate expenditures for members of each sex or unequal expenditures for male and female teams, if a recipient operates or sponsors separate teams, will not constitute noncompliance with this section, but the Director may consider the failure to provide necessary funds for teams of one sex in assessing equality of opportunity for members of each sex."

In the court's view, Count VI does not state a case or controversy that is ripe for judicial determination. In the first place, wholly aside from the question of ripeness, it is doubtful whether any "case or controversy" whatsoever is alleged in Count VI. The factors listed in [Title IX] do not affirmatively impose any substantive duties of compliance upon the NCAA or its members; they merely outline the factual circumstances that will be considered by the Director in ascertaining whether equal athletic opportunity is being provided by those to whom the substantive directives of [Title IX] apply. The factors challenged as being unconstitutionally vague neither add to nor detract from the substantive duties of compliance imposed by statute, nor do they themselves purport to create a statutory offense. [The court found that because no school was being sued to enforce the regulations that there was no case in controversy.] Yet the NCAA does not argue that the relevant statutes are impermissibly vague or that it or its members may be ultimately required to suffer sanctions for conduct that they could not be reasonably apprised would constitute a violation of the law. It is therefore difficult to perceive how regulatory vagueness in itself has caused injury to the plaintiff. No such immediate or threatened injury is in fact alleged, and the court therefore entertains serious doubts that Count VI alleges a case or controversy within the meaning of Article III of the Constitution.

More crucial to the court's view that Count VI is not justiciable, however, is the fact that "declaratory judgment remedies are discretionary, and courts traditionally have been reluctant to apply them to administrative determinations unless these arise in the context of a controversy 'ripe' for judicial resolution." In this case, the regulations purporting to define what factors shall be considered by the Director are not alleged to have any impact upon the primary conduct of regulated entities, and the court is not confronted with a situation in which the promulgations [of the 1975 regulations] can be said "to be felt immediately by those subject to (the challenged regulations) in conducting their day-to-day affairs." The impact of the regulation is therefore not sufficiently direct and immediate as to render the issue appropriate for judicial review at this time. Furthermore, there is no indication in the record that withholding judicial consideration of Count VI at this time will cause hardship to the parties. No administrative proceedings to terminate or refuse to grant federal financial assistance for noncompliance with Title IX and the implementing regulations may be brought until HEW "has advised the appropriate person or persons of the failure to comply with the requirement and has determined that compliance cannot be secured by voluntary means." Relevant regulations further provide that the responsible government official "shall to the fullest extent practicable seek the cooperation of recipients in obtaining compliance . . . and shall provide assistance and guidance to recipients to help them comply voluntarily." Here the plaintiff makes no allegation of having sought administrative elucidation of the statutory standards by which the conduct of it and its members will purportedly be judged. In these circumstances the claim [that] the [1975 regulations are] unconstitutionally vague because it provides no meaningful standards of compliance is not ripe for judicial consideration. Furthermore, there are many procedural bridges that must be crossed before the plaintiff and its members may be sanctioned for any violation of the relevant statutes or regulations. In addition, any administrative enforcement action pursuant to [Title IX] is subject to judicial review. In these circumstances, the allegation that the defendant HEW has "unfettered discretion" to find violations of the substantive requirements of [the 1975 regulation] is clearly not ripe for decision.

The Supreme Court has observed that the "basic rationale" of the ripeness doctrine is "to prevent the courts, through avoidance of premature adjudication, from entangling themselves in abstract disagreements over administrative policies, and also to protect the agencies from judicial interference until an administrative decision has been formalized and its effects felt in a concrete way by the challenging parties." These dual purposes are best served in this case by declining pre-enforcement judicial review of the claims advanced in Count VI.

In summary, for the reasons discussed above, the court finds that Counts I–V of the plaintiff's amended complaint fail to allege any "injuries in fact," both causally related to actions of the defendant and for which the NCAA is an appropriate spokesman, to any of the members of the NCAA. Accordingly, in the absence of any alleged injury to the NCAA itself, the NCAA must be denied standing to litigate Counts I–V in a purely representational capacity. Further, Count VI must be dismissed as being unripe for judicial consideration.

Supreme Court of the United States

Geraldine G. CANNON, Petitioner,
v.
UNIVERSITY OF CHICAGO, et al.*

Decided May 14, 1979

Mr. Justice STEVENS delivered the opinion of the Court.

Petitioner's complaints allege that her applications for admission to medical school were denied by the respondents because she is a woman. Accepting the truth of those allegations for the purpose of its decision, the Court of Appeals held that petitioner has no right of action against respondents that may be asserted in a federal court. We granted certiorari to review that holding.

Only two facts alleged in the complaints are relevant to our decision. First, petitioner was excluded from participation in the respondents' medical education programs because of her sex. Second, these education programs were receiving federal financial assistance at the time of her exclusion. These facts establish a violation of [Title IX].

According to her complaints, petitioner was qualified to attend both of the respondent medical schools based on both objective and subjective criteria. In fact, both schools admitted some persons to the classes to which she applied despite the fact that those persons had less impressive objective qualifications than she did.

Both medical schools receive federal aid, and both have policies against admitting applicants who are more than 30 years old, at least if they do not have advanced degrees. Northwestern Medical School absolutely disqualifies applicants over 35. These policies, it is alleged, prevented petitioner from being asked to an interview at the medical schools, so that she was denied even the

*Cannon v. Univ. of Chicago, 441 U.S. 677 (1979).

92

opportunity to convince the schools that her personal qualifications warranted her admission in place of persons whose objective qualifications were better than hers. Because the incidence of interrupted higher education is higher among women than among men, it is further claimed, the age and advanced-degree criteria operate to exclude women from consideration even though the criteria are not valid predictors of success in medical schools or in medical practice. As such, the existence of the criteria either makes out or evidences a violation of the medical school's duty under Title IX to avoid discrimination on the basis of sex. Petitioner also claimed that the schools accepted a far smaller percentage of women than their percentage in the general population and in the class of persons with bachelor's degrees. Referring to statistics submitted by the University of Chicago in its affidavit accompanying its summary judgment motion indicating that the percentage of women admitted to classes from 1972 to 1975, 18.3%, was virtually identical to the percentage of women applicants. Of course, the dampening impact of a discriminatory rule may undermine the relevance of figures relating to *actual* applicants.

Upon her rejection by both schools, petitioner sought reconsideration of the decisions by way of written and telephonic communications with admissions officials. Finding these avenues of no avail, she filed a complaint with the local office of HEW in April 1975, alleging, *inter alia*, violations of Title IX. Three months later, having received only an acknowledgment of receipt of her letter from HEW, petitioner filed suit in the District Court for the Northern District of Illinois against the private defendants. After she amended her complaints to include the federal defendants and requested injunctive relief ordering them to complete their investigation, she was informed that HEW would not begin its investigation of her complaint until early 1976. In June 1976, HEW informed petitioner that the local stages of its investigation had been completed but that its national headquarters planned to conduct a further "in-depth study of the issues raised" because those issues were "of first impression and national in scope." As far as the record indicates, HEW has announced no further action in this case.

That section, in relevant part, provides: [The Court then quoted the statutory language of Title IX].

The statute does not, however, expressly authorize a private right of action by a person injured by a violation of Section 901.

The Court of Appeals quite properly devoted careful attention to this question of statutory construction. As our recent cases demonstrate, the fact that a federal statute has been violated and some person harmed does not automatically give rise to a private cause of action in favor of that person. Instead, before concluding that Congress intended to make a remedy available to a special class of litigants, a court must carefully analyze the four factors that *Cort* identifies as indicative of such an intent. Our review of those factors persuades us, however, that the Court of Appeals reached the wrong conclusion and that petitioner does have a statutory right to pursue her claim that respondents rejected her application on the basis of her sex.

I

First, the threshold question under *Cort* is whether the statute was enacted for the benefit of a special class of which the plaintiff is a member. That question is answered by looking to the language of the statute itself. [For example,] it was statutory language describing the special class to be benefited by Section 5 of the Voting Rights Act of 1965 that persuaded the Court that private parties within that class were implicitly authorized to seek a declaratory judgment against a covered State. The dispositive language in that statute—"no person shall be denied the right to vote for failure to comply with [a new state enactment covered by, but not approved under, Section 5]"—is remarkably similar to the language used by Congress in Title IX.

[This language]—which expressly identifies the class Congress intended to benefit—contrasts sharply with statutory language customarily found in criminal statutes, such as that construed in *Cort,* and other laws enacted for the protection of the general public. There would be far less reason to infer a private remedy in favor of individual persons if Congress, instead of drafting Title IX with an unmistakable focus on the benefited class, had written it simply as a ban on discriminatory conduct by recipients of federal funds or as a prohibition against the disbursement of public funds to educational institutions engaged in discriminatory practices. Unquestionably, therefore, the first of the four factors identified in *Cort* favors the implication of a private cause of action.

Second, the *Cort* analysis requires consideration of legislative history. We must recognize, however, that the legislative history of a statute that does not expressly create or deny a private remedy will typically be equally silent or ambiguous on the question. But this is not the typical case. Far from evidencing any purpose to *deny* a private cause of action, the history of Title IX rather plainly indicates that Congress intended to create such a remedy.

Title IX was patterned after Title VI of the Civil Rights Act of 1964. Except for the substitution of the word "sex" in Title IX to replace the words "race, color, or national origin" in Title VI, the two statutes use identical language to describe the benefited class. Both statutes provide the same administrative mechanism for terminating federal financial support for institutions engaged in prohibited discrimination. Neither statute expressly mentions a private remedy for the person excluded from participation in a federally funded program. The drafters of Title IX explicitly assumed that it would be interpreted and applied as Title VI had been during the preceding eight years.

In 1972 when Title IX was enacted, the critical language in Title VI had already been construed as creating a private remedy. It is always appropriate to assume that our elected representatives, like other citizens, know the law; in this case, because of their repeated references to Title VI and its modes of enforcement, we are especially justified in presuming both that those representatives were aware of the prior interpretation of Title VI and that that interpretation reflects their intent with respect to Title IX.

It is not, however, necessary to rely on these presumptions. Section 718 of the Education Amendments authorizes federal courts to award attorney's fees to the prevailing parties, other than the United States, in private actions brought against public educational agencies to enforce Title VI in the context of elementary and secondary education. The language of this provision explicitly presumes the availability of private suits to enforce Title VI in the education context. For many such suits, no express cause of action was then available; hence Congress must have assumed that one could be implied under Title VI itself. That assumption was made explicit during the debates on Section 718. It was also aired during the debates on other provisions in the Education Amendments of 1972 and on Title IX itself, and is consistent with the Executive Branch's apparent understanding of Title VI at the time.

Third, under *Cort,* a private remedy should not be implied if it would frustrate the underlying purpose of the legislative scheme. [The court concluded that a private cause of action would further the underlying purposes of Title IX by avoiding the use of federal resources to support discriminatory practices and to provide individual citizens effective protection against those practices.]

[Avoiding the tax dollars for discriminatory purposes] is generally served by the statutory procedure for the termination of federal financial support for institutions engaged in discriminatory practices. That remedy is, however, severe and often may not provide an appropriate means of accomplishing the second purpose if merely an isolated violation has occurred. In that situation, the violation might be remedied more efficiently by an order requiring an institution to accept an applicant who had been improperly excluded.

Moreover, in that kind of situation it makes little sense to impose on an individual, whose only interest is in obtaining a benefit for herself, or on HEW, the burden of demonstrating that an institution's practices are so pervasively discriminatory that a complete cut-off of federal funding is appropriate.

[The Department of Health, Education, and Welfare] takes the unequivocal position that the individual remedy will provide effective assistance to achieving the statutory purposes. The agency's position is unquestionably correct.[1]

Fourth, the final inquiry suggested by *Cort* is whether implying a federal remedy is inappropriate because the subject matter involves an area basically of concern to the States. No such problem is raised by a prohibition against invidious discrimination of any sort, including that on the basis of sex. Since the Civil War, the Federal Government and the federal courts have been the *"primary* and powerful reliances" in protecting citizens against such discrimination. Moreover, it is the expenditure of federal funds that provides the justification for this particular statutory prohibition. There can be no question but that this aspect of the *Cort* analysis supports the implication of a private federal remedy.

In sum, there is no need in this case to weigh the four *Cort* factors; all of them support the same result. Not only the words and history of Title IX, but also its subject matter and underlying purposes, counsel implication of a cause of action in favor of private victims of discrimination.

II

Respondents' principal argument against implying a cause of action under Title IX is that it is unwise to subject admissions decisions of universities to judicial scrutiny at the behest of disappointed applicants on a case-by-case basis. They argue that this kind of litigation is burdensome and inevitably will have an adverse effect on the independence of members of university committees.

This argument is not original to this litigation. It was forcefully advanced in both 1964 and 1972 by the congressional opponents of Title VI and Title IX, and squarely rejected by the congressional majorities that passed the two statutes. In short, respondents' principal contention is not a legal argument at all; it addresses a policy issue that Congress has already resolved.

History has borne out the judgment of Congress. Although victims of discrimination on the basis of race, religion, or national origin have had private Title VI remedies available at least since 1965, respondents have not come for-

---

[1] In its submissions to this Court, as well as in other public statements, HEW has candidly admitted that it does not have the resources necessary to enforce Title IX in a substantial number of circumstances: "As a practical matter, HEW cannot hope to police all federally funded education programs, and even if administrative enforcement were always feasible, it often might not redress individual injuries. An implied private right of action is necessary to ensure that the fundamental purpose of Title IX, the elimination of sex discrimination in federally funded education programs, is achieved."

ward with any demonstration that Title VI litigation has been so costly or voluminous that either the academic community or the courts have been unduly burdened. Nothing but speculation supports the argument that university administrators will be so concerned about the risk of litigation that they will fail to discharge their important responsibilities in an independent and professional manner.

When Congress intends private litigants to have a cause of action to support their statutory rights, the far better course is for it to specify as much when it creates those rights. Title IX presents the atypical situation in which *all* of the circumstances that the Court has previously identified as supportive of an implied remedy are present. We therefore conclude that petitioner may maintain her lawsuit, despite the absence of any express authorization for it in the statute.

It is so ordered.

The Initial Backlash: The 1980s

• INTRODUCTION •

The decade started off with a new landmark: Thirty-three percent of all high school athletes were now girls, a 600-percent increase from pre–Title IX days. While not as spectacular, the growth in female sports participation at the college level was still impressive: Thirty percent of all intercollegiate athletes were now female, a 100-percent increase from pre–Title IX days. Girls and women were filling these new sports opportunities as quickly as schools created new programs.

The wave of legislative and administrative successes of the 1970s was about to be tempered by the Supreme Court and a new presidential administration, which was poised to erect momentous obstacles in the development of Title IX. A backlash against civil rights was occurring generally, and the movement for gender equity in athletic departments was in the crosshairs of many of its opponents. Ronald Reagan was elected president of the United States in 1980, and one of his administration's commitments was to scale back the federal government. At the time, many schools, businesses, and local governments expressed frustration with civil-rights laws that they considered to be legislative and judicial intrusion into their activities. The ideology of a limited federal government encompassed minority rights in employment, housing, voting, and education, and civil rights for the handicapped and the aged. Gender equity in athletics was yet another target. The authority and resources of the federal government had made Title IX and the civil rights movement possible, and the Reagan administration was publicly committed to curtailing that power.

At first, the Reagan administration's beliefs translated into an attempt to abolish several agencies, including the Department of Education. Failing that, the administration accomplished almost as much by substantially cutting the Department of Education's budget. The result was that the Office for Civil Rights (the OCR), the administrative agency responsible for enforcing Title IX, dropped hundreds of complaints regarding discrimination in athletics. The effect was to send a signal to schools that the OCR would not pursue Title IX complaints seriously.

In addition to slashing enforcement budgets, President Reagan's administration attempted to squelch Title IX's broader application with a new limiting interpretation of the law's reach. Whereas the Nixon, Ford, and Carter administrations had all interpreted Title IX to prohibit discrimination throughout any institution if it received any federal funds, Reagan officials rewrote the administrative rules so that only the specific program that received the federal funds was covered by antidiscrimination laws. Soon after the president's inauguration, his administration imposed these limiting interpretations, which started to affect women athletes directly.

In *Univ. of Richmond v. Bell*,[1] female athletes sued after their attempts to get funding for their sports program failed. The OCR initially took the position that the university was covered by Title IX because the university received a $1,900 Library Resource Grant.[2] The appellate court held that the university did not have to turn over athletic records to the OCR because its intercollegiate sports program—which was funded separately from the library—received no federal funds. The new administration, however, did not appeal the case, siding with the school instead of the aggrieved athlete. While the decision in *Univ. of Richmond* had the specific effect of shielding intercollegiate sports from civil-rights enforcement, it also had broad ripple effects on other discrimination cases, because many other civil-rights statutes were premised similarly on the receipt of federal funds. These included: (a) Title VI of the Civil Rights Act of 1964, which prohibited racial discrimination in federally assisted programs or activities; (b) Section 504 of the Rehabilitation Act of 1973, which banned discrimination against qualified handicapped persons in federally assisted programs or activities; and (c) the Age Discrimination Act of 1975, which banned age discrimination in federally assisted programs or activities.

Meanwhile, a similar case had been moving through the courts since 1977. Grove City College was a small Christian college in Pennsylvania. The college had a long history of independence from the government, steadfastly refusing direct government funding, while it boasted one of the lowest tuition charges of private colleges in America. The college website stated:

> Grove City College teaches and advocates free market economic theory. By putting that theory into practice, the College maintains competitively low charges and a superior academic program. Grove City College operates on a balanced budget, refuses federal aid, and remains virtually debt-

---

[1]543 F. Supp. 321 (1982).
[2]Ibid., 322.

free, thereby proving that higher education can operate responsibly by providing an affordable, first-rate education without government funding or mandates.[3]

In April 1977, the college refused to sign a required Title IX assurance of compliance form issued by the administrative agency overseeing Title IX compliance, which would have subjected all the school's activities to federal regulations. Grove City College argued that, unlike the University of Richmond, only its students received federal funds in the form of student loans and grants.[4]

In 1984, the issue made its way to the U.S. Supreme Court in *Grove City College v. Bell*. In a six-to-three decision, excerpted in this section, the Supreme Court accepted the Reagan administration's position that Title IX banned sex discrimination only in the specific programs within an educational institution that directly received federal funding.[5] Thereafter, schools could not discriminate in the administration of the program that directly received federal funds, such as its student loan program or Pell Grant program, but a school's housing, academic, and athletics program were no longer governed by Title IX if those programs did not receive federal funds directly. Athletic departments that previously were believed to be subject to Title IX no longer were. And the absence of any legislation to prohibit discrimination based on sex, race, age, or disability left student athletes without a federal remedy for discriminatory acts.

The impact of *Grove City* on athletic departments around the country was dramatic. The Department of Education dropped almost all of its complaints, as did courts. The rapid growth of women's sports across the country came to an end.

The U.S. Congress, however, reacted swiftly and decisively, introducing legislation that would overturn the *Grove City* decision that same year. While the U.S. House of Representatives passed the Civil Rights Act of 1984 by a vote of 375–32, the Senate failed to garner the necessary votes. The legislation was reintroduced every subsequent session for a few years. During the course of the debate about the Act, it was the issue of women's sports participation that

[3] http://www.gcc.edu/Benefits_of_Independence.php

[4] Judge Paul A. Simmons asked the following questions of the HEW attorney: "Don't you think that there has to be a limit to bureaucratic pressures and meddling with the rights of people? In this day and age, when most institutions have their hands out trying to get money from the government, an institution is saying, 'We don't want the government to give us anything.' The government is discouraging what some might believe a laudable position." In "A History of Bold and Principled Decisions," http://64.233.187.104/search?q=cache:xnm77taxM2QJ:https://www1.gcc.edu/news/facts/main/HISTORY_TIMELINE.pdf+Ronald+Reagan+%22Title+IX%22&hl=en&gl=us&ct=clnk&cd=25 (accessed June 15, 2007).

[5] 465 U.S. 555 (1984). Grove City responded by instituting a fund-raising campaign in order to replace any federal funds with private scholarships and loans. Grove City currently does not allow its students to accept any federal financial aid, including grants, loans, and scholarships.

energized the discourse. Congress held extensive hearings on Title IX's application to athletics and again reviewed the 1975 Regulations and the 1979 Policy Interpretation. The result of these debates was that Congress kept the statute, the Regulations, and the Policy Interpretation intact, thereby solidifying congressional intent to protect athletic departments from discrimination. Finally, in 1987, Congress passed the Civil Rights Restoration Act.

An immediate hurdle presented itself, however, when President Reagan vetoed the legislation. On March 22, 1988, President Reagan said:

> The truth is, this legislation isn't a civil-rights bill. It's a power grab by Washington, designed to take control away from states, localities, communities, parents, and the private sector and give it to federal bureaucrats and judges. One dollar of federal aid, direct or indirect, would bring entire organizations under federal control—from charitable social organizations to churches and synagogues. The Grove City bill would force court-ordered social engineers into every corner of American society. I won't cave to the demagoguery of those who cloak a big government power grab in the mantle of civil rights. I have vetoed the Grove City bill, and I ask every senator and representative to rise above the pressures of an election year, to make a stand for religious liberty by sustaining my veto of this dangerous bill.[6]

Despite the president's remarks, Congress overrode his veto overwhelmingly, easily garnering two-thirds of the legislature's votes, and the Civil Rights Restoration Act, reprinted in this section, became law in 1988. The Act reversed the U.S. Supreme Court's 1984 *Grove City* decision and restored full coverage of Title IX provisions prohibiting sex discrimination in education by recipients of federal funds. The Act also restored the coverage of other statutes that prohibited discrimination based on minority status, disability, and age, which were similarly premised on the receipt of federal funds.[7]

Lawsuits around the country, such as *Haffer v. Temple Univ.*,[8] were directly affected by the passage of the Civil Rights Restoration Act. In *Haffer*, female athletes sued to remedy discrimination throughout the athletic department, including participation opportunities, athletic scholarships, and treatment issues. Originally, the athletes' entire case was based on violations of Title

---

[6] "Remarks to State and Local Republican Officials on Federalism and Aid to the Nicaraguan Democratic Resistance." The President spoke at 11:47 a.m. in Room 450 of the Old Executive Office Building, March 2, 1988. http://www.reagan.utexas.edu/archives/speeches/1988/032288d.htm.

[7] The Civil Rights Restoration Act was not a clear win for many. The Act also included the Danforth Amendment, which authorized federal fund recipients to decline to provide abortion benefits or services, while simultaneously prohibiting them from penalizing any individual who seeks a service related to a legal abortion.

[8] 678 F. Supp. 517 (E.D. Pa. 1987), C.A. No. 80-1362 (E.D. Pa. Sept. 6, 1988).

IX.[9] After the Supreme Court announced its decision in *Grove City,* the female athletes could no longer rely on Title IX to get relief from the court. The judge thereafter ordered the plaintiffs to strike all aspects of their Title IX claim except those regarding the "athletic scholarship and financial aid program" because there may have been federal funds at issue. The athletes were given time to amend their complaint, which added a state constitutional claim and a Fourteenth Amendment claim (guaranteeing equal protection under the law for all citizens).[10] Shortly after the Civil Rights Restoration Act was passed, the case quickly settled favorably for the female athletes.[11]

Whereas the plaintiffs in *Haffer* were able to take advantage of the newly passed Civil Rights Restoration Act, other lawsuits during the time period seeking to advance gender equity survived by relying on state equal-rights statutes and state antidiscrimination statutes. The relief these statutes provided, however, was not as complete as that under Title IX. In 1979, fifty-three coaches and athletes brought suit against Washington State University. At trial in *Blair v. Washington St. Univ.,*[12] the female athletes demonstrated that, despite marked improvements since the early 1970s, women's athletic programs at the university received inferior treatment in funding, fundraising efforts, publicity and promotions, scholarships, facilities, equipment, coaching, uniforms, practice clothing, awards, and administrative staff and support.[13] During the 1980–1981 school year, the total funding available to the men's athletic programs was $3,017,692, versus $689,757 for the women's programs, or roughly 23 percent of the men's.[14] The trial court observed in its memorandum opinion: "The nonemphasis on the women's athletic program was demonstrated in many ways, some subtle, some not so subtle. . . . The message came through loud and clear, women's teams were low priority. . . . [T]he net result was an entirely different sort of participation opportunity for the athletes."[15]

The Washington State Supreme Court effectively held that the men's football program should be included in calculations for determining participation opportunities, scholarships, and distribution of nonrevenue funds.

> To exclude football, an all-male program, from the scope of the Equal Rights Amendment would only serve to perpetuate the discriminatory policies and diminished opportunities for women. . . . The exclusion of football would prevent sex equity from ever being achieved since men would always be guaranteed many more participation opportunities

---

[9]*Haffer v. Temple Univ.,* 524 F. Supp. 531 (E.D. Pa.1981) *aff'd,* 688 F.2d 14 (3d Cir. 1982).
[10]Ibid., 521.
[11]C.A. No. 80-1362 (E.D. Pa. Sept. 6, 1988) (entry of consent order).
[12]740 P.2d 1379 (Wash. 1987).
[13]Ibid., 1380–1381.
[14]Ibid., 1381.
[15]Ibid., 1381.

than women, despite any efforts by the teams, the sex equity committee, or the program to promote women's athletics under the injunction.[16]

The case, however, did not rectify the inferior treatment the female athletes were receiving and was not a true victory for the female athletes. In calculating budgets, the court allowed the football team to preserve its priority by allowing the school to exclude the revenue generated by each sport from its otherwise-equal budgeting process. The court held that the "injunction allows each sport to reap the benefit of the revenues it generates."[17] Thereby, football players would continue to enjoy a superior athletic experience from that provided to female athletes, including the very factors that led to the litigation, such as publicity and promotions, scholarships, facilities, equipment, coaching, uniforms, practice clothing, awards, and administrative staff and support. Given that women were just beginning to claim their rights as sports participants, their ability to generate revenues was severely limited. Men's football could rely on a rich history and lavish resources that stretched back over 100 years. Thus, it is doubtful that under the *Washington State* interpretation of the budgeting process that women's athletics would ever reach parity. A lawsuit brought under Title IX, however, would have reached a different result given its legislative history and implementing regulations.[18] As discussed in Part II, attempts to exclude football or "revenue-producing" sports from a determination of Title IX compliance consistently were rejected.

Meanwhile, states began to pass their own legislation specifically protecting women athletes from discrimination. In 1982, California passed a law similar to but more comprehensive than Title IX. Like its federal counterpart, it outlaws sex discrimination in any program or activity of an educational institution receiving any state financial assistance. But unlike the federal law, it explicitly covers athletics and employment, and covers many other areas such as pregnancy. Many other states were to follow with specific prohibitions against gender discrimination in athletics, including Alaska, Florida, Georgia, Hawaii, Illinois, Iowa, Maine, Minnesota, Nebraska, New Jersey, New York, Rhode Island, South Dakota, Washington, and Wisconsin.[19] In addition, female athletes participating in public schools could rely on state Equal Rights Amendments or general nondiscrimination state statutes to rectify discrimination in a court of law.[20]

[16]Ibid., 1382–1383.
[17]Ibid., 1384.
[18]44 Fed. Reg. at 71422.
[19]Compiled by Nancy Hogshead-Makar, http://www.womenssportsfoundation.org/cgi-bin/iowa/issues/article.html?record=963 (accessed June 15, 2007).
[20]*See,* e.g., *Darrin v. Gould,* 540 P. 2d 882 (Wash. 1975); *O'Conner v. Bd. of Ed. of Sch. Dist. No. 2,* 645 F.2d 578 (7th Cir. 1981); *Petrie v. Ill. High Sch. Assoc.,* 394 N. E. 2d 855 (Ill. App. Ct. 1979).

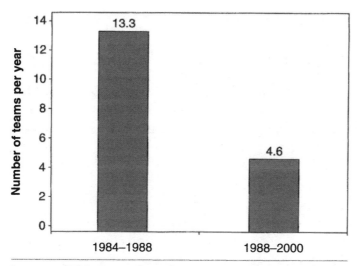

Impact of Title IX on the reduction rate of wrestling teams. When Title IX was not enforced (1984–1988), schools cut wrestling teams at a rate of almost 3 times higher than during the subsequent 12 years, when Title IX was enforced (1988–2000).

The Status of Men's Sports without Title IX

From 1984 to 1988, when the three-part test was not in effect due to *Grove City*, there was effectively no Title IX coverage for women athletes, and a number of interesting trends in certain men's sports emerged. As the table below demonstrates, men's wrestling declined dramatically during this period. Colleges and universities cut wrestling teams at a rate almost three times as high as during the twelve years after Title IX coverage was reestablished through the Civil Rights Restoration Act of 1987. During the four years from 1984 to 1988, the number of NCAA institutions sponsoring men's wrestling teams dropped by 53, from 342 to 289. During the twelve years from 1988 to 2000, the number dropped by 55, from 289 to 234. Men's overall participation also dropped during the years that Title IX did not apply to athletic departments, declining from 201,063 in 1984–1985 to 178,941 in 1987–1988.[21] In addition, it was not until 1993 that Title IX was in effect during a presidential administration favorable toward gender equity. Yet the greatest drop in the number of men's wrestling teams occurred between 1982 and 1992, when it fell from 363 to 275. Similarly, during 1982–1992, men's gymnastics teams decreased from seventy-nine to forty. Why, then, did the number of men's wrestling and gymnastics teams drop so precipitously during 1982–1992 when Title IX was not being enforced with any

[21] NCAA, *1982–2001 Sports Sponsorship and Participation Statistics Report.*

vigor by the courts or the Department of Education? In the case of gymnastics, many have opined that these programs were dropped due to a school's concern with legal liability. Indeed, the number of female-gymnastics teams lost during this period was eighty-three, more than double the loss of thirty-nine in male teams. Whatever the reasons proffered for the decrease in male-athletic participation during 1982–1992, it is doubtful that they had much to do with a school's legal responsibility to provide women with equitable athletic opportunities under Title IX.

The NCAA v. the AIAW

While the three branches of government were engaged in a tug-of-war over gender equity, the viability of the governing body for women's collegiate athletics, the Association for Intercollegiate Athletics for Women (AIAW), came into question.[22] Prior to 1972, the NCAA was happy to let the AIAW control women's intercollegiate athletics. After all, there was little prestige, power, or money that went along with women's sports. As such, men's sports and the NCAA were the de facto voice of intercollegiate athletics within each institution. But after the passage of Title IX and the legal mandate against gender discrimination in education, including athletic departments, the NCAA's attitude gradually changed. The NCAA and the AIAW had sat on opposite sides of the table while Title IX's enactment, retention, and implementation were debated in Congress. The NCAA lobbied against its application to athletic departments, whereas the AIAW lobbied for its application. The NCAA, having lost its legislative attempt to strike the 1975 Regulations and the 1979 Policy Interpretation in their entirety, and having lost its legal attempt to invalidate the law and regulations as they applied to its members in federal court, decided that women's sports had gained sufficient status to take control over them. It became clear that women's sports would be growing in numbers, stature, and resources. But even more important, the women's distinct voice within the athletic department was growing and would threaten the privilege that the men had enjoyed to control the direction of sport.

The NCAA used its relationships with corporate sponsors and television contracts as well as its institutional influence over its member schools to overwhelm the AIAW. In 1982, the AIAW brought suit against the NCAA, arguing that the NCAA unlawfully used its monopoly power in men's college sports to facilitate its entry into women's college sports and to force AIAW out of existence.[23]

---

[22]See Part II for a more thorough discussion of the AIAW and its role in the development of women's athletics.

[23]*Assoc. for Intercollegiate Athletics for Women v. Nat'l. Collegiate Athletic Assoc.*, 735 F.2d 577 (D.C. 1984).

An entity is said to have monopoly power when it, acting alone, has the ability to affect market prices as well as the production or distribution of a product or service. A monopolist can hurt new, smaller competitors with "predatory pricing" by offering a product or service at a price below the amount it costs the monopolist to produce. The AIAW argued this principle, claiming that the NCAA had offered to fund women's championship tournaments without any additional fees from its member schools. Ultimately, the AIAW lost its lawsuit, in part because the NCAA positioned itself as a membership organization of schools offering a superior product rather than a profit-maximizing organization with enough market power to force the AIAW to close its doors.

The loss of the AIAW was to have far-reaching effects for women in leadership positions within athletic departments, including coaches, trainers, promotional positions, and administrators. Newly merged athletic departments dropped many of the female administrators now performing duplicative functions. As the data from the Carpenter and Acosta study show in Part V, the number of women as coaches and athletic administrators continues to decline and is currently at an all-time low.

The AIAW's absorption also ended any effort to put in place a different organizational model and philosophy for women's sports. Albeit at a slower pace than for the men, the commercialized aspects of the NCAA began to penetrate the women's game, especially after the 1984 Supreme Court decision in *Oklahoma v. NCAA*. The piece by Gary Roberts in this section addresses some of these issues.

The AIAW's dissolution did come with a compromise from the NCAA. The organization agreed that it would cease all efforts to try to thwart the goal of gender equity in athletic departments. As we shall see in Part IV, that promise has been fulfilled in many respects.

Supreme Court of the United States

GROVE CITY COLLEGE, Individually and on Behalf of Its Students, et al., Petitioners

v.

Terrel H. BELL, Secretary of Education, et al.*

Decided February 28, 1984

Justice WHITE delivered the opinion of the Court.

Section 901(a) of Title IX of the Education Amendments of 1972 prohibits sex discrimination in "any education program or activity receiving Federal financial assistance," and Section 902 directs agencies awarding most types of assistance to promulgate regulations to ensure that recipients adhere to that prohibition. Compliance with departmental regulations may be secured by termination of assistance "to the particular program, or part thereof, in which . . . noncompliance has been . . . found" or by "any other means authorized by law." Section 902, 20 U.S.C. Section 1682.

This case presents several questions concerning the scope and operation of these provisions and the regulations established by the Department of Education. We must decide, first, whether Title IX applies at all to Grove City College, which accepts no direct assistance but enrolls students who receive federal grants that must be used for educational purposes. If so, we must identify the "education program or activity" at Grove City that is "receiving Federal financial assistance" and determine whether federal assistance to that program may be terminated solely because the College violates the Department's regulations by refusing to execute an Assurance of Compliance with Title IX.

I

Petitioner Grove City College is a private, coeducational, liberal arts college that has sought to preserve its institutional autonomy by consistently refusing state

*Grove City College v. Bell, 465 U.S. 555 (1984).

and federal financial assistance. Grove City's desire to avoid federal oversight has led it to decline to participate not only in direct institutional aid programs, but also in federal student assistance programs under which the College would be required to assess students' eligibility and to determine the amounts of loans, work-study funds, or grants they should receive. Grove City has, however, enrolled a large number of students who receive Basic Educational Opportunity Grants (BEOGs), under the Department of Education's Alternate Disbursement System (ADS). [The grants were made directly to the students through the Department of Education, and the student loans were guaranteed by the federal government.]

The Department concluded that Grove City was a "recipient" of "Federal financial assistance" as those terms are defined in the regulations implementing Title IX, and, in July 1977, it requested that the College execute the Assurance of Compliance required by [government regulations]. If Grove City had signed the Assurance, it would have agreed to "[c]omply, to the extent applicable to it, with Title IX . . . and all applicable requirements imposed by or pursuant to the Department's regulation . . . to the end that . . . no person shall, on the basis of sex, be . . . subjected to discrimination under any education program or activity for which [it] receives or benefits from Federal financial assistance from the Department."

When Grove City persisted in refusing to execute an Assurance, the Department initiated proceedings to declare the College and its students ineligible to receive BEOGs. The Administrative Law Judge held that the federal financial assistance received by Grove City obligated it to execute an Assurance of Compliance and entered an order terminating assistance until Grove City "corrects its noncompliance with Title IX and satisfies the Department that it is in compliance" with the applicable regulations.

II

In defending its refusal to execute the Assurance of Compliance required by the Department's regulations, Grove City first contends that neither it nor any "education program or activity" of the College receives any federal financial assistance within the meaning of Title IX by virtue of the fact that some of its students receive BEOGs and use them to pay for their education. We disagree.

Grove City provides a well-rounded liberal arts education and a variety of educational programs and student services. The question is whether any of those programs or activities "receiv[es] Federal financial assistance" within the meaning of Title IX when students finance their education with BEOGs. The structure of the Education Amendments of 1972, in which Congress both created the BEOG program and imposed Title IX's nondiscrimination requirement, strongly suggests an affirmative conclusion. BEOGs were aptly characterized as

a "centerpiece of the bill," and Title IX "relate[d] directly to [its] central purpose." In view of this connection and Congress' express recognition of discrimination in the administration of student financial-aid programs, it would indeed
be anomalous to discover that one of the primary components of Congress'
comprehensive "package of federal aid" was not intended to trigger coverage
under Title IX.

It is not surprising to find, therefore, that the language of Section 901(a)
contains no hint that Congress perceived a substantive difference between direct
institutional assistance and aid received by a school through its students. The
linchpin of Grove City's argument that none of its programs receives any federal
assistance is a perceived distinction between direct and indirect aid, a distinction that finds no support in the text of Section 901(a). Nothing in Section
901(a) suggests that Congress elevated form over substance by making the
application of the nondiscrimination principle dependent on the manner in
which a program or activity receives federal assistance. There is no basis in the
statute for the view that only institutions that themselves apply for federal aid
or receive checks directly from the federal government are subject to regulation.
As the Court of Appeals observed, "by its all inclusive terminology [Section
901(a)] appears to encompass all forms of federal aid to education, direct or
indirect." We have recognized the need to "'accord [Title IX] a sweep as broad
as its language,'" and we are reluctant to read into Section 901(a) a limitation
not apparent on its face.

Our reluctance grows when we pause to consider the available evidence of
Congress' intent. The economic effect of direct and indirect assistance often is
indistinguishable, and the BEOG program was structured to ensure that it effectively supplements the College's own financial aid program. Congress undoubtedly comprehended this reality in enacting the Education Amendments of
1972. The legislative history of the amendments is replete with statements
evincing Congress' awareness that the student assistance programs established
by the amendments would significantly aid colleges and universities. In fact,
one of the stated purposes of the student aid provisions was to "provid[e] assistance to institutions of higher education."

Congress' awareness of the purpose and effect of its student aid programs
also is reflected in the sparse legislative history of Title IX itself. Title IX was
patterned after Title VI of the Civil Rights Act of 1964. The drafters of Title VI
envisioned that the receipt of student aid funds would trigger coverage, and,
since they approved identical language, we discern no reason to believe that the
Congressmen who voted for Title IX intended a different result.

The few contemporaneous statements that attempted to give content to the
phrase "receiving Federal financial assistance," while admittedly somewhat

ambiguous, are consistent with Senator [Birch] Bayh's declaration that Title IX authorizes the termination of "all aid that comes through the Department of Health, Education, and Welfare." Such statements by individual legislators should not be given controlling effect, but, at least in instances where they are consistent with the plain language of Title IX, Senator Bayh's remarks are "an authoritative guide to the statute's construction." The contemporaneous legislative history, in short, provides no basis for believing that Title IX's broad language is somehow inconsistent with Congress' underlying intent.

Grove City contends that Senator Bayh's statement demonstrates an intent to exclude student aid from coverage under Title IX. We believe that his answer is more plausibly interpreted as suggesting that, although the Secretary is empowered to terminate student aid, he probably would not need to do so where leverage could be exerted by terminating other assistance. The students, of course, always remain free to take their assistance elsewhere.

Persuasive evidence of Congress' intent concerning student financial aid may also be gleaned from its subsequent treatment of Title IX. We have twice recognized the probative value of Title IX's unique postenactment history, and we do so once again. The Department's sex discrimination regulations made clear that "[s]cholarships, loans, [and] grants . . . extended directly to . . . students for payment to" an institution constitute federal financial assistance to that entity. Under the statutory "laying before" procedure of the General Education Provisions Act, Congress was afforded an opportunity to invalidate aspects of the regulations it deemed inconsistent with Title IX. The regulations were clear, and Secretary Weinberger left no doubt concerning the Department's position that "the furnishing of student assistance to a student who uses it at a particular institution . . . [is] Federal aid, which is covered by the statute." Yet, neither House passed a disapproval resolution. Congress' failure to disapprove the regulations is not dispositive, but, as we recognized in *North Haven Board of Education v. Bell*, it strongly implies that the regulations accurately reflect congressional intent. Congress has never disavowed this implication and, in fact, has acted consistently with it on a number of occasions.

It is also significant that in 1976 Congress enacted legislation clarifying the intent of the Privacy Act to ensure that institutions serving as payment agents for the BEOG program are not considered contractors maintaining a system of records to accomplish a function of the Secretary. This legislation responded to concerns expressed by educational institutions over "the additional and unnecessary administrative burdens which would be imposed upon them if [they] were deemed 'contractors.'" In sharp contrast, Congress has failed to respond to repeated requests by colleges in Grove City's position for legislation exempting them from coverage under Title IX.

The statutory authorization for BEOGs, moreover, has been renewed three times. Each time, Congress was well aware of the administrative interpretation under which such grants were believed to trigger coverage under Title IX. The history of these reenactments makes clear that Congress regards BEOGs and other forms of student aid as a critical source of support for educational institutions. In view of Congress' consistent failure to amend either Title IX or the BEOG statute in a way that would support Grove City's argument, we feel fully justified in concluding that "the legislative intent has been correctly discerned."

With the benefit of clear statutory language, powerful evidence of Congress' intent, and a longstanding and coherent administrative construction of the phrase "receiving Federal financial assistance," we have little trouble concluding that Title IX coverage is not foreclosed because federal funds are granted to Grove City's students rather than directly to one of the College's educational programs. There remains the question, however, of identifying the "education program or activity" of the College that can properly be characterized as "receiving" federal assistance through grants to some of the students attending the College.

Grove City asks to be relieved of that judgment on the grounds that none of its educational programs is receiving any federal aid and that if any of its programs is receiving aid, it is only its administration of the BEOG program. Grove City is entitled to have these issues addressed, for otherwise it must deal with the undisturbed judgment of the Court of Appeals that the entire College is subject to Federal oversight under Title IX. Even though the Secretary has changed his position and no longer agrees with the expansive construction accorded the statute by the Court of Appeals, it is still at odds with Grove City as to the extent of the covered program; and in any event, its modified stance can hardly overturn or modify the judgment below or eliminate Grove City's legitimate and substantial interest in having its submissions adjudicated.

III

An analysis of Title IX's language and legislative history led us to conclude in *North Haven Board of Education v. Bell* that "an agency's authority under Title IX both to promulgate regulations and to terminate funds is subject to the program-specific limitations of Sections 901 and 902." Although the legislative history contains isolated suggestions that entire institutions are subject to the nondiscrimination provision whenever one of their programs receives federal assistance, we cannot accept the Court of Appeals' conclusion that in the circumstances present here Grove City itself is a "program or activity" that may be regulated in its entirety. Nevertheless, we find no merit in Grove City's contention that a decision treating BEOGs as "Federal financial assistance" cannot be reconciled with Title IX's program-specific language since BEOGs are not tied to any specific "education program or activity."

Although Grove City does not itself disburse students' awards, BEOGs clearly augment the resources that the College itself devotes to financial aid. The fact that federal funds eventually reach the College's general operating budget cannot subject Grove City to institution-wide coverage. Grove City's choice of administrative mechanisms, we hold, neither expands nor contracts the breadth of the "program or activity"—the financial aid program—that receives federal assistance and that may be regulated under Title IX.

To the extent that the Court of Appeals' holding that BEOGs received by Grove City's students constitute aid to the entire institution rests on the possibility that federal funds received by one program or activity free up the College's own resources for use elsewhere, the Court of Appeals' reasoning is doubly flawed. First, there is no evidence that the federal aid received by Grove City's students results in the diversion of funds from the College's own financial aid program to other areas within the institution. Second, and more important, the Court of Appeals' assumption that Title IX applies to programs receiving a larger share of a school's own limited resources as a result of federal assistance earmarked for use elsewhere within the institution is inconsistent with the program-specific nature of the statute. Most federal educational assistance has economic ripple effects throughout the aided institution, and it would be difficult, if not impossible, to determine which programs or activities derive such indirect benefits. Under the Court of Appeals' theory, an entire school would be subject to Title IX merely because one of its students received a small BEOG or because one of its departments received an earmarked federal grant. This result cannot be squared with Congress' intent.

In neither purpose nor effect can BEOGs be fairly characterized as unrestricted grants that institutions may use for whatever purpose they desire. The BEOG program was designed not merely to increase the total resources available to educational institutions, but to enable them to offer their services to students who had previously been unable to afford higher education. It is true, of course, that substantial portions of the BEOGs received by Grove City's students ultimately find their way into the College's general operating budget and are used to provide a variety of services to the students through whom the funds pass. However, we have found no persuasive evidence suggesting that Congress intended that the Department's regulatory authority follow federally aided students from classroom to classroom, building to building, or activity to activity. In addition, as Congress recognized in considering the Education Amendments of 1972, the economic effect of student aid is far different from the effect of nonearmarked grants to institutions themselves since the former, unlike the latter, increases both an institution's resources and its obligations. In that sense, student financial aid more closely resembles many earmarked grants.

We conclude that the receipt of BEOGs by some of Grove City's students does not trigger institution-wide coverage under Title IX. In purpose and effect, BEOGs represent federal financial assistance to the College's own financial aid program, and it is that program that may properly be regulated under Title IX.

IV

Since Grove City operates an "education program or activity receiving Federal financial assistance," the Department may properly demand that the College execute an Assurance of Compliance with Title IX. Grove City contends, however, that the Assurance it was requested to sign was invalid, both on its face and as interpreted by the Department, in that it failed to comport with Title IX's program-specific character. Whatever merit that objection might have had at the time, it is not now a valid basis for refusing to execute an Assurance of Compliance.

The Assurance of Compliance regulation itself does not, on its face, impose institution-wide obligations. Recipients must provide assurance only that "each education program or activity operated by . . . [them] *and to which this part applies* will be operated in compliance with this part." The regulations apply, by their terms, "to every recipient and to *each education program or activity* operated by such recipient *which receives or benefits from Federal financial assistance.*" Nor does the Department now claim that its regulations reach beyond the College's student aid program. Furthermore, the Assurance of Compliance currently in use, like the one Grove City refused to execute, does not on its face purport to reach the entire College; it certifies compliance with respect to those "education programs and activities receiving Federal financial assistance." Under this opinion, consistent with the program-specific requirements of Title IX, the covered education program is the College's financial aid program.

A refusal to execute a proper program-specific Assurance of Compliance warrants termination of federal assistance to the student financial aid program. The College's contention that termination must be preceded by a finding of actual discrimination finds no support in the language of Section 902, which plainly authorizes that sanction to effect "[c]ompliance with any requirement adopted pursuant to this section." Regulations authorizing termination of assistance for refusal to execute an Assurance of Compliance with Title VI had been promulgated, and upheld, long before Title IX was enacted, and Congress no doubt anticipated that similar regulations would be developed to implement Title IX. We conclude, therefore, that the Department may properly condition federal financial assistance on the recipient's assurance that it will conduct the aided program or activity in accordance with Title IX and the applicable regulations.

Accordingly, the judgment of the Court of Appeals is
Affirmed.

[The concurrences of Justice Powell, Burger, O'Connor and Stevens are omitted, as are the partial concurrences and partial dissents by Justices Brennan and Marshall.]

Public Law 100-259 [S. 557]
March 22, 1988

Civil Rights Restoration Act of 1987*

To restore the broad scope of coverage and to clarify the application of Title IX of the Education Amendments of 1972, section 504 of the Rehabilitation Act of 1973, the Age Discrimination Act of 1975, and Title VI of the Civil Rights Act of 1964.

Be it enacted by the Senate and House of Representatives of the United States of America in Congress assembled,

Short Title

SECTION 1. <20 USC 1681 note> This Act may be cited as the "Civil Rights Restoration Act of 1987."

Findings of Congress

SEC. 2. <20 USC 1687 note> The Congress finds that—

(1) certain aspects of recent decisions and opinions of the Supreme Court have unduly narrowed or cast doubt upon the broad application of Title IX of the Education Amendments of 1972, section 504 of the Rehabilitation Act of 1973, the Age Discrimination Act of 1975, and Title VI of the Civil Rights Act of 1964; and

(2) legislative action is necessary to restore the prior consistent and long-standing executive branch interpretation and broad, institution-wide application of those laws as previously administered.

*20 U.S.C. Section 1687.

Education Amendments Amendment

SEC. 3. (a) Title IX of the Education Amendments of 1972 is amended by adding at the end the following new sections:

"INTERPRETATION OF 'PROGRAM OR ACTIVITY'

"SEC. 908. <20 USC 1687> For the purposes of this title, the term program or activity' and 'program' mean all of the operations of—

"(1)(A) a department, agency, special purpose district, or other instrumentality of a State or of a local government; or
"(B) the entity of such State or local government that distributes such assistance and each such department or agency (and each other State or local government entity) to which the assistance is extended, in the case of assistance to a State or local government;

"(2)(A) a college, university, or other postsecondary institution, or a public system of higher education; or
"(B) a local educational agency (as defined in section 198(a)(10) of the Elementary and Secondary Education Act of 1965), system of vocational education, or other school system;

"(3)(A) an entire corporation, partnership, or other private organization, or an entire sole proprietorship—

"(i) if assistance is extended to such corporation, partnership, private organization, or sole proprietorship as a whole; or
"(ii) which is principally engaged in the business of providing education, health care, housing, social services, or parks and recreation; or

"(B) the entire plant or other comparable, geographically separate facility to which Federal financial assistance is extended, in the case of any other corporation, partnership, private organization, or sole proprietorship; or

"(4) any other entity which is established by two or more of the entities described in paragraph (1), (2), or (3); any part of which is extended Federal financial assistance, except that such term does not include any operation of an entity which is controlled by a religious organization if the application of section 901 to such operation would not be consistent with the religious tenets of such organization."

(b) Notwithstanding any provision of this Act or any amendment adopted thereto:

"NEUTRALITY WITH RESPECT TO ABORTION

"SEC. 909. <20 USC 1688> Nothing in this title shall be construed to require or prohibit any person, or public or private entity, to provide or pay for any benefit or service, including the use of facilities, related to an abortion. Nothing in this section shall be construed to permit a penalty to be imposed on any person or individual because such person or individual is seeking or has received any benefit or service related to a legal abortion."

[The statute then further clarifies the meaning of "Program and Activity" under the Rehabilitation Act, which bars discrimination against the handicapped, and specifies that those with a contagious disease do not qualify under this Act.]

Reducing the Commercialization of Intercollegiate Athletics*

Gary R. Roberts

Preliminary Observation

Perhaps the biggest obstacle to pressing for the set of rather radical recommendations outlined below is the risk that promoting any or all of them might diminish the credibility of the Commission and its ability to influence college athletics. I recognize that these recommendations would change dramatically a highly commercialized culture that is grounded in principles of free-market economics and in turn thrives because of the enormous entertainment value provided to the public. Almost by definition, changing that culture would necessarily mean taking something valued away from the public (great sports entertainment), from highly popular and influential coaches and athletic administrators (large incomes and celebrity status), and from the NFL and NBA (their free "farm systems"). Thus criticism and political risk will inevitably accompany any meaningful effort to diminish commercialism in athletics.

While no entity should commit political suicide, meaningful change to the current unacceptable commercial climate of big-time college sports cannot occur by simply stating platitudes and tinkering with academic "reforms" that threaten no one. The Commission has a substantial amount of credibility and political capital on this general topic. For the sake of the integrity of higher education and society generally, as well as the interests of all real student-athletes, I urge the Commission to spend much of that capital by pushing courageously for difficult but essential reforms—if for no other reason than to shift

*Presented to the Knight Commission, Washington, D.C., May 24, 2004. At the time of the presentation, Gary R. Roberts was Sumter Davis Marks Professor of Law and Director of the Sports Law Program at Tulane Law School. He is currently the Dean of the Indiana University School of Law.

the focus of the conversation about college athletics onto the real issues and away from superficial "window dressing." The Commission may feel that some of the suggested reforms contained herein may be too politically unpalatable to propose at this time, but I include them all here simply to put a wide range of options out on the table for consideration. I hope that the Commission will consider publicly supporting a number of these dramatic proposals because without such leadership, reversing the current trends will be impossible.

Basic Principle

That the commercialization of intercollegiate athletics, particularly at the Division I (and I-A) level, is undesirable at current levels that create exaggerated incentives for schools to abandon their primary academic mission, to exploit many talented athletes who are unable to take advantage of promised educational benefits, and to engage in unethical practices in order to win and thereby to maximize revenues. Meaningful reform of college sports cannot be accomplished unless the imperative of and immense incentives for revenue generation and the "professionalization" of college athletics are diminished.

Opt-Out Principle

If the steps suggested below are adopted, many "major" athletic schools might carry through with a threat they have made before: to leave the NCAA and to form their own (blatantly commercial) organization. If so, that would be their choice. If they do, however, and thereby acknowledge that commercial objectives are of higher priority to them than educational and amateur athletic objectives, they should: (a) be required to recognize their major sport athletes as employees, with the full range of legal implications that accompanies that status (labor laws, occupational health and safety laws, workers' compensation, etc.); (b) not be given any special antitrust status or exemption for any of their rules or practices; (c) have their income from "revenue-producing" sports treated as taxable unrelated business income; (d) not have "gifts" made to their programs be tax deductible to the "donors"; and (e) have their athletic facilities be considered taxable business property. In short, such athletic programs would be treated under the law like the commercial businesses they chose to be. If presented with that choice, every school would remain in the NCAA.

Specific Proposals

1. Antitrust exemption

Background and Rationale: The Supreme Court's 1984 decision in *NCAA v. Bd. of Regents of the Univ. of Oklahoma*, 468 U.S. 85 (1984), was a watershed in the evolution of college athletics. The Court ruled that NCAA rules restricting the number of times a school's football team could appear on television under contracts negotiated solely by the NCAA was an illegal restraint of trade under sec. 1 of the Sherman Act. This immediately prevented the NCAA from regulating the activities of individual members or conferences in selling their athletic entertainment product. The decision established that in this respect schools are commercial business competitors. Freed from any constraints on their individual revenue-seeking activity, and faced with a reality that on-field success means greater revenue that in turn makes it easier to sustain on-field success with top coaches, lavish facilities, and huge recruiting budgets (the well-described "arms race"), schools and conferences began a fundamental transformation in which more and more decisions, many affecting the welfare of the athletes and integrity of the academic process, were made based primarily on commercial considerations.

It is not mere coincidence that after this 1984 decision there was a dramatic increase in both the frequency and severity of rules violations, abuses, and public scandals in Division I, which led in the late 1980s to the creation of the NCAA President's Commission and the beginning of the modern academic reform movement with the adoption of Proposition 16. Sadly, these reform measures (that focused on strengthening the academic side of the enterprise) have done little or nothing to slow the trend of ever-increasing deplorable institutional behavior. This is all undoubtedly attributable in large part to the dramatically increased commercial incentives created by this 1984 Supreme Court antitrust decision.

Two additional antitrust decisions since 1984 have exacerbated this trend. In *Law v. NCAA*, 134 F.3d 1010 (10th Cir. 1998), the so-called "restricted earnings coach" case, a federal appeals court ruled that an NCAA rule capping the salaries of the last assistant coach on various teams also violated Sherman Act Section 1. More recently, in *Worldwide Basketball and Sports Tours, Inc., v. NCAA*, 273 F. Supp. 2d 933 (S.D. Ohio 2003), a federal district court held that rules limiting the number of times a school's basketball team could participate in preseason tournaments exempted from the "twenty-eight-games-a-year" rule also violated antitrust law. Although this second decision is still on appeal,[1] the upshot of these cases (and some others that are pending) is that the NCAA is at substantial risk to be found in violation of antitrust law with respect to any rule regulating its member schools' athletic activities unless it directly involves

[1] Editors' note: Finally, in *Worldwide Basketball and Sports Tours, Inc., v. NCAA*, 388 F.3d 955 (6th Cir. 2004), the U.S. Sixth Circuit Court of Appeals reversed a district court judgment and ruled that the NCAA's "two-in-four" rule did not violate the antitrust laws based on the trial record because the plaintiff tournament operators had failed to establish a relevant market in which there were demonstrable anticompetitive effects.

either academic standards or the definition of amateurism (i.e., generally restrictions directly involving the student-athletes).

This now calls into question the legality of numerous long-standing NCAA cost-containment or competitive-balance-promoting rules that need only to be challenged by aggressive plaintiffs—e.g., limits on the number of coaches, limits on the number of contests and the length of seasons, the ban on playing non-NCAA teams. Efforts to control costs or to place any constraints on the marketing or sale of the athletic "product" are likely to be ruled illegal if they can be characterized as causing a quantitative or qualitative reduction of output, the cornerstone of modern antitrust doctrine. What is supposed to be a student activity that is ancillary to the educational process has now been legally transformed into a distinct consumer product to be made and sold based solely on economic market forces to the detriment of the academic mission and the welfare of the student-athletes. The natural impulse of athletic departments and conferences to pursue maximum revenues is now almost unfettered by antitrust law's disabling of NCAA authority to constrain its member schools' "right" to produce and sell their product (*Bd. of Regents* and *Worldwide Basketball*) and to spend athletic revenues however they want (*Law*) (as long as benefits do not go directly to individual student-athletes). This frames a legal landscape in which commercialism is not only encouraged, it is virtually legally required. Unless the NCAA can regain the legal authority to reign in the pursuit of revenue, excessive expenditures, and the exploitation of the student-athletes, there is little hope of meaningful reform of the system.

Recommendations

- Grant the NCAA (and only the NCAA) an antitrust exemption for all rules that regulate any activity or activities of its member institutions relating to the production, funding, marketing, and distribution of any sports "product" (e.g., by defining an athletic contest between student-athletes at NCAA institutions, tickets to such events, rights to broadcast such events, and any activities ancillary to the production, marketing, or sale of such events as not involving or related to commercial products produced or sold in interstate commerce).
- This exemption, however, could and should be made contingent on the NCAA adopting rules that accomplish certain objectives and that further "decommercialization"—e.g., a minimum degree of revenue sharing (see below), capping major programmatic expenses (e.g., coaches' salaries, program or athletic department budgets, recruiting expenses). If the NCAA failed to meet these contingencies, the law should expressly provide that NCAA restraints on the player-labor market (i.e., its amateurism rules and academic standards) would not enjoy any exemption or protected antitrust

status as they now do, a provision that would guarantee that the NCAA would meet the contingencies.

2. Encourage the NCAA to decrease financial incentives and pressure for winning and to promote greater competitive balance to increase opportunities for student-athletes

Background and Rationale: The vicious cycle of "the arms race" exists largely because winning is dependent on being able to provide the coaches, facilities, recruiting budgets, etc., that attract the best athletes, which depends on generating the most dollars, which is accomplished primarily by winning. While that cycle cannot be broken entirely (i.e., winning will always have benefits for an institution), it can be significantly diminished by removing many of the direct financial incentives for winning and diminishing the pressures to win. (Most of these ideas are at substantial legal risk without an antitrust exemption.)

Recommendations

- Do not tie dollar distributions of NCAA revenues to athletic success:
  - Institutional Distributions—Distribute a major portion of the NCAA pool money to institutions based on factors that do not reward athletic success (e.g., on the number of student-athletes, history of rules compliance, graduation or retention rates). Indeed, a revolutionary and almost un-American, but very effective, approach would be to distribute some money based inversely on the records or computer rankings of a school's major sports teams, much like higher draft choices go to the teams with poorer records in order to promote competitive balance.
  - Distribute a major portion of the NCAA pool money *directly to student-athletes* through programs or benefits (e.g., guaranteed stipends for post-graduate study after eligibility has expired, universal health insurance, disability insurance to cover educational expenses for a first degree even if an injury cuts short the athletic career).
- Adopt a system of extensive revenue sharing among all institutions in each division (esp. Division I):
  - Require 40 percent of all athletically related operating income (game-related revenue like tickets, club seats, suites, concessions, and parking; TV and radio rights revenue; conference distributions; sponsorship revenue; game appearance payments) to be paid into the central NCAA pool, from which distributions will be made in accordance with the above guidelines.
  - Require 20 percent of all athletically related "gifts" to an institution to be paid into the central NCAA pool, from which distributions will be made

in accordance with the above guidelines. (Note: Money received as "gifts" that triggers rights to preferential seating or other athletically related benefits should be treated as operating income, not a gift.)

- Adopt caps on athletic expenditures:
  - Limit coaches salaries
  - Limit recruiting budgets
  - Limit athletic department staff size
  - Regulate recruiting activities
- Reduce the requirements and thus the costs of being a member of Division I-A (e.g., sixteen sports, minimum scholarship, and football attendance requirements), which put substantial pressure on all institutions to generate more revenues and win games so their athletes in all sports can be in the highest division.

3. Encourage the NCAA to discourage athletes whose only or primary interest is preparing for a professional athletic career, and thereby to diminish coaches' incentives to recruit and to exploit such pseudo-professional athletes

Recommendations

- *Freshman Ineligibility*—Bar freshmen from participating in any interschool contests and greatly limit their practice time for one full year of enrollment; limit athletes to three total years of eligibility (in five years of enrollment).
- *Allow Aspiring Professional Athletes to Become Professional Athletes*—Eliminate restrictions on or eligibility implications for football and basketball players who want to declare eligibility for inclusion in the NFL, NBA, or other professional draft (most of whom have little interest and/or ability to take advantage of the college educational experience). (The only significant reason for such restrictions today is that having athletes leave a college program early diminishes the commercial value of the college team's product by causing it to lose talented players and by disrupting the coaches' recruiting planning. Not only does eliminating these restrictions diminish the commercial benefits of recruiting great athletes with little interest or ability to succeed academically, it will have a tendency to enhance competitive balance among member schools' programs.)

4. Restructure NCAA governance

Background and Rationale: A conference-based governance structure greatly tilts the system toward commercialism. Conferences were established and exist primarily to schedule and generate revenue streams, and they have no responsibility for academic or amateurism matters. Commissioners, currently the most powerful individuals in the system, do not work on a college campus and have little or no academic background. Furthermore, a voting structure that gives greater (indeed, controlling) voting power to the larger and more commercialized programs also tends to tilt the rule-making process toward commercial interests.

Finally, the "restructuring" of NCAA governance in 1996 has empowered those who represent the commercial perspective and greatly emasculated the academic voice and perspective. No nonadministrative faculty sits on the Board of Directors, and this past academic year only five of fifty-two members of the Division I Management Council were faculty. Thus, the very participants in the process who would best protect the supposed primary mission of the athletic enterprise from the lure of commercialism have essentially disappeared from the critical decision-making levels. Ultimate de jure authority rests with institutional CEOs on the Board of Directors, but these individuals have left their faculty roles far behind and now have incentives very much rooted in commercial values, and in any event they are busy executives with complex institutions to run who must depend heavily on their athletic administrators and conference commissioners for critical input and advice. It is widely acknowledged today that true power in Division I rests with conference commissioners, especially those in the six largest-revenue-generating (BCS) conferences who control postseason football independently of the NCAA and whose representatives on the Board of Directors and Management Council have controlling voting power. With the ascension of the power of the conference commissioners (mostly businessmen with little or no academic background) and the decline in the role of the faculty, the system has become heavily tilted in favor of commercial interests. Giving faculty a crucial role would be an important element in any effort to reign in excessive commercialization.

Recommendations

- Return each division to a "one school, one vote" system.
- The person holding the vote for each school should be its CEO. In the absence of the CEO, the vote should be held by its FAR.[2] In the absence of both the CEO and FAR, the vote should be delegated to a member of the full-time tenured faculty designated by the CEO.
- Give the Division I faculty athletics representatives the power either to veto (if the current legislative system is retained), or to delay for some significant

---

[2]FAR is an acronym for Faculty Athletics Representative. According to NCAA by-laws, each school is to appoint a faculty member of the institution who does not hold an administrative or coaching position in the athletics department. The FAR is intended to provide outside oversight to better ensure academic integrity and athletics rules compliance.

period (perhaps one or two years—like the British House of Lords) (if the "Town Hall" system were reestablished), any legislation and significant commercial contracts. Also, conferences should be greatly encouraged to give FARs similar veto or delaying authority over all conference rules and contracts.

5. NCAA control over all postseason competition

Background and Rationale: The BCS is the most glaring symbol of over-commercialization in college athletics, and it greatly contributes to the huge gaps in brand prestige and revenue-generating potential between the "haves" and the "have-nots" that will inevitably lead many schools to cut football or reduce overall athletic opportunities for many student-athletes. It also greatly enhances the disproportionate economic incentives for winning. The recent changes negotiated in the BCS structure are merely a Band-Aid that does virtually nothing to correct its fundamental structural imbalances or its commercializing influences. Arguments made against the NCAA taking control of postseason Division I-A football are hypocritical and baseless. (The BCS is only possible because of the conference-based, commissioner-centric structure of Division I generally—it is no coincidence that NCAA "restructuring" and the establishment of the BCS were almost simultaneous. Moving to a system with individual institutions, not conferences, as the foundation blocks, and with faculty, not commissioners, holding the greatest power, would inevitably undermine this perverse commercial influence that operates independently of the NCAA.)

Recommendation

- The NCAA should take control over the operation and regulation of all postseason competition in Division I-A football, just like it does in every sport in every division except I-A football.

Transitional and Regulatory Issues

Taking the above steps would raise serious transitional issues. There are many long-term contractual commitments, expectations upon which people have relied in good faith, and financial obligations incurred in reliance on expected revenue streams that would be unfairly undermined if all of the recommendations were immediately implemented. To alleviate the problems the transition would cause, many reforms would have to be phased in over an appropriate period of time, some relationships and contracts would have to be grandfathered, and a mechanism for granting special exceptions would need to be put in place.

Furthermore, many of the systems advocated here will require complex implementing regulations and a well-staffed enforcement body willing and able to see that they are followed. This is inevitable in any system that attempts to replace market forces with a regulated framework. This, however, is a culture long known to the NCAA, and it currently has such a system with respect to the recruitment, "compensation," and amateur status of its student athletes. Extending that regulatory system to revenues and staff would not be an unreasonably difficult burden.

Recognizing that the above set of proposals would be regarded as radical and strongly resisted by powerful interest groups, it is highly unlikely that such sweeping reform could be accomplished piecemeal through the current (or any) legislative structure set up simultaneously to implement an existing system. Thus, rather than propose specific reforms, and recognizing that reform is the enemy of revolution, there is an alternative approach.

Establish a "Constitutional Commission" to Create a New NCAA Constitution and By-Laws

It is obvious that any comprehensive effort at fundamental reform would require enormous deliberation, thorough consideration of the details relating to both the new system and transitional issues, and careful attention to drafting. Beyond the essential antitrust exemption that only Congress could enact, fundamental reform geared to returning intercollegiate athletics to its stated primary mission and greatly diminishing the corrupting dominance of commercial forces could be greatly facilitated by a comprehensive and coherent plan for a new set of rules, a new structure, and a new governing document. Thus, one approach the Commission could take would be to urge the NCAA to establish a compensated independent "Constitutional Commission," composed of former CEOs, faculty on leave, and individuals representing student-athlete and public interests, entrusted with presenting a new model within some extended time frame. This would produce an alternative to the current system that member institutions could approve or reject on its overall merit. Perhaps simply tinkering with the current system through established processes dominated by persons with their own vested interests may not be capable of getting us where we need to go. We may need to start over, and such a commission might be the best route to enable us to do so.

Accelerated Pace: The 1990s

• INTRODUCTION •

If the 1980s was a time of stagnation for gender equity in athletics, then the 1990s was its renaissance. As the turn of the century approached, more women were working and moving comfortably into positions of influence in every sector of the sports and athletic marketplaces. Although women's sports participation rates were still far from those of men, societal views of women's roles were undergoing a fundamental shift, including the perception of women in athletics.

A new group of athletes and academic writers, who found sports participation exhilarating and empowering, began to make a connection to the feminist movement, even when participating athletes may not have. These writers gathered research from a broad array of scientific journals and evidence from educational institutions to demonstrate the breadth of benefits women gained from sports participation. The excerpt from Mariah Burton Nelson is an exemplar of these writers. The old stereotypes that had once held women back were now subject to ridicule and began to erode.

The National Collegiate Athletic Association (NCAA)

The 1990s was a time of change for the NCAA, the organization of roughly 1,200 colleges' and universities' athletic departments that had fiercely battled the idea of equality for women's athletics in Congress and in the courts. It was now overseeing and controlling most of women's athletic programs nationwide. Now that women's athletics were a larger part of its responsibility, and society and the courts were favoring gender equity, the organization's approach to its women's programs was in the spotlight.

In the early 1990s, women's participation numbers were still quite low. For instance, while in 1991–1992 women accounted for 55 percent of postsecondary school enrollments and 53 percent of bachelor's degrees, they accounted for only 32 percent of intercollegiate athletes in Division I, which was scarcely above the level of 1980. Further, in 1991–1992 women athletes received only 30 percent of scholarship money, 23 percent of operating funds, and 17 percent of recruitment spending at Division I-A schools.

The longitudinal study by Linda Carpenter and Vivian Acosta in this section illustrates the negative effects that the consolidation of women's sports had on women in leadership roles in athletic departments, such as coaches, trainers, and athletic directors. Many women were forced out of their athletic administration and coaching jobs due to the merger of men's and women's programs. The women who remained, however, were able to make some significant changes to the NCAA, turning the organization toward embracing the role of a gender-equity advocate. Judy Sweet, from the University of San Diego, became the first female president of the NCAA in 1991. The next year, the NCAA published its first study on the status of women.[1] The results were discouraging, but they shined a light on what many privately had suspected: that women's second-class status was still prevalent.

As a result, the NCAA established a gender-equity task force and charged it with finding ways the organization could assist institutions in achieving gender equity. Early on, the task force defined gender equity as follows: "An athletics program can be considered gender equitable when the participants in both the men's and women's programs would accept as fair and equitable the overall program of the other gender."

The task force recommended creating a sourcebook for all NCAA members that ultimately was titled *Achieving Gender Equity: A Basic Guide to Title IX and Gender Equity in Athletics for Colleges and Universities.* It is now in its third edition.

In addition, the NCAA adopted *Operating Principle 3.1, Gender Issues,* which states a commitment to demonstrating fair and equitable treatment of both men and women. Consistent with that principle, the NCAA began to require that member schools provide a gender-equity plan as a component of its decennial certification process.[2] Each member institution was required to "[d]emonstrate that it is committed to, and has progressed toward, fair and equitable treatment of both male and female student-athletes and athletics department personnel." If a prior gender-equity plan was either modified or not carried out fully, the institution had to provide an explanation. Concurrent with the NCAA's study,

[1] NCAA, *Gender-Equity Study* (1992).

[2] *2006–2007 Division I Athletics Certification Handbook,* http://www.ncaa.org/library/membership/d1_athletics_cert_handbook/2006-07/2006-07_athletics_certification_handbook.pdf (accessed June 27, 2007).

many conferences undertook their own studies and created plans to increase participation for female athletes.

In 1994, the NCAA enacted guidelines for identifying "emerging sports" for women that had not yet achieved the necessary numbers to qualify for an NCAA-sponsored championship. The intent was to provide more options for schools in terms of available sports for women and encourage schools to increase opportunities. Several of those sports, such as women's collegiate crew, had grown enough to merit a Division I NCAA championship by 1997.

In addition, the NCAA began hosting Title IX seminars in 1995.[3] The seminars were designed to assist schools in understanding Title IX, providing them with needed educational resources. Despite its official policy of strongly supporting the law, enforcement problems among its member schools remained. For example, while the NCAA requires schools to demonstrate a commitment to gender equity, the NCAA has not yet found a violation of its own rules, even when those same schools were found by courts to be in violation of Title IX. Critics charge that if the NCAA were serious about achieving gender equity, they would treat a violation of their gender equity rules as seriously as they treat violation of its principles of amateurism for athletes competing in football or men's basketball. For instance, violations of the latter led to Southern Methodist University's expulsion from the NCAA for a number of years. Additionally, critics charged that the speakers at these seminars were defense lawyers who merely taught schools how to do the minimum to avoid lawsuits, rather than complying with the spirit of the law. Speakers regularly advanced the concept of "roster management," which teaches schools to cut men's programs to the bare bones and then to pump up artificially the numbers supposedly participating on women's teams, rather than comply with the spirit of the law, to add more women's teams.

Critics have also charged that the NCAA is concerned primarily with the appearance of gender equity rather than its reality. Crew, for instance, has become a widely popular sport for women, and crew teams typically are quite large. In 2002, the average women's crew team in Division I had fifty-four participants.[4] This type of women's sport is attractive to NCAA members because the large female squad partially offsets the large squad on the men's side of the ledger that often includes football. But the NCAA could create more opportunities for women to actually compete by mirroring the Olympic crew program. For example, when the NCAA created a national championship for crew, the competition was comprised of only two races, one involving an eight-person

---

[3]The seminars have since been renamed "Gender Equity Seminars" and include a broader range of topics, including hazing, homophobia, and sports guidelines for single-sex institutions.

[4]Interestingly, in 1992 the average women's crew team in Division I had only twenty-nine members.

boat, the other a four-person boat.[5] This configuration translates into only twelve rowers plus a coxswain, for a total of thirteen athletes who have an opportunity to compete at most schools. Nonetheless, some schools try to "count" as many as eighty athletes on the women's side of the ledger, when in other men's and women's sports, most of the athletes have at least the possibility of participating in a competition. If the NCAA added all the races normally run in Olympic competition, which has six women's events and a total of thirty athletes, more athletes would be afforded the opportunity to actually compete. Even with these criticisms, the addition of the sport of crew has been an enormous success story for women, and has demonstrated that women fill athletic opportunities that schools create.

Legal Developments

The 1990s was a time of testing the statutory language of Title IX and the 1979 Policy Interpretation in courtrooms across the country. Statutes and regulations that have been tested in courts of law and emerge intact are akin to a strong metal that has been forged to withstand the heat and hammering of the environment. In America's legal tradition, case law regulates how the common law and statutes are to be understood, based on how prior cases have been decided. A judicial opinion in one case will govern or persuade court decisions in future cases. In addition, courts follow the doctrine of stare decisis by which reported decisions must be consistent with previous decisions of higher, parallel, or the same court. Litigation with consistent outcomes provides certainty in the law, eliminating ambiguities and reducing the need to litigate future disputes. This outcome is desirable because certainty allows people to order their affairs with reduced fear of legal action. Where judicial precedents establish clear rules and standards, affected parties cannot legitimately claim that the law is so vague that they cannot be expected to comply.

During this time, a network of attorneys, led by the National Women's Law Center and Trial Lawyers for Public Justice, began working together to devise litigation strategies to counter the growing lawsuits and to affirm the legal foundations of Title IX. The results of their efforts tested the administrative agency's regulations and defined the scope of the 1979 Policy Interpretation, particularly prong one.

The Supreme Court's 1979 opinion in *Cannon*, presented earlier in this book, held that plaintiffs had a private cause of action under Title IX. A subsequent case would make the parameters of a Title IX lawsuit clearer, paving the way for a wave of Title IX actions. In *Franklin v. Gwinnett County Public Schools*,[6]

---

[5]Some powerhouse schools may send two eight-person boats to the NCAA Championships.
[6]503 U.S. 60 (1992).

a female high-school student alleged she had been the victim of repeated sexual harassment by her teacher. She sued the school under Title IX in an attempt to get monetary damages. In February 1992, a unanimous Supreme Court held that when an institution intentionally violates Title IX, victims could recover damages from that school.[7]

Franklin had important implications for women athletes. Prior to *Franklin*, student-athletes who demonstrated a Title IX violation at their school could only get a court to provide injunctive relief, which means a court will order one of the parties to act or refrain from acting in a particular way. A court ordering injunctive relief in an athletics case could, for example, reinstate a team that was either dropped or recently demoted from varsity to junior varsity. A court could also require that a school add a new team, build new facilities, or provide comparable travel opportunities, among many other possibilities. After *Franklin*, in addition to injunctive relief and damages, student-athletes could also be reimbursed for any funds they had expended while, for example, competing as a club team that had been unfairly denied varsity status. Attorneys working on a contingency-fee basis would also be assured of being better compensated if their clients prevailed in a Title IX lawsuit. (Attorneys representing women athletes were already assured of their hourly fees if they prevailed under Section 718 of the Education Amendments.)

Franklin also required that the school must be found to have *intentionally* violated Title IX. This standard is not generally difficult for female athletes, because collegiate athletics necessarily involves the explicit establishment of separate men's and women's teams and separate men's and women's sports budgets. When a school treats these two groups of teams differently, it will be deemed to have intended the foreseeable outcome of its discrimination. Thus, *Franklin*'s requirement that the discrimination be intentional generally has not posed a significant barrier in an athletics Title IX lawsuit.

Another important lawsuit with wide-ranging repercussions far beyond the individuals involved arose in 1991, when a group of athletes led by Amy Cohen sued Brown University after the school eliminated two women's sports, volleyball and gymnastics, and two men's sports, water polo and golf. The "equal" cuts hurt women disproportionately because their participation was far from "equal" prior to Brown's cuts. The women's overall sports participation was now several percentage points below where it had been prior to the elimination of the two women's teams. Few imagined at the time that Title IX and its implementing regulations were about to be seriously tested and that the participants were about to engage in landmark litigation that would last ten years, would go as far as the Supreme Court (which declined review), and would

[7]Ibid., 76.

become the seminal case on the meaning of "equal" sports participation and treatment. This case is discussed in great detail in a piece by Andrew Zimbalist in this section and in the excerpt from the circuit court's decision.

In the midst of this hotly disputed lawsuit, in January 1996, the OCR released the *Clarification of Intercollegiate Athletics Policy Guidance: The Three-Part Test,* which is excerpted here. The 1996 Clarification was written to eliminate much of the ambiguity regarding the interpretation of the three prongs. For example, schools and student-athletes alike wanted to know what the requirement for "substantial proportionality" in prong one meant, and how close a school's athletic department was required to mirror the school's enrollment. The issue was whether a school had to provide identical participation opportunities, down to the percentage points, or whether a variance of 3 percent to 10 percent was acceptable. As covered by the 1996 Clarification, it also answered the question of how schools were to come into compliance with prongs two and three.

In ruling for the athletes, the First Circuit's decision in *Cohen v. Brown Univ.* referenced the administrative agency's 1996 Clarification, bolstering the plaintiff's arguments that Brown was failing to meet any of the prongs as established by the 1979 Policy Interpretation, and thereby was discriminating against women when it eliminated two women's teams. Today, *Cohen v. Brown Univ.* is a powerful precedent for all current and future female athletes. Instead of litigating Title IX disputes, an expensive and time-consuming process, most complaints are able to be resolved through settlement, particularly as they relate to a school's responsibility to add new teams or continue funding existing teams. After the decade was over, future female athletes had strong case law on the books that validated the statute and OCR's regulations, making it far easier for other female athletes trying to remedy inequities in their schools.

The OCR also released another interpretation of policy in 1996 (which is included in this section of materials) on equitably apportioning scholarship awards, commonly referred to as the "Bowling Green Letter." The letter clarifies the coverage of Title IX and its regulations as they relate to the funding of athletic scholarships for men's and women's intercollegiate athletics programs. According to the 1979 OCR policy, the total amount of scholarship aid made available to the two budgets was required to be "substantially proportionate" to the participation rates of male and female athletes. In clarifying this standard, the OCR set forth a strict standard for schools to meet—plus or minus 1 percent of the student-athlete population, absent some justification for a larger differential.

Even with the many successes women athletes achieved in the courts, suing individual schools for broad relief from systemic discrimination is exceedingly wasteful of economic resources—resources that otherwise could be put toward creating new women's teams. A far better approach is to empower schools with clear legal guidance and educational tools for compliance, and then let schools order their athletic departments accordingly. The courts, the NCAA, the OCR, and many advocacy organizations were doing just that. And yet there was still an enormous amount of foot dragging. In *Cook v. Colgate Univ.*,[8] the court felt the need to affirm the mandate of Title IX: "Equal athletic treatment is not a luxury. It is not a luxury to grant equivalent benefits and opportunities to women. It is not a luxury to comply with the law. Equality and justice are not luxuries. They are essential elements which are woven into the very fiber of this country. They are essential elements now codified under Title IX."[9]

Reverse Discrimination Cases

As female student-athletes like Amy Cohen gained attention with their success in suing schools to enforce Title IX, another series of cases would raise the decibel level in the public debate on the law. In *Kelly v. Bd. of Trustees of Univ. of Ill.*,[10] the university eliminated the men's swimming team in a budget-cutting move. The male swimmers sued their school, claiming that cutting their program discriminated against them because the women's team was not also cut, constituting reverse discrimination. They asserted that Title IX, and specifically prong one, was a "gender-based quota system,"[11] a scheme they asserted was "contrary to the mandates of Title IX."[12] But because the law requires athletic departments to provide men and women with equal athletic opportunities as a whole, meaning that all of men's sports are to be compared with all of women's sports (rather than comparing a specific men's and women's team), the court found that men, as a group, were not being discriminated against. The court found that men overall attending the University of Illinois enjoyed far greater sports-participation opportunities than women. Specifically, men enjoyed 76 percent of the athletic opportunities while representing just 56 percent of the student-body enrollment. Although this and other Title IX reverse-discrimination claims have repeatedly lost in courts across the country,[13] the law's foes continued to raise the same arguments again and again in trying to

[8]802 F. Supp. 737 (N.D.N.Y. 1992), *vacated as moot*, 992 F.2d 17 (2d Cir. 1993).
[9]Ibid., 750.
[10]35 F.3d 265, 270 (7th Cir. 1994), *cert. denied*, 513 U.S. 1128 (1995).
[11]Ibid., 271.
[12]Ibid.
[13]See, e.g., *Miami Univ. Wrestling Club v. Miami Univ.*, 302 F.3d 608 (6th Cir. 2002); *Chalenor v. Univ. of N.D.*, 291 F.2d 1042 (8th Cir. 2002); *Pederson v. La. State Univ.*, 213 F.3d 858, 878 (5th Cir. 2000); *Boulahanis v. Bd. of Regents*, 198 F.3d 633 (7th Cir. 1999); *Neal v. Bd. of Trs. of the Ca. State Univs.*, 198 F.3d 763 (9th Cir. 1999).

weaken Title IX.[14] Because courts deem such matters to have been decided, these detractors have taken their arguments to the public forum and have sought change through the executive and legislative branches of government, as will be seen in Part V.

The OCR's Dispute Resolution Process and Resolution in a Court of Law

The OCR's 1996 Policy Clarification and the Bowling Green Letter went a long way to help women athletes in litigation, as was the case in *Cohen v. Brown Univ.* But, the OCR was still largely ineffective when it came to directly helping women athletes resolve discrimination, whether by adding a team or providing more equitable treatment. It was still not aggressively enforcing its own policies when it came to resolving complaints from female athletes.

The OCR's enforcement lassitude in the 1990s was a continuation of the agency's posture during the previous decade. A study of the OCR during 1988–1991 was performed at the LBJ School of Public Affairs at the University of Texas, which found:

> OCR's conclusions were not only routinely late [often over a year and a half late] but also contradictory. Frequently, OCR overlooked evident disparities between opportunities and resources available to male and female athletes, used arbitrary and varying methods to determine if a "noted" disparity was "significant," claimed no violation if disparities in one area were "offset" by disparities in another without equating the impact of the two areas, and substituted an institution's promise that an equity action plan would be implemented for actual confirmation that violations were remedied. For example, in its 1989 investigation of a complaint alleging sex discrimination in the University of Arkansas at Pine Bluff intercollegiate-athletics program, OCR found disparities favoring male athletes in four components—provision of equipment and supplies, coaching, medical and training facilities and services, and publicity services. In spite of these findings, OCR concluded that the disparities were not substantial enough to show evidence of gender discrimination and that therefore the university was fully in compliance with Title IX.[15]

---

[14]For example, in March 2007, an organization called "Equity in Athletics, Inc." brought a lawsuit against the Department of Education, attempting to make many of the same arguments refuted in *Kelly*: that schools should only be required to accommodate the relative interests between the sexes. *Equity in Athletics, Inc., v. Dept. of Ed.*, Civil Action No. 5:07-CV-00028.

[15]Kenneth Tolo, "Gender Equity in Athletics: The Inadequacy of Title IX Enforcement by the U.S. Office of Civil Rights," LBJ School of Public Affairs, University of Texas, Working Paper No. 69, January 1993, 5. The budget for OCR had funding for 907 full-time employees in fiscal year

Given this ongoing pattern of dormant or ineffectual enforcement, it is not surprising that organizations dedicated to helping women athletes achieve gender equity at their schools, such as the Women's Sports Foundation, the National Association for Girls and Women in Sports, Women's College Basketball Coaches Association, National Women's Law Center, National Organization for Women, Public Justice,[16] and the American Association of University Women, advised aggrieved student-athletes, coaches, and administrators to be aware of these limitations before proceeding, or sidestep the OCR altogether and proceed directly to court. If athletes pursued complaints with the OCR, they were often frustrated with the process, and for good reasons. For example, the person filing the complaint has neither the right to participate in the investigation and enforcement of their complaints nor the right to make sure their evidence or witnesses are heard. The agency is not even required to provide relief to the person making the complaint as part of the compliance agreements it obtains. Thus, if the OCR found that a school needed to add more sports for women, the school might be free to add soccer even if the complainant participated in a different sport, such as tennis. Indeed, the agency could opt not to investigate a particular complaint at all.

Because these athletes could not rely on the basic elements of due process that characterize judicial proceedings, they bypassed the OCR altogether. Court cases repeatedly confirmed the deficiencies in the OCR's review process and findings, holding schools to be in violation of Title IX despite the OCR having found the school to be in compliance.[17] Remarkably, but tellingly, the OCR's *only* disciplinary power—withholding federal funds,[18]—has *never* been exercised in the thirty-four years of Title IX's existence.

Notably, from 1992–2000 under the Clinton administration, the OCR conducted just forty-four athletics-participation-compliance reviews when the NCAA alone has over 1,200 member institutions. The statistical breakdown showed that 25 percent of the institutions investigated agreed to Title IX compliance via prong one, or proportionality; 8 percent agreed to compliance via prong two, or demonstrating a continuous history of expansion for women's opportunities; and 64 percent agreed to comply via prong three, accommodating

---

1986. The appropriation fell so that by fiscal 1991 there was funding for only 820 employees. In fact, the actual level of employment fell to 789 in 1989. Ibid., 21.

[16]Formerly Trial Lawyers for Public Justice.

[17]*Roberts v. Colorado State Univ.*, 814 F. Supp. 1507, 1515–1516 (D. Colo. 1993) (rejecting OCR's conclusion that Colorado State was in compliance with Title IX); *Perdue v. City Univ. of N.Y.*, 13 F. Supp. 2d 326 (E.D.N.Y. 1998) (noting that despite the OCR finding Brooklyn College, a member of the CUNY system, "had committed multiple Title IX violations, there was testimony that CUNY did not implement the modifications promised in its detailed assurances.") Ibid., 335. See Heckman, *Glass Sneaker*, 601–602.

[18]20 U.S.C. Section 1682.

the interests and abilities of women on campus. This data showed that schools were utilizing all three prongs to demonstrate compliance and, indeed, more than two-thirds did not use the much-maligned prong one involving proportionality. While the OCR was now far more aggressive in pursuing Title IX athletics-discrimination cases than during the first Bush administration, it was still not comparable to the record that female athletes were accumulating in court cases.

Congress

Legislative action affecting gender equity was also ongoing. Congress passed the Equity in Athletics Disclosure Act (EADA), as part of the Improving America's Schools Act of 1994,[19] in an effort to force schools to self-evaluate their progress toward the goal of gender equity and to expose gender inequities in athletics to the public. The EADA allows the Department of Education to monitor progress toward gender equity by requiring higher educational institutions that receive federal funds and have intercollegiate-athletic programs to prepare an annual report to the Department. The report includes data on levels of athletic participation, staffing, and revenues and expenses, both by men's and women's teams. Reports are made available to the public on a searchable database through a website: http://ope.ed.gov/athletics/Search.asp. Anyone can retrieve participation and expenditure reports for any two- or four-year institution in the United States. There are currently efforts to expand the EADA to include high schools receiving federal funds as well.

This combination of the slow growth of participation opportunities in women's sports during the 1980s, the recognized lack of help from the OCR, the success of plaintiffs in the *Franklin* and *Brown Univ.* cases, and the changing attitudes regarding women's participation all led toward a surge in private lawsuits brought by athletes and their families in the 1990s.

Students as Enforcers of Title IX?

Without aggressive OCR or NCAA enforcement, student-athletes are largely left alone to remedy discrimination in athletic departments by pursuing lawsuits in court. This places on high-school and collegiate athletes—oftentimes school-aged children—the burden of remedying inequities, rather than on those in educational and athletic-leadership positions. Students generally cannot be expected to know their rights under Title IX, nor are they aware of the enforcement mechanisms the law provides. In a recent study, less than 5 percent of

[19]Pub. L. 103-382.

students had even heard of Title IX.[20] Students are generally unaware of the identity of their school's Title IX coordinator, even if a school has assigned one.[21] Yet students face a wide array of social costs associated with even raising the issue of equitable resources. They typically do not have access to data like budgets or the salary of their coach. Additionally, outspoken students can risk losing an institution's help in providing and securing athletic, academic, or professional recommendations. These effects have been known to extend to a student's younger sibling. Students also face bureaucratic hurdles because complaints often result in several years of legal wrangling to rectify an alleged violation, many times extending beyond a student's graduation date. Finally, attempts to provide a more equitable distribution of resources often result in social scorn. Amy Cohen, who sued Brown University, was ostracized during her litigation. Not only did her school mount a vigorous defense, but the school newspaper and student body came out squarely against her efforts.[22]

But many girls and women, and their families, no longer willing to accept male-athletic entitlement as the status quo, were willing to surmount the formidable obstacles. Combined with a more auspicious political environment, the result was substantial gains in the implementation of Title IX during the 1990s. Unfortunately, as we shall see in the next part, the same cannot be said for the early years of the twenty-first century.

[20]Karen Zittleman, "Title IX and Gender: A Study of the Knowledge, Perceptions, and Experiences of Middle and Junior High School Teachers and Students," *Dissertation Abstracts International* 66, no. 11 (2005), 175 (UMI No. 3194815).

[21]Connecticut Women's Education and Legal Fund, "Keeping Score: A Report Regarding Connecticut Secondary Schools and Title IX's Mandate for Gender Equity in America," *Equity & Excellence in Education* (December 1998), (indicating only 8 percent of students surveyed could identify their Title IX coordinator). Diane Heckman, "The Explosion of Title IX Legal Action in Intercollegiate Athletics During 1992–93: Defining the 'Equal Opportunity' Standard," *Detroit C. L. Rev.* 953, 958 (1994), 958 (concerning "A 1992 report established that the Title IX coordinator played little or no role in the development of intercollegiate athletic budgets at postsecondary institutions, which are members of the City University of New York ['CUNY'], and the report found that there was no central staff member of the CUNY institutions that conducted an oversight role in the process.").

[22]After the case was ultimately resolved, ten years after initiating the litigation, Amy Cohen and the other named plaintiffs have been embraced by Brown University and officially thanked for their contribution to the athletic department.

Testing Title IX:
Amy Cohen and Brown University*

Andrew Zimbalist

The Olympic Games must be reserved for men. . . . [We] must continue to try to achieve the following definition: the solemn and periodic exaltation of male athleticism, with internationalism as a base, loyalty as a means, art for its setting, and female applause as its reward.
—Pierre de Coubertin, founder of the modern Olympic Games[1]

The costs of Title IX and the entry of women into the big time should not be blamed for today's highly publicized financial problems for college sports. At the heart of the problem is an addiction to lavish spending.
—Walter Byers, NCAA executive director 1951–1987[2]

Amy Cohen began competing seriously in gymnastics at the age of eight. She trained three hours a day, five days a week. When she applied to Brown University in 1987, she was led to believe that Brown was a progressive institution committed to women's gymnastics and women's sports in general. During her first semester, Fall 1988, Amy learned differently.

The women's gymnastics team, despite participating in a dangerous sport, did not have its own trainer. It did not have a laundry service for its workout uniforms. Women gymnasts had to schedule their use of the gym around the needs of men's basketball and wrestling. Men's teams frequently traveled to away games a day early to allow for rest and preparation; women made same-day trips.

Virtually all recruiting dollars were spent on men. Student hosts for football recruits, who were transported to the campus at Brown's expense, were given

---

*Adapted from *Unpaid Professionals* (Princeton, N.J.: Princeton University Press, 2001), chapter 3.

[1]Cited in D. Mahoney, "Taking a Shot at the Title," *Connecticut Law Review* 27, no. 3 (Spring 1995).

[2]W. Byers, *Unsportsmanlike Conduct: Exploiting College Athletes* (Ann Arbor: University of Michigan Press, 1995), 247.

$50 to entertain them. The budget for women's recruiting covered only phone calls. While six cars were available for recruiting for men's football and three for men's basketball, none were available for women's sports. John Parry, who served as Brown's athletic director (AD) for eleven years, stated that he believed only 10 percent of Brown's male athletes would have been admitted to the school on the basis of academic merit.

In 1990–1991, the coaches of the sixteen men's teams received a reported $932,227, while the coaches of the fifteen women's teams received only $360,862. Between 1988 and 1992 there was no effort by the school to promote attendance at any of the women's sports. The AD met with the captains of many of the men's teams to discuss how to improve them, but with no captains of the women's teams. The AD did not attend one single women's gymnastics event during the four years Amy Cohen was at Brown.

In Amy's first year at Brown, 1988–1989, Brown hosted the Ivy League Gymnastics Championships. The Brown women's team won the title for the first time in the school's history. Their recognition came in a meeting a few months later with Brown's new AD, Dave Roach. Roach had received instructions from Brown's president Vartan Gregorian to cut $78,000 from the athletic department's $5-million budget. This cut was part of a schoolwide austerity program to deal with a projected budget deficit in excess of $1 million. Gregorian spared only student financial assistance and library acquisitions from his budgetary ax.

Roach decided to eliminate two men's teams (golf and water polo, with a budget of $15,295 together) and two women's teams (gymnastics and volleyball, with a budget of $62,028). Brown, however, upgraded men's squash from club to varsity status in 1989. AD Roach's perception that he was in a financial straitjacket notwithstanding, in the same year that he cut women's gymnastics and volleyball, he increased athlete meal money for away trips from $15 to $22 per day, bought out the contract of the men's soccer coach at a cost of $80,000 and left $62,000 of Brown Sports Foundation money unspent.

The women gymnasts were left with little alternative but to operate as a club, raising $15,000. The school's support services evaporated, scheduling facility use became more difficult, injuries went untreated, prospective gymnasts were no longer interested in Brown and so on. The women gymnasts got together with the volleyball players and decided to take action. They contemplated filing a complaint with the Office of Civil Rights at the Department of Education, but they learned that the Office had insufficient resources to deal with the cases before it and the students needed a quick remedy. Instead, in April 1992, they brought a civil Title IX suit of sex discrimination against Brown.

The students obtained a preliminary injunction in U.S. District Court in December 1992, ordering Brown to restore the two women's teams until the case was decided in trial. Brown, however, appealed the order before the First

Circuit U.S. Court of Appeals and obtained a stay on the decision (Brown did not have to reinstate the teams) until the Court considered the appeal. The students won the appeal in April 1993, but by this time the 1992–1993 season had come and gone, as had recruiting time for the next year. This victory meant the temporary restoration of the two teams until the Title IX case itself went to trial.

The trial began in September 1994 and lasted three months. Judge Pettine decided for the students and ordered Brown to prepare a plan to bring the school into compliance with Title IX. In July 1995, Judge Pettine found Brown's proposed compliance plan unacceptable and ordered it to upgrade four women's teams (gymnastics, fencing, water polo, and skiing) to university-funded varsity status.

Brown appealed again. In November 1996, the First Circuit Appeals Court ruled in a two-to-one vote to uphold Judge Pettine's decision. Brown appealed yet again—this time to the U.S. Supreme Court.

Brown president Gregorian was indignant. He felt that the judges were wearing blinders; apparently, so were the presidents of the other Ivy League schools who chose not to come to Brown's defense on this issue. Gregorian believed that Title IX was a smokescreen for an affirmative action quota and, worse still, it elevated sports above the central academic functions of the university. How, Gregorian wondered, could the courts tell him that it was okay to cut the humanities budget but that it wasn't okay to cut athletics? The courts had said no such thing. Rather, the message was that athletics could be cut, but it was not all right to cut women's sports when women were already being discriminated against.

Why, Gregorian wondered, was Brown being picked on when Brown treated women athletes better than most schools? Amy Cohen answered this query when she testified before Congress in 1993: "If they were above average in preventing date rape yet date rape was still a problem on the campus would that mean that they are fine, that they do not need to make changes and improvements because other schools have a larger date rape problem? I don't think so."[3]

In April 1997, the Supreme Court refused to hear the Brown appeal. Brown proposed yet another compliance plan which again was found to be unacceptable by the female athletes. On the eve of the trial to determine the fitness of Brown's settlement proposal, the parties reached a settlement. Now it was time for Gregorian to wonder why he had spent an estimated $3 million on legal expenses and faced a similar charge to cover expenses for the plaintiff, when he

[3]Ibid., 14.

could have retained the two women's teams in perpetuity with an endowment that size. In July 1998, a federal court approved a settlement that Brown reached the month before, which pledges to maintain women's athletics participation within 3.5 percentage points of women's enrollment at the school and to increase spending on four women's sports.[4]

After being upheld in five previous Appeals Court rulings, Title IX and its implementation guidelines, as promulgated by the Office of Civil Rights, for the first time were sanctioned (if only indirectly) by the highest court in the land.

[4]Available at http://www.tlpj.org/briefs/brown.htm.

United States Court of Appeals, First Circuit

Amy COHEN, et al., Plaintiffs-Appellees,

v.

BROWN UNIVERSITY, et al., Defendants-Appellants*

Decided November 21, 1996

BOWNES, Senior Circuit Judge:

This is a class-action lawsuit charging Brown University, its president, and its athletics director (collectively "Brown") with discrimination against women in the operation of its intercollegiate athletics program, in violation of Title IX of the Education Amendments of 1972, 20 U.S.C. Sections 1681–1688 ("Title IX"), and its implementing regulations, 34 C.F.R. Sections 106.1–106.71. The plaintiff class comprises all present, future, and potential Brown University women students who participate, seek to participate, and/or are deterred from participating in intercollegiate athletics funded by Brown.

This suit was initiated in response to the demotion in May 1991 of Brown's women's gymnastics and volleyball teams from university-funded varsity status to donor-funded varsity status. Contemporaneously, Brown demoted two men's teams, water polo and golf, from university-funded to donor-funded varsity status. As a consequence of these demotions, all four teams lost not only their university funding, but most of the support and privileges that accompany university-funded varsity status at Brown.

Brown contends that the district court misconstrued and misapplied the three-part test. Specifically, Brown argues that the district court's interpretation and application of the test is irreconcilable with the statute, the regulation, and the agency's interpretation of the law, and effectively renders Title IX an "affirmative action statute" that mandates preferential treatment for women by imposing quotas in excess of women's relative interests and abilities in athletics.

*101 F.3d 155 (1st Circ. 1996).

Brown asserts, in the alternative, that if the district court properly construed the test, then the test itself violates Title IX and the United States Constitution.

We emphasize two points at the outset. First, notwithstanding Brown's persistent invocation of the inflammatory terms "affirmative action," "preference," and "quota," this is not an affirmative-action case. Second, Brown's efforts to evade the controlling authority of *Cohen II* by recasting its core legal arguments as challenges to the "district court's interpretation" of the law are unavailing; the primary arguments raised here have already been litigated and decided adversely to Brown in the prior appeal.

Title IX is not an affirmative action-statute; it is an antidiscrimination statute, modeled explicitly after another antidiscrimination statute, Title VI. No aspect of the Title IX regime at issue in this case—inclusive of the statute, the relevant regulation, and the pertinent agency documents—mandates gender-based preferences or quotas, or specific time tables for implementing numerical goals.

Like other antidiscrimination statutory schemes, the Title IX regime *permits* affirmative action. In addition, Title IX, like other antidiscrimination schemes, permits an inference that a significant gender-based statistical disparity may indicate the existence of discrimination. Consistent with the school desegregation cases, the question of substantial proportionality under the Policy Interpretation's three-part test is merely the starting point for analysis, rather than the conclusion: a rebuttable presumption, rather than an inflexible requirement. In short, the substantial proportionality test is but one aspect of the inquiry into whether an institution's athletics program complies with Title IX.

Also consistent with the school desegregation cases, the substantial proportionality test of prong one is applied under the Title IX framework, not mechanically, but case-by-case, in a fact-specific manner. As with other antidiscrimination regimes, Title IX neither mandates a finding of discrimination based solely upon a gender-based statistical disparity nor prohibits gender-conscious remedial measures.

Another important distinction between this case and affirmative action cases is that the district court's remedy requiring Brown to accommodate fully and effectively the athletics interests and abilities of its women students does not raise the concerns underlying the Supreme Court's requirement of a particularized factual predicate to justify voluntary affirmative action plans. In reviewing equal protection challenges to such plans, the Court is concerned that government bodies are reaching out to implement race- or gender-conscious remedial measures that are "ageless in their reach into the past, and timeless in their ability to affect the future."

From a constitutional standpoint, the case before us is altogether different. Here, gender-conscious relief was ordered by an Article III court, constitutionally compelled to have before it litigants with standing to raise the cause of action alleged, for the purpose of providing relief upon a duly adjudicated determination that specific defendants had discriminated against a certified class of women in violation of a federal antidiscrimination statute, based upon findings of fact that were subject to the Federal Rules of Evidence. The factual problem presented in affirmative action cases is, "Does the evidence support a finding of discrimination such that race- or gender-conscious remedial measures are appropriate?" We find these multiple indicia of reliability and specificity to be sufficient to answer that question in the affirmative.

From the mere fact that a remedy flowing from a judicial determination of discrimination is gender conscious, it does not follow that the remedy constitutes "affirmative action." Nor does a "reverse-discrimination" claim arise every time an antidiscrimination statute is enforced. While some gender-conscious relief may adversely impact one gender—a fact that has not been demonstrated in this case—that alone would not make the relief "affirmative action" or the consequence of that relief "reverse discrimination." To the contrary, race- and gender-conscious remedies are both appropriate and constitutionally permissible under a federal antidiscrimination regime, although such remedial measures are still subject to equal protection review.

Cohen II squarely rejected Brown's interpretation of the three-part test and carefully delineated its own, which is now the law of this circuit as well as the law of this case. Brown's rehashed statutory challenge is foreclosed by the law of the case doctrine and we are therefore bound by the prior panel's interpretation of the statute, the regulation, and the relevant agency pronouncements. *Cohen II* held that the Policy Interpretation is entitled to substantial deference because it is the enforcing agency's "considered interpretation of the regulation."

As previously noted, the district court held that, for purposes of the three-part test, the intercollegiate athletics participation opportunities offered by an institution are properly measured by counting the number of actual participants on intercollegiate teams. The Policy Interpretation was designed specifically for intercollegiate athletics. Because the athletics regulation distinguishes between club sports and intercollegiate sports, under the Policy Interpretation, "club teams will not be considered to be intercollegiate teams except in those instances where they regularly participate in varsity competition." Accordingly, the district court excluded club varsity teams from the definition of "intercollegiate teams" and, therefore, from the calculation of participation opportunities, because the evidence was inadequate to show that the club teams regularly participated in varsity competition.

The district court's definition of athletics participation opportunities comports with the agency's own definition. We find no error in the district court's definition and calculation of the intercollegiate athletics participation opportunities afforded to Brown students, and no error in the court's finding of a

13.01 percent disparity between the percentage of women participating in inter-collegiate varsity athletics at Brown and the percentage of women in Brown's undergraduate student body.

Brown contends that an athletics program equally accommodates both genders and complies with Title IX if it accommodates the *relative* interests and abilities of its male and female students. This "relative interests" approach posits that an institution satisfies prong three of the three-part test by meeting the interests and abilities of the underrepresented gender only to the extent that it meets the interests and abilities of the overrepresented gender.

Brown maintains that the district court's decision imposes upon universities the obligation to engage in preferential treatment for women by requiring quotas in excess of women's relative interests and abilities. With respect to prong three, Brown asserts that the district court's interpretation of the word "fully" "requires universities to favor women's teams and treat them better than men's [teams] . . . forces them to eliminate or cap men's teams . . . [and] forces universities to impose athletic quotas in excess of relative interests and abilities."

The prior panel considered and rejected Brown's approach, observing that "Brown reads the 'full' out of the duty to accommodate 'fully and effectively.'" Under *Cohen II*'s controlling interpretation, prong three "demands not merely some accommodation, but full and effective accommodation. If there is sufficient interest and ability among members of the statistically underrepresented gender, not slaked by existing programs, an institution necessarily fails this prong of the test.

Brown's interpretation of full and effective accommodation is "simply not the law." We agree with the prior panel and the district court that Brown's relative interests approach "cannot withstand scrutiny on either legal or policy grounds," because it "disadvantages women and undermines the remedial purposes of Title IX by limiting required program expansion for the underrepresented sex to the status quo level of relative interests." After *Cohen II*, it cannot be maintained that the relative interests approach is compatible with Title IX's equal accommodation principle as it has been interpreted by this circuit.

Brown argues that the district court's interpretation of the three-part test *requires* numerical proportionality, thus imposing a gender-based quota scheme in contravention of the statute. This argument rests, in part, upon Brown's reading of [Title IX] as a categorical proscription against consideration of gender parity. Section 1681(b) [of Title IX] provides:

Nothing contained in subsection (a) of this section shall be interpreted to require any educational institution to grant preferential or disparate treatment to the members of one sex on account of an imbalance which may exist with respect to the total number or percentage of persons of

that sex participating in or receiving the benefits of any federally supported program or activity, in comparison with the total number or percentage of persons of that sex *in any community, State, section or other area*
. . . (emphasis added).

The prior panel, like Brown, assumed without analysis that Section 1681(b)
applies unequivocally to intercollegiate athletics programs. We do not question
Cohen II's application of Section 1681(b). We think it important to bear in
mind, however, the congressional concerns that inform the proper interpretation of this provision. Section 1681(b) was patterned after Section 703(j) of
Title VII, 42 U.S.C. Section 2000e–2(j), and was specifically designed to prohibit quotas in university admissions and hiring, based upon the percentage of
individuals of one gender in a geographical community. Thus, the legislative
history strongly suggests that the underscored language defines what is pro-
scribed (in the contexts of admissions and hiring) in terms of a geographical
area, *beyond the institution,* and does not refer to an imbalance *within the university,* with respect to the representation of each gender in intercollegiate athletics,
as compared to the gender makeup of the student body.

In any event, the three-part test is, on its face, entirely consistent with Section 1681(b) because the test does not *require* preferential or disparate treatment for either gender. Neither the Policy Interpretation's three-part test, nor
the district court's interpretation of it, *mandates* statistical balancing; "[r]ather,
the policy interpretation merely creates a presumption that a school is in compliance with Title IX and the applicable regulation when it achieves such a
statistical balance."

The test is also entirely consistent with Section 1681(b) as applied by the
prior panel and by the district court. As previously noted, *Cohen II* expressly
held that "a court assessing Title IX compliance may not find a violation *solely*
because there is a disparity between the gender composition of an educational
institution's student constituency, on the one hand, and its athletic programs,
on the other hand." The panel then carefully delineated the burden of proof,
which requires a Title IX plaintiff to show, not only "disparity between the
gender composition of the institution's student body and its athletic program,
thereby proving that there is an underrepresented gender," but also "that a second element—unmet interest—is present," meaning that the underrepresented
gender has not been fully and effectively accommodated by the institution's
present athletic program Only where the plaintiff meets the burden of proof
on these elements *and* the institution fails to show as an affirmative defense a
history and continuing practice of program expansion responsive to the interests and abilities of the underrepresented gender will liability be established.
Surely this is a far cry from a one-step imposition of a gender-based quota.

Brown simply ignores the fact that it is required to accommodate fully the interests and abilities of the underrepresented gender, not because the three-part test mandates preferential treatment for women, but because Brown has been found (under prong one) to have allocated its athletics participation opportunities so as to create a significant gender-based disparity with respect to these opportunities, and has failed (under prong two) to show a history and continuing practice of expansion of opportunities for the underrepresented gender. Brown's interpretation conflates prongs one and three and distorts the three-part test by reducing it to an abstract, mechanical determination of strict numerical proportionality. In short, Brown treats the three-part test for compliance as a one-part test for strict liability.

Brown also fails to recognize that Title IX's remedial focus is, quite properly, not on the overrepresented gender, but on the underrepresented gender: in this case, women. Title IX and its implementing regulations protect the class for whose special benefit the statute was enacted. It is women and not men who have historically and who continue to be underrepresented in sports, not only at Brown, but at universities nationwide.

The prior panel held that "[t]he fact that the overrepresented gender is less than fully accommodated will not, in and of itself, excuse a shortfall in the provision of opportunities for the underrepresented gender" (*Cohen II*). Instead, the law requires that, absent a demonstration of continuing program expansion for the underrepresented gender under prong two of the three-part test, an institution must either provide athletics opportunities in proportion to the gender composition of the student body so as to satisfy prong one, or fully accommodate the interests and abilities of athletes of the underrepresented gender under prong three. Id. In other words,

If a school, like Brown, eschews the first two benchmarks of the accommodation test, electing to stray from substantial proportionality and failing to march uninterruptedly in the direction of equal athletic opportunity, it must comply with the third benchmark. To do so, the school must fully and effectively accommodate the underrepresented gender's interests and abilities, even if that requires it to give the underrepresented gender (in this case, women) what amounts to a larger slice of a shrinking athletic-opportunity pie (Ibid., p. 906).

We think it clear that neither the Title IX framework nor the district court's interpretation of it mandates a gender-based quota scheme. In our view, it is Brown's relative interests approach to the three-part test, rather than the district court's interpretation, that contravenes the language and purpose of the test and of the statute itself. To adopt the relative interests approach would be not only to overrule *Cohen II*, but to rewrite the enforcing agency's interpretation of its own regulation so as to incorporate an entirely different standard for Title IX compliance. This relative-interests standard would entrench and fix by law the significant gender-based disparity in athletics opportunities found by the district court to exist at Brown, a finding we have held to be not clearly erroneous. According to Brown's relative-interests interpretation of the equal-accommodation principle, the gender-based disparity in athletics participation opportunities at Brown is due to a lack of interest on the part of its female students, rather than to discrimination, and any attempt to remedy the disparity is, by definition, an unlawful quota. This approach is entirely contrary to "Congress's unmistakably clear mandate that educational institutions not use federal monies to perpetuate gender-based discrimination," and makes it virtually impossible to effectuate Congress's intent to eliminate sex discrimination in intercollegiate athletics.

Brown has contended throughout this litigation that the significant disparity in athletics opportunities for men and women at Brown is the result of a gender-based differential in the level of interest in sports and that the district court's application of the three-part test requires universities to provide athletics opportunities for women to an extent that exceeds their relative interests and abilities in sports. Thus, at the heart of this litigation is the question of whether Title IX permits Brown to deny its female students equal opportunity to participate in sports, based upon its unproven assertion that the district court's finding of a significant disparity in athletics opportunities for male and female students reflects not discrimination in Brown's intercollegiate athletics program, but a lack of interest on the part of its female students that is unrelated to a lack of opportunities.

We view Brown's argument that women are less interested than men in participating in intercollegiate athletics, as well as its conclusion that institutions should be required to accommodate the interests and abilities of its female students only to the extent that it accommodates the interests and abilities of its male students, with great suspicion. To assert that Title IX permits institutions to provide fewer athletics participation opportunities for women than for men, based upon the premise that women are less interested in sports than are men, is (among other things) to ignore the fact that Title IX was enacted in order to remedy discrimination that results from stereotyped notions of women's interests and abilities.

Interest and ability rarely develop in a vacuum; they evolve as a function of opportunity and experience. The Policy Interpretation recognizes that women's lower rate of participation in athletics reflects women's historical lack of opportunities to participate in sports. Moreover, the Supreme Court has repeatedly condemned gender-based discrimination based upon "archaic and overbroad generalizations" about women. The Court has been especially critical of the use of statistical evidence offered to prove generalized, stereotypical notions about men and women. For example, in holding that Oklahoma's 3.2 percent beer statute invidiously discriminated against males eighteen to twenty years of age, the Court in *Craig v. Boren* (1976), stressed that "the principles embodied in the Equal Protection Clause are not to be rendered inapplicable by statistically measured but loose-fitting generalities."

Thus, there exists the danger that, rather than providing a true measure of women's interest in sports, statistical evidence purporting to reflect women's interest instead provides only a measure of the very discrimination that is and has been the basis for women's lack of opportunity to participate in sports. Prong three requires some kind of evidence of interest in athletics, and the Title IX framework permits the use of statistical evidence in assessing the level of interest in sports. Nevertheless, to allow a numbers-based lack-of-interest defense to become the instrument of further discrimination against the under-represented gender would pervert the remedial purpose of Title IX. We conclude that, even if it can be empirically demonstrated that, at a particular time, women have less interest in sports than do men, such evidence, standing alone, cannot justify providing fewer athletics opportunities for women than for men. Furthermore, such evidence is completely irrelevant where, as here, viable and successful women's varsity teams have been demoted or eliminated. We emphasize that, on the facts of this case, Brown's lack-of-interest arguments are of no consequence. As the prior panel recognized, while the question of full and effective accommodation of athletics interests and abilities is potentially a complicated issue where plaintiffs seek to create a new team or to elevate to varsity status a team that has never competed at the varsity level, no such difficulty is presented here, where plaintiffs seek to reinstate what were successful university-funded teams right up until the moment the teams were demoted.

On these facts, Brown's failure to accommodate fully and effectively the interests and abilities of the underrepresented gender is clearly established. Under these circumstances, the district court's finding that there are interested women able to compete at the university-funded varsity level, *Cohen III*, is clearly correct.

Finally, the tremendous growth in women's participation in sports since Title IX was enacted disproves Brown's argument that women are less interested in sports for reasons unrelated to lack of opportunity.

Brown's relative-interests approach is not a reasonable interpretation of the three-part test. This approach contravenes the purpose of the statute and the regulation because it does not permit an institution or a district court to remedy a gender-based disparity in athletics participation opportunities. Instead, this approach freezes that disparity by law, thereby disadvantaging further the underrepresented gender. Had Congress intended to entrench, rather than change, the status quo—with its historical emphasis on men's participation opportunities to the detriment of women's opportunities—it need not have gone to all the trouble of enacting Title IX.

1996 Clarification of Intercollegiate Athletics Policy Guidance: The Three-Part Test*

The Office for Civil Rights (OCR) enforces Title IX of the Education Amendments of 1972, which prohibits discrimination on the basis of sex in education programs and activities by recipients of federal funds. The regulation implementing Title IX contains specific provisions governing athletic programs and the awarding of athletic scholarships. Further clarification of the Title IX regulatory requirements is provided by the Intercollegiate Athletics Policy Interpretation, issued December 11, 1979.[1]

The Title IX regulation provides that if an institution sponsors an athletic program it must provide equal athletic opportunities for members of both sexes. Among other factors, the regulation requires that an institution must effectively accommodate the athletic interests and abilities of students of both sexes to the extent necessary to provide equal athletic opportunity.

The 1979 Policy Interpretation provides that as part of this determination OCR will apply the following three-part test to assess whether an institution is providing nondiscriminatory participation opportunities for individuals of both sexes:

1. Whether intercollegiate-level participation opportunities for male and female students are provided in numbers substantially proportionate to their respective enrollments; or
2. Where the members of one sex have been and are underrepresented among intercollegiate athletes, whether the institution can show a history and con-

*Available at http://www.ed.gov/offices/OCR/docs/clarific.html (accessed June 29, 2007).

[1] The Policy Interpretation is designed for intercollegiate athletics. However, its general principles, and those of this Clarification, often will apply to elementary and secondary interscholastic athletic programs, which are also covered by the regulation.

tinuing practice of program expansion which is demonstrably responsive to
the developing interests and abilities of the members of that sex; or

3. Where the members of one sex are underrepresented among intercollegiate
   athletes, and the institution cannot show a history and continuing practice
   of program expansion, as described above, whether it can be demonstrated
   that the interests and abilities of the members of that sex have been fully
   and effectively accommodated by the present program.

Thus, the three-part test furnishes an institution with three individual avenues to choose from when determining how it will provide individuals of each
sex with nondiscriminatory opportunities to participate in intercollegiate athletics. If an institution has met any part of the three-part test, OCR will determine that the institution is meeting this requirement.

It is important to note that under the Policy Interpretation the requirement
to provide nondiscriminatory participation opportunities is only one of many
factors that OCR examines to determine if an institution is in compliance with
the athletics provision of Title IX. OCR also considers the quality of competition offered to members of both sexes in order to determine whether an institution effectively accommodates the interests and abilities of its students.

In addition, when an "overall determination of compliance" is made by
OCR, OCR examines the institution's program as a whole. Thus, OCR considers
the effective accommodation of interests and abilities in conjunction with
equivalence in the availability, quality, and kinds of other athletic benefits and
opportunities provided male and female athletes to determine whether an institution provides equal athletic opportunity as required by Title IX. These other
benefits include coaching, equipment, practice and competitive facilities,
recruitment, scheduling of games, and publicity, among others. An institution's
failure to provide nondiscriminatory participation opportunities usually
amounts to a denial of equal athletic opportunity because these opportunities
provide access to all other athletic benefits, treatment, and services.

This Clarification provides specific factors that guide an analysis of each part
of the three-part test. In addition, it provides examples to demonstrate, in concrete terms, how these factors will be considered. These examples are intended
to be illustrative, and the conclusions drawn in each example are based solely
on the facts included in the example.

Part One: Are Participation Opportunities
Substantially Proportionate to Enrollment?

Under part one of the three-part test, where an institution provides intercollegiate-level athletic participation opportunities for male and female students in
numbers substantially proportionate to their respective full-time undergraduate

enrollments, OCR will find that the institution is providing nondiscriminatory participation opportunities for individuals of both sexes.

OCR's analysis begins with a determination of the number of participation opportunities afforded to male and female athletes in the intercollegiate athletic program. The Policy Interpretation defines participants as those athletes:

a. Who are receiving the institutionally sponsored support normally provided to athletes competing at the institution involved, e.g., coaching, equipment, medical and training room services, on a regular basis during a sport's season; and

b. Who are participating in organized practice sessions and other team meetings and activities on a regular basis during a sport's season; and

c. Who are listed on the eligibility or squad lists maintained for each sport; or

d. Who, because of injury, cannot meet a, b, or c above but continue to receive financial aid on the basis of athletic ability.

OCR uses this definition of participant to determine the number of participation opportunities provided by an institution for the purposes of the three-part test.

Under this definition, OCR considers a sport's season to commence on the date of a team's first intercollegiate competitive event and to conclude on the date of the team's final intercollegiate competitive event. As a general rule, all athletes who are listed on a team's squad or eligibility list are counted as participants by OCR. In determining the number of participation opportunities for the purposes of the interests and abilities analysis, an athlete who participates in more than one sport will be counted as a participant in each sport in which he or she participates.

In determining participation opportunities, OCR includes, among others, those athletes who do not receive scholarships (e.g., walk-ons), those athletes who compete on teams sponsored by the institution even though the team may be required to raise some or all of its operating funds, and those athletes who practice but may not compete. OCR's investigations reveal that these athletes receive numerous benefits and services, such as training and practice time, coaching, tutoring services, locker-room facilities, and equipment, as well as important nontangible benefits derived from being a member of an intercollegiate athletic team. Because these are significant benefits, and because receipt of these benefits does not depend on their cost to the institution or whether the athlete competes, it is necessary to count all athletes who receive such benefits when determining the number of athletic opportunities provided to men and women.

OCR's analysis next determines whether athletic opportunities are substantially proportionate. The Title IX regulation allows institutions to operate separate athletic programs for men and women. Accordingly, the regulation allows an institution to control the respective number of participation opportunities offered to men and women. Thus, it could be argued that to satisfy part one, there should be no difference between the participation rate in an institution's intercollegiate athletic program and its full-time undergraduate student enrollment.

However, because in some circumstances it may be unreasonable to expect an institution to achieve exact proportionality—for instance, because of natural fluctuations in enrollment and participation rates, or because it would be unreasonable to expect an institution to add athletic opportunities in light of the small number of students that would have to be accommodated to achieve exact proportionality—the Policy Interpretation examines whether participation opportunities are "substantially" proportionate to enrollment rates. Because this determination depends on the institution's specific circumstances and the size of its athletic program, OCR makes this determination on a case-by-case basis, rather than through use of a statistical test.

As an example of a determination under part one: If an institution's enrollment is 52 percent male and 48 percent female, and 52 percent of the participants in the athletic program are male and 48 percent female, then the institution would clearly satisfy part one. However, OCR recognizes that natural fluctuations in an institution's enrollment and/or participation rates may affect the percentages in a subsequent year. For instance, if the institution's admissions the following year resulted in an enrollment rate of 51 percent males and 49 percent females, while the participation rates of males and females in the athletic program remained constant, the institution would continue to satisfy part one because it would be unreasonable to expect the institution to fine tune its program in response to this change in enrollment.

As another example, over the past five years an institution has had a consistent enrollment rate for women of 50 percent. During this time period, it has been expanding its program for women in order to reach proportionality. In the year that the institution reaches its goal—i.e., 50 percent of the participants in its athletic program are female—its enrollment rate for women increases to 52 percent. Under these circumstances, the institution would satisfy part one.

OCR would also consider opportunities to be substantially proportionate when the number of opportunities that would be required to achieve proportionality would not be sufficient to sustain a viable team, i.e., a team for which there is a sufficient number of interested and able students and enough available competition to sustain an intercollegiate team. As a frame of reference in assessing this situation, OCR may consider the average size of teams offered for the underrepresented sex, which would vary by institution.

For instance, Institution A is a university with a total of 600 athletes. While women make up 52 percent of the university's enrollment, they only represent

47 percent of its athletes. If the university provided women with 52 percent of athletic opportunities, approximately sixty-two additional women would be able to participate. Because this is a significant number of unaccommodated women, it is likely that a viable sport could be added. If so, Institution A has not met part one.

As another example, at Institution B women also make up 52 percent of the university's enrollment and represent 47 percent of Institution B's athletes. Institution B's athletic program consists of only sixty participants. If the University provided women with 52 percent of athletic opportunities, approximately six additional women would be able to participate. Because six participants are unlikely to support a viable team, Institution B would meet part one.

Part Two: Is There a History and Continuing Practice of Program Expansion for the Underrepresented Sex?

Under part two of the three-part test, an institution can show that it has a history and continuing practice of program expansion that is demonstrably responsive to the developing interests and abilities of the underrepresented sex. In effect, part two looks at an institution's past and continuing remedial efforts to provide nondiscriminatory participation opportunities through program expansion.[2]

OCR will review the entire history of the athletic program, focusing on the participation opportunities provided for the underrepresented sex. First, OCR will assess whether past actions of the institution have expanded participation opportunities for the underrepresented sex in a manner that was demonstrably responsive to their developing interests and abilities. Developing interests include interests that already exist at the institution.[3] There are no fixed intervals of time within which an institution must have added participation opportunities. Neither is a particular number of sports dispositives. Rather, the focus is on whether the program expansion was responsive to developing interests and abilities of the underrepresented sex. In addition, the institution must demonstrate a continuing (i.e., present) practice of program expansion as warranted by developing interests and abilities.

[2]Part two focuses on whether an institution has expanded the number of intercollegiate participation opportunities provided to the underrepresented sex. Improvements in the quality of competition and of other athletic benefits provided to women athletes, while not considered under the three-part test, can be considered by OCR in making an overall determination of compliance with the athletics provision of Title IX.

[3]However, under this part of the test an institution is not required, as it is under part three, to accommodate all interests and abilities of the underrepresented sex. Moreover, under part two an institution has flexibility in choosing which teams it adds for the underrepresented sex, as long as it can show overall a history and continuing practice of program expansion for members of that sex.

OCR will consider the following factors, among others, that may indicate a history of program expansion demonstrably responsive to the developing interests and of the underrepresented sex:

- an institution's record of adding intercollegiate teams, or upgrading teams to intercollegiate status, for the underrepresented sex;
- an institution's record of increasing the numbers of participants in intercollegiate athletics who are members of the underrepresented sex; and
- an institution's affirmative responses to requests by students or others for addition or elevation of sports.

OCR will consider the following factors, among others, as evidence that may indicate a continuing practice of program expansion that is demonstrably responsive to the developing interests and abilities of the underrepresented sex:

- an institution's current implementation of a nondiscriminatory policy's or procedure for requesting the addition of sports (including the elevation of club or intramural teams) and the effective communication of the policy or procedure to students; and
- an institution's current implementation of a plan of program expansion that is responsive to developing interests and abilities.

OCR would also find persuasive an institution's efforts to monitor developing interests and abilities of the underrepresented sex, for example by conducting periodic nondiscriminatory assessments of developing interests and abilities and taking timely actions in response to the results.

In the event that an institution eliminated any team for the underrepresented sex, OCR would evaluate the circumstances surrounding this action in assessing whether the institution could satisfy part two of the test. However, OCR will not find a history and continuing practice of program expansion where an institution increases the proportional participation opportunities for the underrepresented sex by reducing opportunities for the overrepresented sex alone or by reducing participation opportunities for the overrepresented sex to a proportionately greater degree than for the underrepresented sex. This is because part two considers an institution's good faith remedial efforts through actual program expansion. It is only necessary to examine part two if one sex is overrepresented in the athletic program. Cuts in the program for the underrepresented sex, even when coupled with cuts in the program for the overrepresented sex, cannot be considered remedial because they burden members of the sex already disadvantaged by the present program. However, an institution that has eliminated some participation opportunities for the underrepresented sex can still meet part two if, overall, it can show a history and continuing practice of program expansion for that sex.

In addition, OCR will not find that an institution satisfies part two where it established teams for the underrepresented sex only at the initiation of its program for the underrepresented sex or where it merely promises to expand its program for the underrepresented sex at some time in the future.

The following examples are intended to illustrate the principles discussed above. At the inception of its women's program in the mid-1970s, Institution C established seven teams for women. In 1984, it added a women's varsity team at the request of students and coaches. In 1990, it upgraded a women's club sport to varsity-team status based on a request by the club members and an NCAA survey that showed a significant increase in girls' high-school participation in that sport. Institution C is currently implementing a plan to add a varsity women's team in Spring 1996 that has been identified by a regional study as an emerging women's sport in the region. The addition of these teams resulted in an increased percentage of women participating in varsity athletics at the institution. Based on these facts, OCR would find Institution C in compliance with part two because it has a history of program expansion and is continuing to expand its program for women in response to their developing interests and abilities.

By 1980, Institution D established seven teams for women. Institution D added a women's varsity team in 1983 based on the requests of students and coaches. In 1991, it added a women's varsity team after an NCAA survey showed a significant increase in girl's high-school participation in that sport. In 1993, Institution D eliminated a viable women's team and a viable men's team in an effort to reduce its athletic budget. It has taken no action relating to the underrepresented sex since 1993. Based on these facts, OCR would not find Institution D in compliance with part two. Institution D cannot show a continuing practice of program expansion that is responsive to the developing interests and abilities of the underrepresented sex where its only action since 1993 with regard to the underrepresented sex was to eliminate a team for which there was interest, ability, and available competition.

In the mid-1970s, Institution E established five teams for women. In 1979, it added a women's varsity team. In 1984, it upgraded a women's club sport with twenty-five participants to varsity-team status. At that time it eliminated a women's varsity team that had eight members. In 1987 and 1989, Institution E added women's varsity teams that were identified by a significant number of its enrolled and incoming female students when surveyed regarding their athletic interests and abilities. During this time it also increased the size of an existing women's team to provide opportunities for women who expressed interest in playing that sport. Within the past year, it added a women's varsity team based on a nationwide survey of the most popular girls' high-school teams. Based on the addition of these teams, the percentage of women participating in varsity athletics at the institution has increased. Based all these facts, OCR would find Institution E in compliance with part two because it has a history of program expansion and the elimination of the team in 1984 took place within the context of continuing program expansion for the underrepresented sex that is responsive to their developing interests.

Institution F started its women's program in the early 1970s with four teams. It did not add to its women's program until 1987 when, based on requests of students and coaches, it upgraded a women's club sport to varsity-team status and expanded the size of several existing women's teams to accommodate significant expressed interest by students. In 1990, it surveyed its enrolled and incoming female students; based on that survey and a survey of the most popular sports played by women in the region, Institution F agreed to add three new women's teams by 1997. It added a women's team in 1991 and 1994. Institution F is implementing a plan to add a women's team by Spring 1997. Based on these facts, OCR would find Institution F in compliance with part two. Institution F's program history since 1987 shows that it is committed to program expansion for the underrepresented sex and it is continuing to expand its women's program in light of women's developing interests and abilities.

Part Three: Is the Institution Fully and Effectively Accommodating the Interests and Abilities of the Underrepresented Sex?

Under part three of the three-part test, OCR determines whether an institution is fully and effectively accommodating the interests and abilities of its students who are members of the underrepresented sex—including students who are admitted to the institution though not yet enrolled. Title IX provides that a recipient must provide equal athletic opportunity to its students. Accordingly, the Policy Interpretation does not require an institution to accommodate the interests and abilities of potential students.[4]

While disproportionately high athletic-participation rates by an institution's students of the overrepresented sex (as compared to their enrollment rates) may indicate that an institution is not providing equal athletic opportunities to its students of the underrepresented sex, an institution can satisfy part three where there is evidence that the imbalance does not reflect discrimination, i.e.,

---

[4]However, OCR does examine an institution's recruitment practices under another part of the Policy Interpretation. Accordingly, where an institution recruits potential student-athletes for its men's teams, it must ensure that women's teams are provided with substantially equal opportunities to recruit potential student-athletes.

where it can be demonstrated that, notwithstanding disproportionately low participation rates by the institution's students of the underrepresented sex, the interests and abilities of these students are, in fact, being fully and effectively accommodated.

In making this determination, OCR will consider whether there is (a) unmet interest in a particular sport; (b) sufficient ability to sustain a team in the sport; and (c) a reasonable expectation of competition for the team. If all three conditions are present, OCR will find that an institution has not fully and effectively accommodated the interests and abilities of the underrepresented sex.

If an institution has recently eliminated a viable team from the intercollegiate program, OCR will find that there is sufficient interest, ability, and available competition to sustain an intercollegiate team in that sport unless an institution can provide strong evidence that interest, ability, or available competition no longer exists.

a) Is There Sufficient Unmet Interest to Sustain an Intercollegiate Team?

OCR will determine whether there is sufficient unmet interest among the institution's students who are members of the underrepresented sex to sustain an intercollegiate team. OCR will look for interest by the underrepresented sex as expressed through the following indicators, among others:

- requests by students and admitted students that a particular sport be added;
- requests that an existing club sport be elevated to intercollegiate team status;
- participation in particular club or intramural sports;
- interviews with students, admitted students, coaches, administrators, and others regarding interest in particular sports;
- results of questionnaires of students and admitted students regarding interests in particular sports; and
- participation in particular interscholastic sports by admitted students.

In addition, OCR will look at participation rates in sports in high schools, amateur-athletic associations, and community-sports leagues that operate in areas from which the institution draws its students in order to ascertain likely interest and ability of its students and admitted students in particular sport(s).[5] For example, where OCR's investigation finds that a substantial number of high

---

[5]While these indications of interest may be helpful to OCR in ascertaining likely interest on campus, particularly in the absence of more direct indicia, an institution is expected to meet the actual interests and abilities of its students and admitted students.

schools from the relevant region offers a particular sport which the institution does not offer for the underrepresented sex, OCR will ask the institution to provide a basis for any assertion that its students and admitted students are not interested in playing that sport. OCR may also interview students, admitted students, coaches, and others regarding interest in that sport.

An institution may evaluate its athletic program to assess the athletic interest of its students of the underrepresented sex using nondiscriminatory methods of its choosing. Accordingly, institutions have flexibility in choosing a nondiscriminatory method of determining athletic interests and abilities provided they meet certain requirements. These assessments may use straightforward and inexpensive techniques, such as a student questionnaire or an open forum, to identify students' interests and abilities. Thus, while OCR expects that an institution's assessment should reach a wide audience of students and should be open-ended regarding the sports students can express interest in, OCR does net require elaborate scientific validation of assessments.

An institution's evaluation of interest should be done periodically so that the institution can identify in a timely and responsive manner any developing interests and abilities of the underrepresented sex. The evaluation should also take into account sports played in the high schools and communities from which the institution draws its students both as an indication of possible interest on campus and to permit the institution to plan to meet the interests of admitted students of the underrepresented sex.

b) Is There Sufficient Ability to Sustain an Intercollegiate Team?

Second, OCR will determine whether there is sufficient ability among interested students of the underrepresented sex to sustain an intercollegiate team. OCR will examine indications of ability such as:

- the athletic experience and accomplishments—in interscholastic, club, or intramural competition—of students and admitted students interested in playing the sport;
- opinions of coaches, administrators, and athletes at the institution regarding whether interested students and admitted students have the potential to sustain a varsity team; and
- if the team has previously competed at the club or intramural level, whether the competitive experience of the team indicates that it has the potential to sustain an intercollegiate team.

Neither a poor competitive record nor the inability of interested students or admitted students to play at the same level of competition engaged in by the institution's other athletes is conclusive evidence of lack of ability. It is sufficient that interested students and admitted students have the potential to sustain an intercollegiate team.

c) Is There a Reasonable Expectation of Competition for the Team?

Finally, OCR determines whether there is a reasonable expectation of intercollegiate competition for a particular sport in the institution's normal competitive region. In evaluating available competition, OCR will look at available competitive opportunities in the geographic area in which the institution's athletes primarily compete, including:

- competitive opportunities offered by other schools against which the institution competes; and
- competitive opportunities offered by other schools in the institution's geographic area, including those offered by schools against which the institution does not now compete.

Under the Policy Interpretation, the institution may also be required to actively encourage the development of intercollegiate competition for a sport for members of the underrepresented sex when overall athletic opportunities within its competitive region have been historically limited for members of that sex.

Conclusion

This discussion clarifies that institutions have three distinct ways to provide individuals of each sex with nondiscriminatory participation opportunities. The three-part test gives institutions flexibility and control over their athletic programs. For instance, the test allows institutions to respond to different levels of interest by its male and female students. Moreover, nothing in the three-part test requires an institution to eliminate participation opportunities for men.

At the same time, this flexibility must be used by institutions consistent with Title IX's requirement that they not discriminate on the basis of sex. OCR recognizes that institutions face challenges in providing nondiscriminatory participation opportunities for their students and will continue to assist institutions in finding ways to meet these challenges.

Letter from the
U.S. Department of Education
to Bowling Green State University*

UNITED STATES DEPARTMENT OF EDUCATION
WASHINGTON, D.C. 20202

July 23, 1998

Ms. Nancy S. Footer
General Counsel
Bowling Green State University
308 McFall Center
Bowling Green, Ohio 43403-0010

Dear Ms. Footer:

This is in response to your letter requesting guidance in meeting the require-ments of Title IX, specifically as it relates to the equitable apportionment of athletic financial aid. Please accept my apology for the delay in responding. As you know, the Office for Civil Rights (OCR) enforces Title IX of the Education Amendments of 1972, 20 U.S.C. Section 1682, which prohibits discrimination on the basis of sex in education programs and activities.

The regulation implementing Title IX and the Department's Intercollegiate Athletics Policy Interpretation published in 1979—both of which followed publication for notice and the receipt, review, and consideration of extensive

*Office for Civil Rights, U.S. Department of Education (July 23, 1998); http://www.ed.gov/about/offices/list/ocr/docs/bowlgrn.html (accessed July 2, 2007).

comments—specifically address intercollegiate athletics. You have asked us to provide clarification regarding how educational institutions can provide intercollegiate athletes with nondiscriminatory opportunities to receive athletic financial aid. Under the Policy Interpretation, the equitable apportioning of a college's intercollegiate athletics scholarship fund for the separate budgets of its men's and women's programs—which Title IX permits to be segregated— requires that the total amounts of scholarship aid made available to the two budgets are "substantially proportionate" to the participation rates of male and female athletes. 44 Fed. Reg. 71413, 71415 (1979).

In responding, I wish (1) to clarify the coverage of Title IX and its regulations as they apply to both academic and athletic programs, and (2) to provide specific guidance about the existing standards that have guided the enforcement of Title IX in the area of athletic financial aid, particularly the Policy Interpretation's "substantially proportionate" provision as it relates to a college's funding of the athletic scholarships budgets for its men's and women's teams. At the outset, I want to clarify that, wholly apart from any obligation with respect to scholarships, an institution with an intercollegiate athletics program has an independent Title IX obligation to provide its students with nondiscriminatory athletic-participation opportunities. The scope of that separate obligation is not addressed in this letter, but was addressed in a Clarification issued on January 16, 1996.

Title IX Coverage: Athletics vs. Academic Programs

Title IX is an antidiscrimination statute that prohibits discrimination on the basis of sex in any education program or activity receiving federal financial assistance, including athletic programs. Thus, in both academics and athletics, Title IX guarantees that all students, regardless of gender, have equitable opportunities to participate in the education program. This guarantee does not impose quotas based on gender, either in classrooms or in athletic programs. Indeed, the imposition of any such strict numerical requirement concerning students would be inconsistent with Title IX itself, which is designed to protect the rights of all students and to provide equitable opportunities for all students.

Additionally, Title IX recognizes the uniqueness of intercollegiate athletics by permitting a college or university to have separate athletic programs and teams for men and women. This allows colleges and universities to allocate athletic opportunities and benefits on the basis of sex. Because of this unique circumstance, arguments that OCR's athletics compliance standards create quotas are misplaced. In contrast to other antidiscrimination statutes, Title IX compliance cannot be determined simply on the basis of whether an institution makes sex-specific decisions, because invariably they do. Accordingly, the statute instead requires institutions to provide equitable opportunities to both male and female athletes in all aspects of its two separate athletic programs. As the court in the Brown University case stated, "[i]n this unique context, Title IX operates to ensure that the gender-segregated allocation of athletic opportunities does not disadvantage either gender. Rather than create a quota or preference, this unavoidable gender-conscious comparison merely provides for the allocation of athletic resources and participation opportunities between the sexes in a nondiscriminatory manner." *Cohen v. Brown Univ.*, 101 F.3d 155, 177 (1st Cir. 1996), *cert. denied*, 117 S. Ct. 1469 (1997). The remainder of this letter addresses the application of Title IX only to athletic scholarships.

Athletics: Scholarship Requirements

With regard to athletic financial assistance, the regulations promulgated under Title IX provide that, when a college or university awards athletic scholarships, these scholarship awards must be granted to "members of each sex in proportion to the number of students of each sex participating in . . . intercollegiate athletics." 34 C.F.R. 106.37(c). Since 1979, OCR has interpreted this regulation in conformity with its published "Policy Interpretation: Title IX and Intercollegiate Athletics," 44 Fed. Reg. 71413 (Dec. 11, 1979). The Policy Interpretation does not require colleges to grant the same number of scholarships to men and women, nor does it require that individual scholarships be of equal value. What it does require is that, at a particular college or university, "the total amount of scholarship aid made available to men and women must be substantially proportionate to their [overall] participation rates" at that institution. Id. at 71415. It is important to note that the Policy Interpretation only applies to teams that regularly compete in varsity competition. Id. at 71413 and n. 1.

Under the Policy Interpretation, OCR conducts a "financial comparison to determine whether proportionately equal amounts of financial assistance (scholarship aid) are available to men's and women's athletic programs." Id. The Policy Interpretation goes on to state that "[i]nstitutions may be found in compliance if this comparison results in substantially equal amounts or if a disparity can be explained by adjustments to take into account legitimate nondiscriminatory factors." Id.

A "disparity" in awarding athletic financial assistance refers to the difference between the aggregate amount of money athletes of one sex received in one year, and the amount they would have received if their share of the entire annual budget for athletic scholarships had been awarded in proportion to their participation rates. Thus, for example, if men account for 60 percent of a school's intercollegiate athletes, the Policy Interpretation presumes that—absent legitimate nondiscriminatory factors that may cause a disparity—the men's athletic program will receive approximately 60 percent of the entire annual scholarship budget and the women's athletic program will receive approximately 40 percent of those funds. This presumption reflects the fact that colleges typically allocate scholarship funds among their athletic teams, and that such teams are expressly segregated by sex. Colleges' allocation of the scholarship budget among teams, therefore, is invariably sex-based, in the sense that an allocation to a particular team necessarily benefits one sex to the exclusion of the other. See *Brown*, 101 F.3d at 177. Where, as here, disparate treatment is inevitable and a college's allocation of scholarship funds is "at the discretion of the institution," *Brown*, 101 F.3d at 177, the statute's nondiscrimination requirement obliges colleges to ensure that men's and women's separate activities receive equitable treatment. Cf. *United States v. Virginia*, 518 U.S. 515, 554 (1996).

Nevertheless, in keeping with the Policy Interpretation's allowance for disparities from "substantially proportionate" awards to the men's and women's programs based on legitimate nondiscriminatory factors, OCR judges each matter on a case-by-case basis with due regard for the unique factual situation presented by each case. For example, OCR recognizes that disparities may be explained by actions taken to promote athletic program development, and by differences between in-state and out-of-state tuition at public colleges. 44 Fed. Reg. at 71415. Disparities might also be explained, for example, by legitimate efforts undertaken to comply with Title IX requirements, such as participation requirements. See, e.g., *Gonyo v. Drake Univ.*, 879 F. Supp. 1000, 1005–1006 (S.D. Iowa 1995). Similarly, disparities may be explained by unexpected fluctuations in the participation rates of males and females. For example, a disparity may be explained if an athlete who had accepted an athletic scholarship decided at the last minute to enroll at another school. It is important to note that it is not enough for a college or university merely to assert a nondiscriminatory justification. Instead, it will be required to demonstrate that its asserted rationale is in fact reasonable and does not reflect underlying discrimination. For instance, if a college consistently awards a greater number of out-of-state scholarships to men, it may be required to demonstrate that this does not reflect discriminatory recruitment practices. Similarly, if a university asserts the phase-in of scholarships for a new team as a justification for a disparity, the university may be required to demonstrate that the time frame for phasing-in of scholarships is reasonable in light of college sports practices to aggressively recruit athletes to build start-up teams quickly.

In order to ensure equity for athletes of both sexes, the test for determining whether the two scholarship budgets are "substantially proportionate" to the respective participation rates of athletes of each sex necessarily has a high threshold. The Policy Interpretation does not, however, require colleges to achieve exact proportionality down to the last dollar. The "substantially proportionate" test permits a small variance from exact proportionality. OCR recognizes that, in practice, some leeway is necessary to avoid requiring colleges to unreasonably fine-tune their scholarship budgets.

When evaluating each scholarship program on a case-by-case basis, OCR's first step will be to adjust any disparity to take into account all the legitimate nondiscriminatory reasons provided by the college, such as the extra costs for out-of-state tuition discussed earlier. If any unexplained disparity in the scholarship budget for athletes of either gender is 1 percent or less for the entire budget for athletic scholarships, there will be a strong presumption that such a disparity is reasonable and based on legitimate and nondiscriminatory factors. Conversely, there will be a strong presumption that an unexplained disparity of more than 1 percent is in violation of the "substantially proportionate" requirement.

Thus, for example, if men are 60 percent of the athletes, OCR would expect that the men's athletic scholarship budget would be within 59 percent to 61 percent of the total budget for athletic scholarships for all athletes, after accounting for legitimate nondiscriminatory reasons for any larger disparity. Of course, OCR will continue to judge each case in terms of its particular facts. For example, at those colleges where 1 percent of the entire athletic scholarship budget is less than the value of one full scholarship, OCR will presume that a disparity of up to the value of one full scholarship is equitable and nondiscriminatory. On the other hand, even if an institution consistently has less than a 1-percent disparity, the presumption of compliance with Title IX might still be rebutted if, for example, there is direct evidence of discriminatory intent.

OCR recognizes that there has been some confusion in the past with respect to the Title IX compliance standards for scholarships. OCR's 1990 Title IX Investigator's Manual correctly stated that one would expect proportionality in the awarding of scholarships, absent a legitimate, nondiscriminatory justification. But that Manual also indicated that compliance with the "substantially proportionate" test could depend, in part, upon certain statistical tests. In some cases, application of such a statistical test would result in a determination of compliance despite the existence of a disparity as large as 3 to 5 percent.

We would like to clarify that use of such statistical tests is not appropriate in these circumstances. Those tests, which are used in some other discrimination contexts to determine whether the disparities in the allocation of benefits to different groups are the result of chance, are inapposite in the athletic scholarship context because a college has direct control over its allocation of financial aid to men's and women's teams, and because such decisions necessarily are sex based in the sense that an allocation to a particular team will affect only one sex. See *Brown*, 101 F.3d at 176–178 (explaining why college athletics "presents a distinctly different situation from admissions and employment," and why athletics requires a different analysis than that used in such other contexts "in order to determine the existence of discrimination"). In the typical case where aid is expressly allocated among sex-segregated teams, chance simply is not a possible explanation for disproportionate aid to one sex. Where a college does not make a substantially proportionate allocation to sex-segregated teams, the burden should be on the college to provide legitimate, nondiscriminatory reasons for the disproportionate allocation. Therefore, the use of statistical tests will not be helpful in determining whether a disparity in the allocations for the two separate athletic scholarship budgets is nondiscriminatory.

While a statistical test is not relevant in determining discrimination, the confusion caused by the manual's inclusion of a statistical test resulted in misunderstandings. Therefore, OCR is providing this clarification regarding the substantial proportionality provision found in the 1979 Policy Interpretation to confirm the substance of a longstanding standard. In order to ensure full understanding, OCR will apply the presumptions and case-by-case analysis described in this letter for the 1998–1999 academic year. OCR strongly encourages recipients to award athletic financial assistance to women athletes in the 1997–1998 academic year consistent with this policy clarification, both as a matter of fairness and in order to ensure that they are moving towards the policy clarification stated in this letter.

I trust that this letter responds to the questions the University has regarding the "substantially proportionate" provision of the Policy Interpretation in the context of the funding for an institution's two separate athletic scholarship budgets for male and female athletes. I am sending a copy of this letter as technical assistance to the complainants and the other twenty-four recipients also currently involved with OCR on the issue of awarding athletic financial assistance. We will be in contact with you shortly to continue to work with the University regarding this matter and to discuss other points raised in your letter. If you have any questions regarding this letter, please contact me at (312) 886-8387.

Sincerely yours,

Dr. Mary Frances O'Shea
National Coordinator for Title IX Athletics

Women in Intercollegiate Sport:
A Longitudinal, National Study,
Twenty-Nine Year Update, 1977–2006*

Vivian Acosta and Linda Jean Carpenter

In 1972, the year Title IX was enacted, more than 90 percent of women's teams were coached by females. By 1978, the year of mandatory Title IX compliance, the percentage had dropped to 58.25. Some of the large change in the early years from 1972 to 1978 was due to the massive increase in the number of teams offered for women (an increase from 2.5 in 1972 to 5.61 teams per school in 1978).

Today, even though the number of women's teams is at an all-time high, the representation of females among the coaching ranks of women's intercollegiate athletics is at an all-time low.

Percent of Female Head Coaches of Women's Teams in All Divisions, 1972–2006	
1972	90.0%
1978	58.2%
1982	52.4%
1988	48.3%
1992	48.3%
1998	47.4%
2002	44.0%
2006	42.4%

*http://webpages.charter.net/womeninsport (accessed July 2, 2007), excerpt.

Percentage of Female Athletic Directors of Women's Programs

Year	All divisions	Division I	Division II	Division III
1972	90.0+			
1980	20.0			
1992	16.8			
1994	21.0			
1996	18.5			
1998	19.4	9.9	18.6	29.4
2000	17.8	8.5	17.4	25.6
2002	17.9	8.4	16.1	27.6
2004	18.5	8.7	16.9	27.5
2006	18.6	9.3	17.8	26.6

Additionally, the representation of females among the ranks of head coaches for men's teams remains at 2 percent, where it has been since before the passage of Title IX. When we look at intercollegiate coaching as an entire workplace unit, we find that only 17.7 percent of all intercollegiate athletics teams have female head coaches. Another way to say the same thing is that 82.3 percent of all teams are coached by males.

The above table shows that the share of female athletic directors of women's programs has declined since 1972.

Stronger Women*

Mariah Burton Nelson

Boy, don't you men wish you could hit a ball like that!
—Babe Didrikson Zaharias

The way many women gain strength, and keep gaining strength, is through sports. Women can become strong in other ways, without being athletes, but athletic strength holds particular meaning in this culture. It's tangible, visible, measurable. It has a history of symbolic importance. Joe Louis, Jackie Robinson, Jesse Owens, Billie Jean King: Their athletic feats have represented to many Americans key victories over racism and sexism, key "wins" in a game that has historically been dominated by white men.

Sports have particular salience for men, who share childhood memories of having their masculinity confirmed or questioned because of their athletic ability or inability. Along with money and sex, sports in this culture define men to men. Sports embody a language men understand.

Women also understand sports—their power, their allure—but historically, most women were limited to a spectator's perspective. When a woman steps out of the bleachers or slips off her cheerleader's costume and becomes an athlete herself, she implicitly challenges the association between masculinity and sports. She refutes the traditional feminine role (primarily for white women) of passivity, frailty, subservience. If a woman can play a sport—especially if she can play it better than many men—then that sport can no longer be used as a yardstick of masculinity. The more women play a variety of sports, the more the entire notion of masculine and feminine roles—or any roles at all assigned by gender—becomes as ludicrous as the notion of roles assigned by race. Female athletes provide obvious, confrontational evidence—"in your face" evidence, some might say—of women's physical prowess, tangible examples of just what women can achieve.

The Stronger Women Get, the More Men Like Football (Dare Press, 2005), chapter 3, excerpt.

The athlete's feminism begins with the fact that her sports participation is a declaration of independence. Female athletes don't necessarily see it this way. They don't necessarily call themselves feminists. They cycle or swim or surf because it's fun and challenging, because it feels good, because they like the way it makes them look, because it allows them to eat more without gaining weight, because it gives them energy and confidence and time spent with friends, female or male. Many are ignorant about the women's rights movement. I've heard college students confuse feminism with feminine hygiene.

In fact, female athletes have a long tradition of dissociating themselves from feminism. Their desire to be accepted or to acquire or keep a boyfriend or a job has often equaled their passion for sports. Thus athletes have taken great pains—and it can hurt—to send reassuring signals to those who would oppose their play: "Don't worry, we're not feminists. We're not dykes, we're not aggressive, we're not muscular, we're not a threat to you. We just want to play ball." It has been a survival strategy.

It's time to tell the truth. Our behavior is feminist.[1] Some of us—including some pioneers who lobbied for Title IX, some coaches who volunteered to teach girls, and some athletes who competed in the first pro-baseball and -basketball leagues—are lesbians. Some of us are aggressive. Some of us are muscular. All of us, collectively, are a threat—not to men, exactly, but to male privilege and to masculinity as defined through manly sports. By reserving time each day for basketball dribbling, or for runs or rides or rows, women are changing themselves and society. Feminism is rarely an individual's motivating force but always the result: A woman's athletic training, regardless of the factors that lead to her involvement, implicitly challenges patriarchal constraints on her behavior. We take care of ourselves. For a group of people who have historically been defined by our ability to nurture others, the commitment to nurture ourselves is radical. Sport for women changes the woman's experience of herself and others' experience of her. It is feminist: It alters the balance of power between the sexes. It is daring. It is life changing. It is happening every day.

Several writers have used sports as metaphor, depicting women emancipated by the process of building muscle and endurance. In Alice Adams's short story "A Public Pool," a shy, anxious, unemployed woman feels too tall and too fat. She lives with her depressed mother. By swimming laps, she is slowly and subtly transformed. At first she feels embarrassed to appear, even in the locker room, in her bathing suit. Swimming twenty-six laps, a half-mile, seems a struggle. She feels flattered by attention from a blond, bearded swimmer not because he

[1]Susan Greendorfer, "Making Connections: Women's Sport Participation as a Political Act" (paper presented at the National Girls and Women in Sports Symposium, Slippery Rock State University, Slippery Rock, Pennsylvania, February 13, 1993). Susan Greendorfer, professor of kinesiology at the University of Illinois, Urbana-Champaign, was the first or one of the first to assert that women's sports are inherently a political act.

is kind or interesting—in fact he cuts rudely through the water with a "violent crawl"—but because he is male.

By the end of the story, she becomes "aware of a long strong body (mine) pulling through the water, of marvelous muscles, a strong back, and long, long legs." She applies for a job she'll probably get and looks forward to moving out of her mother's house. When she happens upon "Blond Beard" outside a cafe, she realizes that he is a gum-chewing, spiffily dressed jerk. The story ends with his inviting her to join him for coffee, and her declining. "I leave him standing there. I swim away."[2]

Feminism is about bodies: birth control, sexual harassment, child sexual abuse, pornography, rape, date rape, battering, breast cancer, breast enlargement, dieting, Liposuction, abortion, anorexia, bulimia, sexuality.

And then there is sports.

"The repossession by women of our bodies," wrote the poet and author Adrienne Rich in *Of Woman Born*, "will bring far more essential change to human society than the seizing of the means of production by workers."

As athletes, we repossess our bodies. Told that we're weak, we develop our strengths. Told that certain sports are wrong for women, we decide what feels right. Told that our bodies are too dark, big, old, flabby, or wrinkly to be attractive to men, we look at naked women in locker rooms and discover for ourselves the beauty of actual women's bodies in all their colors, shapes, and sizes. Told that certain sports make women look "like men," we notice the truth: Working out doesn't make us look like men, it makes us look happy. It makes us smile. More important, it makes us healthy and powerful. It makes us feel good.

The National Center for Health Statistics reports that physical fitness is linked to a general sense of well-being, a positive mood, and lower levels of anxiety and depression, especially among women. The athlete is more likely than her nonathletic sisters to have self-confidence.[3]

Women who exercise weigh less than nonathletes, and have lower blood pressure and lower levels of cholesterol and triglycerides. They miss fewer days of work.[4]

Female student-athletes in college are more likely to graduate than their nonathletic peers. White female athletes have a graduation rate of 72 percent, compared to 64 percent of white women in the general student body. African American female athletes have a graduation rate of 62 percent, compared to only 46 percent of black women in the general student body.[5]

[2]Alice Adams, "A Public Pool," *Mother Jones,* November 1984, 38.

[3]*Physician and Sportsmedicine* 26, no. 5 (May 1998), 86–97; cited by Women's Sports Foundation, 2004.

[4]*American Journal of Health Promotion* 10 (1996), 171–174; cited by "Women's Sports and Fitness Facts and Statistics," Women's Sports Foundation, June 1, 2004.

[5]*NCAA News,* September 1, 2003; cited by Women's Sports Foundation, 2004.

A Harvard study of more than 72,000 nurses found that the more a woman exercises, the less likely she is to suffer a stroke.[6] A Penn State study found that exercise may be even more important than calcium consumption to ensure bone health.[7]

Exercise reduces an older woman's chances of developing osteoporosis. Postmenopausal women who start exercising report improved health status and fewer chronic diseases than their peers who do not exercise.[8] Pregnant athletes report a lower incidence of back pain, easier labor and delivery, fewer stress-related complaints, and less postpartum depression than women who don't exercise.

According to research by the Women's Sports Foundation, female high school athletes are more likely than nonathletes to do well in high school and college, to feel popular, to be involved in extracurricular activities, to stay involved in sport as adults, and to aspire to community leadership. Female high-school athletes are less likely to get involved with marijuana, cocaine, PCP, and other drugs;[9] less likely to get pregnant;[10] less likely to have sexual intercourse in high school;[11] and three times more likely than their nonathletic peers to graduate from high school.[12]

And the effects of exercise persist throughout a lifetime. As little as one to three hours of weekly exercise can lower a teenage girl's lifelong risk of breast cancer by 20 or 30 percent. Four hours of weekly exercise can reduce the risk by almost 60 percent.[13] Women who were athletic as children report having greater confidence, self-esteem, and pride in their physical and social selves than those who were sedentary as children.[14] If, as a society, we are interested in the health and welfare of women, we should encourage and enable them to play sports.

In a country where male politicians and judges make key decisions about our bodies and all of us are vulnerable to random attacks of male violence, the simple act of taking control of our own bodies—including their health, their

[6]*Journal of the American Medical Association* (June 2000); cited by Women's Sports Foundation, 2004.

[7]*Pediatrics Fitness Bulletin* 23, no. 8 (August 2000), 2; cited by Women's Sports Foundation, 2004.

[8]*Archives of Internal Medicine* 158, no. 15 (August 10–24, 1998), 1695–1701; cited by Women's Sports Foundation, 2004.

[9]The Women's Sport Foundation Report: Health Risks and the Female Athlete, 2001.

[10]The Women's Sport Foundation Report: Sport and Teen Pregnancy, 1998.

[11]Ibid.

[12]The Women's Sport Foundation Report, 2001.

[13]*Journal of the National Cancer Institute* (1994); cited by Women's Sports Foundation, 2004.

[14]L. Jaffee and J. Lutter, "A Change in Attitudes? A Report of Melpomene's Third Membership Survey," *Melpomene Journal* 10, no. 2 (1991), 11–16; and L. Jaffee and R. Mantzer, "Girls' Perspectives: Physical Activity and Self-Esteem," *Melpomene Journal* 11, no. 3 (1992), 14–23.

pleasure, and their power—is radical. In a society in which real female bodies (as opposed to media images of female bodies) are unappreciated at best, the act of enjoying one's own female body is radical. It contradicts all feminine training to move, to extend our arms, to claim public space as our own, to use our bodies aggressively, instrumentally, to make rough contact with other bodies. Temple University doctoral student Frances Johnston interviewed dozens of female ice hockey and rugby players and found that "physicality" was one of the most appealing aspects of the games. "They enjoyed the tackling, the checking, the falling down and getting up, the discovery that they had 'survived' another hard hit or rough game." Besides body contact, they enjoyed "kicking the ball, getting rid of the ball right before a tackle, the power of a well-hit slap shot."[15]

Lunging for a soccer ball, we do not worry if our hair looks attractive. Leaping over a high bar, we do not wish we had bigger breasts. Strapped snugly into a race car, roaring around a track at 220 miles per hour, we do not smile or wave. While playing sports, our bodies are ours to do with as we please. If in that process our bodies look unfeminine—if they become bruised or bloody or simply unattractive—that seems irrelevant. Our bodies are ours. We own them. While running to catch a ball, we remember that.

I have coached recreational, AAU, junior high, and high school basketball. My players have been girls (nine through twelve), teenagers (fifteen through eighteen) and grown women (twenty through forty). Most of these players had trouble with the defensive stance, and with "being big."

The defensive stance requires a player to squat, low to the ground, her legs wide. Her knees should gape open, farther apart than her shoulders, her hands ready to deflect passes or shots. From this position she can react quickly to any moves an offensive player makes.

Why is this difficult for girls and women to learn? It's the leg spread. It's unladylike to yawn one's legs wide open. Even little girls growing up today are receiving this message. I can tell because I tease them, imitating the way they try to squat without separating their legs. "It's okay," I say. "No one's going to look up your skirt." They laugh and I know I've hit the mark. Most little girls don't even wear skirts to school anymore. But their foremothers did, and some of their big sisters in high school do. This concept of "skirt," with its implicit vulnerability, still haunts them, even on the basketball court.

My players are haunted, too, by size taboos. They don't like to feel tall, to seem wide, to make loud noises. They don't feel comfortable inhabiting a big space. Even many young ones talk quietly and act timid. In basketball, you need

[15]Frances Johnson, "Life on the Fringe: The Experience of Rugby and Ice Hockey Playing Women" (paper presented at the annual meeting of the North American Society for the Sociology of Sport, Toledo, Ohio, November 5, 1992).

to snatch a rebound as if you own the ball, as if you're starving and it's the last coconut on the tree. You have to protect the ball, elbows pointed outward like daggers, lest others try to grab it. You have to decide where you want to be, then get there, refusing to let anyone push you out of the way. You have to shout, loudly, to let your teammates know who's cutting through the lane or who's open for a shot. Basketball teaches women and girls to renounce the suffocating vestiges of ladylike behavior and act instead like assertive, honest, forthright human beings. It's about unlearning femininity.

Simone de Beauvoir wrote in *The Second Sex* that the athlete receives from sports a sense of authority and an ability to influence others. "To climb higher than a playmate, to force an arm to yield and bend, is to assert one's sovereignty over the world in general." By contrast, the woman deprived of sports "has no faith in a force she has not experienced in her body; she does not dare to be enterprising, to revolt, to invent; doomed to docility, to resignation . . . she regards the existing state of affairs as something fixed."[16]

Thus the very desire to change the conditions of our lives—to demand the equal rights that are a cornerstone of feminism—may be traceable to our own sense of our physical power. This is supported by "tomboy" studies: Female politicians, business leaders, and other successful women often started out as athletes.

Several pro athletes in the post–Billie Jean King generations have become outspoken advocates for women. Golfer Carol Mann, race car driver Lyn St. James, Olympic swimmers Nancy Hogshead and Donna de Varona, basketball pioneer Nancy Lieberman, and soccer star Julie Foudy have served as Women's Sports Foundation presidents. Zina Garrison has talked openly about a troubling feminist issue: the body/self hatred that in her case led to bulimia.

According to a survey of working women, about 50 percent of women of color believe their sports participation helps them to access decision-making channels outside the office, be accepted by co-workers, advance their careers, and tap into business networks. About 36 percent of white women agree.[17]

Women who played college sports rate themselves higher in their abilities to set objectives, lead a group, motivate others, share credit, and feel comfortable in a competitive environment. Former high-school athletes also rated themselves fairly high in these abilities, followed by former youth-sport athletes. Women with no childhood competitive experience felt least adept.[18]

[16]Simone de Beauvoir, *The Second Sex* (New York: Vintage Books, 1952), 331.

[17]Don Sabo and Marjorie Snyder, "Miller Lite Report on Sports and Fitness in the Lives of Working Women," in cooperation with the Women's Sports Foundation and *Working Woman*, March 8, 1993, 13–15.

[18]Ibid., 5–7.

Psychologists say that the best antidote to depression and helplessness is action. Athletes, with their proud muscles and trained minds, are poised to take those actions, and to provide leadership for women who are sick of living in fear. Sport, by definition, strengthens. The athlete dedicates herself to women's rights, beginning with her own. The team athlete becomes appreciative of women's bodies, beginning with her own. She cares for women, respects women, and becomes willing to take physical risks for and with women. Sport for women represents autonomy, strength, pleasure, community, control, justice, and power. It disrupts men's attempts to elevate themselves above women. It changes everything.

The Second Backlash: 2001–2008

• INTRODUCTION •

An infamous Chinese politician once described the uneven advance of the country's socialist revolution as "two steps forward, one step backward." Alas, like most social change, Title IX has progressed in fits and starts as well. As Parts III and IV show, a court decision can either derail extensive legislative efforts to ensure equality for women in athletics, or provide clarity and certainty for all concerned. Likewise, a presidential administration that is supportive of Title IX translates into greater opportunities for women in both high school and college, while an administration hostile to the law can stagnate growth. Similarly, athletic-governing bodies that put resources toward Title IX compliance will foster an atmosphere of trust between men's and women's athletic departments, rather than one of hostility by challenging the law with high-paid lobbyists and lawsuits in the courts.

But after the 1990s' period of rapid reform with numerous legal victories for women athletes and stronger OCR regulations, Title IX's detractors regrouped and unleashed a new assault.

Before the new offensive, however, the momentum from the 1990s had one more victory to register. On February 20, 2001, the Supreme Court ruled in *Brentwood v. Tenn. Sec. Sch. Athletic Assoc.* that a high-school athletic association is a "state actor" and is thereby subject to the Constitution. The importance of the ruling was that the Equal Protection Clause of the Fourteenth Amendment, which requires the government to treat its citizens equally, applies to large high-school athletic associations in gender-equity suits. (This is in contrast with the NCAA, which has been found not to be a state actor.) For example, in *Communities for Equity v. Mich. St. High Sch. Athletic Assoc.*, the Sixth Circuit relied on *Brentwood* when it held that the MSHSAA's gender-based discriminatory

scheduling of high-school sports seasons violated the Constitution's Equal Protection Clause. Girls, but not boys, played sports in nontraditional seasons,
thereby depriving female athletes of access to tournaments, college recruiting,
and scholarships. MSHSAA tried to argue that the scheduling allowed more girls
to participate because schools could more easily share facilities with girls playing during nontraditional seasons. The court held, however, that the MSHSAA
could require boys and girls to alternate between nontraditional seasons, or
could move a commensurate number of the boys' teams to nontraditional seasons. Thus, it found that the discriminatory scheduling was not substantially
related to achieving any important governmental interest and it was declared
unconstitutional. The ruling is significant for several reasons, but primarily
because it requires large statewide school districts' athletic associations to treat
girls and boys equitably, which enables a far more efficient use of litigation
resources than suing individual schools.

The Backlash

During its first three decades, Title IX enjoyed broad bipartisan support in Congress. Yet, no legislative enactment is free from change. In January 2001, the
stage was set for a multipronged attack on the implementation of Title IX. When
then–Texas governor George W. Bush needed Iowa's votes to reach the White
House, he was approached by a group of Iowa wrestling coaches who felt that
the presidential candidate might be receptive to their interpretation of Title IX.
They were correct, and Title IX reform became a part of the 2000 Republican
platform. Along with then Speaker of the House Dennis Hastert, a former wrestling coach, and former wrestler Donald Rumsfeld, then Secretary of Defense,
the mission of these Title IX detractors was for the Bush administration to
rewrite Title IX's policy interpretations. All three branches of government would
be involved: The judiciary would hear a lawsuit against the Department of
Education challenging Title IX regulations; the administration would try to get
public consensus for the OCR to change Title IX regulations; and certain powerful congressmen would be ready to prevent the legislature from passing legislation to overturn these new, weaker Title IX regulations.

In January 2002, the National Wrestling Coaches Association (NWCA) filed
a lawsuit against the Department of Education, alleging that the athletic regulations interpreting Title IX were responsible for the decrease in men's wrestling
teams, that it discriminated against men, and that the law was based on an
illegal "quota system,"[1] many of the same arguments raised in the *Kelly* decision
(discussed in Part III).

[1]*Nat'l Wrestling Coaches Assoc. v. Dep't of Educ.*, 361 U.S. App. D.C. 257 (D.C. Cir. May 14,
2004).

Before the wrestlers' lawsuit would reach its conclusion, the litigation provided the Department of Education with a reason to weaken Title IX via the benignly titled "Commission on Opportunities in Athletics," which was established on June 27, 2002. The commission's official purpose sounded innocuous enough: "Collect information, analyze issues, and obtain broad public input directed at improving the application of current federal standards for measuring equal opportunity for men and women and boys and girls to participate in athletics under Title IX."[2] As detailed in the excerpt from the Minority Report, the deep biases of the appointed membership exposed the political motive underlying the commission: Thirty-one invited panelists were opposed to Title IX, fifteen were in favor of the law, and six were considered neutral. Many experts, such as the author of the GAO study that found that, overall, opportunities for men were increasing, not decreasing, were not invited to testify. Schools that were sued for compliance problems had a number of their representatives testify, but not a single person who represented plaintiffs in Title IX lawsuits against academic institutions testified. Ten slots on the panel went to organizations or individuals affiliated with men's discontinued sports teams, who unsurprisingly called for the elimination of the current Title IX equal-opportunity standard. No panelist represented any organization with a large number of discontinued women's sports, or with new women's Olympic sports that benefited from Title IX. Four invited panelists were football coaches or representatives of football organizations seeking to protect the advantaged position of their sport. The commission met four times over the ensuing year and a half before issuing its report, which is excerpted in this section. Two members of the commission also wrote a Minority Report, which is also included here, that critiques the Majority Report.

While the commissioners debated, another assault during this time was a rhetorical one. Title IX's detractors deployed once again the same political, philosophical, economic, and legal arguments that had been rejected by the judiciary and the court of public opinion during the 1970s, 1980s, and 1990s. This time no one objected to the idea of women playing sports. Virtually all critics claimed to be big supporters of women's athletics and the original intent of the law, but claimed that Title IX had now gone "too far" by requiring schools to cut men's teams through its quota requirements. Their hope was that these rejected arguments would gain traction in the increasingly conservative mood of the times. Indeed, the major media outlets were receptive to many of these arguments, including segments on *60 Minutes* and articles in the *New York Times*, among others.

The tone of the *60 Minutes'* coverage is indicated by the following commentary by host Bob Simon and his exchange with wrestling coach Leo Kocher:

[2]http://www.ed.gov/about/bdscomm/list/athletics/about.html.

SIMON: But while women have been making giant strides, hundreds of men's teams have been eliminated, and the men say that also trails back to Title IX. Here's what happened. The government told the schools that the only surefire way to abide by Title IX is by achieving what's called proportionality. That means that if half of the student body is female, half of the athletes should be as well.

So, if a college has too many male athletes, it can do one of two things. It can add more women's teams. No problem with that, except money, often a lot of money, which is why many colleges choose the cheap and easy way—just cut the number of men. Colleges have cut hundreds of wrestling teams, along with dozens of men's gymnastics, tennis, and track-and-field teams. Men's swimming is also taking a bath. Remember Olympic-gold-medalist Greg Louganis? He polished his art on the University of Miami's championship swimming and diving team. That team no longer exists.

LEO KOCHER, *wrestling coach*: I don't think that the American public understands what's going on in colleges. I don't think they understand that they're applying the quota law to sports in college.

SIMON: Leo Kocher, a wrestling coach and an architect of the lawsuit, says Title IX has led college athletics into the world of the absurd.

KOCHER: I once talked to a Division III swim coach. She coached both the men and the women. She was told she could only keep as many men out on the team as women stayed out for the team.

SIMON: Does this actually happen, that guys are tossed off of a swim team?

KOCHER: Absolutely. Absolutely.

Prominent conservative writers took up the cause; a new conservative women's group called the Independent Women's Forum, cofounded by Lynne Cheney, Vice-President Dick Cheney's wife, came out against Title IX; and the internet flowered with the idea that men's sports somehow were imperiled by Title IX. The article by Jessica Gavora in this part is an exemplar of the type of criticisms laid at the doorstep of Title IX. The article by Nancy Hogshead-Makar addresses the prominent aspects of these polemics as well as the counteroffensive against them that have arisen since 2000.

The Commission on Opportunities in Athletics released its Majority Report in January 2003, which made a number of recommendations that would have been set backs for gender equity. The recommendations, however, were met with a storm of public protest. In response, Secretary of Education Rodney Paige backed off the most radical proposed recommendations, stating that he would not implement any recommendations that did not receive unanimous support. Some of the remaining recommendations still would have weakened legal protections for females, and some commissioners charged that either the votes were not recorded properly or in other instances that they were given false information just prior to voting.

When the public learned the effect that many of these recommendations would produce, the decibel level got even louder. The NCAA began lobbying for Title IX to remain the same. Over 100 organizations formally opposed any changes to Title IX and sent letters to Congress, the Department of Education, and to President Bush. Members of the House and the Senate sent letters to both Secretary Rodney Paige and to President Bush, urging him not to adopt any of the Commission's proposed changes. All major newspapers have daily sports sections, which provided regular column space to covering the developments within the Commission. Other important public policies like air pollution, tax reform, or AIDS research that were also targeted for change by the Bush administration could not count on this amount of public awareness. This bright public spotlight prevented the Commission from being able to claim that they were merely "tinkering" with Title IX regulations, or that their proposals would not have serious consequences for women. Two major polls taken during the relevant time period concluded that *even if* Title IX harmed men's sports—a proposition that Title IX advocates hotly dispute—the public still resoundingly supported Title IX as it was. President Bush had an election in a few months, and the prospect of explaining why women were no longer entitled to equal opportunities in sports was not an enviable position to defend.

Finally, on July 11, 2003, Secretary Paige issued the Department's "Additional Clarification" stating that the 1979 Policy Interpretation would remain the legal standard for compliance under Title IX, and that the administration would make no changes to the policies. After spending over $700,000 of taxpayer funds, not to mention the sums spent by advocates and opponents of the law, Title IX and its three-part test were left intact. Advocates breathed a sigh of relief, assuming that the battle against the administration had been won.

Shortly after Secretary Paige reaffirmed the current policies regarding Title IX, the wrestlers' lawsuit was thrown out on a motion to dismiss, which occurs at the earliest stages of litigation, long before a trial. The court ruled that *even if* all the wrestlers' allegations were true, the wrestlers would not be entitled to any legal relief. As the decision in this section of the Court of Appeals for the District of Columbia makes clear, the NWCA's position failed for many reasons. The primary one was that the wrestlers could not demonstrate that weakening civil rights for women athletes would restore any discontinued wrestling programs. As a consequence, the wrestlers' lawsuit—which was the initial driving force for the creation of the commission—was dismissed.[3] It was another win for advocates, this time in the judiciary. Advocates now assumed that the

[3]See also the materials on Legal Standing, in the Introduction to Part II.

threat was over, and that they could turn their attention to other issues for women in athletics.

Two years later in 2005, however, the Department reneged on its public position to maintain the status quo by secretly developing and then promulgating a new "interpretation" of its policy that allowed colleges and universities to use e-mail interest surveys *exclusively* to determine whether schools were compliant with Title IX under prong three (i.e., whether a school is fully and effectively meeting its female students' interests and abilities to participate in sports). Remarkably, the Department took this step with no public input whatsoever: no public meetings, hearings, or comments. The articles by Andrew Zimbalist as well as Christine Grant and Don Sabo talk about the problems with this approach to Title IX, and discuss how a seemingly small change in policy could result in dramatic losses for women athletes.

Since then, a wide array of organizations, including athletic, civil-rights, and academic groups, have objected vociferously to the newest Clarification on a number of grounds. These organizations include the Women's Sports Foundation, the National Women's Law Center, the Leadership Conference on Civil Rights, the National Education Association, the YMCA, and the NCAA.[4]

Due to these concerns, the Senate Appropriations Committee requested that the Department prepare a report to address the substantial negative public response to the Clarification. The Department released its report in March 2006. The Zimbalist article discusses the effects of the OCR's presentation, and how it represented a seismic change in course, not a mere explanation or elucidation of existing policy. The overwhelming evidence—including the data underlying the Department's own new report—demonstrated the Clarification's serious methodological flaws. As Neena Chaudhry, senior counsel at the National Women's Law Center, said in response to the report, "The report confirms that the Department set too low a bar for Title IX compliance—and that that standard is unprecedented in OCR's enforcement efforts. The Department of Education should rescind the policy and instead focus on enforcing the law so that women can finally enjoy equal athletic opportunities at our nation's schools and colleges and universities." The NCAA's response was decisive: member schools could not rely exclusively on the Department of Education's model survey to comply with the gender equity portion of the decennial certification process.

Meanwhile, the needless confusion about the law meant it could be blamed for unfortunate circumstances in athletics or even proffered to justify more expenditures on football. Title IX was inevitably blamed when men's teams were dropped from a school's sports offerings, even if those cuts included women's

---

[4]A more complete listing of supporting organizations can be found at http://www.savetitleix .com/who.html.

teams.[5] Ironically, Title IX was said to have played an important role in Western Kentucky University's decision to upgrade its football program from Division I-AA to Division I-A. The school was out of Title IX compliance because it offered approximately twenty too few scholarships for men, and moving its football program to Division I-A would add twenty-two men's scholarships. The school's Board of Regents approved this move in November 2006, to take effect in 2009. The move includes a $70 increase in the required student fee beginning with the fall 2007 semester—a circumstance difficult to imagine for the upgrade of any other athletic team.

Another Attempt to One-Two Punch Title IX

On March 19, 2007, in another déjà vu moment, a group calling themselves "Equity in Athletics" (EIA) filed a lawsuit against the Department of Education in the federal Virginia court, again challenging the validity of the 1979 three-part test. EIA's complaints against the 1979 test were not new. In fact, its claims were remarkably similar to those lawsuits dismissed just three years earlier in *Nat'l Wrestling Coaches Assoc. v. Dep't of Educ.,*[6] as well as those in *Cohen v. Brown Univ.*[7] EIA argues that the 1975 Regulations[8] require schools to provide equal athletic opportunity based on each gender's *relative* interests. It will be some time before the case is resolved, but other courts have rejected this same argument because the test "disadvantages women and undermines the remedial purposes of Title IX by limiting required program expansion for the under-represented sex to the status quo level of relative interests . . ."[9] In addition, this approach would effectively freeze current levels of participation into place. As the court in *Cohen v. Brown Univ.* said, "Had Congress intended to entrench, rather than change, the status quo . . . it need not have gone to all the trouble of enacting Title IX."[10]

Social scientists have also rejected the relative-interest argument. As the materials in this section by researchers Don Sabo and Christine Grant demonstrate, "interest" is not stagnant or immutable. "Interest" in pursuing sports—or any

[5]For example, James Madison University cut seven men's teams and three women's teams, allegedly to comply with Title IX. See "Media Statement, JMU" (February 8, 2007), http://www.jmu.edu/jmuweb/general/news/general8145.shtml (accessed July 6, 2007). But see "James Madison University and Title IX; Myths and Facts" (discussing other options JMU had to comply with the law), http://www.nwlc.org/details.cfm?id=2870&section=athletics (accessed July 6, 2007).

[6]*Nat'l Wrestling Coaches Assoc. v. Dep't of Educ.*; see footnote 1 above.

[7]101 F.3d 155 (1st Circ. 1996).

[8]"Whether the selection of sports and levels of competition effectively accommodate the interests and abilities of both sexes" 45 C.F.R., section 86.41(c)(1).

[9]*Cohen v. Brown Univ.*, see footnote 7 above, 174.

[10]Ibid., 180–181.

academic field of study—depends on a person's life experiences and the opportunities she has encountered. Courts dismissing the relative-interest argument have recognized that "[i]nterest and abilities rarely develop in a vacuum; they evolve as a function of opportunity and experience . . . Women's lower rate of participation in athletics reflects women's historical lack of opportunities to participate in sports."[11]

Much like the Department of Education's formation of the Commission on Opportunities in Athletics in 2002, EIA's lawsuit provided another governmental body, the U.S. Commission on Civil Rights (USCCR), with a pretext to re-examine Title IX and the 1979 three-part test. Although these arguments had been thoroughly vetted in diverse contexts in the past, there was still apprehension that the relative-interest argument might gain traction. "Our fear is that the intention is to create a public record to be used by the Department of Education to say that there is support by the commission for the 2005 clarification," said Donna A. Lopiano, chief executive of the Women's Sports Foundation. "It's a weakening of the spirit of the law. When athletics directors can say, 'Let me wait and see, maybe I'll get some relief,' that's the situation that has the potential to stop progress in its tracks."[12]

Title IX foes knew they would have a receptive audience with Chairman Rodney Paige, the former Secretary of Education who established the Commission on Opportunities in Athletics in 2002, which tried mightily to weaken the law. At the USCCR hearings on May 11, 2007, both sides presented familiar arguments. Advocates used the opportunity to enumerate the flaws in the OCR's model survey. Opponents reiterated the claims in the EIA lawsuit and others, stating that the relative-interest test would be a "small change" in the law, rather than a substantial vitiation of current law. Still, none of the panelists could address how weakening the law for women would help reinstate or expand the men's opportunities, given the rapid escalation of costs in men's football and basketball. These debates continue.

Conclusion

In 1972, Congress adopted the radical idea that girls and women should be treated equitably by educational institutions that receive federal tax dollars. Because sports participation is a part of education and because it provides sig-

---

[11]Ibid., 178–179; see also *Horner v. Kentucky High School Athletic Assoc.*, 43 F.3d 265 (6th Cir. 1994), 275; and *Jeldness v. Pearce*, 30 F.3d 1220 (9th Cir. 1994), in which the court rejected a claim that differing interests between male and female prisoners justified providing female prisoners with fewer educational opportunities.

[12]Elia Powers, "Revisiting Title IX Policy," *Inside Higher Education*, May 11, 2007; http://www.insidehighered.com/news/2007/05/11/titleix (accessed July 6, 2007).

nificant physical, economic, and professional opportunities to all participants, the promise of Title IX must be fulfilled. The strength of civil-rights laws hinges on the ability and willingness of our citizens to prevent and expose violations and to bring the goal of equality to fruition.

To be successful, any social policy—even ones enjoying overwhelming public support like Title IX—must work through all three branches of government. The history of one struggle—equal opportunity in athletics—and how it has worked its way through all three branches of government, demonstrates how government actions can create and shape a policy's evolution. The struggle's accomplishments include the passage of the Title IX statute, writing and adopting viable administrative regulations and interpretations, bringing and defending court cases that would control future interpretations of the law, and attaining additional legislative support when faced with judicial set backs or school inertia.

Yet the articles and materials throughout this book demonstrate that true social change does not come without its set backs. Title IX's set backs have been various. One early set back is that its regulations and interpretations made compliance with the law necessarily complex. Rather than simply requiring equal expenditures for men's and women's athletics, the Javits Amendment requires a far more nuanced analysis—whether a school is providing equal treatment as a whole for each gender within the institution. A second set back was the loss of the AIAW, a powerful female voice within the athletic department that specifically championed female athletes. Importantly, two presidential administrations have been hostile to the enforcement of Title IX, and have used their offices to try to weaken it. Though progress toward gender equity has been slowed at points, it has not been thwarted or fully reversed because supporters of Title IX have been sufficiently cohesive and energetic to fend off its detractors. Title IX advocates have not retreated after numerous defeats and repeated attempts to vitiate the law.

The materials presented in this book show that the fight to achieve gender equity will continue to be a strenuous one. The story is unlikely to end soon. It will play out within our legislatures, our courts, our presidential administrations, and in our public discourse. But despite the Sisyphean challenge, the nobility in Title IX's purpose continues to motivate women and men alike to stay the course.

United States Court of Appeals, District of Columbia Circuit

NATIONAL WRESTLING COACHES ASSOCIATION, et al., Appellants,

v.

DEPARTMENT OF EDUCATION, Appellee*

Decided May 14, 2004

Harry EDWARDS, Circuit Judge:

Title IX of the Education Amendments of 1972 prohibits discrimination on the basis of sex in federally funded educational programs and activities. That prohibition applies to intercollegiate athletics pursuant to regulations promulgated by the Secretary of Health, Education, and Welfare in 1975. Appellee Department of Education ("Department") is charged with enforcing these provisions. The Department assesses universities' compliance with Title IX and the implementing regulations according to various enforcement policies, including a three-part test first issued in 1979 and clarified in 1996.

Appellants are several membership organizations that represent the interests of collegiate men's wrestling coaches, athletes, and alumni who claim to have been injured by the elimination of men's varsity wrestling programs at certain universities. In this action for declaratory and injunctive relief, appellants challenge only the three-part test enunciated in the 1979 Policy Interpretation and the 1996 Clarification on the grounds that they violate the Constitution, Title IX, the 1975 regulations, and the Administrative Procedure Act ("APA"). Appellants do not challenge the 1975 regulations or any other regulations promulgated pursuant to Title IX. The District Court granted the Department's motion to dismiss for lack of subject matter jurisdiction, on the grounds that appellants lack standing under Article III of the Constitution.

We affirm the decision of the District Court in all respects. Appellants' alleged injury results from the independent decisions of federally funded educational

*Nat'l Wrestling Coaches Assoc. v. Dept. of Educ., 366 F.3d 930 (D.C. Cir. 2004).

institutions that choose to eliminate or reduce the size of men's wrestling teams in order to comply with Title IX. Assuming that this allegation satisfies [the Constitution's] Article III's injury-in-fact requirement, we hold that appellants nevertheless lack standing because they have failed to demonstrate how a favorable judicial decision on the merits of their claims will redress this injury. The Supreme Court has made it clear that "when the plaintiff is not himself the object of the government action or inaction he challenges, standing is not precluded, but it is ordinarily 'substantially more difficult' to establish."

In this case, appellants offer nothing but speculation to substantiate their assertion that a favorable judicial decision would result in schools altering their independent choices regarding the restoration or preservation of men's wrestling programs. Appellants do not contest the constitutionality of Title IX, nor do they challenge the 1975 regulations. Therefore, that legal regime, which requires schools to take gender-equity concerns into account when structuring their athletic programs, would remain in place even if the disputed 1996 Clarification and the 1979 Policy Interpretation were revoked. And under that legal regime, schools would still have the discretion to eliminate men's wrestling programs, as necessary, to comply with the gender-equity mandate of Title IX. A judicial decision striking down the 1996 Clarification and the 1979 Policy Interpretation would not afford appellants redress sufficient to support standing.

I. Background

Enacted in response to evidence of "massive, persistent patterns of discrimination against women in the academic world," 118 CONG. REC. 5,804 (1972) (statement of Sen. Bayh), Title IX of the Education Amendments of 1972 prohibits discrimination on the basis of sex in federally funded educational programs and activities. Each federal agency with authority to extend federal financial assistance to an educational program or activity is authorized and directed to ensure the recipient's compliance with Title IX's antidiscrimination mandate through the promulgation of regulations. Institutions that fail to comply with Title IX or these regulations face termination of federal funding, although an implementing agency must first attempt to secure voluntary compliance before imposing this ultimate sanction. Title IX does not require recipients of federal funding to grant preferential treatment to members of one sex to remedy any disproportion that may exist in the distribution of resources or benefits between sexes, relative to the gender composition of the relevant community. However, the statute permits the consideration of such an imbalance in enforcement proceedings. ("[T]his subsection shall not be construed to prevent the consideration . . . of statistical evidence tending to show that such an imbalance exists with respect to the participation in, or receipt of the benefits of, any such program or activity by the members of one sex.")

In 1974, Congress directed the Secretary of Health, Education, and Welfare ("HEW"), the Department's predecessor agency, to promulgate regulations implementing Title IX in the area of intercollegiate athletics. As issued in 1975, these regulations prohibit sex-based discrimination in any interscholastic, intercollegiate, club, or intramural athletic program. [See the 1975 Regulations.] To that end, the regulations require that recipients of federal funding provide "equal athletic opportunity for members of both sexes." The Department determines whether an institution provides equal athletic opportunities to both sexes by examining, *inter alia*, "[w]hether the selection of sports and levels of competition effectively accommodate the interests and abilities of members of both sexes." These regulations were recodified without substantial change in 1980, after HEW's responsibility for implementing Title IX was transferred to the newly organized Department of Education.

The dispute in this case concerns a policy interpretation adopted by HEW in 1979 and clarified by the Department in 1996, which provides further guidance as to how the Department assesses compliance with Title IX and the 1975 Regulations. [See the 1979 Policy Interpretation.] The Policy Interpretation explains that an institution's compliance with the "interests and abilities" requirement of subsection (c)(1) of the 1975 Regulations will be assessed in part pursuant to a three-part test that asks: [the court then reviews the Three-Part Test].

In 1996, after notice and a period for comment, the Department issued a Clarification to illuminate the Three-Part Test. The Department's Office for Civil Rights ("OCR") then sent a "Dear Colleague" letter to interested parties explaining that the 1996 Clarification confirmed that institutions may comply with the Three-Part Test by meeting any one of the three prongs, and that the Three-Part Test is only one of many factors the Department examines to assess an institution's overall compliance with Title IX and the 1975 Regulations. *See Clarification of Intercollegiate Athletics Policy Guidance: The Three-Part Test* (Jan. 16, 1996), *transmitted by* Letter from Norma V. Cantú, Assistant Secretary for Civil Rights, Department of Education (Jan. 16, 1996) ("1996 Clarification"). In response to inquiries regarding schools' elimination or capping of men's sports teams as a method of compliance, the letter stated:

> The rules here are straightforward. An institution can choose to eliminate or cap teams as a way of complying with part one of the three-part test. However, nothing in the Clarification requires that an institution cap or eliminate participation opportunities for men. . . . Ultimately, Title IX provides institutions with flexibility and choice regarding how they will provide nondiscriminatory participation opportunities.

Appellants, the National Wrestling Coaches Association ("NWCA"), the Committee to Save Bucknell Wrestling, the Marquette Wrestling Club, the Yale Wrestling Association, and the College Sports Council, are membership organizations representing the interests of collegiate men's wrestling coaches, athletes, and alumni. They assert injuries arising from decisions by educational institutions to eliminate or reduce the size of men's wrestling programs to comply with the Department's interpretive rules implementing Title IX, specifically the Three-Part Test.

Appellants do not challenge Title IX itself or the 1975 Regulations. As they emphasized throughout their pleadings before the District Court and in their briefs and oral argument before this court, appellants' central premise is that the enforcement policy embodied in the 1979 Policy Interpretation and the 1996 Clarification—i.e., the Three-Part Test—violates the equal protection component of the Due Process Clause of the Fifth Amendment and exceeds the Department's statutory authority by requiring the very same intentional discrimination that Title IX prohibits. Alternatively, appellants claim that the Department's policies amount to an abdication of its duty to enforce Title IX. Appellants further argue that these policy statements violate the 1975 Regulations by replacing that regime of "equal opportunity based on interest," a standard appellants embrace, with a regime of "equal participation based on enrollment," a standard appellants denounce as an impermissible preference in favor of women.

II. Analysis

A. Standing

Appellants' attacks in this lawsuit are aimed solely at the Department's 1979 Policy Interpretation and the 1996 Clarification. They do not challenge Title IX or the 1975 Regulations. Indeed, a central theory of their argument on the merits is that the Department's 1979 and 1996 actions are unlawful, in part, because they violate the statute and the 1975 Regulations. With this context in mind, it is clear that appellants have no standing to pursue this challenge, because they have not demonstrated that their alleged injuries will be redressed by the requested relief. The direct causes of appellants' asserted injuries—loss of collegiate-level wrestling opportunities for male student-athletes—are the independent decisions of educational institutions that choose to eliminate or reduce the size of men's wrestling teams. Appellants offer nothing but speculation to substantiate their claim that a favorable decision from this court will redress their injuries by altering these schools' independent decisions. Absent a showing of redressability, appellants have no standing to challenge the Department's enforcement policies, and we have no jurisdiction to consider their claims.

To satisfy the requirements of Article III standing in a case challenging government action, a party must allege an injury in fact that is fairly traceable to the challenged government action, and "it must be 'likely,' as opposed to merely 'speculative,' that the injury will be 'redressed by a favorable decision.'" Where, as here, the plaintiff is an association seeking to sue on behalf of its members, that plaintiff must demonstrate that (1) at least one of its members would have standing to sue in his own right, (2) the interests the association seeks to protect are germane to its purpose, and (3) neither the claim asserted nor the relief requested requires that an individual member of the association participate in the lawsuit. Accordingly, appellants must establish that at least one of their members has suffered a cognizable injury that is fairly traceable to the Department's Three-Part Test and likely to be redressed by a judicial decision declaring the Three-Part Test to be unlawful and enjoining its use.

Appellants' principal theory of injury is that the Department's interpretive rules harm their member coaches, athletes, and alumni by causing educational institutions to eliminate or reduce the size of men's wrestling teams. Under appellants' view, schools comply with the Three-Part Test not by offering increased athletic opportunities to female students, but by reducing the opportunities available to male students. In support of this theory, appellants point to recent actions by Bucknell, Marquette, and Yale Universities either eliminating their men's wrestling teams or demoting them to nonvarsity status. Appellants contend that these schools took these adverse actions in order to satisfy the Three-Part Test, which permits a finding that a school is in compliance with Title IX if, among other things, it offers athletic opportunities to members of both sexes in numbers that are substantially proportionate to the gender composition of the student body as a whole. For example, appellants assert that a press release accompanying Bucknell University's announcement in May 2001 that it would discontinue its intercollegiate wrestling program "cite[d] Title IX's proportionality requirements as Bucknell's reason for eliminating the wrestling team." Similarly, appellants allege that after Marquette University announced the disbanding of its wrestling program in 2001, the Marquette athletic director made a statement at a dinner party "indicat [ing] that Marquette might bring back its wrestling program if the legal requirements changed." Finally, appellants allege that when Yale University demoted its intercollegiate varsity wrestling team to club status in 1991 for budgetary reasons, it refused offers of private funding, and, "[o]n information and belief, Yale declined to accept the endowment because of Title IX."

[W]e find that appellants' factual allegations are insufficient to establish standing, because appellants have not shown how a favorable decision vacating the 1979 Policy Interpretation and the 1996 Clarification would redress their injuries.

When a plaintiff's asserted injury arises from the Government's regulation of a third party that is not before the court, it becomes "substantially more difficult" to establish standing. Because the necessary elements of causation and redressability in such a case hinge on the independent choices of the regulated third party, "it becomes the burden of the plaintiff to adduce facts showing that those choices have been or will be made in such manner as to produce causation and permit redressability of injury." In other words, mere "unadorned speculation" as to the existence of a relationship between the challenged government action and the third-party conduct "will not suffice to invoke the federal judicial power."

In this case, appellants offer nothing to substantiate their assertion that a decision from the court vacating the 1979 Policy Interpretation and the 1996 Clarification will redress their injuries by altering schools' independent decisions whether to eliminate or retain their men's wrestling programs. As the Department emphasized when issuing its 1996 Clarification, nothing in the Three-Part Test requires schools to eliminate or cap men's wrestling or any other athletic program. *This Clarification is consistent with the fact that Bucknell and Marquette maintained their men's wrestling programs for decades after the adoption of the Three-Part Test.* [emphasis in original]

Appellants do not suggest that any particular school necessarily would forego elimination of a wrestling team or reinstate a previously disbanded program in the absence of these interpretive rules, except to say that Marquette University "might bring back its wrestling program if the legal requirements changed." Indeed, appellants appear to understand that judicial relief in this case would not afford the remedy that they seek. At oral argument, counsel for appellants candidly said that, if his clients prevail, appellants think they may have "better odds" of retaining their desired wrestling programs. Counsel's candor was admirable, but a quest for ill-defined "better odds" is not close to what is required to satisfy the redressability prong of Article III.

On the record at hand, appellants fall far short of establishing the requisite likelihood that the educational institutions whose choices lie at the root of appellants' alleged injuries will behave any differently with respect to men's wrestling if appellants prevailed on the merits and secured their requested relief. Indeed, in the posture of this case, it is difficult to imagine how appellants could make such a showing. Even if appellants prevailed on the merits in their challenge to the Three-Part Test, Title IX and the 1975 Regulations would still be in place. Federally funded schools would still be required to provide athletic opportunities in a manner that equally accommodated both genders. As a consequence, nothing but speculation suggests that schools would act any differently than they do with the Three-Part Test in place. Schools would remain free to eliminate or cap men's wrestling teams and may in some circumstances feel compelled to do so to comply with the statute and the 1975 Regulations. This is particularly so since Title IX itself permits evidence of disproportion in the distribution of benefits between sexes to be considered in enforcement proceedings against recipients of federal funding. Moreover, other reasons unrelated to the challenged legal requirements may continue to motivate schools to take such actions. *See* Bucknell Univ. News Release (May 2, 2001), *reprinted in* J.A. 573 (explaining that Bucknell's gender equity plan was not only "a matter of federal law," but also "morally . . . the right thing to do").

Appellants' request for a judicial order compelling the Department to undertake notice-and-comment rulemaking to amend its enforcement policies does not alter this analysis. The challenged policies—the 1979 Policy Interpretation and the 1996 Clarification—are interpretive guidelines that the Department was not obligated to issue in the first place. Appellants point to no basis for the notion that the Department would be required to replace the challenged policies with anything new were the court to invalidate the existing 1979 Policy Interpretation and the 1996 Clarification. And, in any event, appellants do not even challenge the underlying 1975 Regulations, which, as we have noted, clearly permit universities to follow some of the practices that appellants oppose. Accordingly, appellants have failed to establish that it is likely that a favorable decision from the court on the merits of their claims would provide any redress for their alleged injuries.

We recognize that courts occasionally find the elements of standing to be satisfied in cases challenging government action on the basis of third-party conduct. . . . These cases would only support appellants' assertion of standing if appellants took the position that gender-conscious elimination of men's sports teams would be illegal in the absence of the challenged enforcement policies. Appellants make no such claim. As we have emphasized, appellants do not challenge Title IX or the 1975 Regulations; indeed, they embrace those regulations, which they characterize as properly requiring schools to provide "equal opportunity based on interest." Necessarily, then, they must concede that schools *may* make gender-conscious decisions in order to remedy discrimination and equally accommodate both sexes, in compliance with the statute and regulations. This includes considering "statistical evidence tending to show that . . . an imbalance exists [between men and women] with respect to the participation in" intercollegiate-athletic programs in a school. Therefore, even if the Three-Part Test were vacated, schools would remain free to take gender into account when designing and funding their athletic programs. The "causation by authorization" theory of this first category of cases thus lends no support to appellants' claim of standing.

Second, some cases have held that plaintiffs have standing to challenge government action on the basis of injuries caused by regulated third parties where the record presented substantial evidence of a causal relationship between the government policy and the third-party conduct, leaving little doubt as to causation and the likelihood of redress.

Appellants' reliance in this case on the *possibility* that their members may have "better odds" of retaining their desired wrestling programs plainly falls far short of the mark set by . . . other such cases. While our discussion thus far has emphasized the lack of redressability in appellants' complaint, appellants' submissions similarly fail to demonstrate that causation is so clear that redressability inexorably follows. For example, appellants' amended complaint cited a press release in which Bucknell University announced the elimination of its men's wrestling team—some 22 years after the adoption of the Three-Part Test—and cited gender proportionality as one reason for its decision. That same press release, however, also cites the absence of league sponsorship for wrestling, budgetary concerns, and the need to balance the athletic program with other University priorities as other factors contributing to the decision.

Appellants also rely on a report issued by the General Accounting Office ("GAO") in March 2001 discussing the experiences of four-year colleges in adding and discontinuing men's and women's athletic teams between 1981 and 1999. This report does not advance appellants' case. First, although the GAO found evidence that numerous men's athletic teams were eliminated over the period covered in the study—519 teams discontinued between the 1981–1982 and 1998–1999 academic years, to be precise—the GAO also found that even more new men's teams were created in that same time frame (555 men's teams between the 1981–1982 and 1998–1999 years). What is more telling, however, is that the GAO's discussion of the role that gender-equity concerns played in schools' decisions to add or eliminate teams, upon which appellants rely heavily, is utterly inconclusive as to whether the Three-Part Test caused the elimination of any men's athletic teams. The GAO notes that a majority of surveyed schools cited "gender-equity considerations" as an influential factor in their decisions to discontinue men's teams. The report does not define "gender-equity concerns." We do not know, on the basis of this report, whether these concerns are self imposed or legally required. To the extent they reflect legal requirements, we do not know whether they refer to the Three-Part Test or to Title IX and the 1975 Regulations, which appellants do not challenge. Finally, the GAO also found that several other factors also contributed to schools' decisions as much or more than "gender-equity considerations," including levels of student interest and limits on funding and other resources. *See id.*

In sum, appellants' allegations of causation are far from persuasive. If causation were the only issue in this case, appellants' proffers might be adequate to survive a motion to dismiss. The problem here is that appellants have failed completely to satisfy the redressability prong of Article III standing, for there is nothing to support appellants' claim that a favorable ruling would alter the schools' conduct. To survive a motion to dismiss, a plaintiff "must allege facts from which it reasonably could be inferred that, absent the [challenged policy], there is a substantial probability that . . . if the court affords the relief requested, the asserted [injury] will be removed." Appellants' attempts to show redress-ability are based on nothing but "unadorned speculation."

B. Adequate Remedy

In the alternative, even if appellants had standing to pursue these claims, the availability of a private cause of action directly against universities that discriminate in violation of Title IX constitutes an adequate remedy that bars appellants' case. In *Cannon v. Univ. of Chicago*, 441 U.S. 677, 99 S. Ct. 1946, 60 L.Ed.2d 560 (1979), the Supreme Court held that plaintiffs have a private cause of action for sex discrimination under Title IX against universities.

III. Conclusion

We affirm on the merits the District Court's rejection of appellants' claim that the Department unlawfully denied their petition to amend or repeal the Three-Part Test. As to their remaining claims, we hold that appellants lack standing under Article III.

[Stephen F. Williams, Senior Circuit Judge dissent omitted.]

Tilting the Playing Field:
Schools, Sports, Sex and Title IX*

Jessica Gavora

Mike Scott came to Providence College in Rhode Island for one reason: to play baseball. His dad had played college ball, spent some time in the minors, and was now a high school baseball coach. The younger Scott had been playing baseball since he was old enough to hold a bat. Now he had his eye on a chance at the big time: to play in the majors.

Providence, Mike thought, was the place to begin his journey. Since joining the program as an assistant coach in 1991, head coach Charlie Hickey had worked to build the eighty-year-old Friars program into a Northeast powerhouse. In the 1990s, the team began to attract NCAA tournament bids and recorded just one losing season. And although it was college baseball in New England, where players roughed out the cold spring seasons for the sheer love of the game, Providence began to attract high-quality recruits like Mike Scott. "We were beginning to threaten Northeast powerhouses like Seton Hall and St. John's," says Hickey. "We had what I think what most people in New England consider one of the elite programs."

Recruited as a standout high-school hitter, Scott briefly considered the baseball program at the University of New Hampshire. But when UNH announced that it was cutting baseball in order to comply with Title IX, he turned to Providence College. And although Coach Hickey couldn't offer him a scholarship, only a spot on the team and a chance to play, that was enough. Scott entered Providence in 1997, was injured, and had to sit out his freshman season. Then, one crisp fall day in October 1998, just two weeks into the preseason practice schedule of Scott's sophomore year, Coach Hickey was summoned from the

*New York: Encounter Books (2002), 43–69, excerpt.

practice field into Providence athletic director John Marinatto's office. A few minutes later, he returned to the practice diamond to present Scott and his teammates with shocking news: The 1998–1999 baseball season would be the Friars' last.

The reason was Title IX. Because Providence—like virtually every college and university—receives some federal money in some form, the school was legally bound to comply with the provisions of the law.

But Scott and his teammates were confused: What women had faced discrimination at Providence? The Catholic university had a strong program of athletics for females. Of the twenty varsity programs carried by the college, half were for women, including the latest hot women's intercollegiate sport, ice hockey. No female athlete had filed a complaint of discrimination at Providence, and no investigation had found a pattern of discrimination that somehow had escaped complaint. What, Scott and his teammates wondered, was wrong at Providence College?

The answer could be found in a set of statistics that Marinatto had compiled that fall and submitted to the Department of Education in Washington, D.C. The Equity in Athletics Disclosure Act (EADA) requires that all colleges and universities submit a mind-boggling array of detailed information on their sports programs, broken down by sex. Schools report the number of athletic participants by sex, the assignment of head coaches by sex, operating expenses by sex, recruitment expenses by sex, coaches' salaries by sex, and on and on. In addition, the EADA demands one statistic that has nothing to do with athletics: Schools must compile and submit the number of full-time undergraduates, by sex.

Feminist women's groups like the American Association of University Women pushed hard for passage of the EADA—with data on the gender balance of the student body included—in order to expedite the process of bringing lawsuits against schools under Title IX. By framing the issue in terms of "equity" they were able to convince Congress to impose yet another bookkeeping burden on colleges and universities, and create a taxpayer-funded database with which to pursue Title IX "proportionality." Previously, finding the data needed to bring a lawsuit under Title IX necessitated a little digging; but the EADA created a ready-made client shopping list for trial lawyers. One glance at a school's EADA submission shows a would-be plaintiff's attorney whether or not a school is vulnerable to a Title IX lawsuit.

When Providence College filled out its EADA form in Fall 1998, the findings set off alarm bells in the administration. Like the majority of colleges and universities today, Providence's student body was majority female and growing more so, but its athletic program had failed to keep pace. Drawn by the security of Providence's Catholic tradition, women comprised a whopping 59 percent of all students in Fall 1998. Female student-athletes, however, were only

48 percent of all varsity athletes. This was well above the national average of 40 percent female-athletic participation, but not enough to pass the Title IX "proportionality" test. Adding enough women's teams to meet proportionality, Providence's Gender Equity Compliance Committee calculated, would cost $3 million, a prohibitive expense for the school. Providence had "too many" male athletes—11 percent too many, to be exact. Something had to give.

Seven years earlier, Providence's crosstown rival, Brown University, was sued by a group of female athletes when it attempted to de-fund two men's and two women's varsity teams in a cost-saving effort. The female athletes at Brown argued that cutting women's teams was illegal under Title IX because the university had not yet achieved proportionality—despite offering more teams for women than any other school in the country except Harvard. Brown decided to fight the lawsuit, arguing that Title IX required it to provide women equal opportunity to participate in athletics, not guarantee that they actually participate at the same rate as men. A series of adverse rulings led Brown all the way to the Supreme Court, which declined to hear the case. The result was that the rulings of the lower courts stood: Title IX was interpreted to mean that the university did, in fact, have an obligation to see that women participated in sports as enthusiastically as men. The case was a landmark in the institutionalization of quotas under Title IX. Colleges and universities across the country began to cut men's teams to comply with what the Court had decreed was the correct interpretation of the law.

Mindful of Brown's experience, Providence College did what all colleges and universities are today increasingly forced to do: Consult its lawyers. Their advice was direct: The only way for Providence to insulate itself from a Title IX lawsuit or federal investigation was somehow to add enough female athletes, or subtract enough male athletes, to close the gap. So instead of imposing double-digit tuition increases to raise the funds for new women's teams, Providence chose to boost the number of its women athletes artificially by subtracting from the men's side of the sports ledger.

"They were looking for three things," says Coach Hickey. "They were looking for which sports had the number of participants to cut to bring them closer to proportionality, which sports had the scholarships they could transfer to the women's side, and which sports had the operating budget they could save money on."

Providence baseball had it all: twenty-eight bodies on the playing field, seven scholarships split among them, and $380,000 in operating expenses. Coach Hickey implored the Providence administration to save baseball by allowing the program to raise the necessary funds itself. He was informed that if such a dispensation were granted, Providence baseball would also have to raise enough funds to cover the creation of one or more women's teams necessary to "compensate" for retaining twenty-eight male athletes. "We were originally told, go ahead and raise the $380,000, but on top of that you have to raise 59 percent more," says Hickey. "We're talking about having to come up with $750,000 every year, just to guarantee to play." In the end, the only feasible solution was to cut, not add. By eliminating baseball, men's golf, and men's tennis, and capping the number of men who competed on the remaining eight men's programs, Providence achieved "proportionality." Without the addition of a single women's athletic opportunity, the percentage of female athletes rose from 47 percent to 57 percent.

Suddenly, a season that had begun so hopefully for Mike Scott and Charlie Hickey took on even more importance. Determined to go out with a bang, not a whimper, Scott and his teammates redoubled their efforts on the playing field. Second baseman Paul Costello recalled a line from *Major League,* a movie about a faltering group of professional baseball players: "There's only one thing left to do: Win the whole #$%&* thing!" The team adopted it as their unofficial motto. "We wanted to make a statement," says Scott, "and that was perfect."

And Providence baseball did indeed go on to win the whole thing. The 1998–1999 season was the most successful in the school's history. Scott's team won forty-three games in the regular season and then four more to capture the Big East championship. With Mike Scott setting the pace, they led the nation in hits and were ranked twenty-first in the country. At the NCAA regional championship tournament in Tallahassee, the Friars took on Florida State, ranked second nationally, to conclude their season. "We played like there was no tomorrow because there literally was no tomorrow," says Hickey. But in the end, it didn't matter. Reverend Philip A. Smith, president of Providence College, skipped the last home game. The Friars lost to Florida State, and Scott and his teammates decided not to turn in their uniforms.

Feminists call the struggle for proportionality under Title IX the pursuit of "gender equity." The Women's Sports Foundation (WSF) is perhaps the strongest advocate of Title IX and "gender equity" in sports, having as its mission to "increase and enhance sports and fitness opportunities for all girls and women."

Founded by tennis player Billie Jean King in 1974 in the afterglow of her victory over Bobby Riggs in the "Battle of the Sexes," the WSF is the most powerful advocacy group for female athletes in the country. Like most women's groups, it has benefited from friendly press coverage. But unlike most women's groups, the WSF has made genuine heroes its public face: women like Mia Hamm, Julie Foudy, and Michelle Akers of the championship U.S. Women's World Cup soccer team; Kym Hampton and Rebecca Lobo of the Women's National Basketball Association; two-time heptathlon winner Jackie Joyner-Kersee; sprinter Gail

Devers; swimmer Summer Sanders; and Olympic-gold-medal-winning gymnast Dominique Moceanu. This strategy of capitalizing on the popularity of female athletes has made the WSF a magnet for corporate giving. General Motors and Merrill Lynch are generous supporters. Representatives of Reebok, Mervyn's of California, and the Sporting Goods Manufacturers Association sit on its board of trustees. Their support allows the WSF to rake in additional contributions at a glittering gala each year in New York City and dole out more than $1 million a year in grants and scholarships to female athletes.

But behind the appealing image of strong female athleticism that is the group's public face, the Women's Sports Foundation pursues a relentlessly political agenda: to turn the grant of opportunity for women guaranteed under Title IX into a grant of preference. Under the leadership of its street-fighting executive director, Donna Lopiano, a former All-American softball player and the former women's athletic director at the University of Texas, the WSF has done more than any other group to convince colleges and universities that compliance with Title IX means manipulating the numbers of male and female athletes.

Lopiano, who calls those who disagree with her version of equity "dinosaurs," came to the WSF in 1992 fresh from Austin, where she was instrumental in fomenting a landmark Title IX lawsuit against her own university for its failure to achieve proportionality. Lopiano was the first to admit that [the University of] Texas wasn't guilty of any bias against women, only of failing to give them the preferences she believes they deserve. "Texas did a better job with women's athletics than anybody in the country," she said after the lawsuit had been filed. "Did they make their best effort? Yes. Did they comply with federal law? No."[1]

The Texas case was a landmark because, up to that point, court victories won by female athletes to create Title IX quotas had been limited to mandating the reinstatement of teams that had been cut. The Lopiano-inspired Texas case, in contrast, demanded that women's teams be *added* to fill the gender quota. Thanks to revenues brought in by Longhorn football, Texas had a bigger women's athletic budget than any other two schools in its conference combined. Still, female athletic participation—the responsibility of the recently departed Lopiano—was stuck at around 23 percent in the early 1990s. So even though the administration was already in the process of adding two women's sports, it settled before the case got to court, agreeing to reach proportionality by the 1995–1996 academic year. Additional women's teams were added, while non-scholarship male athletes—who, by outnumbering female nonscholarship athletes 81 to 1, accounted for much of Texas's "Title IX gap"—were cut.

[1] Jonathan Feigen, "Texas Lawsuit May Change Face of College Athletics across U.S.," *Houston Chronicle*, June 27, 1993, 1.

Lopiano brought the same passion for gender engineering to the Women's Sports Foundation. Her strategy, she told reporters in 1992, was to "break the bank," forcing schools to spend so much to meet the gender quota that what she regarded as the corrupt, male-dominated edifice of collegiate sports would fall entirely and be replaced by "gender equity." And if schools wouldn't spend on athletics, Lopiano made sure they spent on litigation. Moreover, according to former OCR investigator Lamar Daniel, she is credited with "taking over" the NCAA Gender Equity Task Force that declared proportionality the "ultimate goal" of member institutions in 1993—a requirement that has led to regular "gender-equity" certification of schools by the NCAA.

In addition, under Lopiano the WSF has worked tirelessly to cultivate future litigants and future complainants in Title IX cases. It maintains an "Equity Hotline" complete with a staff ready to help with attorney referrals, and "how-to" literature and expert assistance on everything from the rights of local girls' softball leagues to the arcana of federal regulations. There is an online database that ranks schools according to their commitment to gender equity and allows users to automatically share that ranking with local media and state and federal politicians. To keep Congress and the media aware of its efforts, the WSF sponsors National Girls and Women in Sports Day. Events are staged across the country and female athletes flood their congressperson's and senator's offices to remind them of the importance of gender equity in athletics.

But the Women's Sports Foundation, however formidable, is only one part of a coalition of liberal women's groups, trial lawyers, and "gender-equity" advocates and consultants for whom Title IX is the sine qua non of existence. The American Association of University Women (AAUW) focuses on Title IX issues outside sports. And the National Women's Law Center (NWLC), another major player in the battle for gender equity, provides critical legal support.

Any attempt to change Title IX enforcement, even in a small way, will meet with great resistance from these groups. "The law means everything," says Donna de Varona, former Olympic swimming champ and WSF founding member. "Sports is the most visible affirmation of what Title IX did. But if you look behind it—if you look at the success of women in business, the success of women as lawyers, as leaders and, hopefully, as politicians—our very lifeblood depends on Title IX."

Nationwide, 41 percent of college athletes are women and 56 percent of undergraduates are women. For the eager gender feminist, these statistics mean that for the entire United States to become "proportional" under Title IX—that is, for the share of female athletes to mirror the 56 percent female share of all students—the number of female athletes would need to increase by 15 percent of all athletes, or just over 59,000. The alternative, in the binary world of Title IX, is that the number of male athletes must *decrease* by over 59,000.

What would that mean in real terms?

- eliminating every football program in the country, or;
- eliminating almost ten times the number of young men who wrestle, or;
- cutting more than the total number of men who play basketball, wrestle, run track, play tennis, swim, do gymnastics, and play water polo combined.

Cuts to men's teams under Title IX proportionality are slowly moving high school and college athletics toward this feminist utopia. A look at high-school athletics shows that, in contrast to the almost-nine-fold increase in girls, the number of boys who play sports today is just about the same as it was in 1971, having grown by less than 200,000, from 3,666,917 to 3,832,352. After decreasing significantly upon passage of Title IX, the number of boys who play sports leveled off in the 1980s and began to climb back up in the mid-1990s.

On the intercollegiate level, where Title IX enforcement has been focused, particularly in the 1990s, the record is much darker. Although about only one in sixteen high school athletes will go on to play varsity sports in college, it would be expected that male intercollegiate-athletic participation would generally rise when high-school participation rises, all other things being equal. Since Title IX was enacted, however, at a time when high-school participation has been rising, men's involvement in intercollegiate athletics has actually dropped from 248,000 or 10.4 percent of total male undergraduates, to 234, 000 or 9.5 percent of all college men.

Using data from a 1997 NCAA Gender Equity report, Leo Kocher found that more than 200 men's teams and over 20,000 male athletes disappeared from the ranks of the NCAA between 1992 and 1997. During the same period, only 5,800 women's athletic spots were added. To use the numbers-obsessed language of the Title IX feminists, this translates into 3.4 men's opportunities lost for every 1 opportunity gained for women.

More recent data released by the NCAA indicate that men's opportunities have actually risen in recent years. But the problem with this data is that when new schools become members of the NCAA by leaving other national collegiate associations like the National Small College Athletic Association (NSCAA), they bring already-existing teams with them, thus artificially inflating the "growth" of men's opportunities.

Last year, for instance, the NCAA claimed that the number of men's basketball teams in the NCAA had increased by forty-four over the previous two years. "I asked for a list of the new basketball teams and every one of those teams had been in existence for a decade or more," says Kocher. "So these were not newly created NCAA athletic opportunities for men. They were already existing and just being counted as new. That's very, very discouraging when the NCAA resorts to bogus statistics because they're the ones who keep the records."

To penetrate the tricky arithmetic of the NCAA, House Speaker Dennis Hastert, a former wrestling coach, asked the nonpartisan government General Accounting Office to look at changes in athletic opportunities for men and women. The GAO investigated the sports programs of 725 colleges and universities and found that from 1985–1986 to 1996–1997, 21,000 men's spots disappeared, a drop of 12 percent. Men's athletic scholarship aid declined by 10 percent. For their part, women gained 14,500 spots, a jump of 16 percent driven by a 66-percent increase in scholarships at NCAA Division I schools and a 73-percent increase at Division II colleges and universities.

The Independent Women's Forum, which has been documenting Title IX quotas in sports since 1997, keeps a running list of discontinued men's sports programs. In 1999, the total since 1992 stood at 359, including 43 wrestling teams, 53 golf programs, 16 baseball teams, 23 swimming programs, and 39 tennis squads.

With the exception of football and basketball, both high-profile, revenue-generating sports, no men's program is exempted, no matter how successful or established. In 1993, UCLA, citing Title IX pressure, dropped its men's swimming and diving teams, which had produced 22 Olympic medalists, including 16 golds. Boston University ended a hundred-year-old tradition of football in 1997. Brigham Young University eliminated its top-10-ranked men's gymnastics team and its top-25-ranked wrestling team.

In Spring 2000, the University of Miami decided to sacrifice its men's swimming program—which had sent competitors to every Olympic Games since 1972 (including gold-medal winner Greg Louganis)—in order to attain Title IX proportionality. Like most colleges and universities, Miami had a growing female majority on campus that had produced a 10-percent difference between the share of students who were female and the share of athletes who were female. Administrators had elected to add, and students had agreed to fund, three new women's sports in the previous five years. But even that wasn't enough to make the numbers come out right.

"This is the most difficult decision that the athletic department has made in a very long time," said Miami athletic director Paul Dee. "These fine young men are being displaced for reasons over which they have no control and which they did not cause. It is extremely regrettable that this is the necessary solution to the issues we face."

Groups like the Women's Sports Foundation and education bureaucrats maintain consistently and piously that cuts to men's programs are not the result of Title IX. The real culprits, they say, are stingy university administrators and gender-biased athletic directors. If universities would just dust off their checkbooks and fund more programs for women, they insist, they wouldn't have a problem under the law. Instead, feminists say, chauvinist administrators sacrifice nonrevenue men's teams because they refuse to spend more on women's sports, or because they refuse to cut from bloated football and men's basketball budgets.

We will turn later to the topic of football, the Title IX feminists' favorite whipping boy and ultimate target. For now, it is worth taking a hard look at the claim that men's programs are cut strictly for financial reasons.

It is true that colleges and universities are endlessly complicated financial, managerial, legal, and academic enterprises. The pressure to raise money is relentless, and even in the best fundraising environment with the most generous alumni, resources are finite. Money devoted to building a new physics lab or hiring a new eighteenth-century French-literature professor is money some other program or department doesn't get.

In the competition for scarce resources, Title IX has added a double burden to athletic departments. A popular misconception of the law is that it requires schools to spend equal amounts on men's and women's sports. In fact, Title IX regulations impose no such requirement. Gender equity advocates originally pushed for equal average-per-capita spending on male and female athletes as one of the standards of compliance, but colleges and universities were successful in having that requirement deleted from the final regulation.

They believed they had won a victory for fairness and institutional autonomy, but what they ended up with has turned out to be worse. By substituting the principle of equal participation for equal spending, Title IX has effectively made quotas the engine that pulls the "gender-equity" train; proportionality in the body count drives de facto proportionality in all aspects of athletics programs. If participation must be proportionate, then the distribution of athletic scholarships must also be proportionate, and so must the provision of equipment, facilities, training, coaching, and the myriad other aspects of an athletic program.

The pressure to meet participation quotas means that even when men's teams offer to become self supporting in order to avoid being cut, universities are forced to turn a deaf ear. When Princeton and the University of Southern California found themselves on the wrong side of the proportionality requirement and moved to cut wrestling and swimming in the mid-1990s, supporters and alumni rallied to raise money to save the programs. Even so, the universities chose to cut them. Why? As Carol Zaleski, president of United States Swimming, the governing body for U.S. Olympic swimming, told a congressional committee, "It's not a question of money. It's a question of numbers."[2]

[2] "Brown's President Asks for a Clear Policy on Title IX," *New York Times*, May 10, 1995, Final Edition, B19.

Often, the number of bodies that universities cut by eliminating men's teams so far outpaces the money they save that it is clear to coaches that they've been the victim of a numbers game, not a budget crunch. After increasing the number of female athletes on campus by 61 percent in just three years, Miami University of Ohio found itself in 1999 with a $1-million deficit in its sports program and a lingering 13-point Title IX gap. That spring, the university's trustees voted to cut men's soccer, tennis, and wrestling—eliminating 30 wrestlers, 25 men's soccer players, and 10 men's tennis players, who shared a total of 8 scholarships among them. The move saved $441,000, less than half of Miami's budget deficit. And it left behind a mountain of bad feeling.

The same year the cuts went into effect, the Miami women's precision skating team traveled to Europe to compete. Twice. "We went to Iowa this year and Florida," Miami wrestling coach Chuck Angello bitterly told the *Cincinnati Enquirer*. "We drove."[3]

Title IX doesn't concern itself with where funding comes from, just how it is spent. So a men's team that is particularly successful at fundraising and attracting alumni support can't spend all of the money it has raised on itself if doing so creates an imbalance between the men's and women's programs.

The Office for Civil Rights, which prides itself on being a "resource" for schools struggling to comply with Title IX, is very clear on this point. At a "gender-equity" conference sponsored by the NCAA in Indianapolis in May 2000, an associate athletic director of a major Midwestern university put this question to an OCR official: A group of baseball alumni at her university was ready to write a $1.5-million check to the baseball team, she said. But the university was afraid to take the money because their softball field was located off campus. What if they take the money, she asked meekly, to build a new baseball stadium and renovate the old stadium for the softball team? Would that be permissible under the law? The OCR official shook her head. Probably not, she said. The men's and women's facilities must be exactly equivalent. And until the university could guarantee that, they couldn't accept the donation.

But the most poignant and persuasive evidence that the force driving Title IX cuts is not finances but males on the playing field is the fact that the first players to be cut are most often the walk-ons.

"Walk-on" is the term used for unrecruited players who nonetheless try out for and make varsity teams. Overwhelmingly they are men. Most often they are benchwarmers, or what the Women's Sports Foundation's Donna Lopiano likes to call "hapless practice dummies." They receive no scholarship aid. They bring their own practice gear and play for love of the game. The movie *Rudy* is based on a real-life walk-on in the Notre Dame football squad.

[3]Paul Daugherty, "Call Me a Swine: Title IX Is Wrong," *Cincinnati Enquirer*, April 16, 1999.

Virtually every men's intercollegiate athletic program in the country disallows walk-ons today under Title IX through what is euphemistically called "roster management." Both the Office for Civil Rights and the NCAA actively encourage roster management. It involves setting upper limits on the participants in men's squads and lower limits on women's squads. That invariably means turning away men who want to play and providing inducements for women, such as additional scholarships and the opportunity to become involved in "emerging sports" like equestrian and synchronized swimming.

In Fall 1996, the University of Northern Colorado cut ten members of its wrestling team to achieve Title IX proportionality—all walk-ons. UNC football coach Joe Glenn was also forced to cut eleven nonscholarship players. The move had nothing to do with saving money, and everything to do with making the numbers line up right. "These were kids paying their own way," Glenn says. "It was the hardest, most irrational thing I've ever had to do in coaching."

One of the ironies of the proliferation of sex quotas in college and university athletic departments is that the NCAA, which began by fighting to exempt athletics from Title IX and later, failing that, to exempt revenue-producing sports like football and men's basketball, has now become a collaborator with the Department of Education in the gender-driven assault on men's athletic programs.

Each year the NCAA hosts seminars for athletic directors and members of university affirmative-action bureaucracies on how to achieve" gender equity" in general and Title IX compliance in particular. One such gender-equity seminar in Indianapolis in May 2000 attracted over three hundred representatives of colleges and universities, women's sports activists, legal experts, and federal officials for two and a half days of discussion of Title IX. Participants listened to presentations on the law's impact on minority women, pleaded with officials for instruction on how to avoid a federal investigation, and garnered "helpful hints" on how to fill out federal forms required to measure gender equity in their sports programs. At no time was a dissenting voice raised about the bureaucratic hassles—or the systematic injustices—that the law created.

Instead, the seminar was a reflection of how deeply embedded the culture of identity politics has become in colleges and universities. Although the subject is outside the scope of Title IX, many of the presentations dealt with the representation of minorities as coaches and college administrators and in leadership positions within the NCAA itself. Also outside the scope of the law, but nonetheless discussed in detail, was the supposed need for more minority women in "nontraditional" sports such as field hockey, lacrosse, water polo, squash, and tennis. These are among the sports most frequently added by institutions attempting to comply with Title IX. They are also the sports in which minority women tend not to participate.

One might assume that an NCAA seminar on Title IX compliance would focus on how to rid athletic programs of discrimination against women. But in fact the greater part of the conference was devoted to advising athletic officials on how to meet the gender quota—or, more accurately, on how to create the appearance of meeting it.

A breakout session entitled "Scholarships, Financial Aid, and Roster Management" turned out to be a how-to session on manipulating the numbers of male and female athletes in order to comply with Title IX. Gender-equity consultant Elaine Dreidame let the cat out of the bag when she informed her audience that although "opportunity" is a word often used in connection with Title IX, "the spirit of the law is concerned with the actual number of student-athletes who are practicing and competing." The name of the game, she counseled, is retaining female student-athletes and deterring males in order to achieve proportionality.

The statistic that federal regulators take seriously when making a threshold determination of proportionality, Dreidame explained, is the number of athletes listed on the squad roster on the first day of official competition. She encouraged coaches and administrators to manipulate their schedules so as to maximize their female body count and minimize their male numbers. Most female athletes, she explained, "don't want to sit on the bench," and their numbers tend to dwindle over the course of the season as nonplaying women drop out. So Dreidame advised administrators to begin women's teams' official play in the fall, when their numbers are highest. That way, if a women's soccer squad began its season with 35 players but lost 7 over the course of the season and made the finals with only 28 players, it would still be counted as having 35 female athletes for Title IX compliance.

Defenders of Title IX quotas like to argue that none of this bloodshed would be necessary if it weren't for one thing: football. This sport is the feminists' ultimate target because of its symbolic association with raw maleness. They know they can't get rid of football, but they can at least hold it responsible for Title IX's impact on other men's sports. Not only does football cost too much, they say, but it is the biggest, most powerful redoubt of white-male hostility to leveling the playing field for women. When men's teams get cut, they say, the real culprit is football. "If you cut a men's team and blame it on women, that's an easier argument than saying we've been indulgent, we're spending too much on football," says Women's Sports Foundation founder Donna de Varona.

Supporters of football argue that the revenue and excitement generated by the sport are the lifelines that keep many women's teams and men's nonrevenue sports alive. On the other side are people like de Varona, joined by some men's minor sports supporters, who say that football is the black hole of intercollegiate athletics: Resources fall into it, never to be seen again. "Football is not the golden goose," says Donna Lopiano, executive director of the Women's Sports Foundation. "It's a fat goose eating food that could nourish more opportunities far women."[4]

Perhaps fittingly, given this animus, the first time that Title IX was mentioned in the same breath as athletics, the subject was football. The late Senator John Tower of Texas tried twice to pass an amendment to the law to exempt "revenue-producing sports" (read: football) from its provisions. Tower, who was a co-sponsor of the original Title IX legislation, worried that the government, "in its laudable zeal to guarantee equal athletic opportunities to women, is defeating its own purpose by promulgating rules which will damage the financial base of intercollegiate athletics."[5]

The Tower amendment was never passed, and football remains the fat man tipping the canoe of Title IX, a unique obstacle to achieving numerical gender balance in intercollegiate athletic programs. Activists such as Lopiano complain about the resources football consumes, but the real problem is the bodies it supports. At the most competitive level of play, the NCAA Division I-A level, squads typically carry more than 100 players and are allowed 85 scholarships. That's over 100 slots on the male side of the proportionality ledger for which there is no female equivalent. In the binary mathematics of Title IX, this means that schools must have four or five additional women's teams just to "make up" for the numbers added to the men's count by football.

Fresno State University, because it has a football team, was unable to comply with a court order mandating that it reach proportionality by 1998—even though it eliminated two other men's teams, added two women's teams, and offered the maximum number of scholarships to its female athletes allowed by NCAA rules. In every sport except basketball, in which men and women received the same number of scholarships, Fresno offered women more scholarship aid. Still, because of the 85 scholarships offered for football, the school couldn't reach the court-ordered quota. In 1998, Fresno appealed to the NCAA to relax its limitation on athletic scholarships in order to attract more women to its programs. The NCAA refused.

Title IX quota enthusiasts have used the fashionable criticism of an "arms race" in collegiate athletic expenditures, led by big-time football, to help make their case for mandated higher expenditures for women. This argument states that the push for competitive advantage in collegiate football (and the television contracts and alumni dollars that flow to winning teams) is fueling a spiral of profligacy on college campuses that is bankrupting athletic departments. In their desperation to produce winning teams, colleges and universities are pouring

[4]Jonathan Feign, "Gender Equity: Football Coaches Circle the Wagons," *Houston Chronicle*, June 28, 1993.

[5]*Congressional Record*, 15 July 1975, 22777–22778.

money into football programs that should go to women's teams. All this spending, so the argument goes, isn't paying off in winning teams and sufficient revenue to cover the high costs of football for most schools. Still, they keep pouring money into the pigskin money pit in a desperate attempt to outbid their rivals.

While it is true that expenditures in intercollegiate athletics are rising, for both men's and women's programs, the gender-equity landscape in collegiate athletic expenditures and revenues is much more complicated than the "blame football first" argument suggests. In fact, the most recent survey of the finances of NCAA member institutions shows a widening gap between profit-making athletic departments and revenue-losing athletic departments—with no correlation to the presence or absence of football.

The study, undertaken by the *Chronicle of Higher Education*, found that 64 percent of schools in Division I-A reported making a profit in their football programs. In their overall athletic budgets, Division I-A schools with football tended to break even, whereas schools without football lost an average of $2.5 million. Smaller Division I schools with football teams, in Division I-AA, reported losses averaging $2.2 million. At a lower competitive level within the NCAA, Division II, colleges and universities with and without football lost money on athletics.[6]

An exhaustive study of the business of intercollegiate sports by the *Philadelphia Inquirer* confirms that programs are sharply divided between the haves and the have-nots. The *Inquirer* found that the 114 schools of Division I-A accounted for 6 of every 10 dollars in intercollegiate athletic revenue. That leaves about 800 colleges and universities to split the remaining 40 percent of revenue. The paper looked at the top 50 intercollegiate football programs and found that they made total profits of $403 million in 1999—an average of $8 million each. That translates into an average profit margin of 50 percent.[7]

Football programs spend money in addition to earning money, of course. Using data from the 1996–1997 academic year, University of Arizona economics professor R. Bruce Billings calculated that Division I-A football programs on average earn 43 percent of all sports revenues and incur 26 percent of total sports costs. The same analysis shows that the number-two revenue-producing sport, men's basketball, earns 16.1 percent of average total revenues while incurring 7.5 percent of average total costs.[8] These revenues over expenses go back into the system to fund other programs.

[6]Welch Suggs, "Gap Grows between the Haves and Have-Nots in College Sports," *Chronicle of Higher Education*, November 17, 2000, Athletics Section, A73.

[7]Gilbert M. Gaul and Frank Fitzpatrick, "Rise of the Athletic Empires," *Philadelphia Inquirer*, September 10, 2000.

[8]R. Bruce Billings and Donald Aythe, "The Role of Football Profits in Meeting Title IX Gender Equity Regulations and Policy," *Journal of Sport Management* 14, no. 1 (January 2000), 28–40.

Feminists decry the high costs of big-time football programs as if they were robbing the budgets of women's sports. In fact, according to an analysis done by the *Chronicle of Higher Education*, it is the "have" schools, whose budgets are bursting with "tainted" profits from football and men's basketball, that do the best job of providing opportunities and spending for women's athletes.

The schools that belong to what the *Chronicle* calls the "equity" conferences with big-time football and basketball television contracts and bowl games—the Atlantic Coast, Big East, Big Ten, Big 12, Pacific-10 and Southeastern conferences—are those that field the largest and most diverse women's sports programs. These schools earn big profits from football and smaller profits from men's basketball, profits that eventually find their way to women's teams. In these conferences, women are over 50 percent of students and 42 percent of athletes.[9] In contrast, in the smaller, regional colleges and universities of Division II, women are over 55 percent of students and only 38 percent of athletes. In the still smaller, nonscholarship athletic programs of NCAA Division III, women are 41 percent of athletes while also constituting a majority of the students.[10]

Professor Billings looked at the data and found a direct correlation between football profits and "gender equity." Although the size of a school's endowment and whether it is a state or a private institution also has some correlation with proportionality in its athletic program, Billings found that football profits make a big difference, especially in financial aid. Compliance increases by .4 percentage points for each $1 million in football profits. With some institutions earning as much as $10 million a year, this can be a significant influence in the aid that supports "gender equity."

The upshot is that feminists tread on dangerous ground when they seek to demonize football with their frequent charges that (a) it doesn't make as much money as Title IX quota critics claim it does, and (b) it's too expensive. The same *Philadelphia Inquirer* study that showed the unequal distribution of wealth in collegiate athletic programs also found that women's sports kick very little into the coffers. Basketball is the female glamour sport, the women's equivalent of football. Yet according to the study, the top 100 women's basketball teams in the country lost a total of $65 million in 1999 (while men's basketball at the same schools made $150 million). The exception is the national champion University of Connecticut team, which has that rare thing in women's sports: a television contract. In 1999 the Lady Huskies made $1 million.[11] And in terms

---

[9]Welch Suggs, "Uneven Progress for Women's Sports," *Chronicle of Higher Education*, April 7, 2000, Athletics Section, A52.

[10]Welch Suggs, "At Smaller Colleges, Women Get Bigger Share of Sports Funds," *Chronicle of Higher Education*, April 14, 2000, Athletics Section, A69.

[11]Gilbert M. Gaul and Frank Fitzpatrick, "Women's Sports: The Ink Is Mostly Red," *Philadelphia Inquirer*, September 10, 2000.

of costs, a 1997 *USA Today* study of gender equity found that NCAA schools spent more to field the average women's basketball player than the average football player. The analysis reported that schools spent $39,892 for each female basketball player and $28,999 per football player. Female athletes in sports other than basketball were also more expensive for schools than males in sports other than football: $10,867 per athlete compared with $7,767.[12]

Feminists can't clamor for protections and preferences for women's programs in federal law while at the same time demanding that men's programs alone be justified on a profit-making basis. But clamor they do, and at the root of their grievance is a deep antipathy for football and the macho traditions it carries with it. This is why they are willing to claim that the elimination of men's teams under Title IX is a conspiracy orchestrated by big-time football.

"It's a very clever strategy to have men's minor sports being pitted against women," said Mary Jo Kane, director of the Tucker Center for Research on Girls and Women in Sport at the University of Minnesota. "The irony in all this is that if men's nonrevenue sports would team up with women's sports and go after football, [reducing] the size and expenditures in football, you could add sports for women and very comfortably support men's nonrevenue sports."

But taking on the sport that fills the stadiums, brings in the television contracts, and fuels the romantic myth of intercollegiate athletics is, to put it simply, not a winning strategy for men's sports hurt by Title IX. University of Chicago wrestling coach Leo Kocher believes that putting the breaks on the escalating arms race over college football is a worthy goal—and completely beside the point in the" gender equity" debate. If people want to pass legislation that tells Notre Dame that they must spend less on a football program that brings in tens of millions of dollars—good luck. But big-time college football doing with less will not make more women want to play collegiate sports. It will not change the fact that Division III men's baseball teams cut dozens of players in order to get their average squad size down to 30.4 players while women's NCAA softball teams struggle to get their average squad up to 18.

Many women, too, see that buying into the bellicose rhetoric of gender activists is self defeating. Female athletes on campus—if not feminist ideologues in the faculty lounge—understand that their fate, more often than not, is intertwined with that of their male counterparts. Time and again the first group to raise its voices to protest men's Title IX cuts is the women who have traveled with and practiced alongside the men all year. In addition to the camaraderie they feel, these female athletes understand that success in their men's athletic department is good for women. It opens doors to hugely successful programs like the women's soccer team at the University of North Carolina at

---

[12]Special Series on the 25th Anniversary of Title IX, *USA Today*, June 13–20, 1997.

Chapel Hill, for example, which is underwritten with money made by men's basketball, and the University of Tennessee women's basketball team, a dynasty whose seed money came from Tennessee football. Some of these women's programs have gone on to be more successful than the men's programs that provided their genesis. Perhaps one day the University of Connecticut women's basketball team will help underwrite a national champion men's baseball team. When that day comes, it will be a victory for hard work and common sense, not for the us-versus-them philosophy of "gender equity."

The flip side of eliminating opportunities for men to meet Title IX quotas, of course, is the push to entice new women onto the playing field. In many cases, this has resulted in legitimate new opportunities for young women to enjoy the physical and educational benefits of athletics. In too many other cases, however, the rush to make athletes out of uninspired and inexperienced young women in the name of "gender equity" has resulted in new inequities and the athletic equivalent of a charade.

In 1993, the same year its Gender Equity Task Force declared proportionality the "ultimate goal" of NCAA member institutions, the NCAA identified nine "emerging sports" for women to help schools meet the numerical requirement of proportionality. Colleges and universities, said the Gender Equity Task Force, should add at least two additional women's sports from a list of exotic athletic endeavors like synchronized swimming, team handball, water polo, archery, badminton, bowling, ice hockey, and squash. Equestrian, initially overlooked, was added in 1998.

The term "emerging sports" implies that these activities were increasingly pursued by girls in high schools. By adding them to their programs, so the theory went, colleges and universities would not just be engaged in gender bean-counting but would actually be fulfilling the legitimate athletic aspirations of thousands of young girls.

The problem was that very few girls were engaged in any of the NCAA's list of "emerging sports" in 1994. Only 11 high schools in the nation offered archery teams. Just 28 schools had equestrian squads. Fewer than 200 individual girls played ice hockey. And a survey by the National Federation of State High School Associations failed to report the existence of a single high-school-girls' synchronized swimming, handball, or squash team.

Still, with the NCAA's encouragement, colleges and universities began to pour resources into these sports with the hope of attracting sufficient numbers of women to athletics to make their quotas. Adding the twelve women necessary to create a synchronized swimming or a handball team, however, didn't result in sufficient additions to their female body count. The numbers just weren't adding up fast enough. Also, fielding successful teams in these sports required finding women who had experience prior to entering college, a difficult and sometimes impossible task. What they needed, athletic directors realized, was a sport that could accommodate large numbers of women and didn't require previous experience. And there it was, tucked in among the NCAA list of "emerging sports": crew.

From the beginning, women's rowing has occupied a special niche in the history of Title IX. In 1976, twenty members of the Yale women's rowing team, with a *New York Times* reporter in tow, marched into the athletics office to protest their second-class treatment at the university. They read a statement decrying Yale's lack of shower facilities for women's crew members, and then stripped to the waist, revealing the words "Title IX" written on each woman's back and breasts.

When the story ran in the March 4, 1976, edition of the *Times*, it set off what the newspaper later called an "international reaction." Within two weeks, female rowers at Yale had new locker rooms. The event—and the story of one of the rowers, Chris Ernst, who went on to become a two-time Olympic rower—was later portrayed in a film called *A Hero for Daisy*.

By 1994, the days when women's crew teams were left to shiver in the cold while the men showered in the boathouse were a distant memory. Attracted by squad sizes that start at 60 but can reach as high as 200, schools began pouring resources into creating women's rowing programs. The NCAA sanctioned 20 scholarships per team, the highest of any women's sport. And from just 66 programs in 1995, the number of intercollegiate women's rowing teams almost doubled in four years, to 122 in 1999. "The reason we're here—everybody knows it—is for gender equity," said University of Massachusetts women's rowing coach Jim Deitz in 1999.[13]

Complicating the challenge for women's crew coaches like Deitz was the fact that the pool of experienced high-school female rowers he has to recruit from is small and showing little signs of growth. In 1994, the year rowing was designated an "emerging sport" by the NCAA, there were only 36 high-school-girls' teams nationwide. In the years since then, according to the National Federation of State High School Associations, while the number of intercollegiate women's squads has almost doubled, the number of high school teams has actually shrunk, to 34.

This means that coaches like Deitz have routinely had to offer spots on rowing squads, and most often full scholarships to go with them, to women who have never before touched an oar. Schools have been forced to hold open try-outs in which any woman can come and join the team. And although some coaches question how often the last 80 or so women on a 150-woman squad

---

[13]Barbara Carton, "You Don't Need Oars in the Water to Go Out for Crew," *Wall Street Journal*, May 14, 1999.

get to compete—or even if they show up regularly at the boathouse to prac-tice—coaches have instituted "no-cut" policies, all in an effort to attract and keep females on their rosters.

In a devastating profile of the lengths to which some schools are going to cobble together women's rowing teams, the *Wall Street Journal* reported that some coaches are literally walking through the campus in search of tall, broad-shouldered women, recruiting novices in stairwells, campus lunchrooms, and even off-campus diners. When the University of Kansas added women's crew to achieve proportionality under Title IX in the late 1990s, they had no high-school-rowing teams in the Midwest from which to recruit. The athletic director was forced to make an appeal at freshman orientation and managed to con-vince over a hundred women to tryout for the team. At Ohio State they went even further and put an ad in the student newspaper: "Tall athletic women wanted. No experience necessary!"

As schools without a tradition of crew or even access to a body of water seek to create teams (Arizona State University, in the desert city of Tempe, famously flooded a two-mile stretch of dry gulch to provide a place for its new team to practice), coaches are having to look to Canada, Europe, and Australia to find experienced rowers. Some coaches are resorting to recruiting basketball and volleyball players who aren't good enough to earn scholarships in their own sports. But even this outreach often falls short. "We're not getting some of those athletes because, with so many scholarships out there, other schools are offering them full rides," confessed University of Washington women's crew coach Jan Harville in 2000.[14]

Even when the teams and the scholarship aid are available, qualified females—both athletically and academically—can be hard to find. San Diego State University learned this the hard way when it failed to comply with the terms of a consent decree ordering all of the schools in the California State University to achieve proportionality by the 1998–1999 school year. San Diego budgeted the scholarship aid and the necessary funds for its athletic program to match its 55-percent-female student body but couldn't find enough academi-cally qualified athletes to take the money. The school even created a summer school for female athletes who were in need of academic remediation, yet in the words of the CSU/Cal-NOW Consent Decree Final Report, "not enough qualified student-athletes accepted the offer."[15]

The premise of Title IX proportionality is that girls and women, given the opportunity, will participate in athletics at the same rate as men. But for the time being at least, it appears that women need to be offered more scholarship

---

[14]*San Diego Union Tribune*, April 2, 2000.
[15]California State University, "Report under the CSU/Cal-NOW Consent Decree Regarding Equal Opportunity in Athletics for Women Students," February 2000, 16.

aid than men just to participate at their current rate of about 40 percent of collegiate athletes. Why, if all this scholarship money is going into women's sports, do women stubbornly refuse to participate at the same rate as men?

In 1993, a court ordered the California State University at Northridge to achieve Title IX proportionality in its athletic program within five years, forcing CSUN administrators to cut their men's soccer, baseball, swimming, and volleyball teams.[16] Proportionality proponents said the failure of the school's athletic program to mirror its student body was the result of illegal discrimination against women.

But CSUN president Blenda Wilson saw other, less insidious forces at work. "I was at our football game last weekend and I said to a colleague of mine as we looked at what must have been a hundred men lined up in red, black, and white jerseys along the sidelines for Cal State Northridge," Wilson told PBS's *National Desk*, "I said, that's a part of the gender-equity problem. There is no sport where a hundred women will stand along the sidelines when only twenty-two get to play."

It's an often-heard complaint from coaches of women's sports that although there are many fiercely dedicated female athletes, fewer women than men are willing to "ride the bench" for a season without getting a chance to compete. "There's an expectation that there are all these women out there to choose from now. They're all coming out of high school where they participated in sports," CSUN head softball coach Janet Sherman told PBS. "But they don't want to sit the bench. I can't get the women to come out. I can't change that."

"Girls are smarter," says Providence College women's tennis coach Carl LaBranche, who lost his men's team to Title IX cuts in 1998. "They look at the other girls playing and in some cases they say, 'I'm not going to be number nine or number ten.' So even though we have twelve spots [on the team], I can't fill them because the girls ask, 'How many travel?' We say, 'Eight.' And they say, 'That's okay coach. Nice knowing you.'"[17]

Because women are less willing to ride the bench—and less willing to "walk on" to a team and play without receiving an athletic scholarship—women's team sizes tend to be smaller than men's, complicating the task of reaching numerical parity in an athletic program. Even today, when the overwhelming majority of men's teams have been artificially limited in the number of players

[16]The outcry prompted by the elimination of four men's teams was such that the California state legislature intervened and passed legislation providing funding for the men's teams for an additional year, and the men's teams were eventually reinstated. Meanwhile, women became 60 percent of Northridge students but the percentage of women expressing interest in sports remained stuck at 38 percent. As of February 2000, Northridge had not met the terms of the Cal-NOW consent decree.

[17]*National Desk*, PBS, April 1999.

they can carry, the average squad size of men's intercollegiate teams is larger than that of women's teams. While a women's indoor track team on average consists of 27 players, a men's team will attract over 32; typically 22 women will come out for lacrosse, but 31 men will make the same commitment; and women's softball coaches get around 18 participants, whereas over 30 men are drawn to the baseball team.

The result is that schools must offer more sports to women than to men, just to get equal numbers of athletes of both sexes coming out to play. Nationally, NCAA-member schools offer women 553 more athletic programs to choose from than they offer to men. And still, fewer women participate in intercollegiate sports than men—about 77,000 fewer in 1998–1999.

Title IX quota advocates answer the claim that women are less interested than men in athletic competition by saying that such assertions have always been the stock in trade of the patriarchy—and they have a point. It wasn't so long ago that women were denied the opportunity to play sports on the basis of the rock-solid conventional wisdom that they weren't interested in athletics, which were "unfeminine."

Today, a new but not altogether different conventional wisdom holds sway among proponents of Title IX proportionality. It, too, judges women as a group, not as individuals, and it, too, seeks to tell women what their interests and capabilities are instead of allowing them to define those for themselves. Its adherents aren't the male-dominated athletics establishment of old, but the effect is still the same. Much as the patriarchy robbed women of their self-determination in the bad old days, today the government, the courts, and the women's groups, acting through the agency of American educational institutions, are seeking to make girls' and women's decisions for them.

A Critique of *Tilting the Playing Field: Schools, Sports, Sex and Title IX**

Nancy Hogshead-Makar

I. Introduction

Don Quixote, Cervantes' well-known fictional character, is a knight errant who sets about doing great deeds only to end up "tilting at windmills." This phrase arises from an incident where Quixote spots windmills and tries to convince his sidekick, Sancho Panza, that they are evil giants with whom he must do heroic battle. Everywhere he journeys, the quixotic traveler sees imagined evils to be remedied; wrongs "he intended to right, grievances to redress, injustices to repair, abuses to remove, and duties to discharge." In doing so, Quixote engages in combat with perceived enemies of all kinds in pursuit of his illusive vision. His difficulty, though, is that he too often gets absorbed in his mind's figments and blames his pratfalls and set backs on the magic powers of a wicked enchanter he deems is his nemesis.

Tilting the Playing Field: Schools, Sports, Sex and Title IX, a book by Department of Justice speech writer Jessica Gavora,[1] is a fine example of seeing windmills and believing them to be evil giants that must be slain. Gavora's book provides grist for the notion that Title IX of the Education Amendments of 1972[2] (Title IX) is a "quota" law to be blamed for the decisions of schools and universities to eliminate men's sports teams for the sake of women's teams.[3]

---

*Adapted from *UCLA Women's Law Journal* (Fall/Winter 2003), 101–141.

[1]Prior to being hired at the United States Department of Justice, Jessica Gavora worked for the Independent Women's Forum, a conservative women's group. See http://www.iwf.org.

[2]20 U.S.C. Sections 1681–1688 (2000).

[3]In response to these and other claims, in June 2002, the Secretary of the Department of Education created the Commission on Opportunities in Athletics, which issued its final report entitled "Open to All: Title IX at Thirty," available at http://www.ed.gov/inits/commissionboards/

These women's teams, Gavora argues, are populated by indisposed women lacking the robust interest in sports that only men possess. Gavora, a nonlawyer, argues that Title IX is simply an aberration in legal reasoning, characterizing the federal judiciary as engaged in Title IX silliness.

This review of *Tilting the Playing Field* (hereinafter *Tilting*) analyzes some of her attempts to vilify the law and finds her policy arguments against Title IX lacking. Unfortunately, *Tilting* does not shoot straight. It presents seriously incomplete facts and a lack of appreciation for the legal reasoning reflected in the numerous published federal court opinions on the topic, all the while rehashing losing legal arguments as if they were phoenixes that deserve to rise from their long-cold ashes. The hyperbolic and cagey manner in which *Tilting* is written is designed to leave readers wondering how judges and regulators could interpret and apply Title IX in such an absurd way. The reality is, however, that Title IX—as applied to sports—is an area of the law that is marked by uncommon consistency, has never been held to be a "quota" law, has never required that schools discontinue a team for compliance, and is entirely consistent with the country's other nondiscriminatory laws.[4]

Simply stated, *Tilting* misstates the law and facts to make Title IX look like a shameful and silly chapter in this country's civil rights efforts, with its author engaging in a heroic battle to save men's sports from the brink of elimination. Gavora is merely tilting at Title IX windmills.

II. Windmill #1: The Law Requires Schools to Cut Men's Sports

Tilting's major, albeit inaccurate, premise is that athletic department decisions to cut men's sports are required by, and are the direct result of, Title IX. Gavora asserts that this "dirty little secret" of Title IX has led to "unintended consequences." She argues that a "law designed to end discrimination against women is now causing discrimination against men" because schools are now forced to limit or reduce opportunities for men's teams.

Gavora is legally and factually inaccurate in her assertion. Title IX and its regulations have never required a school to cut men's teams or men's sporting

---

athletics. See also "Minority Views on the Report of the Commission on Opportunity in Athletics," available at http://www.savetitleix.com/minorityreport.pdf (finding that the recommendations in the Department of Education's Commission on Opportunities in Athletics weakens Title IX's protections, substantially reduces the opportunities in athletics to which women and girls are entitled under current law, and that all but one of the Commission's recommendations fail to address budgetary problems men's teams face).

[4]Diane Heckman, "The Glass Sneaker: Thirty Years of Victories and Defeats Involving Title IX and Sex Discrimination in Athletics," *Fordham Intell. Prop. Media & Ent. L.J.* 13 (2003).

opportunities. Instead, it is the decisions of athletic directors that are to blame. History illustrates the same concept in the civil rights struggles of the 1950s and 1960s, which saw new desegregation laws that required communities to integrate public parks and swimming pools. Rather than integrate, some communities chose to close these facilities. In *Palmer v. Thompson*,[5] the Supreme Court upheld the decision of the city of Jackson, Mississippi, to cease its operation of five swimming pools after a federal district court had declared segregation of the city's recreational facilities to be unconstitutional.[6] The law did not require that Jackson close its public facilities, but it was a permissible choice (albeit of moral consequence). The blame for Jackson's decisions should be placed on the city for closing its public facilities—for their hostility to the principles of racial equality—not on desegregation laws or African Americans. Likewise, the moral blame lies with the decision-makers at schools that discontinue viable men's teams, not the law or female athletes who have struggled for decades for sports opportunities.

Moreover, Title IX "disadvantages" male athletes to the same extent that a new family member "disadvantages" older siblings, or to the same extent that new labor competition from African Americans in the 1960s "disadvantaged" white workers for jobs. Older siblings must share the family resources with the newly arrived member, and white workers now compete in a larger workforce along with African Americans for jobs. Prior to 1972, boys enjoyed nearly 100 percent of the sports opportunities, and now must share those educational resources with an expanded pool of athletes—their sisters. Sharing limited resources equitably is a basic and fundamental tenet of all civil rights laws. The equality principle allowing entities the choice to either bring up the previously disadvantaged group or to bring down the previously advantaged group is consistent throughout the country's civil rights contexts.

Gavora claims that after the early cases, notably *Cohen*,[7] *Roberts*,[8] and *Favia*,[9] prong one (the proportionality test) became the exclusive test schools

---

[5] 403 U.S. 217 (1971).

[6] *Clark v. Thompson*, 206 F. Supp. 539 (S.D. Miss. 1962), *aff'd per curiam*, 313 F.2d 637 (5th Cir. 1963), *cert. denied*, 375 U.S. 951 (1963) (Justice Black, writing for a five-to-four majority, said the only effect was that public pools that had been segregated were no longer maintained, thus placing whites and blacks in the same position with respect to public facilities.); see also *Neal v. Bd. of Trs. of Cal. State Univ.*, 198 F.3d at 763, 770 (permitting a university to diminish athletic opportunities available to men so as to bring them into line with the lower athletic opportunities available to women).

[7] *Cohen v. Brown Univ.*, 809 F. Supp. 978 (D.R.I. 1992) [hereinafter *Cohen I*] (preliminary injunction), *aff'd*, *Cohen II*, 991 F.2d 888, on remand to 879 F. Supp. 185 (D.R.I. 1995) [hereinafter *Cohen III*] (trial on the merits), *aff'd in part, rev'd in part*, *Cohen IV*, 101 F.3d 155, *cert. denied*, 520 U.S. 1186 (1997).

[8] *Roberts v. Colo. State Bd. of Agric.*, 998 F.2d 824 (10th Cir. 1993), *cert. denied*, 510 U.S. 1004 (1993).

[9] *Favia v. Ind. Univ. of Pa.*, 7 F.3d 332 (3d Cir. 1993).

could use to "'insulate [themselves] from a Title IX lawsuit or federal investigation." But Gavora fails to explore the question of whether the law caused institutions to cut the men's teams that they did. Gavora's misleading presentation of the circumstances surrounding Providence University's decision to cut its men's baseball team, for example, is never put to a legal test. What options for the athletic department did the law permit? Did Providence need to close the 11 percent participation gap between Providence's undergraduate female students, which stood at 59 percent, and its female student-athletes, who represented just 48 percent, when there was no demonstrable unmet interest on the part of their female students?[10] A range of alternatives was permissible under Title IX[11] other than cutting the baseball team, and it is legally inaccurate to claim that Title IX required Providence to make that decision. *Tilting's* premise—that all decisions to eliminate men's sports are required by Title IX—is a false one.

III. Windmill #2: Title IX Discriminates Against Male Athletes in Athletic Departments

Women lag behind men in athletic departments in every measurable criteria by significant margins. Women athletes are not the evil giants that Gavora sees. Rather, it is other men—other athletes at the same school—who currently enjoy the greatest proportion of opportunities, scholarships, budgets, and facilities.

In spite of these statistics, Gavora still argues that men's sports are rapidly declining and need to be saved from the misguided nature of Title IX. She lists the losses that men's teams have suffered over the years due to Title IX, relying on selective but incomplete statistics from a General Accounting Office (GAO) report and arguments presented by Leo Kocher, the plaintiff in the wrestler's lawsuit against the Department of Education. But Gavora presents a seriously misleading picture. She fails to report on the major finding of the research from a related GAO report: When all the men's teams added and dropped are computed,

[10]See U.S. Department of Health, Education, and Welfare, Office for Civil Rights, Office of the Secretary, HEW, Title IX of the Education Amendments of 1972: A Policy Interpretation: Title IX and Intercollegiate Athletics (1979) at http://www.ed.gov/offices/OCR/docs/t9interp.html [hereinafter OCR] (test for whether schools are meeting prong three); Diane Heckman, "The Explosion of Title IX Legal Action in Intercollegiate Athletics During 1992–93: Defining the 'Equal Opportunity' Standard," *Detroit C. L. Rev.* 953 (1994); and Heckman, "The Glass Sneaker," footnote 4 above (both discussing schools' use of Title IX as an excuse to drop men's teams without examining the overall budget and expenses for the men's athletic teams when separate programs are offered for male and female student-athletes).

[11]Women's Sports Foundation, "Know Your Rights, Expanding Opportunities for Girls and Women in Sport without Eliminating Men's Sports: The Foundation Position," http://www.womenssportsfoundation.org/cgi-bin/iowa/issues/rights/article.html?record=84 (accessed July 3, 2007).

the result is a net gain of thirty-six men's teams—not a loss.[12] The report clearly demonstrates that men gained both in numbers of teams and numbers of participation opportunities.[13] While the report shows that indeed 180 men's wrestling teams were discontinued between 1984 and 2001, 120 new men's soccer teams were added.[14] Numerous men's baseball, lacrosse, and football teams were also added.[15] It is deceptive to mention only the data showing some men's teams have been discontinued without the corresponding data demonstrating the greater number of opportunities gained by men.

The same GAO report also undercuts Gavora's position that the increases in men's opportunities reported by the NCAA merely reflect new schools joining the association—for example, teams that were already in existence and merely moved from one association to another. In fact, the GAO report included all four-year colleges' experiences (not just those of the NCAA) of adding and discontinuing sports teams.[16] Gavora fails to explore the many reasons teams are added and dropped at particular schools, other than Title IX. The GAO report found that the most frequent reason for discontinuing a men's or women's team was due to lack of student-interest in that sport.[17] Finally, 72 percent of all schools that added women's sports did not drop any sport. Gavora tilts at the windmill of women's modestly growing opportunities, while defending men's disproportionately larger share of opportunities and budgets.

Finally, Gavora fails to disclose the numerous women's teams that have also been dropped during the same time period. For example, women's gymnastics alone lost 100 teams, while men's gymnastics teams lost 56.[18] Thus, it is misleading and one dimensional to argue that Title IX is responsible for men's team losses, when men overall have made gains in sports teams and opportunities and many women's teams have been dropped during the same time period. It is difficult to swallow *Tilting*'s claim that men are being discriminated against.

A. Unequal Participation

Gavora presents highly selective data suggesting that women are getting more than their fair share of participation opportunities—that they are actually over-

[12]U.S. General Accounting Office, "Intercollegiate Athletics: Four-Year Colleges' Experiences Adding and Discontinuing Teams," GAO No. 01-297, 4 (March 2001); available at http://www .gao.gov [hereinafter GAO].

[13]Ibid.

[14]Ibid.

[15]Ibid.

[16]Ibid.

[17]GAO Report, footnote 11 above.

[18]GAO Report, footnote 11 above.

represented in collegiate athletics. For example, she questions how women can claim that there is gender inequity in athletic departments, when, "NCAA-member colleges and universities sponsor more athletic programs for women than men—553 more, to be precise."

The number of athletic programs is a misleading measure of athletic opportunities. Gender equity does not require men's and women's teams to be mirror images of each other, and has never been measured by equivalent numbers of teams.[19] The number of sponsored teams is unrelated to budgets or total expenditures, as evidenced by the fact that, even including the additional women's teams that *Tilting* condemns, women still receive just 36 percent of the overall athletic department budget.[20] Gavora misses this fact because sports-team membership ranges anywhere from five players on a typical golf team to well over 100 athletes on a men's football or women's rowing team. Theoretically, one sex could have twice as many teams as the other sex, yet have half the opportunities to participate in athletics. Gender equity, instead, has long been measured by numbers of actual participation opportunities provided to each gender.[21] The law permits schools to field a men's football team with 115 athletes without requiring the school to match football with either a women's football team or another team consisting of 115 athletes. Instead, the law looks to a school's entire sports program and asks whether equivalent participation opportunities exist. This is a far more reasoned measurement of how a school provides these educational resources to boys and girls than simply counting numbers of teams.

Other facts omitted by the author—facts necessary for an accurate picture of overall opportunities for boys and girls in athletic departments—are that male collegiate athletes outnumber female athletes 208,866 to 150,916, thus receiving 28 percent more opportunities to participate.[22] In high-school athletics, male athletes receive 1.1 million more participation opportunities than their female counterparts (i.e., 29 percent more).[23] Gavora selectively ignores this data showing a far different picture.

[19] 34 C.F.R. Section 106.41 (2002).

[20] NCAA, "Gender-Equity Report 20" (2000); available at http://www.ncaa.org/library/research/gender_equity_study/1999-00/1999-00_gender_ equity_report.pdf [hereinafter NCAA Report].

[21] *Cohen v. Brown Univ.*, 809 F. Supp. 978, 980 (1992).

[22] NCAA Report, footnote 20 above.

[23] National Association of Collegiate Women's Athletic Administrators, "Women's Sports Foundation Reaction to the U.S. Department of Education Motion to Dismiss Lawsuit Brought by Wrestling Coach's Association," May 30, 2002; available at http://www.aaeww.com/nacwaa/wsfresponsetonwca2.htm; citing N.F.H.S.A.A. and NCAA Participation Statistics (2001) (finding that there were 3,921,069 male student-athletes and 2,784,154 female student-athletes).

B. Unequal Scholarship Dollars

Tilting argues that women receive disproportionate and unjustified levels of athletic scholarships. According to Gavora: "The average female student-athlete now receives more scholarship aid than the average male student-athlete. A GAO study of 532 of the 596 NCAA institutions that grant athletic scholarships showed that these schools spent $4,458 in scholarship per male athlete and $4,861 per female athlete."

What Gavora's selective fact-picking overlooks is that it is schools' unwillingness to add more women's teams that accounts for the disparity. Because schools must give scholarship aid in proportion to athletic participation by gender (e. g., if 41 percent of the student-athletes are women, women should receive 41 percent of the scholarship dollars), and the NCAA caps the number of scholarships a school is allowed to offer per sport, the average per-capita scholarship expenditures for women must be higher. There are fewer female athletes to whom scholarship monies are distributed; therefore the concentration of scholarship dollars is higher for an individual female athlete. More accurate facts regarding gender equity in the area of scholarships reveal that female athletes still receive just 43 percent of the total scholarship dollars, which amounts to men receiving $133 million more scholarship dollars each year than female athletes receive.[24]

It cannot be argued with a straight face, as Gavora attempts to do, that male athletes are being discriminated against and need the help of federal civil rights laws to protect them. Men's athletics participation overall is increasing, men's budgets are increasing at a flat-out sprint, and men still enjoy the largest share of the athletic pie. It is easy to be sympathetic to the male athletes whose teams are cut, but countless female athletes have also had their teams cut or never had teams at all. Historically, resources have been allotted disproportionately to men's and boys' sports, not to women's and girls', as a result of intentional, unjustifiable discrimination.[25] As a normative matter, civil rights laws should not be altered to provide fewer athletic opportunities for women because some of these resources have been shifted and redistributed to women when they were unfairly denied them. Additionally, civil rights laws should not be altered to protect specific sports. Women simply are not overrepresented in collegiate athletics as *Tilting* would have readers believe. Instead, they still receive a

[24]NCAA Report, footnote 20 above, 22, 34, 46, 58, 70.

[25]*Nat'l Wrestling Coaches Assoc. v. Dept. of Educ.*, 263 F. Supp. 2d 82, 87 ("Title IX was enacted as part of the Education Amendments of 1972, following extensive hearings on discrimination in education, during which over 1,200 pages of testimony were gathered, documenting 'massive, persistent patterns of discrimination against women' in colleges and universities"); *Historic Patterns of Intercollegiate Athletics Program Development*, 44 Fed. Reg. 71419 (1979).

demonstrably and substantially smaller share of athletic dollars compared to men in the areas of participation, scholarships, and overall budgets.

IV. Windmill #3: Title IX Is a Quota

Every federal appeals court that has examined the "quota" issue has upheld the regulations and concluded that Title IX does not constitute reverse discrimination and is not a quota law.[26] For example, in *Cohen v. Brown Univ.*, the court held, "No aspect of the Title IX regime at issue in this case—inclusive of the statute, the relevant regulation, and the pertinent agency documents—mandates gender-based preferences or quotas, or specific timetables for implementing numerical goals."[27] The United States Supreme Court's refusal to hear the *Cohen* and the *Roberts* cases, although establishing no precedent, certainly reflects that these lower appellate courts are likely getting the law right. In fact, it is difficult to find greater unanimity of judicial opinion on a topic than this one.[28]

Schools are fundamentally different from employers in that their athletics programs are sex segregated and are responsible for shaping and defining student interests. Indeed, one of the responsibilities of higher education, in exchange for federal and state tax-exempt dollars, is to expose students to new ideas and help them develop new skills to become more productive members of society.[29] Education is a cultural investment in our collective future. Interest and skills follow opportunity, and opportunity does not exist until sex-segregated teams are created.[30]

---

[26]See *Chalenor v. Univ. of N.D.*, 291 F.3d 1042, 1045 (8th Cir. 2002); *Pederson v. La. State Univ.*, 213 F.3d 858, 879 (5th Cir. 2000); *Neal v. Bd. of Trs. of Cal. State Univ.*, 198 F.3d 763, 770 (9th Cir. 1999); *Horner v. Ky. High Sch. Athletic Assoc.*, 43 F.3d 265, 274–275 (6th Cir. 1994), *appeal after remand*, 206 F.3d 685 (6th Cir. 2000), *cert. denied*, 531 U.S. 824 (2000); *Kelley v. Bd. of Trs. of Univ. of Ill.*, 35 F.3d 265, 270 (7th Cir. 1994), *cert. denied*, 513 U.S. 1128 (1995); *Cohen v. Brown Univ.*, 991 F.2d 888 (1st Cir. 1993) [hereinafter *Cohen II*] (upholding the grant of a preliminary injunction to the female student-athletes); *Cohen v. Brown Univ.*, 101 F.3d 155, 170 (1st Cir. 1996), *cert. denied*, 520 U.S. 1186 (1997) [hereinafter *Cohen IV*] (this case was before the First Circuit twice, first on Brown University's appeal of a preliminary injunction granted by the district court [*Cohen I*], and the second time after a trial on the merits [*Cohen III*]); *Roberts v. Colo. St. Bd. of Agric.*, 998 F.2d 824, 828 (10th Cir. 1993), *cert. denied*, 510 U.S. 1004 (1993); *Williams v. Sch. Dist. of Bethlehem*, 998 F.2d 168, 171 (3d Cir. 1993), *cert. denied*, 510 U.S. 1043 (1994); see also Heckman, "The Glass Sneaker," footnote 4 above.

[27]*Cohen IV*, 101 F.3d, 170 (1st Cir. 1996).

[28]Ibid.

[29]Kimberly A. Yuracko, "One for You and One For Me: Is Title IX's Sex-Based Proportionality Requirement for College Varsity Athletic Positions Defensible?," 97 *Nw. U. L. Rev.* 731 (2003), 777–778.

[30]*Cohen IV*, 101 F.3d, 179 ("Interest and ability rarely develop in a vacuum; they evolve as a function of opportunity and experience. The Policy Interpretation recognizes that women's lower rate of participation in athletics reflects women's historical lack of opportunities to participate in sports.").

Yet Gavora ignores this legal scholarship and the concept of stare decisis, the underpinning of the American judicial system. She argues that "The gender-quota logic of Title IX is inexorable. . . . There must be just as many girl athletes per capita at any given school as there are boy athletes. Anything less is prima facie proof that someone is being discriminated against." In examining the Title IX cases of the early 1990s,[31] she states that the "proportionality test took one glance at a school's statistical data, pronounced the school guilty on the basis of unbalanced numbers, and forced it to prove itself innocent."

Certainly, statistics can be a part of the plaintiff's burden of proof to show that the school's decision to either eliminate a viable women's team or to refuse varsity status to a potential team amounts to a denial of an educational oppor-tunity on account of its gender, a prohibited gender-discriminatory practice.[32] But Gavora's legal reasoning goes astray when she asserts that "in each of these [seminal Title IX] cases, female athletes charged that statistics—not any invidi-ous policy or hostile act on the part of the schools—proved they were victims of illegal discrimination." Here, Gavora does not appear to understand the meaning of "intentional discrimination" within a legal or a civil rights context. In order to prove intentional discrimination, plaintiffs need not prove that defendants intended to harm female athletes, nor do plaintiffs need to show that defendants acted with discriminatory animus, malice, or any other evi-dence of motive, whether benevolent or invidious. Rather, intentional discrimi-nation means only an intent to treat girls and boys differently.[33] Organizing collegiate athletics necessarily involves establishing a gender classification, and institutions deciding to eliminate a women's team will be deemed to have intended the foreseeable outcome of discrimination against the female ath-letes.[34] Intentionally and knowingly dispersing resources involves choices that signal valuing one gender's educational opportunities over another.[35] Inten-

---

[31]See footnotes 5–8 above.

[32]*Cohen II*, 991 F.2d, 901–902 (holding that the plaintiff has the burden of proof to show that the school is not complying with proportionality); see 20 U.S.C., Section 1681 ("this subsec-tion shall not be construed to prevent the consideration in any hearing or proceeding under this chapter of statistical evidence tending to show that such imbalance exists with respect to partici-pation in, or receipt of benefits of, any such program or activity by members of one sex").

[33]See e.g., *Pederson v. La. St. Univ.*, 213 F.3d 858, 881 (5th Cir. 2000) ("[The university] need not have intended to violate Title IX, but need only have intended to treat women differently"); see also *UAW v. Johnson Controls, Inc.*, 499 U.S. 187, 199 (1991) ("Whether an employment practice involves disparate treatment through explicit facial discrimination does not depend on why the employer discriminates."); *Bangerter v. Orem City Corp.*, 46 F.3d 1491, 1501 (10th Cir. 1995) ("absence of malevolent intent does not convert a facially discriminatory policy into a neutral policy with a discriminatory effect").

[34]*Haffer v. Temple Univ.*, 678 F. Supp. 517, 527 (E.D. Pa. 1987) ("[T]he intent that Temple urges does not exist is provided by Temple's explicit classification of intercollegiate athletic teams on the basis of gender").

[35]See *Pederson*, 213 F.3d, 881; Education Amendments of 1972, 20 U.S.C., Section 901(a), 20 U.S.C., Section 1681(a) (2000); 34 C.F.R., Section 106.41 (2001).

tional discrimination does not require demonstrating some animus or maliciousness on the part of the defendant, although such evidence would certainly make the athlete's case stronger.[36] In *Cohen, Roberts,* and *Favia,* the universities' intentional conduct—dropping a women's team—caused the women's underrepresentation within the athletic department, and unlawfully denied the women the educational opportunity of sports participation.

While *Tilting* attempts to assert that the only real test for Title IX compliance is prong one, Gavora acknowledges that most schools do not rely on proportionality or prong one to demonstrate compliance with Title IX. She reports that her Freedom of Information Act request of Title IX compliance agreements between the OCR and colleges and universities from 1992 to 2000 produced just forty-four OCR athletics-participation reviews. The statistical breakdown showed that 25 percent agreed to Title IX compliance through prong one, or proportionality; 8 percent agreed to compliance through prong two, or demonstration of a continuous history of expansion for women's opportunities; and 64 percent of the total complied under prong three, accommodation of the interests and abilities of women on campus.

As a preliminary matter, one wonders why she attempts to garner such tremendous outcry about OCR activism, when there were just forty-four participation cases during an eight-year time frame, and no college has ever lost any funds for a violation of Title IX standards, despite OCR being responsible for over 1,200 colleges and universities. This history clearly cannot be considered governmental "activism."

More importantly, the central thesis of *Tilting* regarding the validity and functionality of the three separate tests is dubious. Gavora acknowledges but dismisses the fact that 72 percent of the schools reviewed complied with Title IX without providing as many opportunities to women as were provided to men. She argues that because many of the schools complying under prong three were required to add more women's teams, prong three is not a separate test. Yet her own research does not support this conclusion. It concludes that 72 percent of the schools investigated by the OCR were deemed in compliance with Title IX despite the schools' failure to reach proportionality. This clearly demonstrates that all three tests are viable means of demonstrating compliance with Title IX. That some schools complying under prong three were required to add more women's teams demonstrates that these schools failed to respond adequately to existing unmet interests and abilities among their female student body, not that a "quota" was imposed. Whatever opinion Gavora or others might have on Title IX and alleged "quotas," it is not one shared by the federal judiciary nationwide. Instead, it has been unanimously discredited and rejected.

[36]See footnote 33 above.

[Windmill #4 deals with compliance under prong three, and the certainty that the law provided.][37]

VI. Windmill #5: Women Do Not Deserve Sports Opportunities because They Are Not as Interested in Sports

Tilting asserts that women are not as deserving of new athletic opportunities because they are not as interested in sports. The villainous Title IX, Gavora argues, is out to change the fundamental nature of men and women. She contends that cutting men's sports has "nothing to do with saving money, and everything to do with making the numbers line up right." In other words, it's not economics that determine sports participation, it's sociology—supposedly schools cannot recruit enough women to participate in their sports programs, and that, thereby, the law "punishes men for the fact that women are not as interested in sports." To support her conclusions, she relies on some quasi-social science and the fact that women do not walk-on to teams at rates equivalent to men. But her facts and quotes from a few college coaches fail to support her proposition, and instead just speak to cast-off gender stereotypes.

A. Interest and Walk-On Positions

Tilting cites figures indicating that currently more than six million boys and girls play high school sports, who will then vie for fewer than 400,000 college-athletic participation slots. The cutoff between high-school participation and athletic-scholarship dollars is even steeper. According to the NCAA, not even 1 in 330 high-school athletes will land a college scholarship.[38] With 2.8 million girls playing high-school sports, it is inconceivable that colleges cannot find women to play on the teams they create, particularly when schools spend almost twice as much money getting men to play on their teams as they do on women.[39]

The fact that some schools do not have as many female walk-on participants or "benchwarmers" as those for men's teams does not demonstrate women's lack of interest in sports participation. As Gavora readily admits, women rush to fill genuine competitive athletic opportunities. "[F]ewer women than men are willing to 'ride the bench' for a season without getting a chance to compete. . . . 'Girls are smarter,' says Providence College women's tennis coach. . . .

---

[37]See 1996 Clarification of Intercollegiate Athletics Policy Guidance: The Three-Part Test; http://www.ed.gov/offices/OCR/docs/clarific.html (accessed June 29, 2007); see also Chapter 18 of this book.

[38]NCAA Report, footnote 20 above.

[39]Ibid.

'They look at the other girls playing and in some cases they say, "I'm not going to be number nine or number ten." So even though we have twelve spots [on the team] I can't fill them because the girls ask, "How many travel?" We say, "Eight." And they say, "That's okay coach. Nice knowing you."'"

Gavora's examples illustrate that women are inquiring into sports participation opportunities, and demonstrating their desire to compete on a team. They don't want to be symbolic team members with little utility. Gavora's arguments actually support the opposite of the conclusion she intended—that women are very interested in playing sports—and perhaps their interest in sports participation is different from the way men choose to participate, a result she logically should applaud and one the current law permits.

Gavora argues that walk-ons are not about athletic department finances, they are about making the numbers between men and women come out even for "bureaucratic bean-counters." But almost no one inside sports attempts to argue that walk-on positions are costless. They may be comparatively less expensive, but they are far from free. Costs include equipment, uniforms, additional supervision in the form of assistant coaches and managers, medical care, access to the training room, insurance, food provided to athletes at "training tables," academic tutors, and a host of other benefits related to varsity status. Football walk-ons, in particular, are actually quite expensive. Women's athletic budgets are comparably smaller, giving coaches a disincentive to keep additional athletes on the bench. Of course funding walk-on positions is about finances.

The legal issue facing schools is whether a school's heavy male walk-on roster will prevent that same school from starting and funding a women's team, for which women are expressing a tremendous demand for actual competition. Male walk-ons cost money that could instead be used to field real female-athletic opportunities. Deciding whether and how many walk-on positions to budget reflects how a school chooses to allocate financial resources. Far from being divorced from budgetary considerations, decisions regarding allocating these financial resources are intertwined inexorably with gender equity.

Demonstrating the law's flexibility, Title IX permits (but does not require) unequal expenditures between the sexes when schools are providing the students with equivalent educational opportunities. The 1975 implementing regulations state: "Unequal aggregate expenditures for members of each sex or unequal expenditures for male and female teams if a recipient operates or sponsors separate teams will not constitute noncompliance . . . but the [OCR] may consider the failure to provide necessary funds for teams for one sex in assessing equality of opportunity for members of each sex."[40]

---

[40]34 C.F.R., Section 106.41(c) (2001).

Furthermore, the 1979 policy interpretation recognizes that men's and women's teams will have different financial requirements "because of unique aspects of particular sports or athletic activities."[41] It allows such differences if sport-specific needs are met equivalently in both men's and women's programs.[42] In other words, funding an equestrian team may inherently cost more than a swimming team. So long as schools are providing the sexes with the same quality equipment or facilities, the OCR and the courts have considered this cost-differential to be nondiscriminatory in that both the men in the expensive sport and the women in the inexpensive sport are being provided the same educational opportunity to participate on an athletics team.

While Gavora tries to argue that women demand fewer sports, it is simply that women generally demand a different type of sporting experience. Gavora seems to insist that women demand the same type of athletic competition that men demand. If Title IX does not require cost trade-offs for competing resources as Gavora argues, and consistent with her assertion that unequal outcomes are acceptable if men and women have different interests and abilities, providing women with additional teams in order to meet women's distinctive interests is philosophically consistent. When Gavora tries to argue that schools should not penalize men for the fact that women do not want to walk-on, she is wrong. A closer examination reveals that the argument should be reversed: Women should not be penalized by limiting the number of teams provided to them just because men want to walk-on to their teams.

B. The Science of Interest

Given the enormous changes that have occurred in women's athletics over the past thirty years, it cannot be argued that women's interests in sports are immutable or innate. Yet Gavora tries to solve the nature-vs.-nurture dilemma, and, in her world, nature dictates women's interest. Women are "naturally" more interested in mothering and gathering food than men, who are better at spear-throwing and "clubbing enemies." Gavora uses this evolutionary theory to explain why "90 percent of two-year-old boys can throw farther than same-age girls." While she acknowledges that her assertions are not provable, she would still use it as "evidence" to legally limit girls' opportunities in athletics. This practice is constitutionally impermissible. These are exactly the sorts of unfounded stereotypes that led to the dearth of women's sporting opportunities throughout the 1950s and 1960s. As courts have held: "Interest and ability rarely develop in a vacuum; they evolve as a function of opportunity and experi-

[41]Title IX Policy Interpretation, 44 Fed. Reg. 71415.
[42]Ibid.

ence. . . . [W]omen's lower rate of participation in athletics reflects women's historical lack of opportunities to participate in sports."[43]

Women's participation rates are still increasing. To cap participation rates based on the idea that women are less interested in sports than men would freeze current levels of participation and would prevent current and future growth of women's opportunities.

C. Interest Is Part of Title IX's Legal Test for Compliance

As Gavora admits, interest is factored into Title IX's third prong of the participation test for compliance. If a school does not have unmet demand for a potentially viable competitive team—if it is providing opportunities for the women athletes who attend the school and have the ability to play and want to play— then as a legal matter, the school will be in compliance under the third prong of Title IX's participation test.[44] It is the huge demand for women's sports that keeps particularly large institutions from relying on prong three to provide fewer opportunities for women than required under the proportionality test. But this just proves the point that girls are interested in sports.

Gavora poses the following question: "If universities are willing to jettison aspiring male athletes in the name of equality, why not aspiring male physicists?" Gavora confuses the gender-blind physics department with sex-segregated athletic departments. Because athletic departments are permitted by Title IX to sponsor separate teams for men and women,[45] they cannot functionally operate in the same gender-blind manner as the other departments within a school. While the math department may not care at all that its male and female enrollment swings drastically from year to year, an athletic department has no such flexibility. A college must decide—well in advance of an athlete's high-school-sophomore year—how many teams they will be sponsoring when that high-school athlete eventually becomes a college freshman. As courts have ruled when closely examining this issue, "determining whether discrimination exists in athletic programs requires gender-conscious, groupwide comparisons."[46] A school creates the opportunities and then recruits athletes to fill the opportunities created. Title IX simply requires that schools allocate these school-created slots in a nondiscriminatory manner.

[43] *Cohen IV,* 101 F.3d, 178–179.

[44] "A recipient which operates or sponsors interscholastic, intercollegiate, club, or intramural athletics shall provide equal athletic opportunity for members of both sexes." 34 C.F.R., Section 106.41(c).

[45] The regulations explicitly permit institutions to provide separate-sex athletic teams "where selection for such teams is based upon competitive skill or the activity involved is a contact sport." 34 C.F.R., Section 106.41(b) (1999).

[46] *Neal,* 198 F.3d, 773.

D. Recruiting Interested Athletes

Both courts and legal commentators have discarded Gavora's "relative interests" arguments, also espoused by defense attorneys in *Cohen*:

> [A]ny survey of [the interests of] the student body will be driven by the university's athletic offerings, recruiting practices, admissions preferences, and athletic scholarships, if available. Particularly at Division I schools that rely on recruiting to select their intercollegiate athletes, the results of a survey of athletic interest in the student body is predetermined by the university's selection of sports and recruiting practices. For example, if a university recruits twice as many men as women for its intercollegiate athletic offerings, a survey that finds more men than women who claim to be interested in participating in intercollegiate athletics is not a true measure of relative interest. Similarly, a survey of student applicants to a university will be skewed by that university's existing opportunities. Students who want to participate in a sport not offered at a particular university may not apply there.[47]

Courts have recognized that demand for sports at a particular college is due in part to what sports are provided by the college, and a school's efforts to attract these athletes to the campus.[48] Students interested in playing soccer in college will not apply to schools that do not have soccer programs. Additionally, recruiting provides increased numbers of new students with an interest and ability to participate in sports. Athletic departments determine the relative interests of men and women when it chooses its sports offerings and decides the sums spent on recruiting.[49]

[47]Deborah Brake and Elizabeth Catlin, "The Path of Most Resistance: The Long Road Toward Gender Equity in Intercollegiate Athletics," 3 *Duke J. Gender L. & Pol'y* 51 (1996), 79; see also John C. Weistart, "Can Gender Equity Find a Place in Commercialized College Sport?," 3 *Duke J. Gender L. & Pol'y* 191 (1996), 234 ("[M]ost schools in Division I and Division II create interest in their programs. They do this by recruiting. Their coaches . . . search out appropriate athletic candidates, who are then cajoled, entreated, and given special considerations solely to induce them to come to school to play sports").

[48]*Neal*, 198 F.3d, 769 ("[T]he creation of additional athletic spots for women would prompt universities to recruit more female athletes, in the long run shifting women's demand curve for sports participation. As more women participated, social norms discouraging women's participation in sports presumably would be further eroded, prompting additional increases in women's participation levels"); *Cohen IV*, 101 F.3d, 177 ("[B]ecause recruitment of interested athletes is at the discretion of the institution, there is a risk that the institution will recruit only enough women to fill positions in a program that already under represents women, and that the smaller size of the women's program will have the effect of discouraging women's participation").

[49]NCAA Report, footnote 20 above.

Gavora conveniently ignores the enormous sums athletic departments spend recruiting men to play for their schools. Recruiting for women, however, is evidence of a problem inherent in trying to attract more women to participate in athletics. She offers a list of the efforts that have been made to recruit women athletes, concentrating on the recent popularity of large women's crew squads across the nation: "What [athletic directors] needed was a sport that could accommodate large numbers of women and didn't require previous experience." Efforts to recruit women include scholarships; open tryouts; coaches walking through campus in search of tall, broad-shouldered women; and advertisements in school newspapers. The fact that male rowers have traditionally been recruited to college campuses using precisely these techniques does not seem to have occurred to Gavora.[50] Indeed, at least one football team from Division I-A has never cut a single walk-on player, even when those players have never had any football experience, in order to fill their teams.[51]

The case of Anita DeFrantz provides the clearest example of this principle at work. One of the most powerful American women in sports, DeFrantz[52] was recruited onto the rowing team at Connecticut College using techniques similar to those mentioned above during her sophomore year. She had never seen a crew team on the water before that time. DeFrantz went on to win an Olympic bronze medal, earn her law degree, become the executive director of the Los Angeles Sports Foundation, and become vice president and executive board member of the International Olympic Committee.[53] Without just the sorts of efforts Gavora recites with contempt, DeFrantz would not only have missed out on competition, but also on this gateway to her career in sports-leadership positions. Rather than demonstrating women's inherent lack of interest in sports, recruiting was essential in giving DeFrantz the keys to this important educational experience and sports-career opportunity.

The last thirty years show irrefutably that interest is a function of available opportunities. Girls and women have rushed to fill genuine participation opportunities as schools have created them, despite the oftentimes second-class treatment they receive. One out of every 2.5 high school girls is now an athlete. Girls currently in high school are participating in athletics at a rate of 2.8 million per year, and 150,000 women now compete in college. It is the huge demand for

---

[50]As recognized in *Cohen III*, crew was an example of a sport in which interest commonly develops only after matriculation to college. 879 F. Supp., 207.

[51]Brief of Appellee, p. 12, *Mercer v. Duke Univ.*, No. 01-1512, 2002 WL 31528244 (4th Cir. 2002); see also Heckman, "The Glass Sneaker," footnote 4 above.

[52]Women's Sports Foundation, http://www.womenssportsfoundation.org/cgi-bin/iowa/athletes/article.html?record=68 (accessed July 2, 2007).

[53]The Official Website of the Olympic Movement, http:// www.olympic.org/uk/organisation/ioc/members/bio_uk.asp?id=35 (accessed July 3, 2007).

women's sports that keeps particularly large institutions with a very small percentage of their students participating in the athletic department from relying on prongs two and three to provide fewer opportunities than required under the proportionality test, proving the point that girls are interested in sports. The myth that Gavora perpetuates—that women are not as interested in sports—persists stubbornly despite the powerful reality to the contrary. Young women continue to be hampered by schools that fail to field teams because of these outmoded stereotypes that virtually everyone—including Gavora—agrees are not provable, and, in fact, are inaccurate.

VII. Windmill #6: Football Helps Women's Athletic Programs

Gavora argues that schools that have large football teams do a better job of providing gender-equity to the female athletes on campus. She tries to make the point that institutions with strong football and men's basketball programs "do the best job of providing opportunities and spending for women's athletics."[54] She describes a study showing that Title IX compliance increased by .4 percentage points for each $1 million in football profits.[55] However, she fails to tell her readers that schools with big football programs are the same schools dropping men's minor sports, like wrestling.[56] It is precisely at these big football schools, Division I-A, where men's sports are being cut at the fastest clip.[57] At the Division II and III NCAA schools, where virtually 100 percent of football programs and athletic departments lose money, the number of men's minor sports per school has actually increased over the past twenty years.[58] In contrast, at the Division I-A level the number of nonrevenue men's sports per school has decreased. If Title IX truly places unreasonable financial constraints on athletic departments, schools with small budgets should have been the first schools to drop men's minor sports, rather than these larger schools. Gavora's statistics support the fact that the opposite is true. The oft-repeated proposition by economists and legal commentators alike is that it is football's wasted expenditures and spiraling costs that are actually responsible for cutting men's minor sports,[59] not Title IX.[60]

---

[54]Ibid., 62.

[55]Ibid.

[56]Equity in Athletics Disclosure Act, Pub. L. No. 103-382, Section 360(B), 108 Stat. 3969, 3969-71 (1994).

[57]Ibid.

[58]Welch Suggs, "At Smaller Colleges, Women Get Bigger Share of Sports Funds," *Chronicle of Higher Education* (April 14, 2000), A69.

[59]Fulks, footnote 43 above.

[60]Andrew Zimbalist, "Backlash against Title IX: An End Run around Female Athletes," *Chronicle of Higher Education* (March 3, 2000), B9 (noting that female athletes still play in inferior facilities, stay in cheaper hotels while traveling, eat in cheaper restaurants, have smaller promotional

The topic of football raises two separate and seemingly independent public debates on collegiate athletics occurring simultaneously. In addition to the attention Title IX is receiving, college presidents and governing board directors are appalled by the spiraling costs of operating football programs.[61] These costs have nothing to do with making better athletes or a more exciting spectator event, and everything to do with fierce competition for attracting unpaid athletes to the school.[62] These new monies are directed from student fees, general funds, and donors; what does not go into cherry-wood lockers, solid brass nameplates, plush carpets, and million-dollar weight rooms ends up in the pockets of coaches. The best-paid football coaches now make in excess of $2 million a year.[63] Quite apart from any public discussion about Title IX, schools throughout the country are questioning whether this expensive brand of football can survive within the context of an educational institution while preserving the educational mission of athletics.[64] Economists and legal commentators alike have placed the blame for any dropping of men's sports squarely at the feet of these big football programs.[65] If these big football programs help women at all, it is only because Title IX requires that student-athletes be given the same

budgets, and have fewer assistant coaches); John C. Weistart, "Can Gender Equity Find a Place in Commercialized College Sport?," 3 *Duke J. Gender L. & Pol'y* 191, 221 n. 101 (1996) (revenue sports depend on large taxpayer and institutional investments and the general good will of the university in order to generate revenue); Tom McMillen with Paul Coggins, *Out of Bounds: How the American Sports Establishment Is Being Driven by Greed and Hypocrisy—And What Needs to Be Done About It* (New York: Simon and Schuster, 1992) (arguing for a new distribution of funds, not based on win-loss records, but on such criteria as graduation rates and compliance with Title IX).

[61] Zimbalist, footnote 59 above; Andrew Zimbalist, *Unpaid Professionals: Commercialism and Conflict in Big-Time College Sports* (Princeton: Princeton University Press, 1999); Michael Sokolove, "Football Is a Sucker's Game," *New York Times Magazine*, December 22, 2002, 6.

[62] Zimbalist, *Unpaid Professionals*, footnote 60 above.

[63] Ibid.

[64] Sokolove, footnote 61 above; Welch Suggs, "College Presidents Urged to Take Control of College Sports; Knight Commission Seeks to Create a Coalition, Independent of the NCAA, to Create Reform," *Chronicle of Higher Education* (July 6, 2001), A35; "Tulane Opts to Remain in Division I-A," *Chronicle of Higher Education* (June 20, 2003), A33 (Tulane University announced that it would keep its sports programs in Division I-A of the National Collegiate Athletic Association, ending a two-month debate over whether it should cut its losses—$7 million annually—by dropping football or restructuring its athletics department and switching to the NCAA's Division III).

[65] John C. Weistart, "Can Gender Equity Find a Place in Commercialized College Sport?," 3 *Duke J. Gender L. & Pol'y* 191, 234 (1996) (revenue sports depend on large taxpayer and institutional investments and the general good will of the university in order to generate revenue); see McMillen, *Out of Bounds*; Equity in Athletics Disclosure Act, Pub. L. No. 103-382 Section 360(B), 108 Stat. 3969, 3969–3971 (1994), available at http://ope.ed.gov/athletics/index.asp (arguing for a new distribution of funds, not based on win-loss records, but on such criteria as graduation rates, compliance with Title IX); Brian L. Porto, "Completing the Revolution: Title IX as Catalyst for an Alternative Model of College Sports," 8 *Seton Hall J. Sport L.* 351, 369, 383–399 (1998) (describing the corruption resulting from the commercialism of college sports, and the need for a new model of collegiate athletics).

treatment and benefits.[66] As schools foist benefits such as facilities, equipment, travel perks, access to training tables, and training facilities onto football players, Title IX requires that they provide women athletes with the same benefits.[67] Assuredly, women's advances in schools that have big football programs are not due to the gratuitous nature of schools with football teams. . . .

VIII. Windmill #8: Case Law Turned into Urban Legend

Another problem with *Tilting* is that it inaccurately portrays a number of important Title IX cases by bending the facts and law to create what is best described as the seeds of urban legend. Many of Gavora's assertions are not footnoted, and the ones that are cited come from newspaper stories or editorials, and not from the relevant court opinions themselves. Her factual inaccuracies are numerous and pointless to recount. But I can't resist just one example: *Mercer v. Duke University*.[68]

Gavora so mischaracterizes the litigation in *Mercer*[69] that the resulting picture she paints is fictional silliness. Gavora states: "Coach Goldsmith said that he admired [Mercer's] spunk, but he and several former coaches and kickers testified that she didn't have the strength to boot long field goals against major college competition. Duke denied any bias, but the jury sided with the lady placekicker and awarded Mercer $2 million for her trouble."

Again, published opinions and appellee's brief paint an entirely different story. Heather Sue Mercer was an all-state football placekicker in high school,[70] having been the starting placekicker for Yorktown High School.[71] Yorktown won the 1993 New York state championship, and Mercer was voted All-State placekicker.[72] When she entered Duke University in 1994, she approached Coach Goldsmith and expressed her interest in being a walk-on kicker for the football team.[73] Despite the fact that Goldsmith had never before required another player to try out, he made Mercer do so, and under adverse conditions.[74] After the tryout, he told her she had not qualified for the team, but told her that she could be a manager. In 1995, she was allowed to practice with the team, and she was picked by the seniors (over two male players) to be the kicker during

---

[66] 44 Fed. Reg. 71413 (1979).

[67] 34 C.F.R., Section 106.41 (2002).

[68] *Mercer*, 190 F.3d, 643 (4th Cir. 1999).

[69] Ibid.

[70] *Mercer*, 190 F.3d, 644.

[71] Brief of Appellee at 2, *Mercer*, 2002 WL 31528244.

[72] Ibid.

[73] *Mercer*, 181 F. Supp. 2d 525, 529 (M.D.N.C. 2001), *vacated in part*, 2002 WL 31528244 (4th Cir. 2002).

[74] *Mercer*, 181 F. Supp., 530.

the preseason intrasquad scrimmage game, where Mercer kicked the game-winning field goal. Although Goldsmith then put her on the team, from 1995 to 1997 he continually took steps to discourage Mercer from wanting to be a part of the team. According to the court, these acts included: Goldsmith's prohibiting her from attending preseason training camp in 1995, while allowing the other kickers to do so; his telling her that she should outgrow playing little boys' games and instead consider other activities such as beauty pageants or cheerleading; his refusing to issue her a uniform or pads or allow her to dress for games; his refusing to allow her to sit on the sidelines and telling her instead to go sit with her boyfriend in the stands.

Goldsmith later issued a press release stating Mercer was "not on the active roster"—a designation created specifically for her, whereby she could practice with the other kickers but could not participate at any games. In 1996, Goldsmith dismissed her from the team saying there was no place on the team for her, despite having never cut a single player from the team before.[75]

As Gavora notes, Goldsmith tried to belittle Mercer's athletic abilities both as a trial strategy and publicly. But uncontroverted expert testimony established Mercer's superiority as a kicker over Duke's other kickers.[76] Evidence at trial showed that in March 1995, three walk-on placekickers came out for spring practice: Mercer, Pat Tillou, and Ted Post.[77] Unlike Mercer, Tillou and Post had never kicked for a high school or college football team. Unlike Mercer, Post had not attended winter-conditioning drills, and Tillou attended only the last two weeks of winter conditioning. During spring practice Mercer demonstrated that she was a strong kicker who was more accurate and consistent than Tillou or Post. Evidence at trial also showed that Goldsmith rarely observed Mercer kicking and generally did not allow her to kick from long distances when the other placekickers were all permitted to do so.[78] Even though she was cut from the team in 1996, Mercer practiced with the other players in 1997 in hopes of making the team for the next season; however, Goldsmith told her she had no right to be there and told her to leave.[79]

Now imagine that Mercer had endured the same sort of conduct because of her race—making her the sole African American required to try out for the team

---

[75] Brief of Appellee, 12, *Mercer*, 2002 WL 31528244.

[76] Ibid., 13–14 ("Bill Renner, a former NFL player and nationally recognized kicking expert, observed that Mercer was a good ball-striker, consistent, and disciplined, and had good leg strength, a good trajectory on her kicks, and an effective range from 40 to 45 yards. After reviewing videotapes of Mercer and Jim Mills, Renner concluded that Mercer was a superior kicker to Mills. Likewise, Paul Woodside, a former All-American placekicker at West Virginia University, described Mercer as having outstanding technique, accuracy, and consistency, with a field goal range in the mid-40s. He also concluded that Mercer was 'far superior' to Mills").

[77] Ibid., 4.

[78] *Mercer*, 181 F. Supp., 534.

[79] Ibid.

under adverse conditions. Imagine teammates picking this African American to kick the field-winning goal, or being told that the athlete is on the team but is prohibited from attending preseason training camp, while allowing less qualified white athletes to do so. Imagine telling the African American that she should re-evaluate goals realistically, and should acknowledge the limitations that her race would forever place on her. Imagine not being allowed to get a uniform or to sit with teammates—all because of the athlete's race. Imagine a coach who refused to realistically evaluate skills because of race. This was the importance of Heather Sue Mercer's case for all women.

After evaluating Duke University's "flagrant disregard" of the ongoing acts of "discrimination and humiliating behavior," the jury assessed the University $2 million in punitive damages to deter them and others from similar conduct in the future.[80] Logically, *Tilting* should be praising this decision, because it was an example of a woman competing on a men's team, who was requesting treatment on equal terms with the other male athletes. Instead, Gavora turns the case into yet another example of the law gone wrong.

XI. Conclusion

Tilting the Playing Field is a quixotic, agenda-driven opinion piece that blames Title IX for all the evils in athletic departments. It reads like a speech written for an audience of disgruntled male wrestlers who, rather than seeing the real evil giant that crushed their team, view life one dimensionally with a simple mantra: male sports good, Title IX bad. Gavora's speech-writing background seems to have prevented her from discussing legal cases without putting a harsh antifemale spin on her analysis of judicial opinions. Her writing is awash with political buzzwords like "quota," "victim," "entitlement," and "affirmative action," and harsh adjectives and adverbs that seem designed to get attention through talking trash. *Tilting the Playing Field* is not an academic work, though it pretends to be. That its arguments are riddled with inconsistencies and its facts drawn from spin provided by losing defense attorneys matters little. Its style is as if its writer were auditioning for a column in the *Conservative Chronicle*: hyperbolic rhetoric with frequent flashes of fiction. For those whose lives revolve around tilting at Title IX windmills, it is a must-read.

[80]Ibid., 548–549. This $2-million jury verdict was vacated by the court in November 2002 after the Supreme Court held that punitive damages may not be awarded in private actions brought under Title VI of the Civil Rights Act of 1964. See *Barnes v. Gorman*, 536 U.S. 181 (2002). The Mercer court reasoned that since Title IX, upon which Mercer's claim is based, is also modeled after Title VI and is interpreted and applied in the same manner as Title VI, that the Supreme Court's conclusion that punitive damages are not available under Title VI "compels the conclusion that punitive damages are not available for private actions brought to enforce Title IX." *Mercer*, 2002 WL 31528244, *1.

What to Do about Title IX*

Andrew Zimbalist

[Zimbalist begins with a history behind the most recent attacks on the law and an analysis of other explanations behind wrestling's decline, including a review of the GAO report.]

The athletics' arms' race is alive and well, but it has little to show for itself on the bottom line. The 2002 NCAA Revenues and Expenses study finds that of the 114 reporting DIA[1] schools, the average athletic-department deficit was $600,000 in 2001. If one adds to this the average $1.425 million in student fees going to athletics and the $4.625 million in donations going to athletics, the stand-alone athletic department operating deficit averages $6.05 million. Even this number substantially understates the average subsidy to intercollegiate athletics at DIA schools.

The problem is that the one-sided incentives in DIA lead most schools to chase the Holy Grail of financial gain. But, like the NCAA itself, athletic departments are run by athletic directors, coaches, and conference commissioners who do not have to answer to stockholders and do not face the financial discipline of the marketplace. The consequence is endemic waste.

For example, DIA football does not need eighty-five scholarships. Sixty would do fine. NFL teams have forty-five roster, plus seven reserve, players. The average Division I-A team has thirty-two walk-ons plus eighty-five scholarship

---

*Based on testimony before the U.S. Department of Education's Commission on Title IX, San Diego, California, November 20, 2002.

[1]The NCAA is divided up according to competitive divisions. The most competitive division with the largest, most expensive, and elaborate athletic programs is Division I-A. Divisions II and III comprise the more-than-700 smaller programs.

players. If football scholarships were cut to sixty, the average college would save approximately $750,000 annually, enough to finance more than two wrestling teams (whose average cost is $330,000 per team).

College coaches have protested that college football teams cannot be properly compared to professional teams. The latter, they say, can always call up reserves when players get injured, but college teams must have players on their rosters. This is a red herring. The NCAA Injury Surveillance System Summary reports that for the 2000–2001 season, the serious-injury rate during games in football was 14.1 per 1000 athlete exposures, while the rate in football practices was 1.6 per 1000. If we assume that sixty players enter a game and the team plays thirteen games during the year (i.e., including a postseason game), then the average total number of serious injuries (where a player is out seven or more days) from games is eleven per year. If on average each such player misses two games, then the average number of game-injured players is 1.69 per game.

Performing a similar computation for practice-injured players (assuming eighty exposures per practice, five practices per week, and fifteen weeks of practice) yields 9.6 injured players during the year. If each misses two games on average, then the average number of practice-injured players is 1.48 per game, and the total number of injured players per game is 3.17. To be cautious, one can even double or triple this estimate and there would be fewer than seven or fewer than ten injured players per game. There is no justification here for having eighty-five grants-in-aid for a Division I-A football team, even if the average team did not have thirty-two walk-ons.

But why stop here? The NCAA should seek a congressional antitrust exemption with regard to coaches' salaries. Currently, there are dozens of Division I men's basketball coaches who make over $1 million and some who make over $2 million annually, and there are dozens more football coaches in this category. Knock them down to $200,000 (which would still put them above 99 percent of the faculty) and colleges would be able to add another three to six sports, or, heaven forbid, reduce their large athletic deficits. Lest anyone think that these stratospheric coaches' salaries are justified economically, let me remind you that economic theory predicts a coach will be paid a salary up to his marginal revenue product in a competitive labor market. That said, how can it be that the top-paid coaches in college football and men's basketball get comparable compensation packages to each other when the average DIA football team has revenues fully three times as high as the average DIA basketball team? And, how can it be that the top dozen or two DIA football coaches get paid salaries similar to the NFL coaches, when the average NFL team has revenues more than ten times as high as the average DIA football team? These coaches' compensation packages have more in common with the bloated stock option plans in Enron, WorldCom, and other corporations than they do with a competitive marketplace.

Coaches are reaping part of the value that is produced by their unpaid athletes. If unpaid athletes are subject to a restraint of trade because they are amateurs, then Congress should be willing to allow coaches' salaries also to be restrained.

Other savings are available to athletic programs. Colleges going to bowl games might also consider reducing the size of their traveling entourages (Nebraska took a delegation of 826 to the Rose Bowl last year and spent $2.3 million), eliminating the practice of putting the men's basketball and football teams up at a local hotel before home games, diminishing the size of coaching staffs, cutting the length of the playing season in many sports, and so on.

It is frequently argued that it is inappropriate for supporters of gender equity to attack waste in college football because, without football, athletic departments would have less money to fund women's sports. First, when the proper and full accounting is done, this assertion—that football generates a large surplus—only holds for two or three dozen out of well over 500 football teams in the NCAA. Second, even for these two or three dozen teams that generate several million dollars of surplus for their athletic departments, there is no reason why they should not produce still larger surpluses by running a less extravagant and less wasteful program.

Let me conclude with a final comment about DIA football. One often hears that gender equity is fine, but football should be taken out of the equation—that is, remove football's eighty-five scholarships and its operating budget before judging parity between men's and women's sports. There is no justification for such a policy. One might as well argue that women's crew should be taken out before the gender participation numbers are compared. Title IX does not state that there shall be no gender discrimination where revenue generation is equal. It simply states that there shall be no gender discrimination—period. A sport's presumed profitability is plainly not a relevant criterion. As stated in Article I of the NCAA Constitution, college sports are based on the principle of amateurism and the subordination of athletic to academic goals. As such, Division I and II schools benefit mightily from not directly paying their athletes, from tax exemptions on facility bonds, and from special tax treatment of UBIT[2] income. Further, in 1984 the Supreme Court determined that the NCAA may legitimately restrain trade in many areas because, *due to its amateur branding,* college sports increase output and enhance consumer welfare.

---

[2]UBIT is an acronym that stands for unrelated business income taxation.

If college sports were to professionalize and separate out their football programs, using nonmatriculated athletes and paying them salaries and benefits, then there would be a case to eliminate football from gender-equity reckonings. As long as football benefits from the umbrellas of amateurism and the academy, however, the only rational course is to treat it the same as all sports programs for Title IX purposes.

In sum, the financial problem with college sports today is not Title IX or its implementation guidelines. The problem is waste.

Open to All: Title IX at Thirty*

Commission Findings

Question One: Are Title IX standards for assessing equal opportunity in athletics working to promote opportunities for male and female athletes?

Finding 1

After 30 years of Title IX, great progress has been made, but more needs to be done to create opportunities for women and girls and retain opportunities for boys and men.

Given the impassioned testimony presented to this Commission, there is universal consensus on one critical point: Every person who testified stated their full support for Title IX of the Education Amendments of 1972. It is uniformly agreed that this landmark law, enacted 30 years ago, has contributed greatly to opening doors of opportunity for women in our society.

Finding 2

Current Title IX policy provides for three separate ways for institutions to demonstrate that they are in compliance with Title IX's participation requirement.

The policy interpretation issued by the Office for Civil Rights in 1979 created a three-part test for an institution to demonstrate compliance with the athletic participation requirement of Title IX. . . .

*The Secretary of Education's Commission on Opportunity in Athletics, February 28, 2003, excerpt; www.ed.gov/about/bdscomm/list/athletics/title9report.pdf (accessed July 3, 2007).

If properly enforced, the three-part test can be a flexible way for schools to comply with Title IX. On numerous occasions, the Commission has heard strong support for retaining the three-part test to give schools flexibility in structuring their athletics programs while guarding against freezing discrimination into place. The three-part test in theory provides flexibility for educational institutions by providing more than one way to demonstrate compliance, while also establishing attainable goals for eliminating discrimination. The Commission has heard testimony from a number of sources that many educational institutions attempt to comply solely with the proportionality part of the test while others seek to rely on parts two or three.

As will be discussed in more detail later, though, the Commission has heard numerous complaints about the three-part test. Many have argued to the Commission that because the guidance concerning the second and third parts of the test is so ambiguous, the proportionality part is the only meaningful test. Moreover many witnesses argued that the Office for Civil Rights and private litigants have transformed substantial proportionality into strict proportionality. The Commission also concluded that the test for compliance can be revitalized if the Secretary of Education will provide new guidance, while also significantly increasing efforts to reach out with educational materials.

Finding 3

Many practitioners feel that their institutions must meet the proportionality test to ensure a "safe harbor" and avoid expensive litigation.

Witnesses and Commissioners stated on numerous occasions that attorneys and consultants have told them that the only safe way to demonstrate compliance with Title IX's participation requirement is to show that they meet the proportionality requirement of the three-part test. This part assumes that an educational institution is not discriminating in offering participation opportunities if the male-female ratio of athletes at an institution is proportional to the male-female ratio of undergraduate enrollment at that institution. It is true that many federal courts have emphasized the proportionality requirement in Title IX litigation. The facts of the *Cohen* case underscore the challenge institutions may face in meeting the evidentiary requirements of parts two and three of the three-part test, which are by their nature more subjective than part one.

Finding 4

Although, in a strict sense, the proportionality part of the three-part test does not require that opportunities for boys and men be limited, it has been a factor, along with other factors, in the decision to cut or cap teams.

The 1996 Clarification letter advised educational institutions that they may "choose to eliminate or cap teams as a way of complying with part one of the three-part test." Cutting teams or limiting the available places on teams is not a requirement for complying with Title IX. However, the Commission was told that when faced with a complaint regarding its athletics programs, an institution may feel that cutting a team or capping opportunities is an easy way to gain compliance.

Testimony to the Commission established that there has been an unfortunate loss of teams, particularly in nonrevenue or Olympic sports. The Commission found that it is extremely difficult to obtain a set of data that is accepted by all parties. However, all agree that there has been a troubling decrease in athletic opportunities for boys and men.

The correlation between the enforcement of Title IX and this loss of teams has also been hotly contested. Many witnesses told the Commission that they believe that teams on which they participated were cut in order to comply with Title IX. The Commission believes that it is unfair to blame the loss of teams wholly on Title IX enforcement, though. Facility limitations and budgetary concerns put heavy pressure on educational institutions to cut back their athletic programs. However, when institutions feel they must make cuts for budgetary reasons, they cannot ignore the potential effect of their decision on Title IX compliance. For instance, a school may be concerned about litigation if it cuts a women's team without being in compliance with the proportionality test. . . .

Finding 5

Escalating operational costs in intercollegiate athletics threaten the effort to end discrimination in athletics and preserve athletic opportunities.

Title IX does not limit an institution's flexibility in deciding how budgets will be allocated among sports or teams. This flexibility should not be subjected to government interference, as long as those decisions are not discriminatory. There can be no question, though, that the cost of operations in intercollegiate athletics has escalated rapidly. This escalation in expenditures is often referred to as the "arms race" because as one school escalates its spending on revenue-producing sports, its competitors are required to match that move to retain competitiveness. It is clear that in some cases, this "arms race" has been the catalyst for the discontinuation of some teams.

While necessary, control of the "arms race" in athletic expenditures is well beyond the province of this Commission to control. It is also clear that many, if not most, of those involved with the leadership of intercollegiate athletics already recognize the need for national action related to the escalation. This Commission, though, would like to state its sense that all avenues must be explored in order to allow institutions to realize potentially great savings by reining in the "arms race." This savings could be the means of retaining some opportunities that might otherwise be lost.

Question Two: Is there adequate Title IX guidance that enables colleges and school districts to know what is expected of them and to plan for an athletic program that effectively meets the needs and interests of their students?

Finding 1

There is great confusion about Title IX requirements caused by a lack of clarity in guidance from the Office for Civil Rights.

Discussion among Commissioners and testimony offered to the Commission has indicated a widespread sense that the Office for Civil Rights has not provided enough clarity to help institutions to understand how they can establish compliance with Title IX. The confusion has involved each portion of the three-part test, but particularly the second and third parts. This confusion may result from a number of factors. Among these might be: (1) misunderstanding or ignorance about the exact nature of the requirements for Title IX compliance, (2) a lack of education by the Office for Civil Rights on the nature of the three-part test, (3) a lack of clarity in the second and third parts of the test, and (4) a need for additional technical assistance and practical examples of the ways in which institutions can comply. Some have suggested that the Equity in Athletics Disclosure Act contributes to confusion about Title IX compliance by focusing only on the relative rates of participation that would be used for the first part of the test. This might give the impression that this first part is the only effective part of the test.

With regard to the first part of the three-part test, some administrators and others felt they had received conflicting information about the nature of the "safe harbor" concept and the meaning of strict proportionality. As described above, the first part of the three-part test has been designated by the Office for Civil Rights as a "safe harbor" for demonstrating compliance with Title IX's participation requirement. Some have suggested that this gives institutions the sense that only by complying with the first part of the test can they avoid a finding of discrimination in their athletic programs. Thus, schools may feel pressure to achieve proportionality as quickly as possible regardless of how it is accomplished.

With regard to the second part of the test, there has been confusion expressed about how an institution can determine whether it is in compliance. Specifically, clarity is needed regarding the phrase "continuous expansion," and in the requirement that an educational institution must create a new women's team to comply with this test. . . .

With regard to the third part of the test, some administrators express confusion about the possibility of using interest surveys to periodically determine levels of student interest in athletics, which then must be met with matching levels of athletic opportunity. In addition, schools expressed some concern about whether they must approve every request for recognition of a new women's team regardless of financial limitations to accommodate student interest. Thus, some witnesses have argued that if an educational institution is involved with litigation for dropping or failing to add a women's team, that fact alone would preclude a finding that they had accommodated student interest.

This wide range of confusion about the three-part test indicates a need for further information from the Office for Civil Rights about the precise meaning of these tests and the available means for complying with them. Indeed, some schools may be making decisions that may limit the athletic opportunities of their students because those schools do not understand what Title IX actually requires of them.

It is also extremely important to note that any confusion institutions feel about Title IX guidance is greatly exacerbated when schools receive contradictory guidance on compliance from different regions of the Office for Civil Rights. Because administrators may seek information on compliance from their peers in other institutions, differing standards in the regional offices of the Office for Civil Rights can have wide repercussions. Consistency across regions should be a high priority in the effort to clarify the requirements of the three-part test. . . .

Finding 2

The Office for Civil Rights' enforcement of Title IX can be strengthened.

Complaints to the Commission about enforcement of Title IX by the Office for Civil Rights have focused on a few areas. First, some have complained that the process of enforcement is not sufficiently transparent and that sharing of settlement letters might add transparency to the process. Second, concern has been expressed that the enforcement of Title IX is not sufficiently strong because federal funding has never been withheld from a school for failure to comply. Obviously, the hesitancy to use this penalty might be explained by the enormous effects it would have on a school's educational mission. However, some have suggested that the Office for Civil Rights may have other available sanctions short of this with which to encourage compliance. . . .

Question Five: How do revenue-producing and large-roster teams affect the provision of equal athletic opportunities?

The Department has heard from some parties that whereas some men athletes will "walk-on" to intercollegiate teams—without athletic financial aid and without having been recruited—women rarely do this. Is this accurate and, if so, what are its implications for Title IX analysis?

Finding 1

Title IX does not require mirror-image men's and women's sports programs.

Current Title IX enforcement standards consider the total participation opportunities afforded each gender by an institution's athletics program, rather than the numbers or sizes of teams sponsored by the school. So, when the Office for Civil Rights examines whether an athletic program complies with Title IX's participation requirement, it does not look at the relative similarity of teams offered to either sex, but at the ways in which the school accommodates the interests and abilities of athletes. This means that Title IX does not impose a requirement that each women's team be matched by a corresponding men's team or vice versa. This appropriately allows institutions to structure their programs to reflect the relative interests on that specific campus. This allows for nondiscriminatory reasons to be factored into an institutional decision to offer opportunities that might otherwise appear inequitable (such as a team with equipment expenses or roster sizes higher than another team).

Finding 2

Artificial limits on walk-on opportunities do not benefit anyone.

Although no statistical analysis of this issue has been performed, there has been much testimony about the relative rates at which men and women walk-on to teams. A walk-on athlete is one who participates in a sport without either full or partial scholarship support for their participation. A number of witnesses have told Commissioners that male athletes currently walk-on to teams at greater levels than do females. It has been alleged that this has led institutions to limit the number of men allowed to walk-on to teams, a practice known as roster management. Roster management may control the appearance of disproportional participation, but it does not create any corresponding benefit for the sex not subject to roster management.

The relative differences in rates at which men and women walk-on to teams has been explained by reference to cultural forces encouraging male sports participation, which are not matched by a corresponding set of forces for women. It has also been suggested that since women are more involved in a number of other extracurricular activities, they may be simply exercising their choices in ways different to those of men. . . .

A situation where one sex loses the opportunity to walk-on to teams where no corresponding benefit to the other sex is gained is not the intent of Title IX enforcement. Limiting walk-ons for reasons other than those related to lack of institutional resources or coaching decisions has serious ramifications for students who are not allowed to participate in athletics. Schools should not impose these kinds of artificial barriers to such participation.

Finding 3

Since Congress has previously declined to exempt revenue-producing sports from Title IX consideration, any change in that policy would have to be generated by Congressional action.

Commission Recommendations

Based on its findings, the Commission provides the following recommendations to the Secretary of Education. The Commission urges the Secretary to give these recommendations serious consideration and study. Recommendations unanimously approved by the Commission are noted with an asterisk.

Recommendation 1*

The Department of Education should reaffirm its strong commitment to equal opportunity and the elimination of discrimination for girls and boys, women and men.

A clear consensus emerged that affirmed Title IX's importance as a major federal civil rights statute that has brought about tremendous advancements in our society. The Commission heard no testimony recommending that Title IX be repealed or even revised. The Commission recognizes that while women and girls have had many new opportunities, there is much more that must be done. Title IX will continue to be a critical component of our nation's quest for fairness.

Recommendation 2

Any clarification or policy interpretation should consider the recommendations that are approved by this Commission, and substantive adjustments to current enforcement of Title IX should be developed through the normal federal rule-making process.

The Commission heard criticism that the current interpretation of Title IX was implemented through nonregulatory processes. The Commission strongly recommends that any new Title IX policies or procedures be subject to public notice and comment, and that the Administrative Procedures Act be strictly adhered to. When the public is given an opportunity to comment on proposed rules, the new rules can be improved by those comments. Moreover, the new rules are given legitimacy when this process is followed. . . .

Recommendation 4*

The Office for Civil Rights should not, directly or indirectly, change current policies in ways that would undermine Title IX enforcement regarding nondiscriminatory treatment in participation, support services, and scholarships.

Given the widespread support for and success of Title IX, the Department of Education should not change policies in a way that would threaten any progress in creating athletic opportunities for women. It should also be understood that the Commission in no way seeks to lessen the importance of institutional requirements related to nondiscrimination in facilities and support services although these are not discussed at length in this report.

Recommendation 5*

The Office for Civil Rights should make clear that cutting teams in order to demonstrate compliance with Title IX is a disfavored practice.

The loss of teams described in the Commission's findings, and eloquently described by many of the people affected, has caused the Commission great concern. Although the Commission recognizes that that the decision to drop a team is affected by many factors, it should be made clear to schools that it is not a favored way of complying with Title IX. The fundamental premise of Title IX is that decisions to limit opportunities should not be made on the basis of gender. Therefore, educational institutions should pursue all other alternatives before cutting or capping any team when Title IX compliance is a factor in that decision. If indeed teams have to be cut, student athletes should be given justification and adequate notice.

Recommendation 6*

The Office for Civil Rights should aggressively enforce Title IX standards, including implementing sanctions for institutions that do not comply. The Department of Education should also explore ways to encourage compliance with Title IX, rather than merely threatening sanctions.

Testimony before the Commission has noted that no school has been denied federal funding for failure to comply with Title IX. Although this is a dramatic enforcement mechanism, it is still available when there is no compliance. Other mechanisms should be pursued with educational institutions that encourage compliance and are not necessarily punitive.

Recommendation 7*

The Department of Education should encourage educational and sports leaders to promote male- and female-student interest in athletics at the elementary and secondary levels to encourage participation in physical education and explore ways of encouraging women to walk-on to teams.

In addition to enforcement of Title IX, much should be done to encourage interest in athletics. The Commission recommends that the Department of Education explore innovative programs to support and nurture a strong interest in athletics and physical fitness. The Commission recommends that the Department explore this issue closely with the President's Council on Physical Fitness.

The Department should also consult with national sports organizations, foundations, and professional sports leagues about increasing their commitment to developing youth sports programs. The Commission believes that if young girls and boys are participating in large numbers in youth sports programs, our culture will continue to change so that athletic opportunities at the intercollegiate level will come to include equal opportunities for women.

Recommendation 8

The Department of Education should encourage educational institutions and national athletic governance organizations to address the issue of reducing excessive expenditures in intercollegiate athletics. Possible areas to explore might include an antitrust exemption for college athletics.

One of the major factors identified by the Commission in the decision to cut teams is the lack of resources at some schools. The Commission has also heard much testimony about ever-mounting expenditures on college athletics that may exacerbate the problem. Sound use of financial resources will contribute to the continuation of broad sports programs that include Olympic sports. The Commission believes that the Department of Education could make helpful suggestions related to this matter. One Commissioner expressed opposition to an antitrust exemption for college athletics.

Recommendation 9*

The Department of Education should encourage the redesign of the Equity in Athletics Disclosure Act so that it provides the public with a relevant and simplified tool to evaluate the status of Title IX compliance in the nation's postsecondary institutions.

The Commission has heard that the current form for Equity in Athletics Disclosure Act reporting may contribute to the sense that schools need to comply solely with the first part of the three-part test. The Commission also felt that the form should be significantly simplified. Since this form was created legislatively, any change would come about through Congress, so this recommendation is framed as a suggestion of encouragement the Department of Education can give to Congress. . . .

Recommendation 12

The Office for Civil Rights should reexamine its regulations regarding the standards governing private funding of particular sports aimed at preventing those sports from being dropped or to allow specific teams to be added.

This recommendation reflects the same concerns as that of the previous one. It encourages the Office for Civil Rights to review the standards by which outside individuals or groups may make contributions to sports programs at educational institutions. The Commissioners noted in regard to this recommendation that total exemption of sport-specific funding would not be appropriate under this recommendation.

In contrast, some Commissioners were concerned that the current regulations are adequate and need not be revisited. They opposed this recommendation because they felt that revisiting current rules might open the door to discriminatory funding practices where teams would receive large donations that would only benefit one sex. One Commissioner felt this would be analogous to a race-specific scholarship donation.

Recommendation 13*

The Department of Education should encourage the NCAA to review its scholarship and other guidelines to determine if they adequately promote or hinder athletic-participation opportunities.

The last finding of the Commission noted that changes in scholarship limits by the NCAA might provide opportunities for schools to promote opportunities in athletics. This recommendation is aimed at the NCAA, which determines allowable scholarships.

Recommendation 14*

If substantial proportionality is retained as a way of complying with Title IX, the Office for Civil Rights should clarify the meaning of substantial proportionality to allow for a reasonable variance in the relative ratio of athletic participation of men and women while adhering to the nondiscriminatory tenets of Title IX.

The Commission has been told that the meaning of the term "substantial proportionality" in the first part of the three-part test has been adjusted in practice to require "strict proportionality." This recommendation would clarify the meaning of "substantial proportionality."

Recommendation 15

The Office for Civil Rights should consider a different way of measuring participation opportunities for purposes of allowing an institution to demonstrate that it has complied with the first part of the three-part test. An institution could establish that it has complied with the first part of the test by showing that the available slots for men and women, as demonstrated by the predetermined number of participants for each team offered by the institution, are proportional to the male-female ratio in enrollment.

This option would allow a school to demonstrate that it has made athletic opportunities available. Even if the slots a program makes available are not filled, the school could still be in compliance with the first part of the three-part test. It would also remove artificial limitations on the walk-on athletes at an institution.

Some Commissioners who opposed this recommendation argued that since walk-on athletes receive institutional resources, they should be treated the same as other athletes. In response to the concern with capping men's opportunities, they said that teams may be capped for reasons unrelated to Title IX. Finally, they stated that this recommendation did not take into consideration the possibility that female enrollment may be lower due to disparities in recruiting men and women to educational institutions. . . .

Recommendation 17

For the purpose of calculating proportionality with the male-female ratio of enrollment in both scholarships and participation, these ratios will exclude walk-on athletes as defined by the NCAA. Proportionality ratios will be calculated through a comparison of full or partial scholarship recipients and recruited walk-ons.

As described in the findings, the Commission feels that artificial limitations on the number of walk-ons may limit opportunities without any corresponding gain for the underrepresented sex. This recommendation aims at removing those artificial limitations.

Some commissioners expressed a concern with this recommendation because they believe that differential treatment for walk-on athletes would not be appropriate since these athletes receive resources from their institutions, as do other athletes.

Recommendation 18

The Office for Civil Rights should allow institutions to conduct continuous interest surveys on a regular basis as a way of (1) demonstrating compliance with the three-part test, (2) allowing schools to accurately predict and reflect men's and women's interest in athletics over time, and (3) stimulating student interest in varsity sports. The Office should specify the criteria necessary for conducting such a survey in a way that is clear and understandable.

Some schools have complained that they have no quantifiable way of demonstrating compliance with the third part of the three-part test. This recommendation directs the Department of Education to develop specific guidance on interest surveys and how these surveys could establish compliance with the three-part test.

Those Commissioners opposed to this recommendation believe that allowing interest surveys may prevent future progress in providing opportunities for women because offering opportunities regardless of interest may encourage participation even where none currently exists. They felt that any use of interest surveys should be limited to demonstrating compliance with the third part of the three-part test. They also faulted the recommendation for not taking into consideration the effect of historical patterns of discrimination on women's interest in athletics.

Recommendation 19*

The Office for Civil Rights should study the possibility of allowing institutions to demonstrate that they are in compliance with the third part of the three-part test by comparing the ratio of male-female athletic participation at the institution with the demonstrated interests and abilities shown by regional, state, or national youth or high-school participation rates or national governing bodies, or by the interest levels indicated in surveys of prospective or enrolled students at that institution.

This recommendation provides another way for schools to quantify compliance with the three-part test.

Recommendation 20

In demonstrating compliance with the proportionality requirement of the first part of the three-part test, the male-female ratio of athletic participation should be measured against the male-female ratio of an institution's undergraduate population minus nontraditional students.

The Commission has heard testimony indicating that nontraditional students are much less likely to participate in athletics than other students. This recommendation recognizes that phenomenon and is aimed at allowing colleges to comply with Title IX where it would be difficult to do so based on large numbers of students who, based on their circumstances, are extremely unlikely to participate in varsity sports.

The Commissioners opposing this recommendation believe that nontraditional students may be as interested in sports as any other students and should thus not be excluded from consideration in determining proportionality under the first part of the three-part test. They also argued that part three of the three-part test already allows for variances caused by nontraditional students at an educational institution.

Recommendation 21*

The designation of one part of the three-part test as a "safe harbor" should be abandoned in favor of a way of demonstrating compliance with Title IX's participation requirement that treats each part of the test equally. In addition, the evaluation of compliance should include looking at all three parts of the test, in aggregate or in balance, as well as individually.

Many who have testified before the Commission have complained that the emphasis of the Office for Civil Rights on encouraging compliance with the first part of the three-part test by designating it as a "safe harbor" is leading institutions to limit opportunities rather than expand them. This recommendation aims to allow schools to demonstrate compliance using the other parts of the test without having to be concerned about later complaints for noncompliance with the first part.

Recommendation 22*

The Office for Civil Rights should be urged to consider reshaping the second part of the three-part test, including by designating a point at which a school can no longer establish compliance through this part.

The Commission has heard testimony that the second part of the three-part test may no longer be necessary because schools have had since 1972 to comply with Title IX and there is no longer a need to allow them to phase in compliance. It has also heard that the second part is so unclear as to make it almost impossible to use to demonstrate compliance with Title IX. This recommendation urges the Office for Civil Rights to examine the continued viability of the second part of the test and ways of making it more understandable.

Recommendation 23*

Additional ways of demonstrating equity beyond the existing three-part test should be explored by the Department of Education.

Over the years, changes in the demographics of athletic participation and college enrollment have made Title IX enforcement more complicated. As these kinds of changes continue, there may be further need to allow educational institutions to comply with Title IX requirements beyond those currently in place.

Minority Views on the Report of the Commission on Opportunity in Athletics*

Donna de Varona and Julie Foudy

Introduction

In June 2002, Secretary of Education Roderick Paige created the Commission on Opportunity in Athletics to evaluate whether and how current standards governing Title IX's application to athletics should be revised. The Commission is today transmitting its report to the Secretary, a report that includes recommendations for substantial changes to current Title IX guidelines and policies.

After careful review and deliberation and unsuccessful efforts to include adequate discussion of our minority views within the majority report, we have reached the conclusion that we cannot join the report of the Commission. We are instead releasing this Minority Report and request that the Secretary include this document in the official records of the Commission's proceedings.

Our decision is based on (1) our fundamental disagreement with the tenor, structure, and significant portions of the content of the Commission's report, which fails to present a full and fair consideration of the issues or a clear statement of the discrimination women and girls still face in obtaining equal opportunity in athletics; (2) our belief that many of the recommendations made by the majority would seriously weaken Title IX's protections and substantially reduce the opportunities to which women and girls are entitled under current law; and (3) our belief that only one of the proposals would address the budgetary causes underlying the discontinuation of some men's teams, and that others would not restore opportunities that have been lost.

---

*Report submitted February 26, 2003; available at http://www.savetitleix.com/minority report.pdf (accessed July 11, 2007), excerpt.

This Minority Report is divided into three sections. The first presents the findings and recommendations that we believe the Commission should have included in its report—a substitute report. The second section addresses the reasons that we cannot support a number of the Commission's key recommendations. The third section identifies some of the problems with the Commission's process that we believe contributed to the problems with the report and with the recommendations that will weaken Title IX's protections.

With regard to this last point, in our view, the problems with the report are the result of a process, established by the Commission staff, that did not adequately focus on critical issues, did not compile all of the evidence necessary to fully address the state of gender equity in our nation's schools, and did not allow sufficient time for Commissioners to conduct either a careful review of the evidence that *was* compiled or an assessment of the potential impact of various recommendations.

We ask that the Commissioners and Secretary give careful consideration to this Minority Report. Title IX has been one of our country's most important and most effective civil rights laws, and the public deserves the fullest possible education about, access to, and consideration of the issues at stake in the important debate about the law's application to athletics. Ensuring that Title IX's goal of equal opportunity is reached demands no less.

Part I: Findings and Recommendations

A. Findings

Finding 1

Title IX and the three-part test have promoted great advances for women and girls to participate in sports.

Title IX, and the three-part test that implements it, have opened doors for millions of women and girls to obtain the benefits of participating in competitive athletics. While fewer than 32,000 women participated in college sports prior to the enactment of Title IX,[1] today that number has expanded nearly five-fold—or more than 400%—to approximately 163,000 women.[2] Opportunities for girls at the high-school level have grown even more dramatically; since 1972, female participation in high-school athletics has skyrocketed by 847%, from 294,000 to almost 2.8 million.[3]

[1] Department of Health, Education and Welfare, *Policy Interpretation*, 44 Fed. Reg., 71419 (1979).

[2] U.S. General Accounting Office, No. 01-297, *Intercollegiate Athletics: Four-Year Colleges' Experiences Adding and Discontinuing Teams* (hereafter "GAO Report"), March 2001, 7.

[3] National Federation of State High School Associations (NFHS), *2001 High School Athletics Participation Survey.*

Finding 2

Despite these advances, discrimination still limits athletics opportunities for girls and women at both the high-school and college levels today.

Despite Title IX's success in opening doors to women and girls, the playing field is far from level for them. For example, although women in Division I colleges are 53% of the student body, they receive only 41% of the opportunities to play sports, 36% of overall athletic operating budgets, and 32% of the dollars spent to recruit new athletes.[4] Girls at the high-school level receive 1.1 million fewer opportunities to play sports than their male counterparts.

Among other things, these disparities affect women's access to the financial assistance that can increase the ability to pursue a college education; it has been estimated that men receive $133 million more *per year* than women in athletic scholarships.[5] Additionally, women at all educational levels continue to be subjected to inequities in the treatment of their teams, from inferior equipment and facilities to disadvantageous scheduling and opportunities to receive coaching.

Finding 3

Enhancing athletic opportunities for young women and girls is of vital importance because of the significant benefits those opportunities provide.

Competitive athletics promotes physical and psychological health, responsible social behaviors, greater academic success, and increased personal skills.[6] A recent study by the Oppenheimer Fund found that more than four out of five executive businesswomen (82%) played sports growing up—and the vast majority say lessons learned on the playing field have contributed to their success in business.[7] And for low-income women and girls, the financial support made available through athletic scholarships can mean the difference in being able to attend college at all.

Finding 4

The fact that women and girls have fewer opportunities in athletics than men reflects the persistent discrimination against them, not lack of interest.

[4]NCAA, *Gender Equity Report* (2000), 20.

[5]NCAA, *Gender Equity Report* (2000), tables, 16, 28, 40, 52, 64.

[6]See, e.g., Teegarden, Proulx, et al., *Medicine and Science in Sports and Exercise*, 28 (1996), 105–113 (citing health benefits); D. Sabo, et al., *Women's Sports Foundation Report: Sport and Teen Pregnancy* (1998) (adolescent female athletes have lower rates of sexual activity and pregnancy); NCAA, "Study on Graduation Rates," in *NCAA News* (June 28, 1995) (female student-athletes have higher grades, are less likely to drop out, and have higher graduation rates than their non-athletic peers).

[7]"From the Locker Room to the Boardroom: A Survey on Sports in the Lives of Women Business Executives," *Game Face* (February 2002).

Although the Commission heard allegations that women are less interested in participating in sports than men, the history of Title IX flatly contradicts this assertion. The dramatic increases in participation at both the high-school and college levels since Title IX was passed show that when doors are opened to them, women and girls will rush through. And the fact that 2.8 million girls play sports in high school refutes any claim that there is insufficient interest to fill the approximately 170,000 slots now available to participate in intercollegiate athletics or the additional opportunities to which they are entitled under the law.

Courts have repeatedly recognized that the stereotype that women are less interested in sports than men is unfounded and unlawful. As one court stated, "interest and ability rarely develop in a vacuum; they evolve as a function of opportunity and experience. . . . [W]omen's lower rate of participation in athletics reflects women's historical lack of opportunities to participate in sports."[8]

Finding 7

The three-part test, adopted by the Department of Education in 1979 and in force since that time, is flexible and fair. All three prongs of the test have been used successfully by schools to comply with Title IX, and each is necessary to give schools flexibility in structuring their athletics programs while guarding against freezing discrimination into place.

The three-part test offers three wholly independent ways that schools can show that they are providing equal opportunities to their male and female students to participate in athletics. . . . Indeed, the General Accounting Office has found that between 1994 and 1998, more than two-thirds of the schools investigated by the Office for Civil Rights at the Department of Education complied with Title IX's participation requirements under prong two or prong three.[9]

The three-part test as a whole provides substantial flexibility. The first part of the test stands for the basic principle that a school that provides equal opportunity to the women and the men in its student body is, by definition, not discriminating against any of those students. It does not mandate proportionality; it simply authorizes a school to treat women equally with men and says the law will approve it when they do. It is this common-sense principle that has led courts to call this prong of the test a "safe harbor." But if members of one gender are underrepresented among an institution's athletes, this does not mean that the school has not complied with Title IX; it simply means that the school could use one of the other two prongs to demonstrate that it meets Title IX requirements.

[8] *Cohen v. Brown Univ.*, 101 F.3d 155, 178–179 (1st Cir. 1996), *cert. denied*, 520 U.S. 1186 (1997).
[9] GAO Report, 14.

The second prong allows schools to show that they have made, and are continuing to make, progress toward equality. And the third prong permits schools to customize equal opportunity requirements to their own campuses by providing a lower level of opportunity to women where that lower level nonetheless satisfies the interests and abilities that exist. It is difficult to conceive of an enforcement mechanism that could more flexibly accommodate the myriad types of athletic programs that exist on our nation's campuses, as well as the differences among student bodies at different schools, and still be true to the core principles of Title IX's mandate of equality.

Finding 8

The Office for Civil Rights (OCR) has provided extensive guidance on the operation of each prong of the three-part test, but should provide enhanced technical assistance, consistent with that guidance, on the means by which schools can comply with the test. OCR can also do more to ensure consistent interpretation of Title IX by all regional offices.

When it was adopted in 1979, the three-part test was part of a larger Policy Interpretation that described in detail the OCR approach to assessing compliance with Title IX in the area of athletics. In January 1996, the OCR issued a Clarification of the 1979 Policy Interpretation. This Clarification provides specific factors to guide an analysis of each prong, as well as multiple examples to demonstrate, in concrete terms, how each of these factors is applied. Among other issues, the Clarification addresses in detail (a) how to define an "athlete" for purposes of evaluating proportionality; (b) circumstances in which schools will be given leeway and need not provide precisely proportional opportunities, under prong one of the test; (c) factors that OCR will consider in assessing whether a school has a history and continuing practice of expanding opportunities; (d) the means by which schools should assess the interests of their students under prong three; and (e) the means by which schools should assess whether there is sufficient ability and expectation of competition to sustain a team under that prong. The numerous examples included throughout the Clarification offer a valuable road map for schools seeking to understand the operation of each prong of the test.

The Commission heard testimony that there is confusion about the terms of the three-part test and about the flexibility provided by current Department policies. More technical assistance about the means by which schools can comply with the test, as well as about best practices—as identified, for example, in the 2001 GAO report—might help to address any confusion that exists. In addition, OCR should ensure that any complaints about inconsistent enforcement by different OCR regional offices are addressed.

Finding 9

The term "safe harbor," used by some courts and OCR to describe the operation of the first prong of the three-part test, is a legal term of art that does not mean that the first prong is the only effective way to comply with the test. OCR can do more to provide enhanced technical assistance to ensure that educational institutions understand that compliance is possible under prongs one, two, or three.

In its 1996 Clarification, OCR—using language from the court's decision in *Cohen v. Brown Univ.*—described the first prong of the three-part test as a "safe harbor" for schools. By that designation, OCR used a well-known legal term that, in this context, means simply that schools that can meet the terms of the first prong can evaluate their compliance with no additional inquiry. The term "safe harbor" is a protection for the institution, but it does not mean that the first prong is the only "safe" way to comply with Title IX's participation requirements or that it is more difficult to meet the standards of prongs two and three of the test. The term is a merely descriptive one that adds no legal weight to the operation of the first prong.

Finding 10

The lawfulness of the three-part test has been affirmed by every federal appellate court to consider the issue.

The three-part test has been the subject of substantial litigation since its adoption, in cases brought both by women who assert that they have been denied participation opportunities and by men who claim that the three-part test has resulted in cuts to their teams. In *every* case that has been brought, the federal court of appeals hearing the case has upheld the three-part test and the policies then in place to implement it. Eight out of eight circuit courts have considered the issue and found that the test appropriately implements Title IX requirements.[10] It is well-settled law, and to change it would unleash a new round of litigation, causing real confusion and uncertainty.

---

[10]*See Chalenor v. Univ. of N. Dakota*, 2002 U.S. App. LEXIS 14404 (8th Cir. May 30, 2002); *Pederson v. La. St. Univ.*, 213 F.3d 858, 879 (5th Cir. 2000); *Neal v. Bd. of Trustees of Calif. St. Univs.*, 198 F.3d 763, 770 (9th Cir. 1999); *Horner v. Ky. High Sch. Athletic Assoc.*, 43 F.3d 265, 274–275 (6th Cir. 1994); *Kelley v. Bd. of Trustees, Univ. of Ill.*, 35 F.3d 265, 270 (7th Cir. 1994), *cert. denied*, 513 U.S. 1128 (1995); *Cohen v. Brown Univ.*, 991 F. 2d 888 (1st Cir. 1993), and 101 F.3d 155, 170 (1st Cir. 1996), *cert. denied*, 520 U.S. 1186 (1997) (this case was before the First Circuit twice, first on Brown University's appeal of a preliminary injunction granted by the district court, and the second time after a trial on the merits); *Roberts v. Colo. St. Bd. of Agriculture*, 998 F.2d 824, 828 (10th Cir. 1993), *cert. denied*, 510 U.S. 1004 (1993); *Williams v. Sch. Dist. of Bethlehem*, 998 F.2d 168, 171 (3d Cir. 1993).

Finding 11

OCR has never imposed a financial penalty on a school for failing to comply with the three-part test.

Although permitted to do so by Title IX, OCR has never imposed on a school the penalty authorized for a failure to comply with Title IX: the loss of federal funding.

Finding 12

The three-part test does not impose quotas or require preferential treatment.

Because athletic teams are sex segregated, schools *themselves* decide how many slots they will allocate to men and how many to women. The proportionality prong does not dictate how many slots, that would otherwise be open to all, must be set aside for women—it merely offers a means of measuring whether the school is dividing the sex-segregated slots it has created on an equal basis. As every appellate court to address the issue has recognized, "determining whether discrimination exists in [sex-segregated] athletic programs *requires* gender-conscious, groupwide comparisons." (emphasis added)[11]

Finding 13

Title IX does not require mirror-image men's and women's sports programs.

Current Title IX enforcement standards consider the total participation opportunities afforded each gender by an institution's athletics program rather than the numbers or sizes of teams sponsored by the schools. Title IX does not impose a requirement that each women's team be matched by a corresponding men's team or vice versa. Similarly, Title IX does not require that men and women be granted equal numbers of athletic scholarships, but only that overall scholarship dollars be allocated equitably among male and female athletes.

Finding 14

Title IX does not cause cuts to men's teams.

Nothing in Title IX or its policies requires schools to reduce men's opportunities to come into compliance with participation requirements. In fact, GAO data confirm that 72% of colleges and universities that have added women's teams have done so without cutting any teams for men.[12] Additionally, although the Commission was provided with less information on this issue, women's teams have also suffered cuts over the last twenty years. For example, the number of

---

[11]*Neal v. Bd. of Trustees of Calif. St. Univs.*, 198 F.3d 763, 770 (9th Cir. 1999).
[12]GAO Report, 14.

schools sponsoring women's gymnastics dropped from 190 in 1981–1982 to 90 in 1998–1999—a decline of more than 50%.[13]

Finding 15

To the extent that schools have discontinued men's—and women's—athletic teams since Title IX was passed, there are many reasons for those decisions. Most notably, budgetary decisions, the athletics "arms race," excessive expenditures, and philosophical decisions related to the appropriate quality and size of athletic programs have resulted in the loss of opportunities for other sports.

Title IX does not limit an institution's flexibility in deciding how budgets will be allocated among sports or teams. There can be no question, though, that the cost of operations in intercollegiate athletics has escalated rapidly. This escalation in expenditures is often referred to as the "arms race" because as one school escalates its spending on revenue-producing sports, its competitors feel required to match that move to retain competitiveness. It is clear from testimony that this "arms race" has been the catalyst for the discontinuation of many teams. And the Commission received substantial information on the spiraling costs of coaching salaries, prerequisites for players, and luxurious athletic facilities that increasingly strap college-athletics budgets and force reductions in other expenditures for sports.

Finding 17

"Walk-on" student-athletes cost money and receive the benefits of participating in intercollegiate athletics. To the extent that men walk on more than women, intangible benefits accorded to men's teams and the persistent budgetary barriers that limit the extent to which women's teams can support additional players have been identified as causes.

Walk-on athletes—typically, those players who do not receive athletic scholarships—receive the benefits that stem from participation in athletics, including coaching, practice, training services, medical benefits, equipment, uniforms, preferential course scheduling, academic support programs, preseason-training-period room and board, access to weight rooms, and the like. It is clear that provision of these services to additional athletes costs money. In addition, the addition of walk-on athletes to a team forces a school to reconsider its coaching ratios to ensure that all players receive adequate attention. As a result, there are costs and competitive considerations that influence a school's decision whether to limit the permissible number of walk-ons.

---

[13]GAO Report, 12.

Women's teams often lack the resources to provide for more than the minimum number of athletes slated by the school for the team. Additionally, because of the history of discrimination to which female athletes have been subject, women's teams sometimes lack the status of their men's counterparts To the extent that men walk-on to teams to a greater degree than women, these factors have been identified as causes.

Finding 19

There is a mechanism by which the Department of Education can systematically monitor participation in athletics and athletic program expenditures at the college levels, the Equity in Athletics Disclosure Act. There is no mechanism in place by which the Department of Education or the public can systematically monitor these variables at the high-school level.

The Equity in Athletics Disclosure Act requires colleges and universities to compile data about the gender breakdown of their participation opportunities and scholarship dollars, as well as about their expenditures on, and recruiting and coaching expenses for, men's and women's teams. Because the EADA does not apply to secondary schools, there is no comparable requirement that high schools monitor how they are allocating sports opportunities between their male and female students.

B. Recommendations

Recommendation 1

The Department of Education's current Title IX athletics policies, which have promoted advances toward equality for women in sports, should be preserved without change.

The Department's current athletics policies, in place through Republican and Democratic administrations and upheld by every federal appellate court to examine them, have worked to open doors to millions of girls and women to gain the benefits of participating in competitive sports. The playing field is not yet level, however, and the policies must be maintained in order to ensure that women and girls receive the truly equal opportunity they are afforded by the law.

Recommendation 2

The Department of Education should strongly enforce Title IX standards, including implementing sanctions for institutions that do not comply.

Enforcement should be strengthened, and resources increased, to ensure that discrimination is investigated and addressed in an effective and timely way.

Recommendation 3

Using existing guidance, Department of Education staff should undertake an educational campaign to help educational institutions understand the flexibility of the law, explain that each prong of the three-part test is a viable and independent means of compliance, and give practical examples of the ways in which schools can comply.

Recommendation 4

In educating schools about current policies, the Department of Education should advise them that nothing in Title IX requires the cutting or reduction of men's teams, and that to do so is disfavored.

Numerous civil rights laws apply the principle of "equalizing up" in authorizing remedies for discrimination—that is, raising opportunities for the disadvantaged group, rather than diminishing them for the previously benefited group, as a means of achieving civil rights compliance. In providing technical assistance, the Department should advise schools of this principle, as well as providing information on techniques other schools have used to achieve this goal.

Recommendation 5

The Department of Education should encourage educational institutions and national athletic governance organizations to address the issue of reducing the escalating costs of intercollegiate athletics, particularly in some parts of the men's athletics programs, and fostering agreement on reforms.

The Department of Education should play a critical role in establishing and facilitating forums in which these issues can be addressed, as well as in publicizing and seeking agreement to their results. The reduction of excessive athletics expenditures would go a long way toward freeing up resources to support both women's teams and men's lower profile sports. The Department should also initiate conversations about more systemic reforms to eliminate the "arms race" in athletics—reforms that would allow reallocation of resources to support broad-based sports participation by both male and female students.

Recommendation 6

The Department of Education should encourage educational institutions and national athletic governance organizations to address whether organization rules, such as limitations on the numbers of athletics scholarships, hamper compliance with Title IX participation requirements and, if so, to take corrective action.

Part II: Responses to Commission Recommendations

The Commission's Majority Report asserts that the recommendations made by the Commission are the product of "strong consensus." However, we strongly disagree with the Commission's major recommendations, and, for a number of them, were joined by other Commissioners as well. We believe that these recommendations are contrary to the intent of Title IX, would critically weaken this important civil rights law, and would result in substantial losses of participation opportunities and scholarships for women. We summarize our concerns below.

A. Three Recommendations Would Substantially Reduce the Number of Athletic Opportunities to Which Women and Girls Are Entitled by Permitting Schools to Count Male and Female Students and Athletes in New Ways

A number of the Commission's recommendations authorize schools to change the ways in which they count the men and women in their student bodies, on the one hand, and the men and women to whom they provide athletic opportunities, on the other. Singly and together, these recommendations would allow schools to be deemed as complying with Title IX while substantially reducing the number of participation opportunities they are obliged to provide to women under current standards.

Recommendation 15 would modify the proportionality prong of the three-part test by allowing each school to identify a "predetermined number of participants for each team offered by the institution" and then to count that number of slots as filled—regardless of how many athletes in fact participate on the team. This proposal would allow schools to artificially inflate the percentage of athletic opportunities they give to women by counting opportunities they never actually fill or seek to fill.

The potential for abuse that is inherent in this proposal has long been recognized. In fact, the Office for Civil Rights rejected just such a recommendation in issuing the 1996 Policy Clarification. In determining the number of participation opportunities offered by a school, OCR refused to count "unfilled slots, i.e., those positions on a team that an institution claims the team can support but which are not filled by actual athletes," because "participation opportunities must be real, not illusory" and because "OCR must consider actual benefits provided to real students."[14] To allow a school to count slots which provide *no* actual benefits to *any* real student would make a mockery of any claim that the school was providing equal opportunity.

[14]U.S. Department of Education, *Clarification of Intercollegiate Athletics Policy Guidance: The Three-Part Test*, 3.

The recommendation is all the more problematic because women lag significantly behind men in the receipt of dollars spent to recruit new athletes. The average Division I college allocates only 32% of its athletic-recruiting budget to women's teams.[15] It is particularly troubling for a school that spends 112% more recruiting men than women—and that then, as a result, has fewer women participating on its women's teams—to be able to claim credit for providing a "predetermined," but unfilled, number of slots. If Title IX's participation requirements are interpreted in a way that provides no check on these disparities, women will continue to be treated as second-class citizens in schools' recruiting efforts.

Recommendation 17 would also allow schools to change the ways in which they count the athletic opportunities they provide, by allowing schools *not* to count athletic opportunities for men that the schools actually *do* provide. Recommendation 17 provides that proportionality ratios should be "calculated through a comparison of full or partial scholarship recipients and recruited walk-ons," excluding from the count opportunities provided to walk-on athletes as defined by the NCAA.

This proposal would enable schools to pretend that they are *not* giving athletics opportunities to men, and then to reduce their obligation to female athletes accordingly, even though walk-on athletes receive the benefits of sports participation, including coaching, training, tutoring, equipment, and uniforms. In fact, by one estimate, a school that excluded from its count athletes who did not receive scholarships could reduce its participation gap and thereby reduce by 32 the number of slots to which women would be entitled under current law.[16] This decline in the participation gap is a wholly illusory and artificial reduction; it does not signify that the school has in fact made any progress whatsoever in providing equal opportunities to its male and female students.

Further, it is unclear, as a practical matter, how this recommendation would apply to Division III colleges or to high schools, where athletes are provided no scholarships. Under Recommendation 17, therefore, only "recruited walk-ons" would count in the school's totals. But unlike Division I and II schools, Division III colleges are not required by the NCAA to monitor contacts between coaches and prospective students; as a result, they do not have the means to evaluate whether their walk-on athletes are "recruited" under the NCAA definition. Moreover, Division III schools often lack the funding to send coaches on recruiting trips or to phone or bring prospective athletes to campus. Consequently, large numbers of athletes are likely *not* to have been recruited under NCAA standards, even though they may have been recruited in other ways. Because this proposal does not address whether Division III schools could

---

[15]NCAA, *Gender Equity Report 1999–2000*, 15.

[16]Welch Suggs, "Getting Ready for the Next Round," *Chronicle of Higher Education* 49, no. 23 (February 14, 2003), A39.

claim that their athletes are *not* recruited, or what standards regarding recruitment would apply, there could be an even larger loophole in Title IX's protections at Division III colleges—even beyond the impact of the proposal on Division I and Division II schools.

Recommendation 20 provides that in demonstrating compliance with the proportionality prong of the three-part test, "the male-female ratio of athletic participation should be measured against the male-female ratio of an institution's undergraduate population minus nontraditional students." Under this proposal, in other words, schools could exclude so-called "nontraditional" students—defined for this purpose to include students who are not between the ages of 18 and 24,[17] and students of any age who have children—as members of the student body whose interests and abilities the schools are obligated to accommodate.

The stereotype that students over a certain age or students who are parents are not interested in participating in sports is both inaccurate and contrary to many Supreme Court cases that have struck down these types of stereotypes. This recommendation would allow every school to presume, for purposes of Title IX, that all students who are over the age of 24 or who have children are uninterested in playing sports. That is unfair to women, who are disproportionately likely to be the "nontraditional" older students excluded under this proposal. Available data show, for example, that among individuals older than 24 who were enrolled in degree-granting institutions in 2001, women outnumbered men by 37%.[18] It is also impractical; in order to equitably apply the principle of exclusion based on parental status, the school would have to identify and exclude not only mothers, but also male undergraduates, of any age, who have fathered children.

The recommendation is also unnecessary, because schools that enroll large numbers of "nontraditional" students are, like other schools, specifically authorized under prong three of the test to consider the interests of that population in allocating their athletic opportunities. To the extent that a school's female students, including those who are "nontraditional," are in fact less interested in participating in sports than men, the school will be in compliance with Title IX if it fully accommodates the interest that exists—even if it falls short of proportionality.

[17]The Commission's report suggests that nontraditional students are those over the age of thirty-two. We assume that this is a typographical error, because the Commission clearly intended to exclude those who are "older than the traditional, full-time undergraduate college athlete," and specifically defined those students as students over the age of twenty-four in the draft report that the majority approved.

[18]U.S. Department of Education, National Center for Education Statistics; http://nces.ed.gov/pubs2002/digest2001/tables/dt174.asp.

B. Two Recommendations Would Treat Schools as Having Provided Equal Opportunity Even Where They Do Not Actually Provide It

Two of the recommendations would authorize schools to comply with a proportionality standard without actually providing equal opportunity to their female students—and without satisfying any other prong of the three-part test.

An *unnumbered proposal*, which is included in the report although it received only a tie vote, would direct schools to allocate 50% of their participation opportunities to men and 50% to women regardless of the actual percentage of males and females in the student body, and then authorize schools to fall short of that allocation by 2 to 3 percentage points. This proposal would, in effect, allow schools to impose a ceiling of 47% of athletic opportunities and scholarships for women—no matter how large the percentage of women in the student body or how many women want to play. Because women typically comprise 53% of the student body at Division I-A schools, and 49% of the students at the high-school level, this proposal will inevitably result in losses from the opportunities to which women and girls would be entitled under current law. The losses are, of course, likely to be greater at the numerous colleges at which women comprise a higher percentage than 53% of undergraduates—including some powerhouse institutions, such as Florida State University and the University of Georgia, where women are 57% of the student body. The chart below illustrates the projected *annual* losses at each educational level, assuming no reduction in current participation or scholarship opportunities for men, college enrollment of 53% female (average enrollment at Division I-A schools), and high-school enrollment of 49.1% female (national average enrollment in grades 9–12).

Similarly, *Recommendation 14* urges the Secretary to allow for a "reasonable variance" from equality if proportionality is retained as a way of complying with Title IX. Because the language is open-ended, it is impossible to put a limit on the losses that girls and women would endure were this recommendation to be adopted; in fact, this proposal could result in greater losses than those anticipated under the unnumbered proposal. This recommendation would authorize the Secretary to treat as sufficient for Title IX compliance a level of participation that falls far short of true equality—subject only to his own subjective judgment about what is a "reasonable" variance. While we did not object to this recommendation when it was proposed following a confused and truncated Commission discussion, our review of it as drafted in the Commission's report convinces us that it could create damaging results that would not be consistent with Title IX and that we cannot support.

	50/50 standard with ±2% variance (females = 48%)	50/50 standard with ±3% variance (females = 47%)
Lost Opportunities and Scholarships Under Unnumbered Recommendation, Which Could Be Even Greater Under Recommendation 14		
Participation losses for collegiate female athletes	43,000	50,000
Scholarship losses for collegiate female athletes	$103,000,000	$122,000,000
Participation losses for high-school female athletes	163,000	305,000

C. Two Recommendations Would Authorize Improper Use of "Interest Surveys" to Limit Opportunities for Girls and Women and to Weaken Prong Three of the Three-Part Test

Recommendation 18 would allow schools to use "interest surveys" to (a) demonstrate compliance with the three-part test, (b) "accurately predict and reflect men's and women's interest in athletics over time," and (c) stimulate student interest in sports. Because it would authorize the use of such surveys to reduce schools' obligations to provide equal opportunity to women and girls, this recommendation is fundamentally flawed in numerous respects.

First, the use of interest surveys to reduce the basic obligation of educational institutions to provide equal opportunity is invalid and has been unequivocally rejected by the courts. Using interest surveys is a way to force girls and women to *prove* their right to equal opportunity before giving them a chance to play. The proposal rests on the stereotyped notion that women are inherently less interested in sports than men—a notion that contradicts Title IX and fundamental principles of civil rights law.

As courts have repeatedly recognized, what interest surveys measure is the discrimination that has limited opportunities for girls and women to participate in sports—*not* the interest that exists when girls are given unfettered opportunities to play. As the court in *Cohen v. Brown Univ.* put it, "interest and ability rarely develop in a vacuum; they evolve as a function of opportunity and experience. . . . [W]omen's lower rate of participation in athletics reflects women's historical lack of opportunities to participate in sports."[19] To allow the use of

[19]*Cohen v. Brown Univ.*, 101 F.3d 155, 178–179 (1st Cir. 1996), *cert. denied*, 520 U.S. 1186 (1997).

surveys to limit opportunities for women is simply to freeze prior discrimination into place—it certainly is not to "accurately predict and reflect men's and women's interest in athletics over time."

Additionally, the evidence proves that women are *not* less interested in sports than men; when the doors of opportunity are opened, women rush through them. As noted above, girls' and women's participation in sports has increased dramatically since the passage of Title IX thirty years ago. Moreover, it is simply illogical to claim that women are less interested in obtaining the economic, physical, psychological, and social benefits that stem from participation in athletics. There are 2.8 million girls participating in high-school sports, and fewer than 170,000 opportunities to play in college; this fact alone is sufficient to demonstrate that the argument that women are not interested in sports is simply an effort to continue an outmoded stereotype.

Recommendation 19, as described in the Commission's report, suffers from some of the same flaws as Recommendation 18. Recommendation 19 advises the Secretary to study allowing schools to assess compliance with the third prong of the three-part test by comparing the school's ratio of male-female athletic participation to the "demonstrated interests and abilities" shown by high-school and other participation rates or by interest levels shown in surveys of current or prospective students at the school. To the extent that this recommendation was intended or would be used to authorize restriction of opportunities for girls and women based on the results of an interest survey—or to modify the third prong of the test to allow merely "relative" rather than full accommodation of the women's interests and abilities that exist—it directly contradicts the court's ruling in *Cohen v. Brown Univ.* In its 1996 Clarification, OCR set forth explicit and detailed guidance on the appropriate and lawful ways to evaluate interest and abilities under the third prong of the test, and that guidance must be maintained intact. Upon review of the report's treatment of this recommendation, we cannot agree to it unless the understanding set forth above is made clear.

D. One Recommendation Would Allow Schools to Use Private Funding to Subvert Equal Opportunity for Girls and Women

Recommendation 12 requests the Office for Civil Rights to reexamine its policies governing the private funding of teams to prevent sports from being dropped or to allow specific teams to be added. Current law is more than adequate to allow such private funding; what supporters of this recommendation apparently have in mind is to enable the Secretary to rewrite long-standing policy to permit private donors to underwrite men's teams without triggering any obligation that schools then treat their women's teams equally. Were the Secretary to accept this invitation, schools could also be authorized to steer private slush funds to male teams without counting them as athletes—or, in other words, to create a loophole that would justify discrimination if subsidized by private funds.

We support having the Office for Civil Rights provide technical assistance to educate schools and the public about the existing standards governing private funding of teams—but only to the extent that Title IX principles and limitations are respected and conveyed in the process.

E. One Recommendation Offers the Secretary an Open-Ended Invitation to Add New Ways to Comply with Title IX Not Even Considered by the Commission

Recommendation 23 advocates that the Secretary explore "additional ways of demonstrating equity beyond the existing three-part test." This open-ended proposal could be used to authorize changes to Title IX enforcement mechanisms that the Commission never even addressed, much less approved. Given that the three-part test has stood the test of time—and has been affirmed by both Republican and Democratic administrations and uniformly upheld in the courts—it is inappropriate, particularly when substantial discrimination still exists to be remedied, for the Commission to be proposing what could amount to a wholesale abandonment of this critical enforcement tool. Our careful review of this recommendation in the report—and our analysis of the threat it represents to current policies, which we were unable to conduct under the time constraints of the Commission meeting—convince us that we must withdraw our original consent to this proposal.

There are other recommendations whose meaning, upon review of the Commission's written report, seems ambiguous. Recommendation 9, for example, encourages redesign of the Equity in Athletics Disclosure Act to provide the public with a "relevant and simplified tool" to evaluate a school's Title IX compliance. While it would be unobjectionable to change EADA reporting requirements to allow schools to supply additional information about their compliance with the three-part test, it would be contrary to our intent in consenting to this recommendation, and contrary to the purpose of the reporting obligation, to use this recommendation to justify an overhaul of the reporting form that would delete key information. We would strongly disagree with any interpretation of this or any other recommendation that would lead to a reduction of the protections in place for girls and women to achieve equal opportunities to participate in athletics.

Part III: Problems in the Commission's Process

We have set forth above some of the concerns that trouble us about the recommendations that the Commission has now approved. We believe that the problems with the recommendations reflect problems in the Commission process that prevented full consideration of the relevant issues:

- *The Commission's charge failed to ask the critical question: whether discrimination against girls and women persists, and how it can be remedied.* The Commission's charter did not contain the question that should have informed the Commission's efforts from the beginning. Instead, the Commission's focus was on addressing losses to some men's teams. As a result, the Commission made no inquiry into the question of whether the original goals of Title IX have been met—and if not, why.
- *The Commission lacked representatives of important constituencies.* There was no Commissioner who represented the interests and perspectives of Division II or Division III schools, or junior and community colleges. Most significantly, the Commission lacked any representative of high-school athletics programs. The Commission's report itself acknowledges the Commission's inability to reach conclusions about the application of Title IX at the high-school level; this is a particularly troubling omission because the recommendations, if adopted by the Secretary, will affect the nearly 6 million students who play sports in high school.
- *Witnesses selected by the Department of Education testified two-to-one against current policies, and other expert testimony that was requested was not provided.* The witnesses who were invited to testify were overwhelmingly opposed to current Title IX policies, while witness testimony from supporters of the law was limited. For example, the Department of Education invited at least five panelists from schools sued for failure to comply with Title IX, but selected no witnesses to represent plaintiffs who were victims of discrimination or women whose teams had been cut.

  Moreover, Commissioners requested specific experts whose testimony would have helped inform critical components of the Commission's inquiry. The Department of Education declined to invite these requested experts. To choose just two examples, the Commission did not hear from the author of the authoritative GAO report on participation trends, who would have testified that men's participation opportunities and number of teams have increased, not decreased, over time. In addition, the only witness who was asked to testify about current law was a recent law graduate who was, by her own admission, not well informed about the 1996 Clarification. We believe that Commissioners were thereby thwarted in their efforts to obtain the best information from the best sources.

- *The Commission had inadequate time for serious review.* Deadlines for Commission consideration of issues and decision-making did not allow Commissioners to do the kind of careful study warranted by the issues. For example, Commissioners had only 6 working days after the last public hearing to list and explain each of their proposed recommendations. Commissioners also had only two working days before the final decision-making meeting in Washington, D.C., to review the first draft of the proposed report. Commissioners were given less than a week to respond to the final draft of the report. We specifically urged another meeting of the full Commission to carefully review the language and impact of the final report, to no avail.

- *The Commission was not provided information on, nor therefore was able to consider, the impact of its recommendations.* The Commission was not provided with any data on the effect of its recommendations, including their impact on participation opportunities and scholarships for female athletes. Additionally, recommendations to change the 1996 Clarification were made without an accommodation to the Commissioners who requested, on several occasions, to circulate and discuss the extensive guidance provided in that Clarification. Commissioners were told that there was insufficient time for this type of analysis.

- *The arrangements made for expression of minority views were insufficient.* The Commission authorized inclusion of short statements of minority views following the recommendations on which there was dissent, but did not allow for any fuller statement of the dissenters' rationales or inclusion of concerns about the drafting of other portions of the report. As a result, the report does not reflect a full statement of the views of each of the Commissioners.

Conclusion

Equal opportunity for women and girls in education is of the utmost importance to our nation. The opportunity to participate in athletics is a critical component of that equality, since it opens the door for millions to play sports, receive college scholarships, and obtain other important benefits—including increased health, self-esteem, academic performance, responsible social behaviors, and leadership skills—that flow from sports participation.

Women and girls have made substantial strides toward equality in the 30 years since Title IX was passed. There is much more to be done, however, before Title IX's goals are achieved. Those goals are too important to be compromised by any weakening of the policies that have promoted the advances that have occurred or by anything less than the strongest enforcement of current law.

For these reasons, we ask the Secretary specifically to reject Recommendations 12, 14, 15, 17, 18, 19, 20, 23, and the unnumbered proposal in the Majority Report and to keep current policies in place without change. Rather than changing the policies that have been so important in opening opportunities for women and girls—when their job is not yet done and when their validity has been consistently upheld—the Department of Education should focus on using those policies to educate schools and the public about the importance of equal opportunity, the need to keep working to achieve it, and the flexibility of the means by which schools can provide it. Women and girls who play sports—and the fathers and brothers who support them—deserve no less.

Limitations of the Department of Education's On-Line Survey Method for Measuring Athletic Interest and Ability on U.S.A. Campuses*

Don Sabo and Christine Grant[1]

The Department of Education has endorsed using an online survey method as the sole means of assessing student interest in additional athletic participation opportunities. The March 17, 2005, *Additional Clarification on Intercollegiate Athletics Policy: Three-Part Test—Part Three* would allow colleges and universities to use a "Model Survey" alone to claim compliance with Title IX's mandate that schools provide equal participation opportunities to male and female students. In particular, the results of the Department's survey could be used to determine institutional compliance with the third prong of Title IX's three-part participation test. Under this prong, an institution may comply if it can show that its athletics program fully and effectively accommodates the interests and abilities of the underrepresented sex.

Until it issued its new Clarification, the Department had interpreted the third prong of the test to require a systematic evaluation of a host of factors, beyond surveys, to assess whether institutions had fully met the interests and abilities of their female students. *See Clarification of Intercollegiate Athletics Policy Guidance: The Three-Part Test* (Jan. 1996). The Department's new "Additional" Clarification would eviscerate that interpretation and allow educational institutions to rely exclusively on a survey to measure unmet interest. But it would be methodologically misguided for institutions to utilize the Department's on-line survey method as the sole measure of compliance with prong three.

---

*Buffalo, NY: Center for Research on Physical Activity, Sport & Health, D'Youville College, June 2005.

[1]Don Sabo is the Director of the Center for Research on Physical Activity, Sport & Health at D'Youville College. Christine Grant is an Associate Professor of Health and Sports Studies and the Women's Athletics Director Emerita at the University of Iowa.

Instead, sound methodological guidelines dictate that multiple approaches to assessing the athletic interests and abilities of students be deployed. Moreover, the on-line survey authorized by the new Clarification suffers from serious methodological flaws.

Sound Methodology Requires the Use of Multiple Measures to Evaluate Interest and Ability and Shows the Limitations of a Survey

Basic methodological principles, as well as substantial research, demonstrate that exclusive reliance on a survey to evaluate women's interests and ability to participate in sports is not likely to fairly reveal the true extent of those interests and abilities. This is so for several reasons:

1. Research shows that an individual's disposition and willingness to express personal interest in athletics is influenced by social norms, culture, gender, race, and ethnicity. For example:

   a. Boys and men are apt to express interest in sports and identify as athletes because these interests are traditionally associated with appropriately "masculine" behavior and identity.[2]

   b. Girls and women often have a higher set of behavioral standards for what it means to be an "athlete." Researcher and author Catherine McKinnon, for example, practiced the martial arts for five years, two hours per night, and five nights a week before she began to consider herself an "athlete."[3] For many young women, increased involvement with sports entails rethinking traditional cultural notions about femininity.[4]

   c. The pervasiveness of "Marianisma" in some Latina/Hispanic cultures (which emphasizes conformity to housewife-motherhood and discourages

---

[2]R. W. Connell, *The Men and the Boys* (Berkeley, CA: University of California Press, 2000); M. A. Messner, *Taking the Field: Women, Men, and Sports* (Minneapolis, MN: University of Minnesota Press, 2002); W. Pollack, *Real Boys: Rescuing Our Sons from the Myths of Boyhood* (New York: Henry Holt and Company, 1998); E. Senay and R. Waters, *From Boys to Men: A Woman's Guide to the Health of Husbands, Partners, Sons, Fathers, and Brothers* (New York: Scribner, 2004).

[3]C. R. Stimpson, "The Atalanta Syndrome: Women, Sports, and Cultural Values," Inaugural Helen Pond McIntyre Lecture, *Scholar & Feminist Online* (Oct. 2006). www.barnard.columbia .edu/sfonline/sport/index.htm (accessed July 3, 2007).

[4]See The President's Council on Physical Fitness and Sports Report, *Physical Activity & Sport in the Lives of Girls: Physical and Mental Health Dimensions from an Interdisciplinary Approach* (Washington, D.C.: Department of Health and Human Services, 1997); D. Sabo, K. E. Miller, M. J. Melnick, and L. Heywood, *Her Life Depends On It: Sport, Physical Activity, and the Health and Well-Being of American Girls* (East Meadow, N.Y.: Women's Sports Foundation, 2004).

nontraditional roles for girls and women) can lead some Latinas to down-play interest and involvement in athletics.[5]

2. Any failure to express interest likely reflects a lack of prior exposure, which in turn is the result of discriminatory limitations on women's opportunities. Interest cannot be measured apart from opportunity, particularly in the context of sports, where women's interest in athletics has been limited by the discrimination to which they have been—and continue to be—subjected. As a result, surveys cannot measure the extent to which women would show interest and ability if nondiscriminatory opportunities were made available to them.

3. As a related matter, any survey of athletic interests is based on the problematic theoretical assumption that surveys of interest can be used to predict athletic behavior. Behavioral scientists have long observed the discrepancy between attitude and behavior. For example, millions of Americans who profess a keen interest in quitting smoking or losing weight continue to smoke and overeat. Particularly in the context of athletics, where women's opportunities have historically been limited, the converse is also true: Individuals who fail to express interest in participating in sports will often embrace the chance to play if offered the opportunity. Many girls who would have expressed no interest in sports, for example, become enthusiastic participants after joining a team because a friend did so, because they were actively recruited by an enthusiastic coach, or because they were taken to tryouts by a pro-sport parent.

For all of these reasons, the Department's long-standing prior policies, including its 1996 Clarification, make clear that a survey of students is only one of many factors that schools must consider in evaluating whether they are fully meeting the interests and abilities of their female students. The 1996 Clarification also requires schools to consider requests by students to add a sport; participation rates in club or intramural sports; participation rates in sports in high schools, amateur athletic associations, and community sports leagues in areas from which the school draws its students; and interviews with students, coaches, teachers, and administrators.

[5]M. Melnick, D. Sabo, and B. Vanfossen, "Educational Effects of Interscholastic Athletic Participation on African-American and Hispanic Youth," *Journal of Adolescence* 27, no. 106 (1992), 295–308; ———, "Effects of Interscholastic Athletic Participation on the Social, Educational, and Career Mobility of Hispanic Boys and Girls," *International Review of Sport Sociology* 17, no. 1 (1992), 57–75; ———, "The Influence of High School Athletic Participation on Post-Secondary Educational and Occupational Mobility: A Focus on Race and Gender," *Sociology of Sport Journal* (Winter 1993).

The use of multiple measures, as set forth in the Department's 1996 Clarification, is methodologically sound and enhances the likelihood that schools will accurately assess the extent of their students' interest in additional sports opportunities. Moreover, this approach has worked as a practical matter. According to the Additional Clarification, between 1992 and 2002, approximately two-thirds of schools complied with Title IX's athletic participation requirements under the third prong of the three-part test. The evidence thus supports the overall efficacy of the Department's long-standing policies, and their reliance on a multiple-measure approach, for promoting athletic opportunity and assessing compliance with Title IX for both sexes.

The Department's Survey Suffers from Methodological Flaws

Although the Department's Additional Clarification was issued with 177 pages of policy and text, the methodological procedures it authorizes and the rationales for those procedures need systematic review and assessment. Even a preliminary review of the Clarification, however, reveals serious concerns about the methodological efficacy of the Department's proposed survey.

1. *The Department's Survey Is Likely to Generate Low Response Rates.* Online surveys often result in low response rates, thereby creating the risk of drawing conclusions based on inadequate sample sizes. Many campuses experience difficulty generating full responses to online surveys, which makes it likely that relatively few students would participate in the Department's online survey.

The problem of low response rates is exacerbated because the Department's survey does not take into account variation in student access to or use of e-mail. The Department's design deploys erroneous sampling logic by assuming that use of campus-based e-mail services is either supplied or utilized uniformly across student populations. But student access to and use of university and college e-mail services is varied and uneven. Some students frequently use college-based online services for e-mail; others do not use it at all. At institutions where frequent disruptions or periodic shutdowns of e-mail services occur, students may seek and secure commercial e-mail suppliers. Students who work full-time or part-time jobs may spend less time on-line or check e-mail less frequently. Poor students may not own a computer or be able to pay for convenient e-mail services. And numerous students may ignore campus e-mail systems in order to avoid real or perceived encounters with what they regard as bureaucratic or commercially invasive spam.

Some (but not all) campuses maintain policies requiring students to check e-mail at certain intervals—for example, once a week or once a day. But even on campuses that do have policies that require students to check e-mail regularly, one cannot guarantee that students actually conform to such policies, or that the institution maintains current (and reliably accurate) directories of e-mail.

Moreover, the Department's survey methodology does not take into account the accelerating diversity in telecommunication preferences among college students. The campus-based online survey design ignores both national and international trends among young and tech-savvy consumers to increasingly rely on text messaging through cell phones as a vehicle for interpersonal communication. Those students who are opting for these regional, "off-campus" communication vehicles would likely not be included in campus-based online surveys.

For all of these reasons, the Department's survey is likely to yield a low response rate. Additionally, nothing in the new Clarification makes clear how policymakers will determine when a large enough sample has been generated by a particular administration of the Department's survey.

2. *The Department's Methodological Procedure to Count Nonrespondents Is Misguided.* The User's Guide for the Department's survey recommends that institutions conduct a "census" of the student population. Under a census methodology, there is no attempt to draw a sample from the student population. Rather, a census involves polling *all* students. But unless completing the online survey is somehow made mandatory (e.g., student registration is blocked until the survey is completed),[6] it is highly unlikely that all students will complete it, based on the reasons set forth above, among others.

Recognizing this reality, the Department's survey guidelines treat the survey methodology as a "census" if all students are simply contacted and asked to go to a website and complete the questionnaire. If a student does not respond to the request, the Clarification specifically states that schools may interpret the nonresponse as evidence of lack of interest—in other words, that student is still "counted" as a respondent and, furthermore, operationally defined as someone with no interest in athletics. By equating nonresponses to a lack of athletic interest (past, present, and future), the Office for Civil Rights' methodological procedures do not meet basic scientific criteria for establishing reliable and valid survey results and interpretations.

---

[6]Even if the on-line survey is made mandatory, students who do not want to participate (irrespective of their interest or participation in athletics) may "protest" the requirement by providing inaccurate information (e.g., indicating "no interest/experience" at the beginning). This may be particularly likely because the survey will probably take many students more time to complete than is stated in the Clarification. The difficulty is that analysts would not know the extent of the inaccuracy.

Furthermore, even if students are screened at the point of registration using a campus ID, one cannot be certain that the person completing the registration is the student who is being targeted; e.g., it is not uncommon for students to have other people register for them. On many campuses, some students, faculty, and staff share their campus IDs and passwords, even though doing so is against University policy.

3. *The Department's Survey Is Properly Understood to Embody a Sampling Methodology, but Is Unlikely to Generate a Representative Sample.* Based on the foregoing analysis, what the Department's survey really relies on is a sampling methodology. But unfortunately, there is nothing in the new Clarification that ensures that the sample that responds to the on-line survey will be representative of the student population. One major problem is referred to as the "coverage error," which occurs, for example, when a researcher assumes that those who did not respond to the survey are similar in all other respects to those who did respond. In many instances, however, the respondents may be very different from the nonrespondents in ways that remain hidden or are not measured. When this occurs, the sample is compromised and the empirical results become suspect.

In addition, the Department's survey suffers from blind recruitment of respondents. A methodological bias often inherent in an on-line survey method is that participants are blind-recruited on-line, and, thus, respondents self-select for participation rather than being randomly or strategically preselected from an existing population roster and individually targeted for recruitment by researchers. Much on-line survey research is done by posting a link to a survey on web pages visited by the target demographic—e.g., a link to the National Basketball Association website, a website for cat or dog lovers, or CNN.com. Analysis and inferences based on resulting data are limited in value because the respondents are entirely self-selected, compared to research designs in which respondents are contacted directly by phone, e-mail, or face-to-face and then enlisted in a study.

4. *Some Students May Misinterpret the Purpose of the Department's Survey.* The Department of Education survey is called "Assessment of Students' Athletic Interests & Abilities." Because those terms are undefined, some students may misinterpret the goal of the survey as an assessment of their interest in participating in *intercollegiate* sports rather than the broad spectrum of real and potential recreational, intramural, club, or junior-varsity activities that might be part of campus life. But schools have an obligation to ensure gender equity in all athletic offerings, not just intercollegiate teams. Moreover, to the extent that these latter athletic activities are historically marginalized or comparatively

underfunded within a specific campus community, students could fail to see them as viable or realistic choices in comparison with the notoriety and institutional centrality of the major intercollegiate sports. Personal interest in participating in a wide array of athletic activities could be skewed or dampened by a realistic assessment of the institutional inequalities that actually exist on campus. As a result, surveys are unlikely to capture the full range of athletic interests that institutions should consider in structuring each level of their sports programs.

Conclusion

The above deficits of the Department's on-line survey method call into question its empirical efficacy. As a result, it would be methodologically misguided for institutions to utilize the Department's online survey method as a sole measure of compliance with prong three. Moreover, the Clarification states that the Department "is not requiring that individual schools conduct elaborate scientific validation" of the procedures and results of the on-line survey.[7] But the procedures and results are suspect unless they are validated based on established scientific and methodological criteria.

We encourage policymakers, government officials, educators, and researchers to fully evaluate the Department's proposed use of the on-line survey method to further elucidate these and other methodological issues.

[7] See http://www.ed.gov/about/offices/list/ocr/docs/title9guidanceadditional.pdf (accessed July 3, 2007).

Bush Administration Uses Stealth Tactics to Subvert Title IX*

Andrew Zimbalist

The true March Madness happens behind the scene. On March 17, 2005, the Office for Civil Rights (OCR) of the U.S. Department of Education (DOE) issued a "Clarification" of the implementation guidelines for colleges to comply with Title IX in athletics. One year later, on March 17, 2006, pursuant to a request from the Senate Appropriations Committee, the OCR released a study that laid bare the nonsense of its previous "Clarification."

Title IX of the 1972 Educational Amendments to the Civil Rights Act requires that schools receiving federal assistance not discriminate against either gender. For colleges to meet this nondiscrimination standard in their athletics programs, they have to meet any one of three tests:

One, a school will be in compliance if the proportion of female athletes roughly equals the proportion of female students at the school (the so-called proportionality standard). Two, the school must have a history and continuing practice of expanding participation opportunities for women. Or, three, the school must fully and effectively accommodate the interests and abilities of the underrepresented sex—typically women.

In January 2002, the National Wrestling Coaches Association (NWCA) sued the Department of Education claiming that Title IX was being implemented as an illegal quota system. The basis for this claim was the proportionality standard.

Every federal appellate court that has looked at the issue has rejected the claim that Department of Education policies create quotas. Nothing in any prong requires schools to maintain a certain number of slots for women. And

*Adapted from *Sports Business Journal*, May 15–21, 2006.

schools may satisfy Title IX requirements by meeting either standard two or standard three. Indeed, of the 132 cases reviewed by OCR between 1992 and 2002, over two-thirds of the schools complied on the basis of standard three.

As the NWCA suit made its way through the courts, the Bush administration launched an investigation into Title IX. Education Secretary Rod Paige established a commission in June 2002 to make recommendations on how the implementation of Title IX should be reformed.

The Commission's membership was stacked and its procedures were prejudicial, so its recommendations to weaken the enforcement of Title IX came as no surprise. Among its twenty-three recommendations were two that proposed the use of a stand-alone survey to be the basis for assessing student interests.

In response to the Commission's 2003 report, there was a massive political outcry and the Bush administration retreated. Secretary Paige announced that the DOE would not alter its implementation of Title IX.

However, after its reelection in November 2004, the Bush administration was less concerned about public opinion. Less than two months after being sworn in for his second term, Bush's DOE, without notice or public input, promulgated its "Clarification."

The Clarification declared that henceforth the OCR would accept the use of an e-mail survey sent to students to be the *sole* determinant of their interest level in sports. Not only had the courts repeatedly rejected such a procedure, Bush's own OCR had done so a year and a half earlier, and the 1996 OCR Clarification made it clear that e-mail interest surveys could only be used as one of several criteria to determine interest level.

The problems with e-mail surveys are multiple, and they only magnify if the surveys are used without other evidence. According to the March 2006 report that the OCR provided to the Senate, after reviewing fifty-four schools that used surveys between 1992 and January 2006, the OCR found that the student response rates on surveys varied from 1 percent to 78 percent. In more than two-thirds of the surveys, the response rate was below 40 percent, and in only two surveys did the rate exceed 75 percent.

Further, the March 2005 Clarification stipulates that nonresponses can be construed as lack of interest. It also states that there will be a "presumption of compliance [with Title IX]" that can only be overturned in the face of "direct and very persuasive evidence of unmet interest sufficient to sustain a varsity team." That is, the burden of proof now lies with the students, not the university.

More alarming still, the Clarification says not a word about the OCR or any other body providing oversight to ensure that the surveys are properly carried out.

Out of the fifty-four cases studied in the March 2006 report, there were only six schools that tried to certify compliance on the basis of using a survey alone.

In each of these cases, the OCR investigated additional evidence (such as requests by students to add sports; participation rates in club or intramural sports; participation rates in high school, amateur associations, or community sports leagues; or interviews with students, coaches, and administrators) and rejected these schools' claims of compliance.

Indeed, between 1992 and 2005, in no case did the OCR certify a school's compliance on the basis of an interest survey alone.

Two facts stand out. First, between 1971 and 2005 the number of women participating in intercollegiate sports increased five-fold, from 32,000 to more than 160,000. Over the same period the number of girls participating in high-school sports increased 9.3-fold, from 300,000 to 2.8 million. Thus, today for every 100 girls playing high-school sports, there are only 5.8 playing in college. This is strong evidence that the interest and ability level is there to support continued growth in intercollegiate-athletic opportunities for women.

Second, even if interest surveys told the whole truth, it would be problematic to rely solely on them. If that was done back in 1972, the participation levels of women would have been frozen at woefully low levels.

According to the last NCAA gender-equity study, women were 54 percent of college students but, in Division I, they were only 43 percent of athletes and they received only 38 percent of athletic department operating funds. This is no time to break the progress of Title IX with manipulative and disingenuous "Clarifications" from the DOE.

Fortunately, the U.S. Congress seems to agree. In late 2006, Congress passed a bill that stipulated e-mail surveys could only be used as part of a broader inquiry.

Football Is a Sucker's Game*

Michael Sokolove

The University of South Florida sprawls over nearly 1,500 acres in a once sparsely populated section of Tampa, close to where the city bleeds into unincorporated Hillsborough County. The campus is pancake flat and in desperate need of more trees and shade. Grass comes up in stubborn clumps through sandy soil. I can't say that I was shocked when I learned of a previous use of this parcel of land: a practice bombing range.

In many other ways, though, the University of South Florida is attractive—and useful. It has produced about 170,000 graduates in its four-decade history. It has a medical school and some well-regarded academic programs. Current enrollment stands at 39,000, and students tend to be grounded and hardworking rather than rich and entitled. (A professor told me that one challenge of his job is teaching morning classes to students who may have worked the late shift at Chili's.) What U.S.F. does not have is any kind of national profile. It has no standing. No buzz. The latest edition of the *Princeton Review*'s "Best 345 Colleges" does not rank it low on the list—it leaves it off entirely.

University officials want U.S.F. in the guidebooks. They want fewer commuters, more out-of-state students, more residence halls, and more of a "traditional" campus feel, by which they mean a campus with a soul and some spirit. It is a big job, and the burden for getting it done has fallen, largely, to Jim Leavitt.

"Sit down," he says as I enter his office one morning this fall. It's clear to me that I'm not only supposed to sit, but to do so in silence. His office is a mess. Clothes are strewn everywhere. About 50 videotapes are scattered on the floor by his desk. Leavitt himself doesn't look so great, either. His brown hair

*New York Times Magazine, December 22, 2002.

is a tousled mop, a modified crew cut gone to seed. He gives the impression of being simultaneously weary and wired.

Leavitt continues at what he was doing before I arrived, drawing with a red pen on an unlined sheet of paper. At one point he reaches behind him on the floor for his Pepsi, which he drinks by the two-liter bottle. When he finally speaks again, his voice leaks out in the weak rasp of someone who does more yelling than sleeping. "I'm sorry," he says, "but I was in here late last night and I never even got to this. To be honest with you, there aren't enough hours in the day. But I've really got to get through it. It's important."

After several more minutes, when he is finally done, I walk around behind Leavitt to inspect his handiwork. On the white paper are a series of squiggles and arrows, eleven on each side of the page.

"What is it?" I inquire.

"A punt return," he says.

Football is the S.U.V. of the college campus: aggressively big, resource-guzzling, lots and lots of fun, and potentially destructive of everything around it. Big-time teams award 85 scholarships and, with walk-ons, field rosters of 100 or more players. (National Football League teams make do with half that.) At the highest level, universities wage what has been called an "athletic arms race" to see who can build the most lavish facilities to attract the highest-quality players. Dollars are directed from general funds and wrestled from donors, and what does not go into cherry-wood lockers, plush carpets, and million-dollar weight rooms ends up in the pockets of coaches, the most exalted of whom now make upward of $2 million a year.

The current college-sports landscape is meaner than ever, more overtly commercial, more winner-take-all. And just as in the rest of the economy, the gap between rich and poor is widening. College sports now consists of a class of super-behemoths—perhaps a dozen or so athletic departments with budgets of $40 million and up—and a much larger group of schools that face the choice of spending themselves into oblivion or being embarrassed on the field. (Which may happen in any case.) It is common for lesser-college football teams to play at places like Tennessee or Michigan, where average attendance exceeds 100,000, in return for "guarantees" from the host school of as much as $500,000. They are paid, in other words, to take a beating.

Any thought of becoming one of the giants and sharing in the real money is, in most cases, a fantasy. Universities new to Division I-A football (in addition to U.S.F., the University of Connecticut and the University of Buffalo have just stepped up to the big time) know that the first level of competition is financial. It is a dangerous game. "The mantra of the need to 'spend money to make money' can be used to justify a great deal of spending, without leading an institution to any destination other than a deeper financial hole," write James

Shulman and William Bowen in *The Game of Life: College Sports and Educational Values*, their 2001 examination of the finances of college athletics.

The current college bowl season began last week and ends January 3 with the national championship game, the Fiesta Bowl. This year, the cartel of teams belonging to the Bowl Championship Series—members of the six most prominent conferences plus independent Notre Dame, a total of 63 teams—will split a guaranteed payoff of at least $120 million from the Fiesta, Orange, Sugar, and Rose Bowls. Teams outside the B.C.S. are eligible to play in such low-wattage affairs as the Humanitarian Bowl, the Motor City Bowl, and the Continental Tire Bowl. For the privilege, they will almost certainly lose money, because the bowl payouts will not even cover travel and other expenses.

"We are receiving letters and calls from conferences that want in," Mike Tranghese, coordinator of the five-year-old B.C.S., told me. "And we have formed a presidential oversight panel to form an answer." But letting more members in would mean splitting up the money more ways. I asked Tranghese if I was missing something in assuming the B.C.S. had no incentive to cut more schools in. "If you were missing something, I would let you know," he said. "The B.C.S. consists of the major teams as determined by the marketplace. Any other system is socialism. And if we're going to have socialism, then why don't we share our endowments?"

One reason B.C.S. members do not want to share is that college sports have become so immensely expensive that even some of the biggest of the big lose money. The University of Michigan, which averages more than 110,000 fans for home football games, lost an estimated $7 million on athletics over the course of two seasons, between 1998 and 2000. Ohio State had athletic revenues of $73 million in 1999–2000 and "barely managed to break even," according to the book *Unpaid Professionals: Commercialism and Conflict in Big-Time College Sports*, by Andrew Zimbalist, a Smith College economics professor. A state audit revealed that the University of Wisconsin lost $286,700 on its Rose Bowl appearance in 1998 because it took a small army, a traveling party of 832, to Pasadena.

The endemic criminal and ethical scandals of college sports are connected by a straight line to the money. Teams that do not win do not excite their boosters, fill up stadiums, appear on national TV, or get into postseason play, thereby endangering the revenue stream that supports the immense infrastructure. It is the desperation for cash, every bit as much as the pursuit of victory, that causes university athletic departments to overlook all kinds of rule-breaking until it splatters out into the open.

One day this fall I opened my morning sports page and, in glancing at the college football briefs, took note that it was a particularly bad day for the Big Ten. The headlines were: "Spartan Tailback Dismissed"; "Iowa Player Arrested"; "Wisconsin Back Stabbed." The Michigan State Spartans dismissed two co-captains within ten days: the starting quarterback, who checked into rehab for a substance-abuse problem, as well as the tailback, who was accused of drunken driving and eluding arrest by dragging a police officer with his car. The next day, the head coach, Bobby Williams, with his team's record at 3–6, was fired—and sent off with a $550,000 buyout.

At tiny Gardner-Webb University in Boiling Springs, North Carolina—a Baptist institution in its first season of Division I basketball—the university president resigned in the fall after acknowledging that he ordered a change in the calculation of a star basketball player's grade-point average. At Florida State University, quarterback Adrian McPherson was suspended days before his arrest for supposedly stealing a blank check, then expressed shock at the discipline meted out by the normally lenient head coach, Bobby Bowden. (When a star player was accused of theft a few years back, Bowden said, "I'm praying for a misdemeanor.") The University of Alabama at Birmingham, which started football just over a decade ago, is playing this season under a cloud. The trustees of the Alabama higher-education system have given the university two years to reverse a $7.6-million budget deficit or face being shut down. In addition, pending civil suits charge that a 15-year-old girl who enrolled at U.A.B. was sexually assaulted, repeatedly, by a large number of football and basketball players, as well as by the person who performed as the school's mascot, a dragon.

The list goes on. Ohio State's thrilling 14–9 victory over Michigan on November 23 occasioned a full-scale riot by inebriated Buckeye fans who burned cars, looted businesses, and caused tens of thousands of dollars in damage before 250 police officers finally restored order at 5 a.m. These sorts of things have become the background music of college sports.

Being a striving team trying to keep up in a big-time conference can be a particular kind of debacle. Rutgers University, in this regard, is Exhibit A. It belongs to the Big East, a B.C.S. football conference that also boasts powerful basketball programs. Rutgers can't compete in either sport. Its cellar-dwelling teams draw poor crowds, and the athletic department ran a deficit of about $13 million last year.

A dissident group, the Rutgers 1,000, has waged a passionate campaign to get Rutgers to leave the Big East and to de-emphasize athletics. This has led, indirectly, to yet an entirely new way of throwing money away on sports. The administration tried to block publication of a Rutgers 1,000 advertisement in an alumni magazine. Not only did Rutgers lose the ensuing court battle, but it also spent $375,000 fighting it, including court-ordered reimbursement of legal fees to the A.C.L.U., which took up the case of the Rutgers 1,000 as a free-speech issue.

"Schools get on a treadmill, and there's no getting off," says James Shulman, an author of *The Game of Life*. "They have to stay on; they have too much invested." The former Princeton basketball coach Pete Carill once said of the big-time programs: "If you want to get into the rat race, you've got to be a rat."

Another way to look at big-time college sports is as a sucker's game, one with many more losers than winners. Notre Dame, a great football team before it was a great university, is the prototype for all schools hoping to hitch a ride on the back of a popular sports team. Duke certainly has become more cele-brated and academically selective in the years its basketball team has been a perennial Final Four participant. But Notre Dame and Duke are exceptions. For every Notre Dame and Duke, there are many more like Rutgers and U.A.B., schools that spend millions in a hopeless mission to reach the top.

The University of South Florida, nonetheless, wants in on the gamble and in on the perceived spoils. The new gospel there is that football is "the tip of the marketing sword." I heard the phrase from several administrators at U.S.F. Vicki Mitchell explained the concept to me. She had directed a highly successful university-wide fund-raising campaign, but in May, not long after the team jumped to Division I-A, she moved to the athletic department to raise money specifically for sports. Under Mitchell, the office devoted to sports fund-raising was ramped up from three staff members to eight, and in the first three months of this fiscal year she and her team brought in $1.6 million, just $200,000 less than the total raised in the previous 12 months. "The easiest way to build a U.S.F. brand is to build an athletic program that is known, and that means football," Mitchell said. "Maybe that's not what the university wants to be known for, but it's reality."

Nearly two decades ago, the exploits of the Boston College quarterback Doug Flutie and the success of the team were credited with increasing applica-tions by 25 percent and transforming B.C. from a regional to a national univer-sity. The syndrome was even given a name: the Flutie effect. That's the kind of magic U.S.F. is trying to catch.

U.S.F. didn't play football at any level until 1997. Its founding president, John Allen, who presided over the university from 1957 to 1970, was that rare thing in football-crazed Florida—a staunch opponent of the sport. In the 1980s, U.S.F. alumni and Tampa businessmen began pushing for football, and the U.S.F. administration began lobbying a reluctant state Board of Regents for a team. In 1993, the outgoing president, Frank Borkowski, in his final weeks at U.S.F. and with the Regents' decision on football pending, hired Lee Roy Sel-mon—a former N.F.L. star and one of the most admired men in Tampa—to lead football fund-raising. That was the pivotal moment. "I was in a pretty tight box," recalls Borkowski, now chancellor at Appalachian State University. "The Regents did not want us to have a team." But to deny football would have been a slap to Selmon.

Jim Leavitt was hired in 1995, two years before the University of South Florida Bulls played their first game. From the start, the university intended to move quickly to the N.C.A.A.'s highest level and eventually challenge football factories like Florida State, the University of Florida, and the University of Miami. By the time the current U.S.F. president, Judy Genshaft, arrived in 2000, the program was in full bloom. Genshaft's term has so far been marked by a thorny dispute spawned by her suspension of Sami Al-Arian, a tenured professor of computer science, over charges that he had ties to terrorism. Compared to the fallout from that, football has been pure pleasure.

Genshaft, who attends the team's games and keeps a jersey in her office with her name on the back, was an undergraduate at Wisconsin and a longtime administrator at Ohio State. "I know big sports," she says, "and I love big sports. It brings more visibility, more spirit, more community engagement. Even researchers coming to us from other big universities, they are expecting sports to be part of campus life."

The rationales put forth for big-time sports are not easily proved or disproved. One example is the assumption that successful teams spur giving to the general funds of universities. "The logic is reasonable enough," Zimbalist wrote in *Unpaid Professionals.* "A school goes to the Rose Bowl or to the Final Four. Alumni feel proud and open up their pocketbooks." But Zimbalist looked at the available evidence and concluded that winning teams, at best, shake loose dollars given specifically for sports. And only for a time; when on-field fortunes reverse, or a scandal occurs, the money often dries up.

Genshaft says that U.S.F. can play football at the highest level without financial or ethical ruin. "It's a risk and it is expensive," she says. "But we've decided that football is part of who we are and where we're going."

But others see disaster as the only possible result. At Rutgers, the sports program has split the campus community and spawned an angry and unusually organized opposition. "The reality of sports at this level is it can't be done right," says William C. Dowling, an English professor and one of the leaders of the Rutgers 1,000. "It's not possible, anywhere, even at the so-called best places. Look at the differences in SAT levels."

One study showed the SAT scores of football players at Division I-A schools to be 271 points lower than incoming nonathletes. "You have kids brought to campus and maybe, maybe they could be real students if they studied 60 hours a week and did nothing else," Dowling says. "But everyone knows that's not happening. It's not their fault. They've been lied to in high school, all these African American kids who get told that playing ball is their way up in society, even though it's never been that for any other ethnic group in America. It's dishonest. It's filthy."

When Vicki Mitchell pitches U.S.F. donors, however, she sells the program as if it were in a state of grace—unsullied by scandal, at least so far, and still operating with a degree of fiscal sanity. She begins by painting a picture of what life is like at the really big football powers. To secure a season ticket at one of those schools in a desirable part of the stadium, if that's even possible, can set a donor back tens of thousands of dollars. "I'll say to someone: 'You're a sports fan. You need to get on board, because everyone knows what it costs at those other places. Our aspirations are no less, but we're not there yet. We're young. We're fun. We're a growth stock. Get in now while it's still affordable.'"

I met head coach Jim Leavitt for the first time just a few days before the biggest home game in the history of University of South Florida football. The opponent, Southern Mississippi, was the strongest team ever to visit U.S.F. and a favorite to break its 15-game home-winning streak. U.S.F. had lost an early-season road game at Oklahoma, then the second-ranked team in the nation, but outplayed the powerful Sooners for long stretches. Leavitt's team was surging in the national polls; the *New York Times* computer rankings would place it as high as 18th in the nation, ahead of such tradition-rich football powers as Tennessee, Florida State, Auburn, Clemson, and Nebraska. These accomplishments, for a program playing just its sixth season, were nothing short of astounding.

As the showdown against Southern Mississippi loomed, two things obsessed Leavitt: winning the game, and money. "The kind of money we need is big, big money," he said to me not long after saying hello. He kept returning to the same point. "We have what we need for a beginning program, but we're not a beginning program anymore." Then: "I don't know what this program will look like in the future. It can be big. But you've got to have money. You've got to have facilities. If you don't, it ain't gonna happen."

Leavitt, 46, grew up in nearby St. Petersburg. He was a high-school sports star, a defensive back at the University of Missouri, then an assistant coach at several universities before he came home to be the first coach of U.S.F. football.

Leavitt has won praise not just for winning, but also for doing so on the cheap. He and his nine assistant coaches work out of a complex of four trailers, in front of which Leavitt erected a split-rail fence "to make it look like the Ponderosa." Leavitt proudly told me that the couch in his office, on which he sometimes lies down for the night, is a $700 vinyl number rather than one of those $5,000 leather cruise ships to be found in the offices of so many other coaches.

This era of frugality, though, has just ended. In early November, the university unveiled drawings for a long-hoped-for training and office complex that will be as big as a football field—104,000 square feet over two floors that will serve most of the university's men's and women's teams but will be dominated by football.

Leavitt views this as natural and right. He tells me about Oklahoma, coached by his close friend Bob Stoops, which already has "an outrageous setup, everything you can imagine," and has just raised yet another $100 million. "I imagine they'll tell you it's not for football only, and I would assume it's not," Leavitt says. "But I'm pretty sure football will get what it needs first. As it should, in my opinion."

Like many football coaches, Leavitt is no fan of Title IX regulations that mandate equal opportunity for female athletes. "Don't get me wrong," he says, "I am a big proponent of women's sports. I want us to be great at women's sports. But football should be separate from the Title IX thing, because nobody else operates like we do. We're revenue producing."

To build the U.S.F. athletic complex will cost as much as $15 million. To furnish it—starting with $425,000 in weight-training equipment, a $65,000 hydrotherapy tub, portable X-ray machines, satellite uplinks and downlinks, trophy cases for a U.S.F. sports hall of fame in the atrium entrance—will cost up to $5 million more.

Despite aggressive fund-raising, private pledges for this facility have reached only $5 million, so it will be built on borrowed money. The construction bond will be backed partly by the "athletic fee" charged to students, which for those who attend full time has reached $224 a year—a fairly substantial add-on to a tuition of only $2,159.

Mitchell says the university considers students "its biggest donor," and student leaders are, in fact, courted like boosters. In October, the student-government president and vice president flew on a private jet with President Genshaft to the big game at Oklahoma.

U.S.F. calculates that the football team brings in, roughly, $4 million in revenue and spends about the same amount. But as in most athletic departments, the accounting makes no attempt to measure the true resources used.

One day, I stood in a humid basement room and watched the laundry—muddy Bulls jerseys and pants, T-shirts, sweat socks, wrist- and headbands, jockstraps—from 105 football players being cleaned. Several colossal washers and dryers were fed by three athletic-department employees. They perform this task early August through late November, six days a week, ten hours a day.

None of this—the salaries, the utility costs, the $8,000 a year just in laundry detergent—is charged against football. Nor is there any attempt to break out football's share of such costs as sports medicine, academic tutoring, strength and conditioning, insurance, field upkeep, or the rest of its share of the more than $5 million in general expenses of the athletic department not assigned to a specific sport.

In the papers I was shown, I also could find no evidence that a $2-million fee to join Conference USA (which is not a B.C.S. conference) as a football-playing member in 2003 was accounted for in football's expense ledger. The money was borrowed from the university's general endowment, and the athletic department is paying the interest.

So when Jim Leavitt says that his football team is revenue producing, that should not be understood as profit generating. I would not pretend to know what football really costs at U.S.F., but it's clearly a lot more than $4 million, maybe even twice that. And another big bill is about to come due: Leavitt's next contract.

Just in case Judy Genshaft didn't know she had a hot coach on her hands who needed a big raise, she could have learned it from reading the local press. The articles began after the end of the 2001 season, when Leavitt entertained some job feelers. "U.S.F. Needs to Make Commitment to Leavitt," read a headline in the *Tampa Tribune.* "U.S.F. said it wanted to play in the big leagues and built an impressive foundation," the columnist Joe Henderson wrote. "Now it has to finish the job, or risk that Leavitt will listen the next time someone calls."

Columns like these are the essential component of setting the market for a coach and driving up his price. An echo chamber of sports journalists, boosters, alumni, fans, and national sports pundits anoints the coach a civic treasure and then campaigns that this indispensable figure must be properly rewarded lest the community risk having him stolen away. This is how it happens everywhere.

As Leavitt's Bulls piled up victory after victory this season, it got ever noisier in the echo chamber. A story by the *Tampa Tribune'*s U.S.F. beat man noted that Leavitt's $180,000 salary was way out of whack, that the average for Conference USA coaches was $410,000, that the coach at Houston—whose team Leavitt's slaughtered, 45–6!—could approach $1 million, and that Leavitt was in fact one of the lowest-paid coaches in all of Division I-A.

A *St. Petersburg Times* columnist, Gary Shelton, celebrated Leavitt's single-mindedness—he has never purchased a CD, doesn't go to the movies, was barely aware of the Florida governor's race—and implied that the coach was too dedicated to the next game and next victory to properly focus on his own self-interest.

The drumbeat on Leavitt's behalf overlooked two things. One is that Leavitt's original contract runs through 2005, although that probably doesn't matter because college coaches are rarely held to the deals they sign. The other unaddressed question was more significant: How would U.S.F. square its big-time ambitions with its still-small-time revenues?

For all the fevered energy and earnest expectations behind U.S.F. football, attendance at home games has long been stuck between 20,000 and 30,000. The team plays way across town, at the 65,000-seat Raymond James Stadium, home of the N.F.L.'s Tampa Bay Buccaneers. "We've flatlined," says Tom Veit, associate athletic director. "We had tire-kickers in the beginning, something like 50,000 at the first game in '97, and we need to bring them back in."

Students have not been dependable fans. About 3,500 live on campus; nearly 10,000 more live in off-campus garden apartments, most of which have swimming pools and frequent keg parties. Fifty-nine percent of U.S.F. students are female, so young men, the natural college-football audience, may have a particular incentive not to stray too far from home. "If you want it to be," says the student-government vice president, Dave Mincberg, "it's like spring break 24/7 around here."

One function that U.S.F. football does serve is as content, cheap programming in the 500-channel universe. Under a contract with ESPN Plus, U.S.F. football (and basketball) games are constantly up on the satellite—along with dozens of other games to be pulled down by viewers with a dish and a college-sports package. The ubiquity of these televised college games makes the dream of a marketing bonanza—Jim Leavitt's fightin' Bulls as the tip of the sword—all the more difficult to achieve. Instead of becoming a "brand" like the well-known sports schools, U.S.F. is more likely to blend in with its anonymous brethren in Sports Satellite World, the Northern Arizonas, Coastal Carolinas, and Boise States.

But U.S.F. has set its course. It's on the treadmill. It plays Alabama next season, Penn State in 2005, and the University of Florida in 2008. It didn't schedule these games to be embarrassed. Rebuilding with a new coach would be difficult competitively and, even more so, commercially. "If we lose Jim Leavitt, from a marketing point of view, that's not a place I want to be," Veit says. "I don't want to be me at that point. He's a hometown guy. He wins. People like him."

When the local sportswriters ask Leavitt about his contract, he gives carefully bland responses. He doesn't have an agent, and it could be argued that with his fawning press, he hardly needs one. The articles clearly please him. One day he says to me: "The Tampa paper is going to have another piece coming up on my salary. But you know, I don't pay too much attention. I don't deserve anything. I'm just glad I have a job. I'm blessed.

"And I mean that. I have zero interest in leaving here. But then people say to me, 'What if you were offered $1 million to go somewhere else?' Well, then I'd probably leave. Let's be realistic."

I asked him what he thought his market value was, and he did not hesitate. "About $500,000 or $600,000," he said. "At least."

The biggest of the big-time college sporting events are intoxicating. The swirl of colors, the marching bands, the deafening roars, the over-the-top political incorrectness—Florida State's Seminole mascot riding in on horseback;

a Mississippi State coach some years back, on the eve of a game against the Texas Longhorns, castrating a bull. The whole thing is a little reminiscent of what I've heard some Catholic friends of mine say: Even if you're a little ambivalent about the message, the pageantry will get you every time.

In college sports, the heady mix of anticipation, adrenaline, camaraderie, and school pride is the gloss over the grubby reality. Pro sports operates within some financial parameters, governed by a profit motive. College sport, by contrast, is a mad cash scramble with squishy rules. Universities run from conference to conference, chasing richer TV deals; coaches from school to school, chasing cash. It's a game of mergers and acquisitions—of running out on your partners before they run out on you.

It's understandable why universities with hundreds of millions already invested in sports can't find a way out. Far less understandable is why a school like U.S.F. would, with eyes wide open, walk in. "I felt then and still feel that U.S.F. could be a model football program," says Frank Borkowski, the former president. "One with clear policies and rules, attractive to bright students, that would not go the way of so many programs—a corrupt way."

But the whole framework of college sports, with its out-of-control spending and lax academic and ethical standards, is rotten; it's difficult to be clean within it. The "student-athletes," as the N.C.A.A. insists on calling them, feel the hypocrisy. When one is caught taking the wrong thing from the wrong person—not the usual perks but actual money—what ensues is a "Casablanca"-like overabundance of shock, then a bizarre penalty phase that almost always punishes everyone but the guilty parties. Thus, when the University of Michigan finally acknowledged this fall that some members of its famed "Fab Five" basketball teams of the early 1990s may have accepted payments from a booster, the university tried to get out in front of N.C.A.A. sanctions by disqualifying this year's team—whose players were about 8 years old in the Fab Five years—from participating in the 2003 N.C.A.A. tournament.

With the greater opportunities being afforded female athletes, it should be no surprise that an outsize sense of entitlement now extends to the women. Deborah Yow, the athletic director at the University of Maryland (and one of the few women leading a big athletic department), told me about a conversation she had with an athlete who had rejected Maryland.

"We just lost a great recruit in the sport of women's lacrosse, in which we have won seven national championships," Yow said. "And one of the comments that the recruit made was that the school she had chosen over us had a beautiful new lacrosse stadium with a lovely locker room, and she even described the lockers in some detail. They were wood; that was the word she kept using. And, as she said, they all had that Nike gear hanging everywhere. And I've been to that facility. And I know that what she said was true."

In theory, Yow could have been pleased to be rejected by such a spoiled child. But she does not have that luxury. Instead, she felt relieved that a planned complex to be used by the Maryland's women's lacrosse team would be the equal of this other palace. "We, as athletic directors, are interested in having the best possible facilities because we have noticed along the way that recruits are interested in this, that it does matter," she says.

College sport could not survive if it were viewed only as mass entertainment. On another level, it serves as a salvation story. The enterprise rests mostly on a narrative of young men pulled from hopeless situations, installed at universities, schooled in values by coaches, and sent off into the world as productive citizens.

No one is better suited to tell the story than Lee Roy Selmon. The youngest of nine children in Eufala, Oklahoma, he excelled in athletics and earned a football scholarship, as did two of his brothers, to the University of Oklahoma. Lee Roy Selmon became the first-ever draft pick of the new Tampa Bay Buccaneers, an N.F.L. Hall of Famer, then a Tampa banker. The Lee Roy Selmon Expressway is one of the city's major thoroughfares.

To Selmon, who became U.S.F.'s athletic director a year and a half ago, college sports is a giant scholarship program for needy children. Of football's 100-player rosters, he says, "The more people here, the more people getting an education, the better. It's about generations—about student-athletes developing abilities, being citizens, having families, and being able to nurture their children."

One evening, I visited with some U.S.F. football players at their mandatory study hall, which takes place inside a wide-open rectangular room as big as a good-size banquet hall. Their monitor, Vik Bhide, a trim engineering student, sat just inside the front door, paging through a book called *The Dimensions of Parking*. The players clustered at round tables, reading textbooks or writing. Most had started their day very early and had already attended classes, lifted weights, endured a three-hour practice, and gone to meetings in which they watched game film with coaches.

I took a walk through the room and peeked at the players' coursework. John Miller, a freshman offensive lineman, was studying vocabulary words from a textbook. On his list were "burgeoning," "inflection," "emanate," "insidious," and "obscenity." "It's a lot of hard words," he said. "But they're good for you."

Vince Brewer, a junior running back, was about to start an informative speech, which he thought he'd write on the subject of what causes a player to pass out during practice. "We get told a lot about dehydration, and the professor said to pick something you know a lot about." Chris Carothers, a massive offensive lineman, told me bluntly that he does not much like school, "but as a football player, it's something you've got to do."

In all of my interactions with U.S.F. football players, I was struck at how mannerly they were. Nearly all are from Florida, many from small towns, and in a classically Southern way, they are yes-sir, no-sir types. Maybe because U.S.F. has not yet reached its ambitions and neither the team nor its players are widely famous—not even on their own campus—there wasn't a lot of swagger.

"My mom and dad had me when they were in 11th grade," Marquel Blackwell, the Bulls' star quarterback, said. "I was raised, basically, by my two grandmothers. The main thing they taught me was how to respect other people."

Not a whole lot of trouble has attached to Jim Leavitt's boys in the six years of U.S.F. football, nothing of the sort that occurs at some places and serves to indict a whole program. There have been some scuffles, as well as a gunplay accident in which a player was wounded.

"We encourage the players to be as much a part of normal campus life as possible," said Phyllis LaBaw, the associate athletic director for academic support. But no one pretends that they really are much like the typical U.S.F. student.

Nearly 70 percent of the U.S.F. football team is black on a campus that is otherwise 70 percent white. (Only 11 percent of U.S.F. students are black; the rest of the minority population is Hispanic, Asian, and Native American.) The football players tend to be poorer than other students and more in need of academic help.

To be a football player at U.S.F., or an athlete of any kind, is like taking your mother to school with you—or several mothers. Academic counselors meet with athletes at least weekly. They sometimes follow them right to the door of a classroom, which in the trade is known as "eyeballing" a player to class. Where a lot of players are grouped in one class, tutors sometimes sit in and take notes. Counselors communicate directly with professors. "We don't ever ask for favors," LaBaw said. "but professors do provide us with information, which is vital."

Football players who miss a class or a mandatory study session get "run" by coaches—meaning they must show up on the practice field at 6 a.m. to be put through a series of sprints by a coach who is not happy to be there at that hour. "It is very punitive," LaBaw said.

LaBaw's department employs four full-time counselors and about 40 tutors and has an annual budget of $400,000. The staff serves all 450 intercollegiate athletes at U.S.F., so the 105 football players are less than a quarter of the clients—but, as is the case with so much else, football sucks up more resources than its raw numbers would indicate. "They need more help," LaBaw said of the footballers, "but what we're doing works. Last year our football players had a mean G.P.A. of 2.52, which if we were already in Conference USA would have been the best in the conference—including Army."

LaBaw is part den mother, part drill sergeant—loving and supportive or confrontational and blunt, depending on the needs of the moment. Under her desk, she keeps a big box; when the season began, it had 5,000 condoms in it, all different colors. She hands them out like lollipops along with however much sex education she can blurt out.

Her effort, while well intentioned, is a version of closing the barn door after the horses have run out. Of the 105 players on U.S.F.'s football team—most of them between 18 and 23 years old—about 30 are fathers and many have produced multiple children. "I would say there's a total of 60 children from this team, and that's a conservative estimate," said LaBaw. "It's amazing how quickly it occurs, usually in the first year. Or they come to school already fathers."

What this means is that the recipients of Lee Roy Selmon's scholarship program for needy young men are recreating the need that many of them came from—children living in poverty, without fathers at home. With their five hours per day of football-related activity on top of class and studying, the fathers have no time even to change a diaper, let alone work to financially support their children. Most of the children live with their mothers or aunts or grandmothers. Some who are nearby spend the day at the university's day-care center, yet another cost of college football since the service is offered virtually free to U.S.F. students.

In DeAndrew Rubin's portrait in the U.S.F. football media guide, it says that his father drowned when he was 11 months old. It adds, "Father had given him a teddy bear for his first Christmas in 1978, and he places it in his locker during every game."

Rubin, 24, has two children, 3 years old and 10 months, and is engaged to their mother, his girlfriend since high school. They live just 30 minutes away in St. Petersburg. "I see them as often as I can, so if I would pass, they would remember me," he said. "I can't help that much financially, but emotionally I want to be there for them."

Unlike several other U.S.F. fathers who said they planned to make the N.F.L., Rubin is considered a prospect, although no sure thing. "It would be good for our situation," he said. "I don't want to have to work a 9-to-5; I guess nobody really does."

LaBaw spends a lot of time talking to the players. "Those who are fathers, there's a comfort aspect—having children is an opportunity to be surrounded by more love, which is what they've always had, from grandmothers and aunts and cousins. But there is also this trophy aspect. It's let me show you the pictures, or the multiple pictures."

Football is at the center of Jim Leavitt's world, so he is not one to question the time or money devoted to it. He does not seem to have a great deal of interest in the nonfootball world. Leavitt makes appearances on campus and in the community, often related to fund-raising, but several people told me he can be brusque. If he says he has 20 minutes to give, then he's normally out the door in 20 minutes. There is always a practice to conduct or a football tape to be watched. He watches game tapes, and tapes of practices. "I sit and watch film all day long," he says. "I'm a recluse."

Because football is so central to him, he assumes his team's success is widely known and that it translates into other realms—he believes, without a doubt, in the concept of football as tip of the marketing sword. "We've had guys drafted into the N.F.L.," he says. "We have two guys with Super Bowl rings. How much does the university spend for that? What's it worth? That's worldwide publicity for the University of South Florida, right?"

I asked Leavitt if his long football hours left him much time with his 7-year-old daughter. "Quality time," he said, then repeated it as if trying to convince himself. "Quality time. It's got to be quality time."

There is one slice of humanity that Leavitt connects with—his players. "That's why I'm in this," he says. "The players. The relationships I have with those young men and the ability to make a difference in their lives. My mission is to help young people in every aspect of life. If I lose sight of that, I'll get out of coaching. The other reason I coach is for that moment when you are victorious. That's hard to create in any other part of life. You feel such contentment. That moment is so powerful." At halftime of U.S.F.'s season finale against Houston, Leavitt grew so agitated that he excitedly head-butted several of his helmeted players and came away bloody.

Beyond the field, Leavitt has reason to believe he had made a difference. His players respond to him as an authority figure and as a friend. They have absorbed his laser focus. They play football. They go to class and mandatory study hall. When the season is over, they lift weights and run. Marquel Blackwell, the quarterback, told me that more established programs like Florida and Nebraska showed interest in him but wanted to switch his position. Of Leavitt, he says: "He believed in me, and I believe in him back. I've given my heart to that man."

On the night of the big game, with U.S.F.'s home-winning streak on the line against Southern Mississippi, President Genshaft played host to a couple of dozen guests in a luxury box at Raymond James Stadium—a crowd that included Florida's lieutenant governor and an assortment of local business types and politicos. Mike Griffin, the student-government president, was in the box, too, wearing a "Bulls for Jeb" campaign button.

Because of Selmon's icon status, his box is the more coveted invitation, and Vicki Mitchell and her staff put together his list for maximum impact. They had targeted a wealthy U.S.F. graduate and Los Angeles lawyer as a potential big donor, but he had become critical of the athletic program on chat rooms devoted to U.S.F. sports. (Fund-raisers monitor such things.) Selmon called the lawyer during a trip to Los Angeles, just to warm him up, then invited him to fly in and sit in his box for the game. The lawyer accepted and showed up at the game with a friend who wore a muscle shirt. But both men fidgeted and looked impatient, then bolted at halftime.

The large-framed woman sitting in a corner of the box paid much more interest and stayed to the end. Selmon spent time visiting with her, at one point positioning himself on one knee in the aisle next to her. She was another potentially deep-pocketed donor: Lucille Harrison, a Florida resident and Shaquille O'Neal's mother.

U.S.F. beat the odds. It preserved its home-winning streak in a stirring game decided on the last play, a missed Southern Mississippi field-goal attempt. By season's end, Leavitt's long hours had paid off beyond what any football prognosticator could have predicted. The Bulls finished the season with a record of 9–2, including a dismantling of Bowling Green, then ranked 25th in the nation. A bid to a minor bowl, the money-losing kind, looked possible, but the bowls snubbed U.S.F. in favor of teams with lesser records but bigger names. Leavitt immediately surfaced as a possibility to fill open coaching jobs at marquee schools, including Alabama and Michigan State. The new program was at a crossroads. Was it going to ante up for its coach, and his assistants, too, which could easily add an instant $500,000 or more to the annual football budget? Or would it start all over with someone new?

As the field goal flew wide in the Southern Miss game, one of Selmon's guests, an alum and successful stockbroker, jumped out of his seat, threw his arms around the U.S.F. athletic director, and got right to the point. "We've got to keep this man!" he shouted, referring to Leavitt. "Let's raise this man some money and keep him here!"

On December 12, the University of South Florida ripped up Jim Leavitt's contract and signed him to a new five-year deal that more than doubled his salary. If he keeps winning, he probably won't make it to the final year of this contract, either, when he's scheduled to make nearly $700,000. U.S.F. will have to pay more to keep him, or other programs will come looking to steal him away. That's how it is when you decide to play with the big boys. The bills just keep on getting bigger.

Title IX by the Numbers

Andrew Zimbalist

Much debate about Title IX swirls around the statistics and financial data used by proponents and opponents of the law to make their respective cases. This data comes from a number of sources. Since the mid-1990s, the NCAA has published an annual gender equity report. This yearly report is based on a survey that responds not only to the NCAA's particular interests and concerns, but also to those related to the Equity in Athletics Disclosure Act that Congress enacted in 1994. The report provides an excellent starting point to review some of the progress that is being made toward the provision of equal athletic opportunity for male and female student-athletes.

The numbers from these reports reveal a clear pattern. After rapid progress in the 1970s (women's participation rate in Division I athletics rose from 15 percent in 1971 to 30 percent in 1981–1982), the decade of the 1980s showed only a minor gain (the Division I participation rose only to 31 percent by 1991–1992). Substantial gender equity gains, however, were registered once again during the period 1993–2001. For instance, in Division I-A, the proportion of women among all athletes rose from 29 percent in 1991–1992 to 43 percent in 2001–2002; the increase in all of Division I was similar, rising from 31 percent in 1991–1992 to 44 percent in 2001–2002. The higher proportion for all of Division I (relative to Division I-A) is due to the greater female participation in Division I-AAA, which is the subdivision that does not allow football.

Along with higher participation ratios, the 1993–2001 period also showed increases in the areas of recruitment expenditures (the women's share in Division I-A rose from 16 percent in 1991–1992 to 30 percent in 2001–2002), head coaches' base salaries (the women's share rose from 34 percent to 36 percent), and scholarship spending (the women's share rose from 28 percent to 41 per-

Table One

	Division I-A athletics participation average per institution		
	Men's	Women's	% Total
1991–1992	323	130	0.29
1995–1996	289	151	0.34
1997–1998	310	191	0.38
1999–2000	297	193	0.39
2001–2002	330	250	0.43
2002–2003	325	253	0.44
2003–2004	322	255	0.44

cent). These improvements were not an accident. The Office of Civil Rights (OCR) under the Clinton administration played an active role during this time, issuing new implementation guidelines and letters of interpretation, and participating in educational efforts to promote Title IX. This posture, in turn, created an environment in which female athletes stood up for their interests, sometimes by making complaints to the OCR and sometimes by initiating litigation against offending schools. The courts, as detailed elsewhere in this book, almost uniformly sided with the female athletes.

The gender equity record under the Bush administration from 2000 to the present, however, has shown little or no progress. As shown in Part V, the Bush administration's Department of Education appointed a commission to "study" Title IX's implementation and through its OCR issued a "clarification" in 2005 that allowed the use of e-mail interest surveys to show compliance. Both actions clearly were driven by the political forces opposed to Title IX's advance. Similarly, during 2002–2006 the OCR initiated just 1 out of 416 complaints filed regarding Title IX's implementation. Not surprisingly, the numerical record since 2001 suggests stagnation.

The most recent NCAA Gender Equity Report, which was published in August 2006, goes through the academic year 2003–2004. Table One above displays the results for gender participation rates in Division I-A. After increasing by fourteen points from 1991–1992 to 2001–2002, the proportion of female athletes has stabilized in the 43 to 44 percent range. Women represent 51.8 percent of the student body at Division I-A institutions (and 53.4 percent in Division I overall). The general picture of stagnation is reinforced when considering the evidence on recruiting expenditures, head coaches' salaries, and scholarships (Table Two).

Table Two

	Division I-A recruiting expenses average per institution			Women's % total
	Men's	Women's	Difference	
1991–1992	$268,996	$49,406	$219,590	0.16
1995–1996	$256,511	$84,550	$171,961	0.25
1997–1998	$324,706	$123,633	$201,073	0.28
1999–2000	$346,500	$142,800	$203,700	0.29
2001–2002	$369,200	$159,300	$209,900	0.30
2002–2003	$382,600	$164,800	$217,800	0.30
2003–2004	$412,700	$175,100	$237,600	0.30

Table Three

	Division I-A head coaches' salaries average per institution			Women's % total
	Men's	Women's	Difference	
1991–1992	$396,791	$206,106	$190,685	0.34
1995–1996	$505,127	$320,965	$184,162	0.39
1997–1998	$629,598	$391,012	$238,586	0.38
1999–2000	$776,500	$480,000	$296,500	0.38
2001–2002	$1,034,900	$577,000	$457,900	0.36
2002–2003	$1,167,000	$620,000	$547,000	0.35
2003–2004	$1,783,100	$850,400	$932,700	0.32

The share of recruiting expenses in Division I-A spent on female athletes surged from 16 percent in 1991–1992 to 30 percent in 2001–2002, but has since remained at 30 percent. More strikingly, the absolute difference between recruiting expenditures on men and women, after falling by roughly $10,000 per institution between 1991–1992 and 2001–2002, began to rise again thereafter, increasing by almost $18,000 per institution over two years.

The pattern for head coaches' salaries is similar, though the relative improvement for women's head coaches between 1991–1992 and 2001–2002 was more modest, and the decline since 2001–2002 has been sharper. Indeed, the absolute difference in head coaches' salaries (including benefits) between

Table Four

| | Division I-A scholarships average per institution | | | Women's |
	Men's	Women's	Difference	% total
1991–1992	$1,291,118	$505,246	$785,872	0.28
1995–1996	$1,575,821	$824,889	$750,932	0.34
1997–1998	$1,986,097	$1,193,730	$792,367	0.38
1999–2000	$2,118,400	$1,402,100	$716,300	0.40
2001–2002	$2,472,500	$1,735,500	$737,000	0.41
2002–2003	$2,602,200	$1,878,700	$723,500	0.42
2003–2004	$2,943,400	$2,130,400	$813,000	0.42

men's and women's teams more than doubled between 2001–2002 and 2003–2004 (Table Three).[1]

The women's share in total athletic scholarships rose significantly from 28 percent in 1991–1992 to 41 percent in 2002–2003, and then remained in the 41 to 42 percent range the next two years. Repeating the pattern with recruiting expenses and head coaches' salaries, the absolute difference between the amount spent on men's and women's scholarships in Division I-A, after falling from $875,872 in 1991–1992 to $737,000 in 2001–2002, widened to $813,000 in 2003–2004 (Table Four).

Thus, gender equity results compiled during the Bush administration are consistent and dismal. Women's share of recruiting expenditures, head coaches' salaries, and scholarships has stalled and relative to men in some instances declined. The data shows that these measures either stayed the same or increased 1 percentage point in participation rates, for recruiting expenses and scholarships, but it fell by 4 percentage points in relative coaches' salaries.[2] In all spending categories, however, the *absolute* gap between expenditures for men's and for women's sports has continued to grow.

These trends are not supported by popular opinion. Opinion polls over the years have indicated strong support for Title IX from the U.S. population. Title IX's general acceptance as well as the momentum it gained during the Clinton years have prevented any dramatic backsliding under the Bush administration. Nonetheless, the nonsupportive, if not antagonistic, posture of some within the Bush administration has succeeded in stalling gender equity's steady progress.

[1] Part of this increase is due to the inclusion of outside sources of funds and of benefits in the most recent survey.

[2] Note again that some of this drop is attributable to new accounting methods.

Index

NANCY HOGSHEAD-MAKAR is a Professor at the Florida Coastal School of Law. She is a former President of the Women's Sports Foundation (1992–1994) and currently serves as its legal advisor. She has testified in Congress numerous times on the topic of gender equity in athletics, written numerous scholarly and lay articles, serves as an expert witness in Title IX cases, and has written amicus briefs representing athletic organizations in the U.S. Supreme Court. Professor Hogshead-Makar is an Olympic Champion from the 1984 Los Angeles Olympics, winning three gold medals and one silver medal in swimming.

ANDREW ZIMBALIST is Robert A. Woods Professor of Economics at Smith College. He is the author or editor of eighteen previous books, including *The Bottom Line: Observations and Arguments on the Sports Business* (Temple) and *In the Best Interest of Baseball? The Revolutionary Reign of Bud Selig.* He is a member of the Editorial Board of *The Journal of Sports Economics,* and has consulted extensively in the sports industry for players associations, leagues, cities, and owners.